W9-BSB-124

THE NATION'S BEST SCHOOLS

THE NATION'S BEST SCHOOLS

BLUEPRINTS FOR EXCELLENCE

Volume 1
Elementary and
Middle Schools

Evelyn Hunt Ogden, Ed.D.
Vito Germinario, Ed.D.

TECHNOMIC
PUBLISHING CO., INC.
LANCASTER · BASEL

The Nation's Best Schools—Volume 1
a **TECHNOMIC** publication

Published in the Western Hemisphere by
Technomic Publishing Company, Inc.
851 New Holland Avenue, Box 3535
Lancaster, Pennsylvania 17604 U.S.A.

Distributed in the Rest of the World by
Technomic Publishing AG
Missionsstrasse 44
CH-4055 Basel, Switzerland

Printed in the United States of America
10 9 8 7 6 5 4 3 2 1

Main entry under title:
    The Nation's Best Schools: Blueprints for Excellence—
    Volume 1/Elementary and Middle Schools

A Technomic Publishing Company book
Bibliography: p.
Includes index p. 353

Library of Congress Catalog Card No. 94-60605
ISBN No. 1-56676-148-4

To Jean D. Narayanan who has truly made a difference in the educational lives of children and in the profession of education through her untiring support of the development and dissemination of Programs, Practices, and Schools That Work.

Evelyn Hunt Ogden

To my daughter, Laura, who has been a constant source of joy, pride, and love.

Vito Germinario

PART THREE: THE ROLE OF THE DISTRICT IN EFFECTIVE SCHOOL DEVELOPMENT

13. THE EFFECTIVE SCHOOL DISTRICT   243

PART FOUR: THE NATIONAL RECOGNITION PROCESS

14. ON BECOMING A BLUE RIBBON SCHOOL OF EXCELLENCE   255

THERE is good news in education in the United States. In every state in every type of community, there are schools that meet the highest standards of excellence—Blue Ribbon Schools—world-class schools: schools where children learn where education prepares children for active participation in the national and the world community of today and the twenty-first century of tomorrow. Within these schools are effective programs, processes, curricula, and instruction. This book focuses on what is good about education in the United States. It looks at what makes great schools great. It provides school staff, central administrators, boards of education, and parents with a standard and a process for assessing their own schools. It provides blueprints for transforming poor schools into good schools and good schools into great schools. To paraphrase President Clinton's inaugural address, there is nothing wrong with American education that cannot be cured with what is right with American education. In recognizing the Blue Ribbon Schools in 1993, the President stated:

> The winners of the Blue Ribbon Awards . . . represent what is best in American education. If we could multiply the . . . schools . . . we could really revolutionize education in America. These are schools producing world-class results by any rigorous measure.

> [We have] to recognize the plain fact that notwithstanding the funding problems, notwithstanding the inequalities, notwithstanding all the problems of American education, you can find virtually every problem in our country solved . . . in an astonishingly effective fashion if you look at these schools. . . . The challenge for us . . . is to figure out how to replicate them.

Blue Ribbon Schools, the Best Schools, can play an important role in bringing about the needed educational reform required to prepare children for the twenty-first century. While representing only 2.5% of the total number of the 110,000 public and private elementary and secondary schools in the nation, these 2809 world-class schools—located in every state; in suburban, urban, and rural communities; serving children from the highest to lowest socioeconomic areas—serve as a powerful repudiation of the often heard cry from less effective schools that "We can't do that here because . . .!" Another important role of the Best Schools is to serve as demonstration sites, operational blueprints, for other schools striving to improve education. Educators want to "see it in action" as they contemplate new ways to meet needs. Theoretical research on learning has little widespread effect until examples of applications appear in "real" schools and classrooms. The movement from research-supported and -validated practice to mainstream school practice has, unfortunately, often taken as much as twenty years.

Transforming a less than effective school to a world-class school involves long-term planned change involving the whole of the organization, as well as change and development in a multiplicity of specific practices and programs. There is no magic bullet. Blue Ribbon Schools serve as models of the whole—models of how to conduct the business of learning—as well as models for the plethora of significant parts that are essential for school effectiveness. What they also model is that even the Best Schools must have the habit of mind to continually review progress against outcomes and be continuously open to change. The Best Schools constantly reach out for models (in nearby schools, across the state, across the nation, in other countries), network with other schools, seek examples of how others have solved problems (i.e., the National Diffusion Network programs), and adopt or adapt practices from other schools that connect with their total vision for school development. The geographical proximity of at least one Blue Ribbon School, with similar demographics, to virtually all other schools in the nation provides the potential for a powerful network of demonstration and training sites. This book seeks to hasten the process of school development by showing the connections among educational goals, objectives, and standards; current research and theory; and the practices, processes, and programs already in place in the Best Schools.

The book is based on the following premises:

- We learn more from focusing on success than on failure.
- The wealth of great schools in the United States, in each and every state, in rich and poor districts, in cities, suburbs, and rural areas is evidence that we in the education profession know enough about what it takes to create effective schools in all types of communities and for all children.
- Principals, teachers, central office staff, boards of education, and parents are interested in and can use what the Best Schools do to make their own schools more effective.
- Frequently, the most credible source of standards, practices, processes, and programs for school improvement are those found in another school.

The Nation's Best Schools: Blueprints for Excellence consists of two volumes. Volume 1 focuses on elementary education, and Volume 2 on secondary education (to be published in 1995). Middle school practices appear in both volumes. The books are designed as guides for promoting school effectiveness; providing practical frameworks for evaluating practices, programs, processes, and student outcomes in schools; and serving as guidelines for school improvement, as well as serving as desk references of effective practice.

The purpose of the school is to maximize learning for all children. The most obvious way schools do this is through direct instruction in the curriculum areas. However, the organizational climate and the systems that support the learner play powerful roles in determining learning outcomes for students. Part One: Environments, Structures, and Supports That Promote Student Learning addresses the roles of school vitality, school leadership, teaching environment, and student environment in maximizing school success for all children.

Children spend approximately 8500 hours in direct instruction in their passage from kindergarten through eighth grade. How this time is spent in the study of the language arts, mathematics, social studies, science, the arts, information processing, and other subjects determines what they know and what they can do at any given point in their elementary school experience. The instructional program is addressed in Part Two: 8500 Instructional Hours — The Elementary Curriculum.

The 110,000 schools in this country are parts of some 16,000 school districts or umbrella organizations. The role of the district in school development and learner outcomes is addressed in Part Three: The Role of the District in Effective School Development.

How Blue Ribbon Schools of Excellence are identified, how schools can use the Blue Ribbon Standards as a basis for self-evaluation and how schools can become Blue Ribbon Schools are the questions answered in Part Four: On Becoming a Blue Ribbon School of Excellence.

Within the chapters, information concerning what children should learn, how they should be taught, and how learning should be assessed was based on the National Goals, National

Standards Projects, educational research and theory, and national and international assessments. Each chapter consists of a section describing how the Best Schools have translated theory into practice. Descriptions of practices, processes, and programs in the Best Schools were based on Blue Ribbon School applications; on-site school validation reports; interviews with principals and staff from recognized schools; and materials provided by the schools, districts, states, and the U.S. Department of Education. While descriptions of practices in all recognized schools were available, it was obvious that not all schools could be included among the illustrations of specific practices. The 228 elementary schools recognized in 1993 represent a cross section of public and private education in the United States. These schools are located in large central cities (22%), mid-size cities (22%), suburbs (40%), small towns (12%), and rural areas (4%). The smallest of the schools had 102 students and the largest 1334 students, with an average of 515 students. Eighty-two percent of these recognized schools were public and 18% were private; they included schools from forty-five states, the District of Columbia, the U. S. Virgin Islands, and Department of Defense Dependent Schools.

Illustrations of practices were drawn primarily from this group of 228 elementary schools. In most cases, the schools were randomly selected from the applications. The decision about which school was picked to feature for a particular program was based upon the degree of detail provided in the application and a desire to use schools representing different community types and examples from as many states as possible. Schools featured in one section could just as easily have been used to illustrate a different practice in another chapter. In other words, while not a scientific sample of Blue Ribbon Schools, the full range and scope of the successful schools are included. In some cases where the same approach, practice, or program was found to be widely used, the names of several schools using that approach, practice, or program are included in parentheses in the chapter. Again, these specific lists in no way indicate that these are the only schools using the program or practice; to the contrary, they are indicators of widely used specific programs and practices in Blue Ribbon Schools.

The Appendices of the book are designed to be a resource. They include a list of the names and addresses of all (2809) Blue Ribbon Schools across the country (recognized 1982 – 1983 through 1993 – 1994), a list of State Liaisons for Blue Ribbon Schools, a description of National Diffusion Network programs and a few other programs used widely in Blue Ribbon Schools, and a list of the State Facilitators in the National Diffusion Network.

THIS is a book that was born out of the knowledge and frustration that, each year over 200 world-class schools—schools in which children are highly successful and whose programs and practices reflect the best of what is known about effective educational practices—are identified, and yet there has been only the most limited dissemination of what these schools do or acknowledgement that these schools represent the national standard for education. This is particularly frustrating in light of the constant stream of reports and press coverage that often lead the public and educators alike to the belief that nothing works in education. Granted, only 2.5% of the nation's schools have been identified as meeting the criteria of a national Blue Ribbon School of Excellence; however, there are undoubtedly many other schools that will be identified in the future. This book is an attempt to open the door on the Nation's Best Schools.

It would not have been possible to write this book without the cooperation and assistance of the recognized schools. The illustrations of programs and practices were drawn directly from their own reports and from the reports of the on-site evaluators. We are sure that, in many cases, a school would have selected a different program as most representative of its programs or practices than the one we used as an example. However, time, resources, and book space required that the authors limit illustrations. We would like to thank the principals who provided us with additional information about their schools and who took time to discuss their practices with us. The book contains illustrations from over 100 different schools, mostly from those recognized in 1993; we wish we could have used an example from each of the 228 schools. To those not used for illustration, we apologize; it was the luck of the draw, not the quality of your schools, which accounts for your not being specifically referenced.

The authors wish to acknowledge the contributions of the staff of the Blue Ribbon School Program: J. Stephen O'Brien, Kathryn E. Crossely; Diane L. Jones; Patricia A. Hobbs; Betty S. Baten; and Jean D. Narayanan, Director of the Recognition Division. This dedicated and highly knowledgeable group provides the vision and the backbone of the Blue Ribbon School Program, and without their encouragement, assistance, and cooperation, this book could not have been written.

The authors also wish to thank Dr. Robert Hendricks, Superintendent of Flowing Wells Schools, for his insights on the role of the district in school development; Susan Stewart, Chamberlain School, for extensive information on the Vermont assessment process; Dr. Liz Schmitz, former principal of Midway Heights, for material concerning the development of technology-based programs; Willa Spicer, Director of Curriculum and Instruction, South Brunswick, for assistance in developing the format for the book; Amy Fisher, Director of Community Relations/Affirmative Action, East Brunswick Public Schools, for photographs; and Faye Webb, Principal of Mirabeau B. Lamar, for special inspiration.

Finally, the authors are indebted to Diana Robinson for her hundreds of hours of editing and rewriting; Karen Phillips and Mary Ann Spillane for their friendship and assistance in typing the manuscript; and Cheryl Haines for her support, encouragement, and assistance in research and editing.

PART ONE

ENVIRONMENTS, STRUCTURES, AND SUPPORTS THAT PROMOTE STUDENT LEARNING

CHAPTER 1

The Essence of Schools: Organizational Vitality

THEY fly a flag proclaiming excellence; the President of the United States calls them the "world-class schools of now and the 21st century . . . the models of what schools should be"; states honor them; communities applaud them; parents cherish them; children learn in them; they are the Blue Ribbon Schools of Excellence, they are the nation's Best Schools. What makes the Best Schools stand head and shoulders above, unfortunately, the majority of schools? It is necessary to look at the myriad specific practices, programs, and outcomes that are the parts of the place we call school. However, the Best Schools are far more than the sum of their individual parts; they are schools bound together by intricate webs of connected and integrated practices, programs, curricula, and support systems. In order to understand the "essence" of these schools, to understand why they are so successful, it is necessary to understand: a) what drives them — to know how they see the world, what they believe, what they value; b) how what they believe and value affects daily, as well as long-range, decisions concerning leadership, teaching, curriculum, student support, and, most importantly, student outcomes. Chapter 1 looks at the following questions:

- How do beliefs about learning, teaching, students, parents, and community determine values, and, therefore, roles, practices, procedures, rewards, and outcomes that define the "essence" of all schools?
- What are the characteristics of effective schools?
- How does the vitality of the school as an organization serve to determine actions and outcomes in the Best Schools?
- What is the process for school improvement in the Best Schools?
- How do the Best Schools respond to research findings, local state and national assessments, standards and goals?
- What are the problems the Best Schools have encountered and overcome?
- What do the Best Schools identify as future challenges and improvement agendas?

CONVENTIONAL, CONGENIAL, AND EFFECTIVE SCHOOLS

Formal studies of effective and ineffective schools and the observations of those who have worked with "failing," "ho-hum," "emerging," and "knock-your-socks-off" schools generally identify three types of schools. The set of characteristics of each type of school supersedes the importance of any individual practice or program in determining the outcomes of instruction. The dominant value and belief systems of a school determine the observable characteristics and the essence of the school as an organization, a place. These underlying values and beliefs define "what we do in this school," "how we make decisions," "how we respond to parents and the community," "what the real operating objectives are that we act upon in this school," "what we perceive as our accountability for what students learn," "what we consider important for children to learn," "how we interact with our colleagues," "what we believe about what children can learn," "why the staff works here," and "what we perceive as valued by the board of education, the central office, parents, and community." No school or district is purely one type; however, how the school leadership and staff, how district leadership and staff, and how boards of education act on the answers to these questions creates the culture, the climate, the character, and ultimately, the degree of effectiveness of the school and school district in terms of student learning.

THE "CONVENTIONAL" OR "COLLECTED" SCHOOL

In the "conventional" or "collected" school, classrooms function largely as autonomous units: the school is a loose "collection" of these separate classrooms. These are schools that have no common goals, no collective sense of what they are trying to accomplish as a whole, as a school. Each classroom is like a mini-school. Teachers work in insolation within their own rooms. Although people usually work very hard, they view their work as what they do in their own classroom or maybe at their own grade level. What happens in the individual classroom depends on the beliefs, values, knowledge, and experiences of the individual teacher. Most of the staff believe that everyone else in the school shares the same beliefs about teaching and learning that they do; however, this is rarely the case.

The principal views his/her role primarily as that of a manager, that is, someone who makes sure that the school runs well, teachers have the materials they want, discipline is maintained, parent complaints are handled, and the PTA receives assistance for projects they undertake. Rules and sets of operational procedures often give the impression of strong building-level leadership and control. However, what are controlled are the operational aspects of the school. The principal's beliefs, often shared by district administration, form the basis of how he/she interprets his/her role, what he/she values, and the basic climate and culture of the school. Among these underlying beliefs are the following:

(1) Instructional Leadership
   - Good teachers make good schools; teaching is an "art"; either you have good teachers or you don't; what goes on in the classroom is the prerogative of the teacher; the principal can do little to affect what goes on in the classroom, other than hire "good" new teachers when there is an opening, prevent "bad" teachers from getting tenure, and encourage older "bad" teachers to retire.
   - Teachers are the ones who know instruction and the needs of students in their class; a good principal is one who lets teachers alone, insures that the teachers have the materials they want for instruction, supports his/her teachers with parents and the district administration, and insures that the school is orderly, clean, and safe.
(2) Management
   - Ensuring a safe and orderly school environment is the most important function of the principal; in order to operate efficiently, the school needs sets of common procedures and practices such as disciplinary policies and processes, schedules for specials such as art, physical education, and pull-out instruction, written curriculum and textbooks for each grade level standard report card and parent conference procedures and the means for reporting standardized test scores to parents.
(3) Instructional Accountability
   - The effectiveness of the school in terms of learning is the responsibility of the

individual teacher; however, effectiveness is llimited by the motivation, ability, and the "problems" children bring to school.

— Ultimately, the degree of effectiveness of the school and the individual classroom is largely a matter of "perception"; if the parents, central office staff, and the board of education are satisfied with the teachers, the classes, and the school, then it is a good school; median standardized test scores, at or above the national norm, serve as confirmation of effectiveness and support current practice; poor test scores are rationalized largely as a reflection of the quality of the students.

(4) Educational Research

— There is little useful knowledge outside of the school or district, which is available to educators; research has little potential for impacting on classroom practice, since most schools are pretty much the same; schools touted as exemplary have more resources and are "lucky" to have better kids and maybe better teachers; national reports recommending the need for change and new approaches to education are developed by people who don't know what the world of the school is "really" like.

(5) School Improvement and Planning

— The schools can always be improved by increased fiscal resources to enhance the building, hire more staff, and/or buy more materials.

— "You shouldn't try and fix it if it can't be proven that its broken"; mandates for change in program, practice, or curriculum originate from outside of the school — such as parents' complaints about the way something is being done or the lack of computers in classrooms; changes in procedures emanate from the central office, or new state testing mandates; all these can be expected to have little positive effect; however, they hold the potential of "rocking the boat" — a good year is one in which there have been few calls for change.

These underlying beliefs create the climate of the school and directly affect decisions concerning what will be valued and reinforced, how people will interact with each other and for what reasons, what the faculty talks about, how outsiders are viewed, and the school's relationship with the district. It follows from the beliefs associated with the conventional school that "leadership" will be defined in terms of efficient operational management and public relations. Stability, lack of conflict, and minimal intervention in terms of the instructional process will be valued. Broad-based instructional planning, for example, conflicts with the value placed on individual teacher autonomy and stability and, therefore, will not be characteristic of these schools. Even where the district has "installed" site-based management in these conventional schools, planning is usually confined to such areas as development of a new disciplinary policy, bus loading and unloading procedures, or student scheduling. Planning for change in instructional practice is considered inconsistent with the "belief" that this area is the prerogative of the individual teacher. Since the concept of development of staff is inconsistent with beliefs concerning the importance or, in fact, the ability of teachers to make major changes in practice, little value is placed on staff development and teacher evaluation in the conventional school. Inservice opportunities are usually limited to specific days in the district calendar and provide a smorgasbord of activities designed to allow for maximum options for individual teachers to make decisions about what to attend. Staff meetings are kept to a minimum and focus mainly on procedures and events involving the entire school, i.e., schedules for "back-to school" night. Teacher evaluation is considered a bureaucratic requirement; at best, the formal evaluation process provides the opportunity to support, in writing, what teachers are doing and a means for weeding out weak nontenured teachers; at worst, the formal evaluation process is viewed by the principal and teachers as an unwelcome and unnecessary interference into the individual classroom and a waste of valuable time.

In conventional school districts, positive assessment of the school by district administration is often in terms of what is not happening; i.e., there were no major problems at the school, no major parent complaints, no grievances filed by staff, and no violence or major vandalism. The perception that the school's effectiveness is judged largely and informally by parent, public, central office, and board of education opinion discourages the indepth analysis of data that might identify and expose problem areas. Standardized norm-referenced tests may be criticized by staff for not measuring what is important in what they teach; however, when the median score is above the 50th percentile, these tests are used to reassure parents and the community that the school is doing well. Lower standardized test scores, however, are explained in terms of the "problems" students bring to school. This is reflective of a pervasive belief that the school can only have a limited impact on the child's innate ability and a tacit acceptance that some will succeed, most will do okay and invariably some will fail.

Unfortunately, most of the schools in America are "conventional" schools (Glickman, 1993). They predominate in suburban, urban, and rural settings, in rich and poor districts, and in high and low socioeconomic communities.

THE CONGENIAL SCHOOL

The congenial school gives the impression of being a cohesive unit with common goals. There is a lot of communication and a lot of meetings. The employees have a strong sense of being a school; it is a nice place to work. However, close inspection of the operational goals and priorities reveals that the focus is on the adults: improving the climate for adults, improving communication among teachers, relieving teacher stress (Glickman, 1993). The belief is that the school should also be a nice place for children—friendly, supportive, concerned with self-esteem and that there should be a friendly relationship between staff and parents. In other words, the "happy" school is the "good" school. However, when you get past the focus on affect, particularly for the adults, there is little difference between the congenial school and the conventional school in terms of beliefs about how children should learn, how instruction should be delivered, or how learning should be assessed. Means frequently are confused with ends. According to Glickman (1993), most of what is seen around the country as site-based management takes place in congenial schools and has more to do with adult needs than student needs.

As in the conventional school, the principal's role is defined mostly in operational and management terms. His/her role is to provide support for individual teachers in terms of classroom material, discipline, and support with parents; however, greater emphasis is placed on pleasing and being liked by parents and teachers. The value placed on public relations leads to actions that minimize the potential for conflict, to an even greater extent then in the conventional school. Value is placed on getting along by going along with the school as a clean, safe, and fun place to be. Change is viewed as having the potential of "rocking the boat." Since common goals concerning the instructional outcomes of education are missing, classroom practices reflect beliefs concerning the autonomy of teachers within the classroom; the idea that learning is limited, based on what the child brings to school; lack of relevance of knowledge and practice outside the school; and satisfaction with the status quo. The emphasis on affect frequently leads to lower standards for at least some children, justified by the belief that, if children are challenged, they may experience failure and low self-esteem. The reward for working in the congenial school for staff comes from the "family-type" atmosphere throughout the school. However, the rewards for children in terms of learning may be no greater than in the conventional school.

THE EFFECTIVE STUDENT OUTCOME-BASED, PROFESSIONAL, COLLEGIAL KNOWLEDGE-BASED SCHOOL

The third type of school, frequently referred to in the literature as the effective "professional school," "collegial school," or "student outcome-based school," operates from a very different belief system concerning the nature and purposes of the school. Satisfaction is derived from professional work accomplished together and from the achievement of children. These schools are bound by a strong sense of common mission and student learning outcome goals. A characteristic of the professional school staff is that they are never satisfied, that it can always be better. They believe the following:

(1) Instructional Leadership
  — The purpose of the school is student learning; all children can learn to a very high set of standards.
  — The most important roles of the principal are to make explicit the belief and value systems of the school, exhibit behaviors that reflect the beliefs of the school, lead the continuing effort at improvement, foster staff development, find "time" for planning and analysis, and communicate the mission and outcomes to parents, the community, and central office.
  — The principal is the instructional leader of the school instructional team—we know more together about effective practice than any one person alone.
(2) Management
  — Ensuring a safe and orderly school environment is an important function of the principal; in order to operate efficiently, the school needs sets of common procedures and practices such as disciplinary policies and procedures, schedules for specials such as art and physical education, written curriculum and textbooks for each grade level, standard report card and parent conference procedures, and means for reporting assessment results to parents.
(3) Instructional Accountability
  — The staff of the school is accountable for the learning of students—if we only work hard enough and are smart enough and creative enough, then every last child will achieve mastery in every content area.
  — Standards for student achievement proposed by professional associations, national committees, and states are valuable for determining what children should learn.
(4) Research on Instruction and Learning
  — As a profession, educators know a great deal about how children learn and how they should be taught; their findings are applicable to what happens in this school.
  — Teachers and principals continue to learn, to get better at what they do.
  — Colleagues have valuable lessons to share—working together will improve education for children.
(5) School Improvement and Planning
  — "Education is never totally fixed and we shouldn't wait until it breaks to work at improving it"; data concerning the outcomes and processes of education should

be continually probed to identify areas of need; it is okay to share flaws with staff, parents, and the community, as they can be trusted to know that the school is working on continuous improvement.

— The change process takes time: time to study data, time to ask fundamental questions, time to research solutions, time to make connections among programs and practices, time to plan, time to train staff, time to implement, and time to reassess; participating in these activities is a vital part of being in the education profession.

— The staff needs to share a common vocabulary and set of common definitions so that they can communicate effectively among themselves, with children, and with parents.

— Change brings an expected degree of anxiety and stress; however, change is essential; not everyone will be totally happy with everyone else's position on every issue; not everyone will agree on certain means or even the value of certain ends, but that is the price we are willing to pay on the road to creating a more effective school.

— Carefully thought-out risk taking is encouraged—it is okay to "play" with new ideas.

— Outside agencies, universities, businesses, parents, and other schools can help in the quest.

— The highest form of satisfaction, as a professional, comes from the intrinsic knowledge that you have made a difference—been part of something beyond personal goals.

These underlying beliefs create the climate of the student outcome-based or professional school and determine what is valued, what is reinforced, what is done, and what the outcomes are. It follows, then, that in these schools, "leadership" is defined largely in terms of instruction. Therefore, the principal needs to know a lot about how children learn; about instructional practice and curriculum; and how he/she can assess outcome data, monitor instruction, study the research, and network with instructional leaders outside of the school. Teachers believe in the benefits of the collegial process of instructional improvement; it follows, then, that they must be actively involved in ongoing learning and staff development, as well as be participants in planning. As a result, staff development is a high priority in professional schools. Since staff act on the belief that every child will learn, data concerning the outcomes of learning are disaggregated and studied. Since standards for learning are valued, the staff is concerned with setting standards and therefore, is willing to look outside for proposed standards for instruction and learning.

EFFECTIVE AND LESS THAN EFFECTIVE SCHOOLS

For more than twenty years researchers have produced studies that identify the factors associated with effective and less effective schools (Edmonds, 1978; Brookover and Lezotte, 1977; Rutter, 1985). The factors associated with effective schools are clearly those characteristic of "professional/collegial/student outcome-based" schools. These schools have the intrinsic ability and habits of mind to continually renew themselves. They have the organizational vitality to self-assess, to set and revise student-centered objectives, to plan, to act in unity, and to reassess. It is interesting that studies show that effective schools have the greatest "dissatisfaction" with their own teaching and learning (Brookover, reported by Glickman,

1993). They believe that "seeking improvement . . . enlivens the organization for adults and students alike and [that] improvement is possible regardless of the current state of the organization" (Joyce et al., 1993).

On the other hand, research on less effective schools shows that they have the greatest satisfaction with their teaching and learning (Brookover, reported by Glickman, 1993). Because less effective schools do not share common goals within the schools, they leave teachers alone to plan what they teach with little guidance from colleagues or articulation of program from year to year (Oates, reported by Glickman, 1993). These practices are consistent with the beliefs held in both the "conventional/collected" and "congenial" school. Such "self-satisfied" schools lack intrinsic organizational vitality; they respond only to external forces, such as central office and state mandates or parental dissatisfaction. They make changes only when the "cost" in terms of disruption and conflict is perceived as less than the "cost" of maintaining the status quo. However, change in response to these externally identified crises or intrusions are apt to be quickly planned, inadequately implemented, and frequently represent more form than substance.

Can conventional and congenial schools become student effective outcome-based schools? The literature is full of case studies of successful turn-around-schools, including many schools designated as Blue Ribbon Schools. Within every school, there are individual teachers who hold the beliefs and values associated with effective schools, and their classrooms are successful places where students learn a great deal. However, leadership is needed to unite not only these effective teachers but also their less effective colleagues, behind a mission that supersedes individual interests. Leadership that values self-criticism, models continuous learning, rewards professional risk taking, initiates and supports broad-based child-centered planning and development, and accepts accountability is essential for effective school development.

Leadership is the most important role of the principal. In case after case, it has been demonstrated that it was the principal who has made the most significant difference in the transformation of a school from a loose collection of individual classrooms to an effective connected school with a shared mission and successful student outcomes. This is not to say, however, that others both inside and outside the school do not participate in very significant ways in the transformation of the school; nevertheless, at the elementary level, the principal is usually the sole administrator, the sole individual who on a day-to-day basis, can establish the school climate, set the level of professional standards and expectations for the school and largely define what roles others will play in the operation and development of the school. Effective principals have a vision of what they want the school to become; a long view of the process of becoming; extensive knowledge of educational practice and program, which allows them to see the connections among decisions, practices, programs and outcomes; a drive to know more; and a belief that the school can do better. These professional characteristics need to be combined with a leadership style, personality, and "people skills" that can motivate others and engage them in the mission of the school and the management skills necessary to successfully maintain the operational aspects of the school.

Unfortunately, in most schools principals have been hired, and once hired, reinforced based on their ability to "run a tight unrocking ship" and their "people skills" are directed at being "liked" by parents and staff. However, without the instructional leadership piece, the status quo will be valued and maintained. Changes that do take place in response to pressure are usually inadequately understood and disconnected enhancements that mainly provide the illusion of effective practice, i.e., "We 'did' cooperative learning last year; this year we are 'doing' higher order thinking skills; next year we are 'doing' manipulatives."

THE BEST SCHOOLS—ORGANIZATIONAL VITALITY

On-site visitors to schools nominated for Blue Ribbon Schools recognition and others who evaluate effective and less effective schools frequently say they can "smell an effective school within five minutes of entering the building." What they mean by this is that, through experience with observing in many different schools, they have learned to pick up a host of clues in what they see, hear, and sense, which signal that this is an "effective school," "a developing school," or a "less effective school." This sense of the school comes from such things as what people are talking about; observed interactions between children, staff and children, principal and staff, and parents and staff; and what is displayed in the school, in the classroom, in the principal's office. Taken together, these clues reflect the vitality of the school. In some cases, the more systematic review of the school's programs, practices, and processes of the school, which follows the first impression, results in a change in that initial impression. This can be particularly true in schools that have recently developed the organizational vitality characteristics of the most effective schools, but have not had the time to align and connect all programs and practices in a manner that maximizes effective learning for all students. Getting even most of it "right" takes time—usually three to five years to move a less effective school to Blue Ribbon standards under the best of leadership. Getting it right is also affected by the context of the school. The presence of large numbers of at-risk students and negative factors outside of the school undoubtedly makes the job more difficult and complex than in contexts, where most children come to school prepared for learning and where parents themselves have had successful associations with education. However, all schools have to face challenges that make the job of school improvement difficult. Among the Blue Ribbon Schools are many schools that have met the most challenging of environmental problems successfully under the most difficult circumstances. One of these is Mirabeau Lamar Elementary Schools, Texas, located in a neighborhood struggling with urban blight, where residents are constant victims of drugs and violence, where 96% of the students qualify for free lunch and there is a greater than 30% turnover of students each year, where the average daily attendance rate is 99%, and where 97% of the students score above the 50th percentile on nationally normed tests.

The Best Schools exhibit the beliefs, drives, actions, and outcomes described by researchers as effective professional, collegial, or student outcome-based schools. They are in a continuous state of growth, trying to make it better. A significant reward for staff working in the Best Schools is the participation with colleagues in probing data, researching alternatives, working for something beyond personal goals, and knowing that they are making a difference.

While the teacher is the person who establishes the climate for the classroom, it is the principal who is the force that sets the tone and provides the drive, who clarifies the belief system of the school, who models the values, and who reinforces the staff who seek to improve instruction. Best School principals really believe that "we can get it right in this school, for every kid." Like the principal of a congenial school, he/she places importance on creating a positive teaching environment, positive interactions among staff, a happy place for kids. But this principal also believes that the satisfaction staff derive from their professional success and that the children derive from learning will be valued most. Without professional or outcome-based leadership, it is virtually impossible for a school to become a professional or outcome school. Some great things can happen within individual classrooms or even at a grade level, but the glue is missing for the total school. The role of the principal is well documented in creating the vitality of the Best Schools, as well as in all the research on effective schools. It is interesting that 12% of the principals of elementary schools recognized as Blue Ribbon Schools in 1991 – 1992 had been principals of other schools that had been previously recognized.

The organizational vitality of the Best Schools is reflected in every program, practice, and instructional outcome; illustrations abound throughout the chapters of this book devoted to the specific programs and practices of effective schools. However, how these schools have defined obstacles in the past, how the schools reach out to continue to learn, and how and what they view as future challenges provide a context for understanding the myriad specific approaches used in the Best Schools.

THE BEST SCHOOLS – THE SCHOOL IMPROVEMENT PROCESS

Central to the success of the Best Schools is a well established process for ongoing school improvement focused on the outcomes of the 8500 hours of instruction in which children will be involved in their journey from kindergarten through grade 8. The process includes both formal and informal means for involving the entire staff and, frequently, parents in a continuous cycle of collecting data on the effectiveness of current practice, identifying unmet needs of students, studying research and effective practices generated outside of the school, establishing improvement objectives and priorities, deciding how instructional time will be used, planning specific programs, developing curriculum, training staff, implementing planned change, developing and identifying assessment strategies, and assessing the impact of the changes on students. In many cases, the process itself has emerged within the school; in other cases the process is part of a district-developed planning model, state-disseminated or -mandated process, or a process shared by schools in a school improvement network such as the Network of Essential Schools, Missouri's Network of Accelerated Schools, or the Effective Schools Network.

SCHOOL IMPROVEMENT PROCESS ILLUSTRATIONS FROM THE BEST SCHOOLS

SKYLINE ELEMENTARY SCHOOL, FERNDALE, WA

The Ferndale School District, a semi-isolated agrarian blue-collar community, is located approximately fifteen miles from the Canadian border in northwest Washington State. Most of the district is rural. The Lummi Indian Reservation is an integral part of the district; Skyline elementary has a 30% minority population, most of whom are Lummi Indians. Thirty-seven percent of the students qualify for free lunch. The entire staff is committed to ensuring that all students, regardless of race or socioeconomic conditions, are successful. In mathematics, 79% and in reading, 75% of the students score above the 50th percentile on standardized tests.

School improvement has been an ongoing project at Skyline since 1986 when they developed their first school improvement plan. School improvement became even more intense with the awarding of the Schools for the 21st Century grant during the 1988 – 89 school year. The underlying goal of Washington State Schools for the 21st Century project is to increase student learning through school improvement. In 1989 – 90 the Skyline staff, students, and parents completed a comprehensive three-year school improvement plan. An outside specialist and consultant in school improvement has worked with them in developing a school improvement process that includes a strategic planning stage, an implementation stage, and an evaluation stage utilizing multiple data.

David Boeringa, *Principal, K – 6, 585 Students*

GREENBELT CENTER ELEMENTARY SCHOOL, GREENBELT, MD

Greenbelt Center Elementary School is located in the heart of Greenbelt, Maryland, a planned community developed during the New Deal administration. The school is a wonderful old building of art-deco style that serves as a social, cultural, and education center. The school serves students from two diverse attendance areas. Approximately 40% live in the Greenbelt community, a short walk or drive to school. The remaining 60% of the students live in a Federally subsidized housing development that is located sixteen miles from the school. Over 70% of the school's students live with only one parent. Eighty-one percent of the students score above the 50th percentile on the Prince George's County Public Tests in mathematics and reading.

Greenbelt Center School was the first public school in Prince George's County to adopt the Effective Schools Process. This occurred seven years ago, one year prior to the mandated involvement of all Prince George's County Public Schools in the process. Involvement with the Effective Schools movement has provided specific focus for school improvement practices at Greenbelt Center. This process includes the establishment of a school mission statement, a detailed needs assessment in the seven correlated areas of Effective Schools, the establishment of priorities, and the initiation of specific programs to address and meet identified needs. It also requires the complete involvement of all staff members and is driven by the belief that school improvement must take place primarily at the school building level in order to meet those needs unique to that particular student population, community, and staff. The roles of the principal and other school educational leaders in this continuing activity are those of catalysts and facilitators.

Concepts, strategies, and human resources emerge as staff members assume responsibility for establishing programs and services that meet student and community needs. At Greenbelt Center, ideas are most often generated in small groups with modifications and final decisions resting with the entire staff. It is through these procedures that the staff develops ownership and commitment to the tasks at hand. Decisions are made by consensus in order to ensure a unified effort in implementing priorities, and all decisions are subject to review and change once implementation is underway.

This process has been in effect for the past seven years, and continues as a viable means of identifying needs and focusing resources for meeting these needs. It is a process that is responsible for the establishment of the Language Development Program, the After-School Program, and a climate of student advocacy and support that permeates Greenbelt Center School. This staff involvement and commitment is also the force that brought about the development of "The Human Services Paradigm," a concept that drives current Center School priorities and efforts.

Carolyn Goffy, Principal (John Van Schoonhoven, Principal at the time of recognition),
K—6, 519 Students

ANCILLAE-ASSUMPTA ACADEMY, WYNCOTE, PA

Ancillae-Assumpta Academy is a private co-educational Catholic elementary school within the Archdiocese of Philadelphia. Personal excellence in a warm and friendly environment is tradition. The school is located on a ten-acre site that was formerly a private estate. Students come from seventeen school districts. Graduates of the Academy attend a wide variety of outstanding public, private, and independent schools. Eighty-six percent in mathematics and 88% in reading score above the 50th percentile on standardized tests. The school was recognized as a Blue Ribbon School in 1986 and 1993; in 1989 it received the national Drug Free School Recognition Award.

The vehicle for school improvement that is in place is a restructuring process for community visioning into the twenty-first century. However, long before its inception, a rich history shows that it was a school on the move. The administration and staff work together to encourage school improvement daily. The administrative team meets once a week, and school improvement is a strong focus. The structure is in place to allow ongoing development in all areas; parents are asked formally to evaluate various areas of the school programs and activities, curriculum Council meetings, curriculum area and schoolwide inservice meetings, and the staff development program that provides the opportunity for faculty to participate and initiate improvements. At the end of the year, everyone on staff has an opportunity to formally assess their own goals and the school's focus for the year with the Director.

Sr. Elizabeth McCoy, *Director, Pre-K – 8, 545 Students*

DEEPHAVEN ELEMENTARY SCHOOL, WAYZATA, MN

Deephaven Elementary School is one of nine elementary schools in the Minnetonka Public School District. The district draws from eleven municipalities, which are among the top socioeconomic communities in the state. The parent community is well-educated and actively involved in the school. There is little student mobility. Building-level autonomy is balanced with central office support. The district provides a strong foundation for the school through a district-wide philosophy statement; articulated curriculum expectations with learner outcomes defined for each level; instructional materials that are selected and evaluated on a systematic basis by a committee of teachers, parents, and administrators; a districtwide testing program; and centralized hiring and evaluation process. Eighty-five percent of the students in mathematics and 83% of the students in reading score above the 50th percentile on nationally normed tests. Clear Springs Elementary School (Linda Saukkonen, Principal) in the Minnetonka District was recognized as a Blue Ribbon School at the same time as Deephaven.

Several years ago, Deephaven became a part of the Minnesota Educational Effectiveness Program (MEEP), which meant that they began a process of intentional school improvement. Six members of the staff received training in the characteristics of effective schools and the process related to planned change. Initial stages in the process focused on team-building, establishment of a positive school climate, and mission development. From these beginnings, the school has successfully used task forces or the Deephaven Advisory Committee to make recommendations for changes to the staff. The school also uses these teams to coordinate improvement efforts with the objectives of the district. Parent support has always been strong; however, by tying the fund-raising efforts of the PTO to the mission of that organization, financial support has risen to nearly $25,000 per year. All of these funds go to enrichment for students.

Bradley Board, *Principal, Pre-K – 4, 394 Students*

THE BEST SCHOOLS – THE USE OF EDUCATIONAL RESEARCH FINDINGS, NATIONAL ASSESSMENTS, AND THE NATIONAL GOALS

The Best Schools are constantly asking questions about what their students should be learning, how they can best teach and support student learning, and how well their students are doing. Characteristically, they look outward, as well as at their own resources, practices, and assessment approaches in answering these questions. The Best Schools have formal and informal knowledge concerning the broad goals of education, standards for student achievement, and curriculum-related research generated at the national level or in professional associations, universities, state agencies, and other districts and schools. They share information within the school, visit other sites to observe programs based on research, participate in intensive staff development, and adopt/adapt practices shown to be effective elsewhere. They do not want to reinvent the wheel. Frequently, the staff of the Best Schools is also actively involved in large-scale improvement efforts beyond their school, serving on state and national advisory and development committees, piloting programs and assessment procedures, training staff from other schools and districts, hosting observers from other districts, and developing programs that will be used by other schools. In many cases the school has been designated as a "demonstration site" for effective practices by the district, state, (i.e., Texas, South Carolina) or networks.

Illustrations of the Use of Research, Assessment, and Goals

DEEPHAVEN, MN

The district hires two full-time staff trainers who offer classes for teachers, such as elements of instruction, time management, learning styles, mentorships, and the use of computers in instruction. Staff development takes place in the building through efforts such as teachers who have attended workshops, specialists, or videotapes.

In the early 1980s, it became clear to Deephaven that if they were going to significantly improve performance in specific areas, they couldn't do them all at once. They began focusing district and building energies on one subject area at a time for a period of several years and focused efforts for five years on reading, five on writing, and five on mathematics. Major developments have occurred in each of these subject areas in terms of what is being taught and how it is being taught.

Research reveals that American students graduate from high school at a distinct disadvantage in the fields of math, science, and technology as compared with the rest of the industrialized world. Although Deephaven students compare favorably with students across the country, the district has initiated and the school has implemented concentrated efforts to strengthen experiences in these areas for the students. At the district level, they have done such things as raise the graduation standards by one year and have accelerated algebra for all students from ninth to eighth grade.

Studies show that more children are coming to school unprepared for formal learning. The district sponsors pre-school early childhood special education and early childhood family education programs. Deephaven has hired a half-time social worker from block grant funds to provide direct service to students, as well as consultation and referral service to parents.

National goals are calling for schools to become more accountable by having students demonstrate competency in the basics. The school has written learner outcomes for every curriculum area for every grade level. Some assessment tools are currently in place, but staff members, through district curriculum committees, are in the process of developing a variety of appropriate assessment tools and strategies so as to better assure success for all students. Differentiated strategies are developing as teachers are facing ever-widening student ability and achievement levels.

OSBORN SCHOOL, RYE, NY

Osborn School is located in a small suburban community on Long Island Sound. The diverse population is comprised primarily of middle and upper middle-income families. Due mainly to job transfers, there is an approximately 20% annual mobility rate.

Osborn School believes strongly in an interdisciplinary approach to learning. Their literature-based Language Arts Program was introduced at Osborn in 1989 and extended throughout the district two years later. This model program received the International Reading Association's Exemplary Reading Award for New York State in 1991. Also in 1991, as a result of a staffwide investigation, the district adopted a more rigorous math program based on the standards of the National Council of Teachers of Mathematics. Portfolios, product assessment, and performance assessment are some of the innovation and practical techniques that are used to augment traditional testing methods. Revision of the report card format is presently being explored as a more appropriate means of evaluation. Staff believes that students learn from each other as well as from their teachers; therefore, at Osborn, all students are heterogeneously grouped. Through the use of cooperative grouping, students learn to work with each other, generate higher order thinking, take risks, learn from failure, appreciate their successes, and respect each other's opinions. A literature-based thinking skills program has been instituted for all children in grades 2 through 6, based on Dr. Edward deBono's CORT Thinking Tools. The Rye City Schools adopted D.A.R.E, a program that fosters self-esteem in students and teaches them how to say no to drugs.

Susan Losek, *Principal, K – 6, 419 Students*

THE BEST SCHOOLS—OVERCOMING PROBLEMS AND IMPEDIMENTS

It is easy to believe when you look at the current programs, practices, processes, and outstanding student outcomes that the Best Schools have not had to deal with the myriad problems facing less effective schools. This is not the case. In some schools, there has been a long history of pursuing excellence, while in others something happened, frequently a new or revitalized principal, to change the path of a less than effective school. However, Best Schools exist in all types of communities and collectively serve the full range of children in the United States. They have faced not only instructional problems, but also changing school populations, increasing numbers of children at-risk, facilities problems, staffing problems, community problems, and funding problems. None of these problems ever really go away; however, the Best Schools recognize problems as challenges, not excuses for inaction.

Illustrations of Factors Identified by the Best Schools That Contributed to Their Success

SKYLINE, WA

The following activities have been introduced over the past five years and are ongoing to ensure success:

(1) *Peer Coaching—Collegial Support Groups:* The entire staff participate on voluntary self-selected peer coaching collegial support teams that assist one another in improving instructional strategies, solve behavior problems, and act as a support team. At Skyline, teachers share good ideas and good teaching practices in an organized and highly effective way.

(2) *Strong Staff Development Program:* Each staff member spends fifteen days of each year, outside of district-contracted time, in the improvement of instruction and/or improvement of curriculum activities. This has resulted in greatly improved instructional techniques and a more relevant integrated curriculum.

(3) *Teacher as Facilitator:* A direct result of the staff development program is the increased understanding of how students learn. Cooperative learning, cross-age tutoring, and peer coaching are used extensively. Students form learning teams and work together to solve problems, with teachers moving from group to group to facilitate the learning process. As a result, students are more actively involved in the learning process.

The Washington State Schools for the 21st Century project has given Skyline the opportunity to develop one of the strongest staff development programs in the state. This was pointed out by Dr. Judith Billings, State School Superintendent, who, when giving her legislative report to the public schools in the state of Washington, singled out Skyline as an example of exemplary school practices.

BOWDOIN CENTRAL SCHOOL, BOWDOIN, ME

Bowdoin is a rural area. The school is the pride of the community and is the center of community activities. The percentage of residents living below the poverty level exceeds county and state levels. Thirty-nine percent of the families live in mobile homes. Sixty percent of the school population is housed in temporary facilities.

Clearly, the initiative and leadership roles taken by staff to improve learning for children have contributed most to the overall success of the school. The support for risk taking from the principal and the school district are essential ingredients to the ongoing success.

Robert Cartmill, *Principal, K—6, 269 Students*

DEEPHAVEN, MN

Developing their building mission statement was a process that helped bring staff together and provided a product upon which they can base decisions for kids. Their mission is to: 1) provide meaningful learning experiences, intellectually, physically, socially, and emotionally, in an organized and purposeful manner and 2) provide instruction in a setting in which every individual is treated with dignity and respect. This articulated purpose is verbalized to parents from the moment they walk through the doors, to staff throughout the year, and to students by actions every day. The Deephaven clientele clearly understands what their purpose is, and this allows them to more successfully focus all resources and energies in that direction.

The Deephaven community maintains high expectations for themselves and for the school. The staff at Deephaven is highly professional and works hard every day. The Minnetonka school district is of the highest quality and challenges each school to be the best that it can be. All these demands could overwhelm and paralyze a local school from making meaningful changes. That is not the case at Deephaven. Significant change has occurred because they have carefully planned which changes are most important during a given year, planned how much change can be made in one year, carefully evaluated at the end of each year, and developed meaningful next steps. They have changed at a healthy pace, which has kept their work exciting and at the same time not burned everyone out.

Deephaven has developed a strong and supportive PTO. Personal involvement of parents has more than doubled in the past five years. Not only does this involvement contribute a great deal of additional manpower to carry out goals, but it communicates the quality of education and degree of commitment that the school staff have to quality education.

OSBORN, NY

Four years ago, a new principal came to Osborn School filled with innovative ideas and the belief that teachers can make a difference. She capitalized on the professionalism and talents of each member of the staff and encouraged them to grow, to learn, and to change. They, in turn, have responded to her specific leadership style, and as part of a shared decision-making process, the entire faculty has helped to shape the school improvement.

THE BEST SCHOOLS—MAJOR EDUCATIONAL CHALLENGES FOR THE NEXT FIVE YEARS

The Best Schools take the long view of school improvement. It is not unusual in reading about the development of a specific program or practice to discover that the school has been actively involved in transforming the program or practice continuously for five, ten or even twenty years. Therefore, it is not surprising that the Best Schools are actively working on agendas with five or more year time lines. A survey of the 1991−92 Blue Ribbon Elementary School Principals, conducted by the U.S. Office of Education, identified the areas they plan to devote greatest attention to in the future (see Table 1).

Specific examples from the Best Schools illustrate more specifically what these schools view as challenges for the future.

Illustrations of Future Agendas in the Best Schools

DEEPHAVEN, MN

Managing the changes associated with the national, state, and local restructuring and reform effort presents considerable challenge. They have a solid instructional program and, at the same time, realize: 1) students who will live and work in the twenty-first century will need different kinds of skills, and 2) research on effective teaching suggests new methodologies will make learning more efficient and more effective. The challenge will be to: 1) clearly define student outcomes in a more interdisciplinary way so that students can see connections to the real world

TABLE 1. School improvement topics to receive the greatest attention (by percent of schools).

Rank Order	Among Top Five Priorities	Topics
1	54.0	Student performance assessment (testing, portfolios, exhibits, mastery)
2	53.1	Technology (computers, satellite hookups, VCRs, laster discs, CD ROM)
3	37.9	Visual and performing arts initiatives
4	37.5	Critical/higher order thinking skills
5	32.7	Strengthening curriculum content
6	32.2	Parent involvement
7	31.7	Teacher professionalism/new roles and responsibilities
8	29.4	Multicultural education/education for a pluristic society
9	28.9	At-risk students/dropout prevention
10	26.1	Character education

and are able to transfer skills learned to the world in which they live, 2) organize curriculum/instruction so that learning takes place sequentially, 3) provide staff with training that allows them to utilize new teaching methodologies, and 4) develop assessment techniques that clearly demonstrate that students have mastered objectives.

Another challenge facing Deephaven will be to continue to provide services that adequately address the social and emotional needs of families served. More severe needs (i.e., chemicals, abuse, dysfunctional families) surface each year. These issues all interfere with the teaching/learning process. These issues also often take intensive intervention before children can learn at normal rates. They intend to

- expand their ability to provide referral services to families
- continue to provide teachers with appropriate intervention strategies
- creatively provide more family education for those in need

SKYLINE, WA

The major challenges the school must face over the next five years include

(1) *Changing Demographics:* The student population has increased from 450 to 585 students in the past three years. Due to additional housing developments, student population will continue to grow. With growth, they will experience a wider range of behaviors and values that increase the difficulty of maintaining and improving a positive school culture. The new population is representative of that described in *A Nation At Risk,* which suggests that three out of five students will live with a single parent, and the percentage of children living in poverty will increase. Addressing the special needs of these students will necessitate even more emphasis on affective education (i.e., self-esteem, decision-making, and interpersonal skills). Skyline recognizes that providing for the multitude of unique needs of these students while continuing to maintain and improve programs of excellence will require imaginative and resourceful planning.

(2) *Relations with the Lummi Tribe:* In October 1991, seventeen Skyline staff members acted on their desire to increase their sensitivity to and appreciation for the unique heritage of Native American students by attending a three-day immersion seminar on the Lummi Reservation. This is an exemplary beginning to open new doors of cooperation and understanding between the cultures. Native American students will greatly benefit from the improved effort to understand and appreciate each other's uniqueness.

(3) *Continued Focus on School Improvement*: The school recognizes the challenge to continue to review, revise, and carry out activities specified in the School Improvement Plan. This

means keeping staff members actively involved in improving their skills and continuing to give them ownership in the future direction of the school.

BOWDOIN, ME

The major educational challenges are the increased use of technology and truly restructuring schools to prepare children for the twenty-first century. The challenges will require long-term commitment to change by staff and the board of directors, and the investment in human resources to include time for planning, curriculum work, and staff development. Limited resources and community resistance to change are the barriers to overcome.

SUMMARY

The underlying beliefs and values about education, children, staff, "possibilities," and goals determine the organizational vitality of schools and, ultimately, the learning outcomes for students. The characteristics associated with the less effective conventional and congenial types of schools and the instructionally effective outcome-based schools—the Best Schools (Blue Ribbon Schools) are identified. Illustrations from the Best Schools show how they maintain a continuous state of school improvement, use research, overcome challenges, and plan for the future.

REFERENCES

Brookover, W. B. and L. W. Lezotte, (1977). "Changes in School Characteristics Coincident with Change in Student Achievement," College of Urban Development of Michigan State University and the Michigan State Department of Education, Lansing, Michigan.

Brookover, W. B. (1977). "Elementary School Social Climate and Student Achievement," *American Educational Research Journal,* 15 (2):301–318.

Edmonds, R. R. "A Discussion of the Literature and Issues Related to Effective Schooling," Paper prepared for the National Conference on Urban Education, CEMREL, St. Louis, MO (1978).

Fullan, M. G. (1982). *The Meaning of Educational Change.* Toronto, Canada: Ontario Institute for Studies in Education.

Glickman, C. (1993). "Promoting Good Schools: The Core of Professional Work," Assembly presentation, ASCD Convention.

Joyce, B. et al. (1993). *The Self-Renewing School.* Alexandria, VA: Association for Supervision and Curriculum Development.

Lezotte, L. W. and B. C. Jacoby. (1992). *Sustainable School Reform: The District Context for School Improvement.* Effective Schools, Okemos, Michigan.

Rutter, M. (1985). *Changing Youth in a Changing Society,* Cambridge, MA; Harvard University Press.

CHAPTER 2

Leadership

DURING The past twenty years, educators have generated much research about what constitutes "effective schools." Yet sustained school improvement is an extremely complex process. The demand for educational reform throughout the country has generated much debate concerning the fundamental aspects of the goals of education, school governance structures, and the changing roles of parents, teachers, and administrators in today's schools. This chapter will examine the critical nature of establishing and prioritizing goals as a focus for sustained school improvement. Additionally, this chapter will explore leadership patterns and practices in the nation's best elementary schools.

Specifically, this chapter will address the following questions:

- What are the essential characteristics of productive educational planning?
- How do Best Schools organize and prioritize goals?
- What goals have Best Schools established for their schools and students?
- What are the most important characteristics of school leaders?
- How do principals in Best Schools inspire staff, parents, and students to accomplish school goals?

CHARACTERISTICS OF EFFECTIVE PLANNING

Successful school districts have long known the benefits of systematic planning. These schools look upon planning as an organic, ongoing process, not one initiated by crisis or the need to institutionalize innovations. Instead, successful schools have developed a culture that recognizes what is good about their schools, but they are secure enough to create a level of dissatisfaction that essentially says "we can do better."

Sashkin and Egermeier (1992) have identified the four broad strategies that are most often utilized in the planning for change in schools:

(1) *Fix the Parts by Transferring Innovations:* Get new information into practice by developing and transferring specific curricular or instructional programs.

(2) *Fix the People by Training and Developing Professionals:* This includes the comprehensive remodeling of preservice and inservice training of administrators and teachers.

(3) *Fix the School by Developing the Organization's Capacities to Solve Problems:* Help people in the school to solve their own problems more successfully. This strategy has grown out of the organization development (OD) movement that has schools collect data to identify and solve problems and to evaluate critical outcomes. Frequently, consultants are brought into the school to guide this strategy.

(4) *Fix the System by Comprehensive Restructuring:* Often called systemic change, school districts adopt a multilevel approach which involves the school/district major stakeholders reaching out to examine and change the fundamental culture of the school community.

The Best Schools across the country have utilized individual as well as a combination of these strategies. Yet common themes can be associated with the Best Schools. The goal in planning for success is to create a professional culture in which instructional and curricular decisions are based on informed research; support inquiry, consultation, and cooperative collaboration; and establish a primary concern for the successful achievement of *all* schools.

Following an examination of the writings and activities of proponents of school improvement, Joyce (1991) has identified five major emphases associated with initiatives for school change:

(1) *Collegiality:* developing cohesive and professional relations within school faculties and connecting them more closely to their surrounding neighborhoods.

(2) *Research:* helping school faculties study research findings about effective school practices or instructional alternatives.

(3) *Site-Specific Information:* helping faculties collect and analyze data about their schools and their students' progress.

(4) *Curriculum Initiatives:* introducing changes within subject areas, or, as in the case of the computer, across curriculum areas.

(5) *Instructional Initiatives:* organizing teachers to study teaching skills and strategies.

The Best Schools, whether urban, suburban or rural, utilize a systematic planning process to initiate and sustain school improvement. Through the development of a common understanding of shared beliefs, students, parents, teachers, and administration are empowered to establish a clear vision for their school. This vision becomes the centerpiece by which the quest for school success is based.

Vision provides a clear statement of what the school should look like and deliver, as well as describes the environment in which it will operate. It includes the identification of an "ideal world" or construction of the "best or preferred future" before injecting reality data (Kaufman and Herman, 1991).

Glickman (1992) speaks to a super vision for school success. He states that, for a school to be educationally successful, it must be a community of professionals working together toward a vision of teaching and learning that transcends individual classrooms, grade levels, and departments. The entire school community must develop a covenant to guide future decisions about goals and operation of the school.

The vision of the Best Schools is most often expressed in a mission statement as a broad general description of purpose. It can be motivational, inspirational, and/or directional (Kaufman and Herman, 1991). In developing a mission statement, no single format works equally well for all schools. But whatever process is used, it must be agreed upon by, and actually involve representatives from, all aspects of the school community. Although it can and should be stated in many different ways, it should emphasize that all students in a school are capable of achieving mastery in all areas of the curriculum and that the teachers and administrators accept responsibility for making this a reality (Lezotte and Jacoby, 1992).

An increasing number of schools have endorsed school improvement through school-based management. There are many definitions of this phenomenon that vary with implementation and practice, for example, "a means of empowering the stakeholders of the school to make important decisions" (Henderson and Marburger, 1990); "schools given the freedom and flexibility required to respond creatively to its educational objectives, and above all, to meet the needs of students" (Hanson, 1990); and "a process of decentralization in which the school becomes the primary unit of management and educational improvement" (Educational Research Service, 1991).

Through a collaborative process, school councils are developed to assume an increased governance role in establishing school goals, priorities, and practices. Principals, teachers, parents, and students accept increased ownership in their schools as they realize that their collected views are not only respected, but acted upon.

According to the American Association of School Administrators (AASA), the National Association of Elementary School Principals (NAESP), the National Association of Secondary Principals (NASSP), and other sources, school-based management:

- allows competent individuals in the schools to make decisions that will improve learning
- gives the entire school community a voice in key decisions
- focuses accountability for decisions
- leads to greater creativity in the design of programs
- redirects resources to support the goals developed in each school
- leads to realistic budgeting as parents and teachers become more aware of the school's financial status, spending limitations, and the cost of its programs
- improves morale of teachers and nurtures new leadership at all levels of the school organization

Many school districts across the country have successfully developed school-based planning councils as a means of transferring significant decision-making authority from state and district offices to individual schools. Many of America's Best Schools have embraced the concept and have successfully integrated school-based planning councils as a vehicle for school improvement.

THE BEST SCHOOLS—PLAN AND ORGANIZE FOR SUCCESS

The Best Schools throughout the country have developed clear mission statements that help operationalize the school's collective vision. Additionally, they have developed precise statements of goals and priorities that establish the parameters for school practices.

Schools have used a variety of vehicles to establish goals and priorities. Many utilized broad-based staff, community, and at times, business partnerships in the formative stages of planning to guide school improvement. Examples of strategies used in our Best Schools are illustrated next.

Planning Illustrations

CHRISTA MCAULIFFE ELEMENTARY SCHOOL, LEWISVILLE, TX

McAuliffe Elementary School is one of eighteen elementary schools in the Lewisville Independent School District, located within thirty miles of the Dallas/Fort Worth area. It is situated in one of the five fastest growing counties in the United States. Lewisville can be characterized as a middle income community, with McAuliffe School having an ethnic mix of 96% Caucasian, 2% African-American, 1.5% Hispanic, and .5% Asian.

A Building Leadership Team (composed of the principal, assistant principal, counselor, an elected teacher from each grade, teacher representatives from special education and related arts, parents, and community leaders) uses a "planned change strategy" to develop school goals and priorities. The McAuliffe vision statement, "We are proud to be life-long learners," is posted in every classroom.

Sharing the common conviction that all students at McAuliffe can and will be successful, the school community has utilized a team approach to establish school goals and priorities. These priorities are articulated into five specific goals:

(1) Student achievement, as measured by standardized tests, will be maintained or will increase at Christa McAuliffe Elementary School.

(2) Student self-esteem will be nurtured and increased through activities that include parent and teacher involvement.

(3) All students shall attend school regularly.

(4) Communication will be strengthened between parents and teachers concerning the child's progress and performance in school.

(5) Third and fifth grade students will increase the number of students receiving academic recognition, as measured by the Texas Assessment of Academic Skills (TAAS).

Mary Ann Ritchie, Principal, K−5, 771 Students

Other schools have chosen to develop goals through the professional staff and have then been reviewed and refined by community stakeholders.

LEAWOOD ELEMENTARY SCHOOL, LEAWOOD, KS

Leawood Elementary School serves a middle to upper income neighborhood of suburban Kansas City, Kansas. Leawood has a long-standing tradition of active parent involvement. To focus parental involvement, as well as meaningful involvement of staff, Leawood has developed a school council as part of the district's School-Based Leadership Program.

Made up of a representative group of parents, teachers, classified staff, and the principal, the leadership council surveyed staff and parents to gather information as to feelings and ideas about creating an "ideal school"; the school council used the data to facilitate the following four school goals:

(1) In order to provide educational life-enriching opportunities, Leawood Elementary will continually explore the needs and utilize the resources of the community (children, families, patrons, business).

(2) To develop the social and emotional well-being of each child, Leawood Elementary will provide age appropriate activities that build a healthy self-esteem and a sense of responsibility.

(3) Recognizing the uniqueness of each child, Leawood Elementary will provide an active learning environment that fosters the development of every student's optimal academic potential.

(4) Realizing the need for awareness and acceptance of differences among people (places and events) both near and far, Leawood Elementary will offer opportunities for students to learn about those of other races, religions, and cultures.

"Design teams," composed of both parents and staff members, have been formed to develop action plans to operationalize each goal.

Doug Harris, Principal, K−5, 478 Students

TISKELWAH ELEMENTARY SCHOOL, CHARLESTON, WV

Tiskelwah Elementary is an inner-city school located on the west side of Charleston, West Virginia. Over 80% of the students qualify for free or reduced lunch. Poverty is a major problem for the majority of the families in the school's attendance area. The students all walk to school. A disproportionate number of students enrolled are categorized as at risk for school failure.

During the summer of 1989, the professional staff met for a two-week period of time. A three-year plan of improvement was developed. This plan was developed after the staff had an opportunity to review national exemplary programs and to identify and prioritize the needs of students. Annual review of school goals, priorities, and activities has been essential as the needs of students, staff, and parents continue to change. The three-year plan of improvement and subsequent annual plan updates have been reviewed by executive council of PTA, the School Improvement Council, and community leaders who have become business partners with the school.

The five fundamental goals for the Tiskelwah's School and students are:

(1) To work collaboratively with parents in the identified school communities to set new directions and expectations about student achievement, aspirations, and success;

(2) To develop an equity perspective among students, teachers, administrators, and parents that will address the needs of students who are at risk, by acknowledging diversity and by increasing expectations for student achievement and successes;

(3) To build an integrated skills-based curriculum that includes a core of common learning and provides a program of instruction that most appropriately addresses the special interests, learning programs, and social development needs of the student population;

(4) To find and implement new solutions for restructuring school organization and management, enhancing curriculum offerings, and improving strategies and techniques for delivering instructional programs in at-risk urban school settings;

(5) To provide an ongoing program of professional staff development experience that will enable staff to address the specific learning and teaching needs of the urban school.

Priority objectives for the 1991–92 school included:

- Students will achieve at the 75th percentile in the basic skill areas of reading and mathematics.
- Students will understand and adhere to school and classroom rules.
- Students will be active participants in the learning process.
- Students will develop a positive sense of self-worth.

Dr. Jorea Marple, *Principal, K–6, 101 Students*

ALAMO ELEMENTARY SCHOOL, ALAMO, CA

Alamo School is the smallest of twenty-three schools in the San Ramon Valley Unified School District. The district includes thirteen other elementary schools, four middle schools, three comprehensive high schools, a continuation high school, and an independent study school with a combined enrollment of 16,428. A teacher strike in 1989?90 and severe cutbacks in the educational program and support services in 1990?91, are visible evidence of the fiscal crisis that has plagued the district in recent years. Alamo School is located in a suburban community with an 84% Caucasian student population and an emerging 10% Asian-Pacific student population.

School goals and priorities are established yearly in cooperation with the School Improvement Program site council. Teachers and the principal write formal personal goals to correspond to school goals. The goals and priorities are communicated to the parent community in a variety of ways. They are formally presented at Back to School Night at the beginning of the school year and are reviewed again at parent-teacher conferences, along with the individual student's progress. In addition, goals and priorities are communicated through regular PTA meetings, monthly PTA newsletters, classroom newsletters, and formal and informal meetings with parents.

The principal, teachers, parents, and community have high academic goals for Alamo students. This is clearly reflected in the school's mission statement: "Academic excellence in an atmosphere that promotes leadership, respect for democratic values and a desire to achieve one's potential."

As a result of this process planning program, Alamo School's six goals are:

(1) Plan and coordinate curriculum that provides students with experiences that promote positive

social development, school involvement, and the opportunity to learn and participate in the democratic process.

(2) Revitalize and supplement the curriculum and instructional methods so they are responsive to the changing individual needs of students and the changing character of society and the working world.

(3) Improve the building's instructional effectiveness and maximize operational efficiency of the facility.

(4) Focus resources on insuring high-quality and dedicated staff.

(5) Pursue business and community partnerships that benefit students' educational opportunities.

(6) Promote parents' involvement in the school through a wide variety of opportunities for participation.

Joan Benbow, *Principal, K – 5, 325 Students*

In many of the Best Schools, general goals are developed at the district level. Individual schools then prioritize and operationalize these goals into observable objectives.

JOHN M. GRASSE ELEMENTARY SCHOOL, SELLERSVILLE, PA

The John M. Grasse Elementary School is one of seven elementary schools in the Pennridge School District, located in rural Hilltown Township in Bucks County, Pennsylvania. The school serves children from various ethnic and socioeconomic backgrounds.

The goals and priorities of the J. M. Grasse Elementary School were established in concert with the development of the Pennridge School District's Long Range Plan that was developed in 1986 and finalized in 1991. These goals and priorities were created by an advisory committee composed of staff members, parents, citizens and students. This committee established three priorities: communications, analytical thinking, and health.

Goals were distributed to the staff each school term as both staff development and instructional activities were focused on their accomplishment. At the conclusion of each school year, the staff assessed the school's progress toward the accomplishment of these goals. In the spring of 1991, a final evaluation of the goal activities and the resulting achievements were presented to the advisory committee that recommended submitting the plan to the Pennridge School Board for approval.

In addition to the goals and priorities established through the long-range planning process, the staff also addressed three needs that were specific to the effectiveness of the school's educational program:

(1) Providing a safe and secure environment

(2) Developing in each student a sense of belonging

(3) Providing activities to encourage the development of self-esteem of all students

These needs were communicated to parents through parent-teacher conferencing, meetings of parent groups, and by the school's newsletter. Students were made aware of these priorities through their daily instructional programs, as well as their informal contacts with teachers and other staff members.

Thomas R. Szabo, *Principal (Gregory T. Nolan, Principal at time of recognition),*
K – 6, 473 Students

Another relatively common theme in the Best Schools is to utilize a model from the research to structure the development of school goals and operational plans. An outstanding example that integrated the Effective Schools Model is illustrated below.

ROOT ELEMENTARY SCHOOL, FAYETTEVILLE, AR

Root Elementary School is one of eight elementary schools that serves the Fayetteville community. It is located on the east side of the city in an area that is composed mainly of single family dwellings, although there is one large area of apartment complexes within the attendance area. Root also serves a small number of families from the rural settlements east of Fayetteville. The majority of the students attending Root come from middle-class, Caucasian families who have high academic and social expectations for their children and are very involved in all school activities. The school goals and priorities were formulated as the staff prepared for the self-study portion of the Comprehensive Outcomes Evaluation process undertaken by the Fayetteville School District. Additionally, the staff has been involved in a needs assessment based on the Effective Schools Model in which the faculty rated Effective Schools Criteria in terms of the presence of these criteria at Root School.

The four goals of Root Elementary School are:

(1) To provide a psychologically and emotionally safe learning environment, which is reflective of the society in which we live;

(2) To develop students who will work cooperatively to acquire the basic and challenging core concepts and abilities in the areas of language arts, mathematics, science, history, geography, economics, the fine arts, physical and health education, and existing/emerging technologies;

(3) To have a well-trained professional staff who will use teaching strategies that will require students to apply thinking skills and problem-solving strategies to all subject matter areas;

(4) To have a caring professional staff who will provide the encouragement and support that will help students develop and exhibit attitudes and attributes that will promote mental, physical, and emotional health.

In order to achieve the above goals, the school's priorities are:

- grouping students whenever possible in heterogeneous and cooperative learning environments,
- working closely with the parents of kindergarten students to ensure that all first grade students will be ready for formal learning,
- communicating high learning expectations that will result in quality performances by all students,
- engaging in cooperative, professional development activities that will result in improved learning opportunities for students,
- keeping students and their parents informed of learning progress on a continuous basis using both formal and informal methods,
- guarding the learning environment so that all types of learning disruptions are kept to an absolute minimum,
- involving parents in all aspects of the education of their children,
- implementing curriculum changes in a planned and sequential manner,
- continuing school-based restructuring and renewal activities based upon identified needs resulting from program and school assessment.

Oma Lea Blackwell, *Principal, K – 6, 522 Students*

As one examines the nature of school planning and goal setting in the nation's Best Schools, we see many approaches to the transformation of school culture. A school culture should be guided by a clear vision, expressed through a focused mission statement that is directed by caring committee members within the school communities. Like the schools previously cited, the Best Schools are often centered around a central theme or school motto such as: "I will try my best to do my best for that is the key to success" (Bunker Hill School, Washington,

D.C.); "We care, we share, we shine" (Saigling Elementary School, Plano, Texas); and "Dignity, Pride and Respect" (Princess Likeleke Elementary School, Honolulu, Hawaii). Additionally, the Best Schools also value collaboration and collective improvement, and transcend personal goals for the school and student goals.

In summary, the nation's finest schools can be best characterized as having:

- A clear and focused mission,
- A climate of high expectations for success of all students and staff,
- Curricular and instructional programs that ensure opportunities for every student to learn basic and higher order content and skills,
- A strong commitment to instructional and programmatic leadership,
- A reliance on research and a sense that appropriate information is collected and used to guide school practices,
- A dedication to the emotional well-being of students, including the reinforcing of pride and self-esteem,
- Purposeful and supportive involvement of parents, other citizens, and business and community groups.

DIMENSIONS OF LEADERSHIP

The literature of educational improvement is filled with calls for better and stronger leadership. Yet a categorical model of effective school leadership still remains elusive. In fact, in recent years, the role of school leaders has become somewhat diffused. In the midst of restructuring initiatives, school-based management teams, peer coaching, and teacher empowerment movements, some question the true role (or significance) of today's principal. Despite its critics, the role of school administration, particularly the building principal, continues to be at the core of successful schools. According to Eaker, Ranells and DuFour (1991), "The leadership skills of the principal are critical to a school improvement initiative."

The role of the principal in today's successful schools has transcended the traditional notion of functional management, power, behavioral style, and instructional leadership. The Best Schools have principals who consider their most important task as establishing a school culture. Whether through collaboration, consensus building, personal influence, or modeling, the principal is able to promote a culture where staff members have school goals that become more important than their own self interests and where teachers work together to accomplish the school's mission.

Typically, unsuccessful schools have teachers who see only their own accomplishments and fail to see the relationship of what they do to the greater school mission. Successful schools have principals who focus their staffs to the central theme and priorities of the school and permit all the educators a greater opportunity to make decisions about education.

This change in the leadership role of the principal has prompted a major shift among those who study leadership and among those who practice it. Despite different styles, principals in successful schools have a transformational effect on the people who work in the shadow of their leadership. As Roberts (1985) explains:

> The collective action that transforms leadership generally empowers those who participate in the process. There is hope, there is optimism, there is energy. In essence, transforming leadership is a leadership that facilitates the redefinition of a people's mission and vision, a renewal of their commitment, and the restructuring of their systems for goal accomplishment.

John Gardner (1990) concludes that the primary skill for contemporary leaders is to "understand the kind of world it is and have some acquaintance with the systems other than their own with which they must work." To function in such a world, leaders need critical skills:

(1) *Agreement-Building:* Leaders must have skills in conflict resolution, mediation, compromise, and coalition building. Essential to these activities are the capacity to build trust, judgment, and political skills.

(2) *Networking:* In a swiftly changing environment, traditional linkages among institutions may no longer serve or may have been disrupted. Leaders must create or recreate the linkages needed to get things done.

(3) *Exercising Non-jurisdictional Power:* In an earlier time, corporate or government leaders could exercise almost absolute power over internal decisions. The new leaders must deal on many fronts with groups or constituencies over which they have no control (for educators, that might be taxpayers with no children in the schools). Their power comes from the ability to build consensus and teamwork and to translate others' ideas into action. They must be sensitive to the media and to public opinion. New leaders use "the power that accrues to those who really understand how the system works and perhaps above all, the power available to anyone skilled in the art of leadership."

Sagar (1992) reports that an increasing trend in schools where teachers and students report a culture conducive to school success is a transformational leader as the principal. He goes on to suggest that these principals consistently utilize identifiable strategies:

- A clear and unified focus that empowers professionals to act as both individuals and members of the school.
- A common cultural perspective that enables teachers to view other schools through a similar lens.
- A constant push for improvement emphasizing the importance of the simultaneous application of pressure and support during educational change.

Through the development of schools as more open systems, leaders no longer decide what to do and then set standards in isolation from other major stakeholders. For many successful schools, the principal's role has been redefined by assuming more of a facilitative role. In fact, the ability of principals to make this transition from one leadership perspective to another, to perceive power as something that is multiplied rather than reduced when it is shared, seems to be one of the key issues of school improvement (Goldman, Dunlap, and Donley, 1991).

Despite the emphasis on leadership as a transforming phenomenon, successful principals have a keen sense of the importance of the stresses placed on school stakeholders during the change process. As cultural anthropologist, Jennifer James (1990) concludes, "Change that is too fast tears some of the fabric of the school culture." To be successful, change agents should never abruptly strip people of their illusions of yesterday, but instead permit one step backward before moving two steps forward, keeping those things that they believe are most important for future improvement.

Sergiovanni (1992) concludes that the only thing that makes a leader special is that he or she is a better follower: better at articulating the purposes of the community, more passionate about goals, and more willing to take time to pursue them.

THE BEST SCHOOLS – LEADERSHIP PRACTICES

The examination of our Best Schools uncovers literally hundreds of special leaders, principals who were able to transform the culture of schools, create a shared vision, and empower the school community to act on behalf of its children. There does not appear to be any one specific profile of an effective principal. Principals in the Best Schools have a wide range of total years' experience in administration, with approximately 15% having less than five years, 34% five to nine years, 25% ten to fourteen years, and 26% fifteen or more years. Their experience as the principal of the recognized school varied also, with 26% serving less than five years, 48% five to nine years, 15% ten to fourteen years, and 10% more than fifteen years. It is interesting to note that 43% of these principals had had only one year or less administrative experience prior to becoming the principal of the school that would become a Blue Ribbon School; however, 13% of the principals had been principals of other recognized schools. Finally, while both men and women were principals of recognized elementary schools, the proportion of women principals in recognized schools is 59%, considerably greater than the 40% women principals for all elementary schools.

The role of the principal is of special significance in successful schools. Consistently, the dedicated professionals have been respected, admired, and in many cases, loved by students, parents, and staff. Time and space prohibit an all-inclusive description of the nation's outstanding principals, yet some most closely approximate the characteristics described in this chapter.

Leadership Illustrations

VIRGINIA WHEELER ELEMENTARY SCHOOL, LOUISVILLE, KY

The Virginia Wheeler Elementary School is located in Louisville (Jefferson County), Kentucky. The school serves a basically rural, residential area bordering on Spencer and Bullitt Counties. The racial/ethnic population of the students is represented by 74% Caucasian, 24% African-American, and 2% Hispanic and Asian-Pacific Islander.

A major historical milestone took place in 1987 when the school restructured to a nongraded K−5 environment using multi-age, multi-ability teams. Tracking was eliminated and flexible groupings were utilized. Shared decision making was adopted, allowing the collective wisdom of the community, parents, students, teachers, staff, and the principal to forge the direction and create the vision of the school.

Wheeler's principal is said to exude strength, purpose, integrity, and vision. She is a facilitator, coach, and mentor and, under her leadership, teachers at Wheeler have themselves developed leadership capacity. Several Wheeler teachers have achieved national recognition for the quality of their teaching and for their implementation of innovative and successful programs in the school. Since coming to Wheeler in 1985, the principal has worked untiringly to involve the administrative and teaching staffs and parents in forging a clear definition of the school and its purposes. Her intensive review of the recent literature on educational research and practice has helped design a school community that promotes the success of all members. Developmentally appropriate practices for the teaching of young children, shared decision making, and teaming of teachers in middle schools were considered and adapted for Wheeler. Powerful discussions involving principal, staff, and faculty led to the decision to become a participatory management school.

Charlene D. Bush, *Principal, K−5, 545 Students*

BELMONT ELEMENTARY SCHOOL, GRAND FORKS, ND

The Belmont School was the first elementary school in Grand Forks, North Dakota. Established in 1883, Belmont School preceded statehood. Although a fire burned the original building, the present structure has been used as a school since 1904.

A significant number of Native American students attend the school, with an exceedingly high student mobility of 21−35% each year. This phenomenon has had a dramatic effect on both class size and continuity in learning. Yet the students in the Belmont School continue to achieve at levels significantly above their predicated scores. This is made possible by the tireless efforts of the professional staff and leadership of Belmont's principal.

The teachers characterize their principal's leadership as inspiring. She maintains high expectations for herself and others, instilling a ''can-do'' attitude that has been amazingly contagious. She is said to be a powerful role model for the school.

She has established a climate where human beings matter. Each child, each teacher, each staff member, and each parent is valued and treated with dignity. She recognizes that, for many parents, school may not have been a successful and positive experience and that the staff needs to help parents develop esteem and partnership with the school to succeed with students. She cares about all the individuals that comprise Belmont School, and she encourages them to care about themselves and their education.

The staff at the Belmont School credit the principal for turning student discipline into a learning experience for conflict resolution. To promote a positive climate in the school, one of her first priorities, she works with the students on how to resolve their differences and then praises their efforts. She gives them the skills and confidence to eventually work out many problems on their own. This is also an effective role model for teachers and parents. When the students were having problems getting along with each other (negative climate), the principal worked with the Teacher Assistance Team to develop a program using a story entitled ''The Dipper and the Bucket.'' It was designed to stop ''put-downs'' (dipping in each other's buckets) and give students the skills to give and receive compliments.

Dr. Beth S. Randklev, *Principal, K−6, 314 Students*

O'HARA ELEMENTARY SCHOOL, PITTSBURGH, PA

The O'Hara Elementary School is located in northern suburban Pittsburgh. It represents a wide range of socioeconomic and cultural differences. In 1981, three smaller schools were merged to form the O'Hara School. Despite initial resistance to the merger, children from three separate communities have blended into a school ignited with spirit and endowed with a special harmony. The school principal has played a significant role in the development and maintenance of this very special school culture.

Leading by example, he exhibits professionalism, diligence, and dedication, promoting a positive atmosphere among staff, students, parents, and community members, and taking an active part in every aspect of school operations. Visible in all areas of the building and grounds, he can also be found in his office well before and long after the school day has ended.

The principal frequently attends classroom functions and activities on his own and at the request of teachers and/or students. He also visits classrooms to get to know students individually and personally and knows most students by name. He promotes belief in self, having respect for others, accepting responsibility for choices, and setting high goals.

The principal is always available to lend his support, and all decisions are made with input from a variety of sources, including parents who praise Mr. Delconte for his ability to involve them in the school and his tireless efforts to support their children both in and out of school.

Vincent R. Delconte, *Principal, K−6, 730 Students*

THOMAS JEFFERSON MIDDLE SCHOOL, NORTH MIAMI, FL

Thomas Jefferson Middle School was built in 1958 in North Miami, Florida, at a time when the school system in Florida was segregated and served a largely homogeneous population. Even for many years after schools were desegregated, Thomas Jefferson remained largely a white, middle class school. This changed radically over the last ten years.

Reflecting the situation in Miami, which is a magnet for immigrants from the Caribbean, South and Central America, and Mid-East, Thomas Jefferson Middle School presently claims staff and students of forty-nine distinct national origins. Racially, the student population is approximately

63% African-American, 21% Hispanic, 14.2% Caucasian, and 1.8% Asian. The black student population represents a culturally diverse mixture of students from Haiti, the Caribbean, and the West Indies. Seventeen percent of the students have limited English proficiency.

The principal has established a clear vision for the Thomas Jefferson Middle School family, a vision that everyone knows and shares. She is said to set a positive tone, which signals commitment and dedication.

Allen E. Hindman, *Principal (Geneva K. Williams, Principal at time of recognition),*
Grades 7 – 9, 1193 Students

One of the characteristics of successful principals is their continuing focus on school improvement. A survey conducted by the U.S. Office of Education, Blue Ribbon School Program identified eleven categories of leadership skills these principals believed they would need to develop further in order to meet the challenges of the year 2000.

Leadership Skills Needed to Meet Future Challenges

1. *Communication (20%)* Better communication skills needed to improve listening, networking, and staff- and parent-oriented communications. Developing effective communication strategies with the business community and general public was also a key concern.

2. *Instructional Leadership (18%)* Principals indicated a need for instructional skills to develop performance standards, conduct academic and resource assessments, and improve curriculum. Under the topic of curriculum improvement, they expressed a desire for skills to meet diverse student needs; develop subject-based curriculum standards, e.g., math and science; effectively implement outcome-based education or early childhood curricula; and implement the restructuring processes at their school.

3. *Shared Decision Making (10%)* Principals mentioned needing skills for developing a transformational leadership style and specific skills for more effectively implementing shared decision making, including team building, delegating responsibilities, planning, implementing programs, and managing projects.

4. *School Management (10%)* Responses included time management, priority setting, quality control strategies, funding, marketing and business orientation to school management, efficiency assessment, staff assessments and supervision, and over-all site-based management skill development.

5. *Motivational (10%)* Principals thought that inspirational leadership skills are critical. These skills include developing appropriate modeling behaviors that "create winners" among staff and students. Principals indicated a need for these skills in order to change staff behaviors, improve their morale, and enhance their professional commitment and sense of empowerment.

6. *Technology (8%)* Developing computer literacy was often mentioned. However, in addition to acquiring this knowledge for personal improvement, principals felt it was important to learn a variety of technological applications for a school setting.

7. *Advocacy (7%)* Principals desired advocacy skills for many reasons, but most often to become an advocate for children, an advocate for family and adult literacy, an advocate for early childhood education, or an advocate for education in general. They wanted to develop a better understanding of the political and legislative processes at the local school board level, as well as at state and national levels.

8. *Consensus Building (6%)* This response category included problem solving, negotiations, compromise and consensus generation strategies, and conflict management. Some principals also indicated a need for knowledge of potential conflict areas, e.g., law and litigation.

9. *Positive School Climate Development (3%)* These responses were similar to those in the motivational category, but focus here was on students, parents and community service providers.

10. *Flexible Thinking (4%)* Principals mentioned the need for self-improvement, especially those skills that lead to increased risk-taking, and innovative and visionary thinking.

11. *Other (4%)* This category includes personal skills not easily classified in the other categories; e.g., the need for skills to improve adult education, develop tenacity, increased cultural literacy skills, and maintenance of healthy lifestyles. U.S. Department of Education, "A Profile of Principals," p. 12, 1993.

SUMMARY

The Best Schools consistently demonstrate the ability to plan and organize for success. Although the strategies to produce the plans vary based on the size, traditions, and needs of the school, many common elements exist. America's finest schools have a clear sense of purpose. Great care is given to develop a mission statement that often serves as the focus for school practices and improvements. The mission is always translated into clear goals that are aimed at the development of a school climate that expects each student to be successful. The Best Schools have principals who transcend the managerial tenets of their role—principals who understand that their primary role is to create and maintain a school culture that is student-centered and goal-oriented. Teachers who work in these schools receive satisfaction from the professional work that they accomplish together for the benefit of children. Principals in the Best Schools not only value the students, parents, and teachers, but systematically involve them in a variety of meaningful educational decisions. Teachers are not treated as hierarchical subordinates, but are given the responsibility to make decisions that affect life in the school. Finally, the principals in America's Best Schools instill a belief within the school community that school improvement is an ongoing process of getting better, no matter how good they may perceive themselves to be now!

REFERENCES

American Association of School Administrators, National Association of Elementary School Principals, and National Association of Secondary School Principals. (1988). *School-Based Management: A Strategy for Better Learning.* Arlington, Virginia.

Eaker, Robert, Mary Ann Ranells, and Richard DuFour, (1991). *Utilizing the Effective School Research: Practical Strategies for School Improvement.* Murfreesboro, Tennessee: Middle Tennessee Chapter of Phi Delta Kappa.

Educational Research Service, (1991). *Site-Based Management.* ERS Information Aid, Arlington, VA, ERS.

Gardner, John. (1990). *On Leadership.* New York: The Free Press.

Glickman, Carl D. (1992). "The Essence of School Renewal: The Prose Has Begun," *Educational Leadership,* 501: 24–27.

Goldman, Paul, Diane Dunlap, and David Donley. (1991). "Administrative Facilitation and Site-Based School Reform Projects," Paper presented at the *Annual Conference of the American Educational Research Association,* Chicago, April 4, 1991.

Hanson, E. M. (1990). "School-Based Management and Educational Reform in the United States and Spain," *Comparative Education Review,* 34:523–537.

Henderson, A. and C. Marburger, "Ten Pitfalls of School-Based Improvement," Network of Public Schools 15 (Spring, 1990):3-5.

James, Jennifer. (1990). "How to Cope with Cultural Chaos" (Interview with Jack Blendiner and Linda T. Jones), *The School Administrator,* 3(47):27–29.

Joyce, Bruce R. (1991). "The Doors to School Improvement," *Educational Leadership,* 48(8):59–62.

Kaufman, Roger and Jerry Herman. (1991). *Strategic Planning in Education: Rethinking, Restructuring, Revitalizing.* Lancaster, PA: Technomic Publishing Company, Inc.

Lezotte, Lawrence W. and Barbara C. Jacoby. (1992). *The District Content for School Improvement.* Okemos, Michigan: Effective Schools Products, Ltd.

Roberts, N. (1985). "Transforming Leaders: A Process of Collective Action," *Human Relations*, 38(11):1023–1046.

Sagar, Richard D. (1992). "Three Principals Who Make a Difference," *Educational Leadership*, 49(5):13–18.

Sashkin, M. and J. Egermeier. (1992). School Change Models and Processes: A Review of Research and Practice," Working draft prepared for the United States Department of Education's AMERICA 2000 initiative and for a research symposium presented at the *1992 Annual Meeting of the American Educational Research Association*, Washington, D.C.

Sergiovanni, Thomas J. (1992). "On Rethinking Leadership: A Conversation With Tom Sergiovanni (interview with Ron Brandt)," *Educational Leadership*, 49(5):46–49.

CHAPTER 3

Teaching Environment

AMERICA'S Best Schools have effective principals. These principals have the ability to develop and sustain an organizational culture that focuses their staffs toward the achievement of school goals. Through the creation of a shared vision comes a foundation for the traditions, norms, values, and beliefs that are embodied within the school community.

The perception of this culture, held by staff, students, and parents constitutes the climate of the school (Keefe and Kelley, 1990). These prevailing conditions that establish the parameters for daily practices and routines have proven to have significant impact on school success. The maintenance of a positive climate provides the framework to move the school's mission and objectives from the awareness and planning stages to the implementation and maintenance stages.

This chapter will examine the significance of a professional teaching environment as a focus for achievement of student-based goals. Additionally, special emphasis will be given to common strategies that have promoted productive teaching environments in successful schools. Finally, programs and initiatives from the nation's Best Schools will be provided to illustrate the unique application of research and strategies into enriching teaching environments.

Specifically, this chapter will address the following questions:

- What are the essential characteristics of a productive teaching environment?
- What strategies are utilized to maximize teacher expertise in school decision making?
- What provisions are made in Best Schools to enable staff to engage in collegial planning and implementation of educational programs?
- What do Best Schools do to support and strengthen the skills of beginning teachers and teachers new to the school?
- What procedures for supervision and evaluation of teachers exist in Best Schools?
- How do Best Schools support and encourage the recognition of teachers?
- What strategies are utilized in Best Schools to enhance teachers' effectiveness with students and to improve job satisfaction?
- What are the characteristics of staff development programs in Best Schools?

PRODUCTIVE TEACHING

Teachers' performance in schools is in part determined by the atmosphere or climate in which they work. It can be looked upon as a broad concept referring to teachers' perception of the work environment. There are a number of common terms used to refer to the general surroundings of an individual at work—ecology, milieu, setting, time, field, atmosphere, or climate. They all are used to refer to the internal quality of the workplace as experienced by its members (Hoy and Forsyth, 1986).

In a very real sense, the conceptual environment in which teachers' work can distinguish successful from nonsuccessful schools is because of the impact and direct influence environment has on teachers' perceptions and behaviors. Similarly, a school's environment can have a significant effect on the learning and development of students and, in some cases, student academic achievement.

No single factor accounts for building a successful teaching environment. Yet much research has been aimed at isolating those characteristics that facilitate student learning and school improvement. Research by Lezotte, 1991, has shown seven operational characteristics that seem to be present in the environments of a successful school:

(1) "A safe and orderly environment," including an environment that is conducive to good discipline where rules and procedures are well defined and where students actually help one another

(2) "Climate of high expectation for success," where a commitment to well-defined goals directs the school's resources and where beliefs and behaviors are aimed at successful achievement for all students

(3) "Instructional leadership," characterized by behavior directed toward instructional goals, motivation of instructional improvement, and provisions for opportunities for staff growth and disbursement of leadership throughout the staff

(4) "Clear focus and mission," directing and unifying staff toward the primary goal of learning for all students

(5) "Appropriate opportunity for student learning and time on task" through the design and delivery of an aligned curriculum and instructional strategies that emphasize student-engaged learning time

(6) "Frequent monitoring of student progress," where a variety of evaluation methods are used that provide students feedback on learning and teachers feedback for modifying instruction

(7) "Home-school relations," where the mission and instructional focus of the school is communicated to parents and the community and where their support is elicited and their involvement encouraged

These underlying characteristics of effective schools have long been valued as a conceptual framework for school success. Increasingly, as indicated in the previous chapter, successful schools have instituted collaborative problem solving as a basic ingredient for school improvement. Teachers and administrators working together to make decisions and solve problems has been proven to foster school excellence, as well as to develop a sense of collegiality among staff.

THE BEST SCHOOLS—TEACHER INVOLVEMENT IN DECISION MAKING AND COLLEGIAL PLANNING

The Best Schools actively create opportunities for the involvement of teachers in most every aspect of school decision making. They have capitalized on the skills and experiences of those who are closest to and know most about the teaching-learning process. Although all successful schools have developed strategies for teacher involvement, examples of strategies that have proven beneficial in America's Best Schools are illustrated next.

Teacher Involvement Illustrations

GLENDALE MIDDLE SCHOOL, NASHVILLE, TN

Glendale Middle School is located in the Oak Hill area of Nashville, Tennessee. Its student population includes 82% Caucasian, 13% African-American, 3% Hispanic, and 2% Asian-

American. Included in the population is a high percentage of learning disabled and emotionally handicapped students, as well as a population of multi-handicapped students mainstreamed into the regular educational program.

Teachers at Glendale are involved in decision making in every aspect of the school program. Teachers are asked to work with the building administrator in arranging the master schedule, which because of extended class offerings, can prove to be quite a task. Curriculum and course content are planned the spring before a new school year begins. Teachers on all grade levels meet regularly to discuss ways to enrich curriculum between grade levels for the purpose of program continuity. A school "Pro-Team" plans for scheduled inservice days, as well as for visiting speakers for professional enrichment. Teachers are also invited to team with other teachers to interview new faculty members and then offer support after employment to familiarize them with the way things are generally handled.

Teachers are also involved in the design and development of the schoolwide discipline plan; teachers are basically responsible for its implementation and success. The teachers at Glendale are even provided input in deciding the beginning and ending times for the school day for teachers.

Another opportunity for teacher empowerment was the decision of the faculty to become a pilot school for the new site-based decision-making plan implemented by the Metro Nashville School System. Through this avenue of management, students, parents, teachers, and community members will have more opportunity for input into school decisions.

Dr. Carol M. Hutson, *Principal, Grades 5−6, 341 Students*

LOMA HEIGHTS ELEMENTARY SCHOOL, LAS CRUCES, NM

Loma Heights School was built in 1966 in the midst of a new neighborhood of upper- and middle-class homes. The local country club was in the neighborhood, and the mostly Anglo families were self-employed or worked at New Mexico State University, White Sands Missile Range, or NASA. Eventually, redistricting to meet Office of Civil Rights regulations changed school boundaries and, in the late 1970s, construction of extensive low-income housing changed the socioeconomic and ethnic picture of the school. Rental properties predominate the immediate neighborhood. More than 60% of the students are Spanish-speaking, and approximately 10% begin school as mono-lingual Spanish speakers.

Last school year, the principal created an Action Board. This group consists of a teacher representing each grade level, a representative of the classified employees, the building principal, and three parents. The board is charged with creating a comprehensive school plan and creating a climate for the school that is conducive to learning. The management model is a democratic one addressing the needs of the students, staff, parents, and school community.

Teachers volunteer to sit on committees, chair those committees, and make decisions about their work. These committees are: (1) curriculum, including Young Author's Conference, Science Discovery Week, School Appreciation Week, multi-age grouping, peer tutoring, cultural awareness, and global awareness; (2) budget, including textbook and supplies, fund raising, funding conference attendance, and building inservice; (3) parent involvement including family math, family literacy, classroom volunteers, community resources, and open houses; and (4) inservice for teachers and parents (based on identified needs and textbook selection).

Cynthia Risner-Schiller, *Principal (Sharon Meier, Principal at time of recognition),*
K − 5, 488 Students

L. P. MONTGOMERY ELEMENTARY SCHOOL, FARMERS BRANCH, TX

The Montgomery Elementary School can be characterized as a school that has undergone a dramatic change in the socioeconomic makeup of its student population. (In 1980, the minority enrollment was 11%; in 1991, minority enrollment was 62%. Many of these minority students speak little or no English, and many come from war-torn Central or South American countries where years of violence and upheaval have prevented the parents and their children from receiving an education. This rapid change has not been without conflict or racial tensions, cultural misunderstandings, and feelings of alienation. Like many other elementary schools, Montgomery faces the current societal problems of dysfunctional families, drug and alcohol abuse, student apathy, and gangs.

Yet, through major restructuring efforts, the Montgomery School staff has remained steadfast in their collective efforts to develop an outstanding school and teaching environment. One of the major factors leading to this success is the staff's commitment to shared decision making and site-based management that frame the school's vision, goals, and plans.

Committee titles are formed based on a needs assessment completed by all possible parents, staff and students. Prior to the planning process for the next year, all staff members volunteer to serve on the committees of their interest. Each committee elects its chairman, who then becomes a member of the School Council. The chairman locates current school board policies/procedures related to the topic with which the committee is dealing and keeps the principal informed during the decision-making process. The committees then do preliminary planning and present their ideas to the total staff for input, refinement, and approval. For example, a ''Homework Committee'' was formed based on parent requests for more homework as indicated on 70% of the returned surveys. Site-based management has provided the framework by which Montgomery has met the needs of the school community.

Figure 1 graphically illustrates the organizational structure of Montgomery's site-based management initiative.

Ree McKenzie, *Principal, Pre-K—6, 698 Students*

More than almost any other profession, teaching is practiced in isolation. All too often, teacher opportunities for the development of professional dialogue and collaboration are limited to hurried episodes over plastic lunch trays or periodic moments while supervising students in the hallways or cafeteria. Most teachers are hungry for stimulating professional dialogue and experiences. Yet, in many schools, little attention is devoted to the provision of time or incentive for the sharing of similar dialogue or meaningful educational experiences.

The Best Schools have recognized the value of enabling staff to engage in collegial planning for the implementation of educational programs in their schools. Empowering teachers through release time, shared planning periods, interdisciplinary teaching experiences, etc., has led to a collective autonomy where professionals collaboratively plan for student success. Several specific examples of strategies for collegial planning in Best Schools are provided next.

Collegial Planning Illustrations

EDGEWOOD ELEMENTARY SCHOOL, HOMEWOOD AL

Edgewood Elementary School is located in the Birmingham suburban community of Homewood, which has one high school, one middle school, and three elementary schools. The student population is primarily Caucasian with 7% of the population being African-American and 2% Asian-American. Student mobility roles are approximately 15%, while the staff stability is very high.

Edgewood's class schedule includes a weekly one-hour block of time for grade-level meetings during the school day. While students are participating in activities away from the classroom, teachers have the opportunity to plan, examine, and discuss various aspects of the curriculum and grade-level activities. This time is used to share new ideas and materials. A curriculum support teacher attends all grade-level meetings and keeps each group informed about activities and materials available throughout the school.

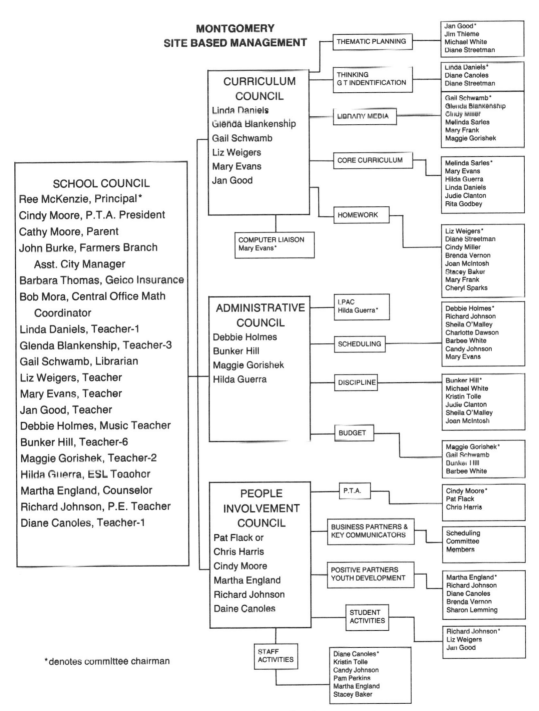

MONTGOMERY SITE BASED MANAGEMENT

SCHOOL COUNCIL
Ree McKenzie, Principal*
Cindy Moore, P.T.A. President
Cathy Moore, Parent
John Burke, Farmers Branch
    Asst. City Manager
Barbara Thomas, Geico Insurance
Bob Mora, Central Office Math
    Coordinator
Linda Daniels, Teacher-1
Glenda Blankenship, Teacher-3
Gail Schwamb, Librarian
Liz Weigers, Teacher
Mary Evans, Teacher
Jan Good, Teacher
Debbie Holmes, Music Teacher
Bunker Hill, Teacher-6
Maggie Gorishek, Teacher-2
Hilda Guerra, ESL Teacher
Martha England, Counselor
Richard Johnson, P.E. Teacher
Diane Canoles, Teacher-1

*denotes committee chairman

CURRICULUM COUNCIL
Linda Daniels
Glenda Blankenship
Gail Schwamb
Liz Weigers
Mary Evans
Jan Good

COMPUTER LIAISON
Mary Evans*

ADMINISTRATIVE COUNCIL
Debbie Holmes
Bunker Hill
Maggie Gorishek
Hilda Guerra

PEOPLE INVOLVEMENT COUNCIL
Pat Flack or
Chris Harris
Cindy Moore
Martha England
Richard Johnson
Daine Canoles

THEMATIC PLANNING — Jan Good*, Jim Thieme, Michael White, Diane Streetman

THINKING G T IDENTIFICATION — Linda Daniels*, Diane Canoles, Diane Streetman

LIBRARY MEDIA — Gail Schwamb*, Glenda Blankenship, Cindy Miller, Melinda Sarles, Mary Frank, Maggie Gorishek

CORE CURRICULUM — Melinda Sarles*, Mary Evans, Hilda Guerra, Linda Daniels, Judie Clanton, Rita Godbey

HOMEWORK — Liz Weigers*, Diane Streetman, Cindy Miller, Brenda Vernon, Joan McIntosh, Stacey Baker, Mary Frank, Cheryl Sparks

LPAC — Hilda Guerra*

SCHEDULING — Debbie Holmes*, Richard Johnson, Sheila O'Malley, Charlotte Dawson, Barbee White, Candy Johnson, Mary Evans

DISCIPLINE — Bunker Hill*, Michael White, Kristin Tolle, Judie Clanton, Sheila O'Malley, Joan McIntosh

BUDGET — Maggie Gorishek*, Gail Schwamb, Bunker Hill, Barbee White

P.T.A. — Cindy Moore*, Pat Flack, Chris Harris

BUSINESS PARTNERS & KEY COMMUNICATORS — Scheduling Committee Members

POSITIVE PARTNERS YOUTH DEVELOPMENT — Martha England*, Richard Johnson, Diane Canoles, Brenda Vernon, Sharon Lemming

STUDENT ACTIVITIES — Richard Johnson*, Liz Weigers, Jan Good

STAFF ACTIVITIES — Diane Canoles*, Kristin Tolle, Candy Johnson, Pam Perkins, Martha England, Stacey Baker

Figure 1. Montgomery site-based management.

By meeting together on a regular basis, teachers are able to share individual talents and areas of expertise. This sharing has resulted in observations in other teachers' classrooms in an effort to develop new strategies for instruction or classroom management. Teachers are also released from classroom responsibilities to conduct demonstration lessons or co-teach at a peer's request.

Recent staff development activities are a direct result of collegial planning. These areas include portfolio assessment, computer assisted instruction, and the construction of math manipulatives.

Ann T. Robbins, *Principal, K – 5, 526 Students*

SAIGLING ELEMENTARY SCHOOL, PLANO, TX

Saigling Elementary is one of twenty-five elementary schools in the Plano Independent School District, a suburban school district in the Dallas, Texas, metropolitan area. The school, which opened in 1977, shares a total campus space with a city park. The population is predominantly white with smaller numbers of Asian, Hispanic, and African-American students. Most households within the Saigling area would be considered upper middle class. Most of the parents are professionals who hold high expectations for the school.

Interestingly, Saigling staff members use a wide variety of strategies to empower teachers and foster collegial planning. These activities are focused around a schoolwide improvement plan and include both extended retreats and the involvement of parents. There is a wide scope of opportunities for professional interaction. The staff engages in collegial planning and implementation of educational programs during team leader retreats, Saigling's Campus Improvement Plan (SCIP) meetings, and team and grade-level meetings. The first team leader retreat created the atmosphere for strong collegial planning. That meeting produced Saigling's "can do" attitude. The planning meeting implemented the development of student programs for citizenship, critical thinking, and increased achievement. The retreat brought about a spirit of high expectations for students and teachers and strong instructional leadership, which increased empowerment of teachers as a direct result.

One of the most exciting collegial planning opportunities that occurs at Saigling is the SCIP program because it broadens collegial planning to include parents. Each of the eight SCIP action teams includes five to six parents and nine to ten staff members. The implementation of the SCIP program created specialist committees – Reading, Math, Writing, History/Geography, Science, Power of Positive Students (POPS), Art, Computers, At-Risk Students, and Clean Campus. The membership of committees, chaired by assistant team leaders, includes teachers from all grades. Teachers select the committees on which they wish to serve; each teacher is a member of two committees. Thus, teachers can view the curriculum across grade levels and special programs. This organization encourages communication and collegial planning throughout the school; also, it reinforces the family concept of a team working to achieve its vision.

The most personally rewarding collaboration occurs during the weekly team meeting attended by the teaching team, the principal, the school counselor, and frequently, the district curriculum coordinator. Discussions center on student achievement, critical thinking, citizenship, students at-risk, curriculum, and educational trends. As needed, grade levels also have meetings for specific academic areas. The team structure and special curriculum committees allow teachers to collaborate in instructional planning and to have opportunities for meaningful interactions.

Janie Milner, *Principal, Pre-K – 5, 679 Students*

MANSFIELD MIDDLE SCHOOL, STORRS , CT

Mansfield Middle School is located in a rural community in the wooded hills of eastern Connecticut. It is in close proximity to both the University of Connecticut and Eastern Connecticut State University. The ease of access to the resources of both universities has had a significant influence on the professionalism and commitment to collegiality among the staff. Mansfield appropriates both time and financial resources to enrich the teaching environment in the school.

Time is set aside for weekly team leader meetings, daily team meetings, monthly faculty meetings, New England Association of Schools and Colleges committee meetings, professional development committee meetings, and meetings held to evaluate the school and to enable staff to engage in collegial planning and in implementation of educational programs at the school. Four afternoon curriculum council meetings and four full common curriculum days are built into the school calendar at a cost of over $53,000 to the district. Teachers participate in decisions affecting the operation of the school with specific emphasis on issues related to curriculum and instruction.

Carole H. Iwanicki, *Principal, Grades 5–8, 489 Students*

SUPERVISION AND EVALUATION OF TEACHERS

For decades, researchers and practitioners have searched for ways to accurately assess teacher performance. The search for a categorical system that meets the needs of both the teacher and the evaluator will forever be elusive. The issues embodied in evaluation are much too complicated to be reduced to checklists or annual narrative statements. Instead, evaluation systems that work have become part of the culture of the school, a culture that values constructive feedback as a vehicle to provide quality education for its students.

The Best Schools see the value of evaluation as a tool for self and school renewal. Additionally, evaluation is looked upon as a collegial activity by which both the teacher and the principal develop a greater understanding of their roles and performance as it relates to the mission of the school. In the Best Schools, evaluation is an ongoing process: something that is systematized and purposeful, something that does not happen just once or twice a year, but, in a very real sense, takes place each day. The Best Schools also realize that the goals of evaluation systems must differentiate for teachers with different levels of expertise, experience, and needs. Finally, it must be recognized that evaluation is not the sole domain of the principal, but that much can be gained through peer observation and coaching. Yet, to provide a conceptual framework to discuss teacher evaluation, a brief description of traditional methods of teacher evaluation would seem appropriate. In a basic way, teacher evaluation in America has two separate functions. The first centers on the improvement of teachers' skills so that they can perform their roles more effectively. This type of evaluation is frequently described as formative teacher evaluation, for its mission is to help modify (form) the teacher's classroom behaviors.

The second function of teacher evaluation centers around decisions such as whether to dismiss a teacher, whether to grant tenure to a teacher, whether to place a teacher on probation, or whether a teacher should advance on a career ladder. This type of evaluation is typically called summative teacher evaluation because it deals more with final, summary decisions about teachers. Summative evaluation is not improvement oriented; instead it is aimed at making judgments about how teacher performance relates to a district's standards for continued employment.

In a more general sense, most writers (Denham, 1987; Harris, 1986; McGreal, 1983) seem to agree that the major purposes of an evaluation are to:

- provide a process that allows and encourages supervisors and teachers to work together to improve and enhance classroom instructional practices
- provide a process for bringing structured assistance to marginal teachers

- provide a basis for making more rational decisions about the retention, transfer, or dismissal of staff members
- provide a basis for making more informed judgments about differing performance levels for use in compensation programs such as merit pay plans or career ladder programs
- provide information for determining the extent of implementation of knowledge and skills gained during staff development activities and for use in judging the degree of maintenance of the acquired knowledge and skills

The supervision and evaluation of teachers have significant roles in a teacher's perception of his/her teaching environment. Bureaucratic systems have long been associated with close organizational environments that tend to inhibit teacher creativity and growth and actually impact negatively on teacher performance. Conversely, laissez-faire or permissive systems tend to communicate misleading information and promote continuation of poor teaching behaviors. Systems that tend to have the most positive effect on professional relations and teaching behaviors tend to be based on the following concepts:

- The supervision/evaluation takes place within a professional context of collegiality and collaboration.
- A clear understanding exists between the supervisor and teacher as to the common language describing good teaching.
- Data collection methods that are utilized in the classroom are clearly understood by both the teacher and the evaluator.
- Data collected through classroom observation are valid (in terms of measuring what they are intended to measure) and reliable (in terms of their intended consistency from one application to another).
- Conferences are held by the teacher and evaluator to share data collection and exchange perceptions of lesson outcomes.
- Consideration is given to differentiated systems of evaluation for beginning, advanced, and expert teachers.

An analysis of America's Best Schools indicates the incorporation of many of the concepts listed above into an ongoing evaluation system. Specifically, many use a version of a Clinical Supervision Model (Cogan, 1973). Although many variations of the model are used, the supervisory cycle in a clinical relationship revolves around eight phases:

(1) Establishing the supervisory relationship: build a relationship of trust and support and induct the teacher into the role of co-supervisor
(2) Planning lessons and units with the teacher: determine objectives, concepts, teaching-learning techniques, materials, and assessment methods
(3) Planning the observation strategy: teacher and supervisor discuss the data to be gathered and the methods for gathering the data
(4) Observing in-class instruction
(5) Analyzing the observational data to determine patterns of behavior and critical incidents of teaching and learning
(6) Planning the conference strategy: set tentative conference objectives and processes
(7) Conferring to analyze data
(8) Resuming the planning: complete the cycle by determining future directions for growth and planning the next unit or lesson

THE BEST SCHOOLS – SUPERVISION AND EVALUATION OF TEACHERS

Best Schools throughout the country utilize a variety of practices and procedures to evaluate teachers. Although stylistically different, each approaches teacher evaluation as an organic learning experience, an experience that closely aligns with the positive outcomes addressed in the research and reviewed in the previous discussion. Several of the evaluation systems utilized in Best Schools are illustrated next.

Supervision and Evaluation Illustrations

GEORGE Q. KNOWLTON ELEMENTARY SCHOOL, FARMINGTON, UT

Knowlton School is located between Utah's two largest metropolitan areas, Salt Lake City and Ogden. It is part of the Davis School District, which services all the public school children between these two major cities. When Knowlton opened its doors thirteen years ago, it welcomed 400 students. It has grown steadily, at one point housing as many as 1000 students; because of a state legislative mandate placing a moratorium on new school construction in order to accommodate the burgeoning student population, Knowlton is now on a year-round school year schedule. This organization allows for a 33% increase in building utilization.

Knowlton School services a middle/upper-class community. Its student population is almost exclusively Caucasian, with various minority groups making up approximately 2% of the student population.

Knowlton uses the Davis Educator Evaluation Program (DEEP), developed by a team of teachers and administrators in the Davis School District. It is based upon the belief that educator evaluation should benefit students by improving classroom instruction and school experiences and that teachers and administrators should be united in working toward that end. The program is based on two approaches: formative evaluation and summative evaluation. The formative approach is based on cooperation, ideally driven by the teacher's desire to improve. Summative measures, on the other hand, are carried out for purposes of accountability, such as official verification of teacher proficiency, documentation of professional status, justification for job retention, need for remediation of teaching deficits, and in the Davis School District, the qualification for Career Ladder funds. The specific features of the evaluation plan include the following:

- A summative evaluation plan is administered every third year to approximately one-third of the school's professional staff.
- A plan of formative evaluation, left essentially in the hands of the teacher, is carried out during the alternate two years. Teachers are free to use any one of several approaches to gathering data for self-assessment of classroom performance, i.e., DEEP category data gathered by means of self-initiated audio or video recordings, data gathered by a peer or mentor teacher, or data gathered with the assistance of the principal. Data is evaluated by the teacher himself/herself.
- A goal-directed activity plan is used in formative, as well as summative, evaluation. Teacher and principal collaborate in the goal setting during summative evaluation.
- A collegial approach to goal-directed activity is used during the alternate (formative) two years. It takes place collaboratively by grades or teams unless precluded by circumstances. Goals are submitted to the principal during the first term. In the final term of the year, the principal is given a report on the outcomes of the goal-directed activity.
- Anonymous feedback from the parents is required in summative evaluations every third year through a survey.
- Evidence of student progress is required every third year in summative evaluations.

Velda S. Morrow, *Principal (L. Glenn Touge, Principal at time of recognition),*
K – 6, 870 Students

LAKE GEORGE ELEMENTARY SCHOOL, LAKE GEORGE, NY

Lake George School is located in the eastern Adirondack Mountains halfway between New York City and Montreal, Canada. The school has serviced a predominantly Caucasian population with an above average socioeconomic strata. Student mobility has increased in recent years, prompting increases in students with special learning needs and students with various at-risk issues. To address student needs, the school has incorporated team teaching, multi-age grouping, and family grouping as vehicles to personalize learning.

The school has embraced a differentiated evaluation system that enables the school principal to concentrate his direct intervention efforts to those in greatest need. Teacher assessment and evaluation are the major means of monitoring the delivery of learning and the process necessary to attain individual teacher improvement, as well as maintain outstanding teacher skills. The faculty in this district developed a mechanism that stresses the important skills of a teacher. As a means to offer teachers independence and recognition, a teacher-directed plan that stresses self-analysis is offered to proficient teachers. The principal can then place emphasis on the teachers needing the most support, which typically includes the new teachers to the district and those least proficient in skills.

The annual performance review is a summary of important skills that are rated as commendable, satisfactory, marginal, or unsatisfactory, with written or oral feedback to support the principal's ratings. The data used to compile this summary is gathered through a minimum of two formal visitations and a minimum of three informal visitations for probationary teachers and teachers identified as needing support. Therefore, need dictates the frequency of evaluation with all staff members.

Other data collected on teacher performance is gathered through comparative results of information gathered through parents and student questionnaires. Test results gathered by teaching teams are summarized and shared with staff members. The results use national curve equivalents to compare scores with the students' previous year's achievement. Also, lesson plans are reviewed when appropriate, student progress reports are monitored, and parental feedback and reactions are considered. With this data, the principal is able to rate a teacher's performance and decide whether a teacher should be on a teacher-directed plan or a principal-directed plan. The teachers on the teacher-directed plan are expected to develop personal growth plans for self-improvement with at least one goal linked to improve student outcomes and at least one to professional development. The principal can then concentrate on developing growth plans with these teachers who are nontenured or in need of support. Structured plans centering around the skills needing improvement are developed and teachers are provided with the most qualified resources to improve that area.

Robert J. Ross, *Principal, K – 6, 535 Students*

BROOKMEADE ELEMENTARY SCHOOL, NASHVILLE, TN

Brookmeade School is part of the Metropolitan Public Schools of Nashville and Davidson County. The school is located on the western edge of the county and has students from the immediate surrounding neighborhood and an urban housing project some twelve miles from the school and from five apartment complexes near the school. The administration and staff of Brookmeade have long been recognized for quality education; in fact, it was selected by *Instructor* Magazine as one of ten schools nationally to receive the Newsworthy School Award.

Like many Best Schools, Brookmeade utilizes a districtwide teacher evaluation system. Brookmeade employs the Metopolitan-Nashville Public Schools' Instructional Improvement Plan (IIP), which was developed in conjunction with the Tennessee Teacher Evaluation System in October, 1986. A work plan, written by each teacher at the beginning of each year with specific individual goals and strategies, is discussed and refined during an individual conference with the principal. During the mid-year (interim) conference and again at the end-of-year (summative) conference, the teacher and administrator look at the documentation of the progress made on these goals. At the summative conference, new goals, achievement, and possible improvements are discussed and recorded on the teacher's summative evaluation.

When the teacher is "on focus," usually every three to four years, two to three formal classroom observations are conducted. Each observation must include a pre-conference, the observation itself, and a post-conference that provides feedback and recommendations. A teacher may be on focus any time a principal or teacher deems it necessary. Lesson plans are reviewed weekly for new teachers and periodically for all other teachers.

The evaluation process is based on a cooperative spirit with open lines of communication. The process recognizes excellence, identifies strengths and weaknesses, and prescribes appropriate staff development. Informal observations are made on a regular basis by the principal, and feedback is given in the form of verbal comments or individual conferences.

Carolyn C. Wood, Principal, K−4, 463 Students

SUPPORT OF BEGINNING TEACHERS AND TEACHERS NEW TO THE BUILDING

It is estimated that 30% of teachers new to the profession leave by the end of their first year. Although the reasons for this phenomenon vary, there is significant evidence to support that the failure to adequately induct, orient, and support these teachers leads to an excessive "dropout rate."

The Best Schools recognize the need to provide activities aimed at successfully integrating teachers into the school and the profession. They realize the critical nature of the first few days of school and the need to provide ongoing support for novice teachers. While the term *induction* is not new, the particular meaning that it has now taken on is somewhat different from meanings it had formerly been given. Whereas induction previously often referred to the informal, often reactionary, and ritualistic socialization of new teachers, it now refers to more sophisticated and systematic efforts to initiate, shape, and sustain the first-week experiences of prospective career teachers (DeBolt, 1992).

Induction programs have become increasingly more popular throughout the last decade. Realizing the greater challenge facing today's novice teachers, school districts have initiated programs to help new teachers meet the demands of current-day teaching. These challenges associated with the diverse nature of children in classrooms, the extensive curricular expectations to teach more, the greater variety of instructional tools from which to choose, and increasing accountability from school officials and parents all lead to the complexities associated in teaching in today's schools.

Once in the classroom, novice teachers experience a sense of panic, feeling that their teacher education programs left them ill-prepared to deal with actual classroom life. Almost invariably, new teachers engage in stressful trial-and-error periods during which they figure out what works, with survival as their primary goal. No longer having the safety nets associated with student teaching, new teachers are awakened to the stark reality that the accountability for planning, organization of instruction, and assessment of students is now their sole responsibility.

Induction programs are aimed at minimizing the stresses associated with beginning teaching by providing programs that seek to add to the experiences of becoming a teacher. Huling-Austen, Odell, et al. (1989) list five common goals of programs designed to assist beginning teachers:

(1) To improve teaching performance
(2) To increase the retention of promising beginning teachers
(3) To promote the personal and professional well-being of beginning teachers
(4) To satisfy mandated requirements related to induction
(5) To transmit the culture of the school (and the teaching profession) to beginning teachers

Sandra Odell (Huling-Austin, Odell, et al., 1989) has condensed a somewhat different set of goals that represent a more comprehensive view of the purpose of induction programs:

- to provide continuing assistance to reduce the problems known to be common to beginning teachers
- to support development of the knowledge and the skills needed by beginning teachers to be successful in their initial teaching positions
- to integrate beginning teachers into the social system of the school district and the community
- to provide an opportunity for beginning teachers to analyze and reflect on their teaching with coaching from veteran support teachers
- to initiate and build a foundation with new teachers for the continued study of teaching
- to increase the positive attitudes of beginning teachers about teaching
- to increase the retention of good beginning teachers in the profession

In pursuit of goals such as these, induction programs have been developed into programs involving new teachers in a wide variety of activities. One promising program, increasingly used by successful schools, is mentoring. While traditionally an informal relationship between new and veteran teachers, mentoring has emerged as a central theme of many induction programs. Mentoring, as the term suggests, provides for an experienced teacher to assist the new teacher as he/she faces the challenges of teaching. Anderson and Shannon (1988) offered a definition of mentoring that includes the following attributes:

- the process of nurturing
- the act of serving as a role model
- provision for the five fundamental functions of the mentor—teaching, sponsoring, encouraging, counseling, and befriending
- a focus on professional and/or personal development
- an ongoing caring relationship

To optimize these concepts, Brooks (1985) has developed a series of strategies that are directed to the critical nature of providing daily successful experiences for new teachers. He provides several such strategies:

(1) Develop a bank of first and second day videotapes of successful, experienced teachers. Require new teachers to review, with an experienced teacher, the tapes before entering class.

(2) Create a beginning teacher staff development day the week prior to the opening of school. The topics should emphasize strategies for getting class/school started and strategies to promote classroom management.

(3) Provide direct supervision, through classroom observation, frequently during the first week of school.

(4) Provide specific contextual recommendations concerning strategies that facilitate the opening of school; improve class climate and promote classroom management.

To a very large degree, the issues facing novice teachers are also areas of concern for experienced teachers who may be new to a particular school/district. Although the experienced teacher comes to the school with a frame of reference that more readily provides the ability to predict classroom events and implement successful teaching and intervention strategies, issues related to integration into the school culture, social support, and a sense of the development of belonging are critical for his/her success. Thus, successful induction programs need to be planned not only around the goals and priorities of the school, but they must be differentiated to meet the unique needs of teachers at different teaching and life stages.

THE BEST SCHOOLS – SUPPORT OF BEGINNING AND NEW TEACHERS

The Best Schools have implemented a wide variety of strategies to meet the needs of their beginning teachers and those experienced teachers new to their districts. The following illustrations provide strategies used in selected Best Schools.

Support of Beginning and New Teachers Illustrations

QUAIL CREEK ELEMENTARY SCHOOL, OKLAHOMA CITY, OK

The Quail Creek Elementary School is the highest achieving school among the fifty-nine elementary schools in Oklahoma City. It prides itself on a philosophy that "all children can learn." The school culture promotes an environment that looks upon teachers as leaders. This process begins with a comprehensive teacher induction program.

The Oklahoma City School District provides inservice for new employees to inform them of policies, goals, and programs unique to their district. Beginning teachers and teachers new to the district complete twenty hours of Effective Schools Training. Curriculum advisors assist new teachers in planning units and lessons in each core subject area. The principal provides teachers with information about duties, policies, and expectations; also assumes leadership in supporting the efforts of teachers who are just beginning their careers. At the building level, grade-level meetings take place to assist new teachers with schedules, routines, and assignments. Grade-level team leaders are expected to provide support and information to new teachers to facilitate a smooth transition to their new working environment. Positive contributions made by teachers new to the building are valued, and individual teachers are recognized for their suggestions during weekly staff meetings.

Entry-Year Assistance Committees (EYAC) are teams of people who are responsible for supporting and nurturing beginning teachers. Each three-member committee is composed of a teacher, an administrator, and a university professional. At least one of these individuals is certified and has experience in the area to which the entry-year teacher is assigned. A consultant will spend an average of two hours each week with the beginning teacher, and part of this time must be spent in observation. Consultants are encouraged to observe the beginning teacher at least every other week. Consultation or observation may occur during the planning period, and time before or after school may also be used.

Each committee has three formal meetings. Each member of the committee also makes three formal observations of the entry-year teacher. At the end of the year, the committee makes a recommendation either for certification or for continuation in the entry-year program. These meetings have been extremely valuable in providing teachers with individual attention to their strengths, weaknesses and concerns.

Ancie Warren, *Principal, K–5, 343 Students*

CHARLES E. TEACH ELEMENTARY SCHOOL, SAN LUIS OBISPO, CA

Teach School is an alternative program for fourth, fifth and sixth grade accelerated learners. These students come from eleven different elementary schools within the San Luis Coastal Unified School District.

The nature of the selected student population makes it critical to quickly and efficiently induct new teachers into the school culture. Following appropriate orientation sessions, new teachers soon participate in the planning process at both the grade and school levels. Mentor teachers provide support through meetings, instructional modeling, and conferences. Additionally, a buddy teacher program is in place in which an experienced teacher provides encouragement and social support.

A district Professional Development Center offers new teachers a five-day workshop on the elements of instruction and principles of learning. Inservices are offered for all teachers in classroom management, cognitive learning styles, curriculum implementation, interdisciplinary/integrated instruction, collegial coaching, and cooperative learning.

John S. Pisula, Jr., Principal, Grades 4 – 6, 285 Students

EDEN INSTITUTE, INC., PRINCETON, NJ

Eden Institute, Inc. is a private, nonprofit school located in Princeton, New Jersey, which educates students with autism. Students typically come from varied backgrounds across the state and are quite varied in their levels of ability. Most students, however, are severely or profoundly retarded and display serious social, communication, and behavioral deficits warranting instruction in a specialized setting.

Because of the unique nature of the student population, specialized recruitment, hiring, and induction procedures are utilized. Selective staff recruitment procedures are extremely important in order to ensure low staff turnover, increased understanding of job responsibilities, and a maintenance of high staff motivation levels. Eden's selection process involves several steps: screening of resumes; screening of potential candidates via telephone; initial interview to discuss program philosophy, job requirements, and expectations for staff performance; second interview to observe experienced staff working with the students; review of all candidates; and final candidate selection.

Eden's training includes both textbook information and practicum experiences. All staff receive a descriptive tour of the program prior to beginning work, as do all visitors. The first part of training is Venture Team. This is comprised of a series of videotapes covering an overview of the following: the Eden Programs, autism, teaching techniques, and speech and language issues. Venture Team also includes a practicum experience. Venture Team is followed by bimonthly training, which includes workshops conducted by the Outreach and Support Services Division covering the areas of autism, teaching techniques, teaching in a group, reinforcement, behavior reduction techniques, professionalism, communication, crisis intervention, a variety of short current topics, and an expanded practicum experience. Following the successful completion of bimonthly training, the staff member is considered to be trained sufficiently to begin working independently in his/her program. Training, however, does not end there.

Ongoing training includes inservice programs, as well as supervisor continuing education. The latter focuses on "fine tuning" technical skills, as well as training staff in supervisory skills. The system offers Eden staff several training options from which they choose a specific number, which enables inservice training to be individualized to meet specific staff needs and interests.

Dr. David L. Holmes, Principal, Special Population, Pre-K – 8, 50 Students

---

SOUTH VALLEY SCHOOL, MOORESTOWN, NJ

Moorestown is a suburban community of almost 20,000 residents located in the southwestern part of New Jersey, approximately twenty miles from center city Philadelphia. The population is largely upper middle class with a significant low-moderate income group. All three of the district's elementary schools have been nationally recognized.

The school recognizes the different career stages of teachers from novice to master teacher. Expectations are high. New teachers attend workshops on instruction conducted by the superintendent, assistant superintendent, and principal. Using a modified clinical supervisory model, four performance evaluations are conducted by central staff, as well as by the principal. New teachers are required to join (at board expense) at least one professional organization, are provided with discretionary funds to enhance their classroom programs, and receive credit on the salary scale for enrollment in district inservice courses. At school level, all new teachers are assigned "mentors" who ease their transition into the district and the high performance expectations. Master teachers are encouraged to play leadership roles in committees and experiment with new programs.

Feedback concerning classroom observations is provided during conferences and in written form. Emphasis is on suggestions for improvement and reinforcement of effective practices. Progress on the teacher's Professional Improvement Plan (PIP) is monitored. At the end of the year, each teacher receives a Summary Evaluation. Teachers have input in the development of PIPs and the Summary Evaluation.

New teachers also receive feedback from central office staff in meetings and at receptions. A survey instrument is used to determine the effectiveness of orientation programs and approaches and is used to improve future efforts. The South Valley principal holds meetings throughout the year to provide continuing inservice and support for new teachers.

Violet Thompson, *Principal, K−4, 289 Students*

STAFF RECOGNITION

Maintaining an effective school system requires the retention of those outstanding teachers who make up the life blood of every school. Approximately 40 to 50% of all teachers leave the profession within seven years. Increasing numbers of teachers state that, if they had it to do over again, they probably would not choose to teach in public schools. In a very real sense, teachers' satisfaction with the workplace depends on the environment in which they work and the success of their experiences in the classrooms. To this end, successful schools have actively engaged and empowered teachers to seek self-fulfillment and satisfaction. Strategies such as improving the management of existing resources, involving teachers in school-based decision making, minimizing bureaucracy, empowering teachers through greater knowledge about teaching and learning, and breaking down teacher isolation through team teaching and planning are all efforts to professionalize teaching so that our best teachers remain in the profession.

Successful schools find ways to recognize the efforts of their outstanding staff members. Through intrinsic and external reward opportunities and incentives, schools have provided teachers with a sense of accomplishment, power, prestige, and in some cases, money, so that children can continue to benefit from a master teacher's expertise. In a general sense, the purpose of recognition incentive programs is to establish an environment in which special achievements and contributions of faculty and staff are recognized and applauded on a regular, systematic basis. In so doing, the faculty and staff will be encouraged to develop and sustain the efforts to teach children.

Many surveys have been taken, with the results usually the same—school personnel desire positive recognition for their efforts (Karpinski, 1985). Some suggestions for recognition that are repeatedly heard include plaques of commendation, recognition in staff notes and district newsletters, written praise with evaluation, written notes of appreciation by the superintendent or principal, verbal compliments, parent-teacher organization awards, and teacher-of-the-month or teacher appreciation days (Karpinski, 1985).

THE BEST SCHOOLS—RECOGNITION OF STAFF

The Best Schools actively seek ways to identify and recognize the accomplishments of their high performing staff members. Through personalized efforts, officials in Best Schools have developed unique ways to applaud the achievements and dedication of those who serve children. Several Best Schools' programs and activities are illustrated next.

Recognition Illustrations

MILL LAKE SCHOOL, SPOTSWOOD, NJ

Mill Lake School is located in the largest residential development in Monroe Township, New Jersey. Monroe Township has a very diverse character, including large rural portions, business sections, and areas that are primarily residential. Four large retirement developments, comprising approximately 50% of the township's adult population, add yet another unique dimension to the community. The student population is primarily Caucasian, with approximately 8% minority population.

A variety of formal and informal strategies are employed to support and encourage excellent teaching skills. Formal measures include:

- Each year, an outstanding teacher is nominated for the Governor's Teacher Recognition Award.
- The Annual Teacher Performance Report includes a category entitled ''Outstanding: consistently demonstrates superior skills and effort'' for teachers deserving of this level. Letters of recognition and appreciation from the principal recognize special effort and accomplishment.
- The districtwide newsletter, *The School Story,* highlights activities and accomplishments of excellent teachers.

Informal measures to support and encourage excellence include:

- Principal's Weekly Bulletin recognizes collegial achievements.
- Personal positive notes are made in the weekly plan book by the principal.
- Outstanding teachers are encouraged to serve on curriculum committees.
- Teachers are encouraged to seek grants and awards that will focus on excellence in the classroom.
- PTA, as well as individual parents, recognize teachers during Teacher Appreciation Week, including a special luncheon.

Nancy Richmond, *Principal, K – 3, 380 Students*

FRANCES R. FUCHS SPECIAL CENTER, BELTSVILLE, MD

Frances Fuchs Special Center is a Special Education Early Childhood Center located in Beltsville, Maryland. Children aged birth to eight years old with handicapping conditions that impact their educational progress are eligible for services. Sources of referrals are parents, physicians, hospitals, and social agencies. The staff includes teachers, speech, occupational and physical therapists, motor and vision specialists, and teacher aides.

Social and economic factors vary greatly among the students who attend the center. The student population is made up of 54% African-American and 35% Caucasian, with the remaining students from Hispanic, Asian, or Native American origins.

To support and recognize the efforts of Fuch's dedicated staff, a wide variety of activities have been developed. The principal and staff believe that recognition of excellence is critical to the ongoing delivery of quality educational programs. The principal makes positive comments regarding excellent performance as part of her daily routine. A pat on the back, an informal comment in the hallway, or recognition at a faculty meeting help to send messages to staff that their efforts and skills are appreciated. A ''Good Things Are Happening'' section of the ''sign-in'' book makes daily reference to staff performance. Both the principal and other staff members may write positive comments about colleagues' performance in this section. Personal sticky notes from the principal are posted on classroom doors or mailboxes. Staff members have been nominated for district-level outstanding teacher competitions.

Outstanding staff are encouraged to share and develop their talents. Many staff deliver inservice to the staff of the school and to other schools' faculties. Several staff, at the suggestion of the principal, are entering graduate studies or participating in district leadership development programs. Excellent staff are encouraged to assume leadership positions in the school as a way of sharing their expertise and bringing public recognition to their contribution to the program.

The staff creates an environment of encouragement and value of excellence. The motor development teacher posted a "no-fault" sign in his classroom to signify that opinions and ideas could be offered without fear of judgment. Monthly breakfasts, birthday celebrations, and secret pals are sponsored by the social committee to help create a feeling of teamwork and collegiality.

Dr. Sherry Lee Liebes, *Principal, Early Childhood Center, 285 Students*

HARLAN ELEMENTARY SCHOOL, BLOOMFIELD HILLS, MI

Harlan School serves a suburban community north of Detroit, Michigan. Students come primarily from homes of middle to upper middle family incomes.

The student enrollment, made up of 92% Caucasian, 4% Asian-American, 3% African-American, and 1% Hispanic, has a very low student mobility rate. Interestingly, the Harlan School is in a district that maintains an open choice of schools for parents throughout the district.

Harlan has been able to attract and maintain an excellent teaching staff. Their dedication and motivation are recognized by the wide variety of activities listed below:

- The formal evaluation process identifies excellence in teaching.
- A "Teacher of the Year" is selected and is honored at a banquet. The recipient is given a monetary award from the board of education.
- A board-sponsored Incentives Grant Program recognizes and rewards outstanding effort.
- The *Harlan Herald* (school newsletter) acknowledges outstanding performance.
- The Parent-Teacher Association acknowledges outstanding contributions during their awards banquet.
- The Board of Education "Briefs" identifies and congratulates any teacher who has made a significant contribution to the system.
- The Principal's Bulletin commends teachers who have performed a special service to the school.
- A Staff Development Bulletin notes exceptional teacher accomplishments.
- Harlan teacher exchange program is available to all qualified teachers.
- Conference expenses and release time are available to those teachers who are making a significant contribution to the educational programs of the school.
- The school's Parent-Teacher Association has teacher enrichment grant funds for significant contributions or projects.
- Teachers are asked to share their expertise in district-, county-, and statewide workshops.
- Parents frequently write letters to the superintendent recognizing teacher dedication and the positive impact made on their child's growth and development.
- The principal both verbalizes and writes "thank you's" in recognition for professional excellence.

Elizabeth Smith, *Principal, K – 5, 416 Students*

STAFF DEVELOPMENT

Despite the widespread interest and school district emphasis on staff development, much remains to be learned about the effectiveness of the process. All too often, schools embark upon one initiative after another, hoping to affect individual and school development.

Similarly, prominent experts move around the country in a series of isolated presentations whose impact on teacher or organizational behavior is, all too often, short-lived.

The Best Schools address staff development with the same vision and commitment afforded all other aspects of school life. Staff development activities are not confined to one or two inservice days when faculty listen to a motivational speaker, attend a show-and-tell workshop, and chat with co-workers over coffee and danish. Instead, staff development promotes true self- and school improvement through thoughtful planning, long-term commitment to specific goals, and appropriate nurturing from school administrators.

Staff development can be defined as those processes that improve job-related knowledge, skills, or attitudes of school employees. Although topics may vary, Sparks and Loucks-Horsley (1989) have identified five major models currently being utilized by staff developers:

(1) Individually guided staff development is where the teacher determines his or her own goals and selects activities that will result in the achievement of those goals. Their model holds that individuals will be most motivated when they select their own personal assessment of their needs.

(2) Observation/assessment is most commonly implemented with a supervisor directly observing the teacher in action, using a predetermined criteria. A basic assumption underlying this approach is that reflection by an individual on his or her own practice can be enhanced by another's observations. Peer coaching where fellow teachers visit one another's classrooms, gather objective data about student performance or teacher behavior, and give feedback in a follow-up conference is an increasingly common form of observation/assessment.

(3) Involvement in a development/improvement process is a combination of learnings that result from the involvement of teachers in the development of curriculum or engagement in systematic school improvement processes that have as their goal the improvement of classroom instruction and/or curriculum. Often, as with many of the Best Schools, teachers serve on school improvement committees where they may be required to conduct research on priority goals of the school, learn group and interpersonal skills, or develop new content knowledge. In each instance, teachers' learning is driven by the demands of problem solving. Teacher involvement and ownership in organic school improvement initiatives provide a strong motivational foundation for this approach.

(4) Training or workshop-type sessions are given in which the presenter is the expert who establishes the content and flow of activities inherent to this strategy in the hope that teachers' decision-making and thinking skills can be enriched through awareness, knowledge, and skill development. The basic assumption that guides this strategy is that teachers can change their behaviors and learn to replicate behaviors in their classroom that were not previously in their repertoire.

(5) Inquiry strategies is where an individual or a group of teachers utilize their basic research techniques to formulate research questions and appropriate studies to improve instruction in their classrooms. Inquiry reflects a basic belief in teachers' ability to formulate valid questions about their own practices and pursue objective answers to those questions.

Although the topics and delivery strategies may vary, there are several common traits that guide effective staff development activities in the Best Schools:

- support of individual self-improvement efforts within a context of school goal setting
- activities closely linked to the mission statement and priority objectives of the school
- activities emphasizing professional and personal growth rather than remediation of specific sub-skills

- incorporation of sound principles derived from research on adult learning
- inclusion of a comprehensive planning process with extensive district, building, and/or individual contributions
- establishment of expectations and climate for successful integration of acquired skills and knowledge into daily practice
- inclusion of an evaluation system with appropriate feedback vehicles to assess the outcomes of activities

These elements of staff development do not evolve without the establishment of an organizational context within which an individual can grow. Thus, the notion of school climate and culture must be systematically nurtured for staff development initiatives to be successful. Loucks-Horsley et al. (1987) attempt to describe that context as one where staff members have a common, coherent set of goals and objectives that they have formulated, reflecting high expectations for themselves and their students. Additionally, administrators exercise strong leadership by promoting a spirit of collegiality, minimizing status differences between themselves and their staff members. Finally, teachers and administrators place a high priority on staff development and continuous improvement.

Staff development is an integral fact of successful schools across the country. Although different in their goals and delivery strategies, all such programs are systematized as part of a total personal/school improvement priority. The Best Schools invest in staff development with the clear expectation that a high yield of return will be realized.

THE BEST SCHOOLS—STAFF DEVELOPMENT

The following illustrations describe examples of specific strategies utilized in the Best Schools.

Staff Development Illustrations

EDGEWOOD ELEMENTARY SCHOOL, HOMEWOOD, AL

A description of major characteristics of the school has been provided earlier in this chapter.

The goals of the instructional staff are consistent with the philosophy and objectives of the school; staff development opportunities are designed with these in mind. The staff development activities help teachers provide for the total growth of each student: academically, morally, emotionally, physically, and socially.

All teachers in the Homewood City School system participate in a minimum of forty-five hours of staff development activities per year. Edgewood teachers consistently go beyond that minimum requirement. Last year, for example, the thirty-six professional staff members participated in a total of 3851 hours of professional development activities. The teachers at Edgewood identify areas of study that are most supportive of the goals and priorities of the school and beneficial to strengthening instructional practices. Schoolwide staff development activities are coordinated by the curriculum support teacher, according to these identified areas. At the end of each school year, teachers evaluate these staff development activities and provide feedback about future offerings. Meetings are held after school in the media center with a majority of the staff attending. Activities are also planned for individual teacher needs.

Examples of staff development offerings include planned weekly meetings, university workshops, observations in other classrooms, schools, or systems, and conferences held in and out of the state. For example, the Schoolwide Enrichment Model Workshop by Joseph Renzulli of the University of Connecticut has been attended by over half of the faculty; several teachers have attended sessions sponsored by the Wright Company in Georgia, Tennessee, and Alabama; one teacher has attended the Northwestern University's Nathan Mayhew Writing Seminar at Martha's Vineyard and, in turn, conducts workshops on portfolio assessment for the system.

The area of English (language arts) has been targeted during the past three years with numerous staff development opportunities. These activities include indepth studies of the writing process and literature-based reading.

The mathematics curriculum has been strengthened by the participation of numerous staff members in summer workshops sponsored by national groups and held in neighboring systems. The use of math manipulatives has also been emphasized. Several teachers used release time from school day responsibilities during the past year to observe outstanding math teachers in the area. Forty-three such observations occurred for math and other areas last year.

Staff development in science-related activities has been provided by university professors, Alabama Power Company, a local computer company, and by classroom teachers. Hands-on materials have been made available for specific units of study from a local museum. This was arranged and demonstrated for teachers by the enrichment teacher. A faculty representative from Homewood High School has also demonstrated and made software available for use with the science curriculum in computer-assisted classes. History and geography activities for teachers during the past several years have focused on a schoolwide program called "Passport Reading." Emphasis is given to methods of incorporating literature with history of cultures throughout the world.

Ann T. Robbins, Principal, K – 5, 526 Students

KLONDIKE ELEMENTARY SCHOOL, WEST LAFAYETTE, IN

Klondike Elementary School houses students from a diverse socioeconomic background. Approximately 28% of the students are from homes where family income is below the poverty level, while almost half of its students are from families of professionals, many of whom are employed by nearby Purdue University. Upwards of 30% student mobility rate is inherent to the school population due to short-term residence of university students and mobile home owners.

Klondike has a strong tradition for excellence in their school. A foundation of this commitment is centered on a strong, financially supported staff development program. In the past three years, the Tippecanoe School Corporation has allocated $10,000 to Klondike for staff development. The School Improvement Committee surveys the staff to determine needs and interests. Since receiving funds in January 1989, every teacher on staff has voluntarily attended at least one, and many have attended nearly all, class offerings, workshops, and conferences. Teachers receive compensation to attend workshops before and after school, on weekends, during summer vacation, and on the two annual staff improvement days. The inservice opportunities taken by members of the staff in the last three years include math problem solving; weekend workshops in geography, portfolio writing, math manipulatives, developmental math, thematic teaching, and integrating math and science activities, a physics workshop, Prime Time (a state initiative that emphasizes small class size and hands-on activities) workshops and fairs, and developmentally appropriate kindergarten, economics, and whole group reading instruction.

Three building-wide opportunities for staff development were held for the first time this school year. A staff "retreat" focused on "Stress Management," "Surviving and Thriving During Construction," and "Conflict Resolution." The staff is also viewing the eight-part video conference series, *Schools That Work: The Research Advantage*, sponsored by the North Central Regional Educational Laboratory and PBS. The staff was particularly interested in this series since it closely addresses the implementation of the National Goals for Education and successful innovations in the basic curriculum areas. The entire staff viewed and discussed Phi Delta Kappa's *National Goals of Education: A Priority for the Year 2000*.

Ardis Wipp, Principal, K – 5, 865 Students

CLEAR SPRINGS ELEMENTARY SCHOOL, MINNETONKA, MN

Clear Springs School can be characterized as a semi-rural, suburban community located west of downtown Minneapolis. Once serving low and middle income families, new housing development has fostered a more diverse socioeconomic population. During the past ten years, student population has increased by 33%. The student population is primarily Caucasian; various minority groups make up approximately 5% of the student body.

Staff development and professional growth opportunities are liberally offered. The Minnetonka School District requires teachers at Clear Springs to take in-district workshops with the following themes: Elements of Instruction (five days), Cooperative Learning (one day), and Classroom Management (two days). The workshops are offered in the summer, during the school day, or during vacation to ensure that every teacher may attend all workshops. The leaders of these workshops make several follow-up visits. Teachers who have a cluster of gifted and talented students receive two days of formal training in curriculum modification techniques for their groups. Much of the staff development is designed and developed by staff at the building level. After building goals are selected by the staff, a team surveys all of the teachers and decides what kind of inservice to provide. In addition, each staff member has had at least two hours each of inservice in special education, the arts, youth service learning, global education, developmentally appropriate curriculum, and math methods. Staff development opportunities in specific content areas include:

(1) *Math:* All K−2 teachers participate in Math Their Way. Two teachers took National Science Foundation PriMath and became trainers for the staff. Two specialists attended a learning disabilities conference in which the focus was math. In the last five years, teachers have taken twenty-seven math classes.

(2) *Language Arts:* All K−4 teachers have attended workshops on student research methods. All teachers have had extensive inservice in literature-based reading programs. In the last five years, teachers have taken thirty-six reading classes. Clear Spring's own teachers have taught process writing to the other staff.

(3) *Science:* Sixteen teachers have attended science workshops. The school employs a scientist-in-residence to teach in all classrooms.

(4) *History:* The integrated study of cultures, which includes the history of the country/people being studied, begins with staff inservice by guest lecturers. The history of Russia, China, and Mexico were presented to the staff. A two-hour inservice highlighted each of these cultures.

Linda Saukkonen, *Principal, K−4, 610 Students*

SUMMARY

The Best Schools value and systematically develop teaching environments that promote goal achievement and student learning. They facilitate a climate where professional involvement and growth are both encouraged and rewarded, actively seeking ways to involve their faculties. Whether through informal processes or formalized school-based management teams, the schools capitalize on the expertise, dedication, and commitment of the entire school staff.

Induction, staff development, evaluation, collaboration, and teacher recognition are all part of an organized process to promote the mission of the school and to foster an environment that promotes success.

REFERENCES

Anderson, E. M., and Shannon, A. C. (1988). "Toward a Conceptualization of Mentoring," *Journal of Teacher Education*, 39(1): 38−42.

Brooks, D. (1985). "The First Day of School," *Educational Leadership*, 42(8): 76–78.

Cogan, M. L. (1973). *Clinical Supervision*. Boston: Houghton Mifflin.

DeBolt, Gary P. (1992). *Teacher Induction and Monitoring*. Albany, New York: State University of New York Press.

Denham, C. (1987). "Perspective on the Major Purposes and Basic Procedures for Teacher Evaluation," *Journal of Personnel Evaluation in Education*, 1:2932.

Harris, B. (1986). *Developmental Teacher Evaluation*. Boston: Allyn and Bacon.

Hoy, Waynek and Patrick B. Forsyth, (1986). *Effective Supervision: Theory into Practice*. New York: Random House.

Huling-Austin, L., S. J. Odell, P. Ishler, L. S. Kay, and R. A. Edelfet, (1989). *Assisting the Beginning Teacher*. Reston, VA: Association of Teacher Educators.

Karpinski, Joseph R. (1985). "Recognizing the Achievements of Your Staff – Ideas on How to Thank, Praise and Reward Employees for Their Accomplishments," *Journal of Educational Public Relations*, 8(1): 22–26.

Keefe, James W. and Edgar A. Kelley, (1990). "Comprehensive Assessment and School Improvement," *NAASP Bulletin*, 74(530): 54–63.

Lezotte, Lawrence W., 1991. *Correlates of Effective Schools: The First and Second Generation*. Effective Schools Products Ltd., Okimos, MI, 1991.

Lezotte, Lawrence W. and Barbara C. Jacoby, (1990). *A Guide to the School Improvement Process Based on Effective Schools Research*. Okemos, Michigan: Effective Schools Products, Ltd.

Loucks-Horsley S., C. Harding, M. Arbuckle, L. Murray, C. Dubea, and M. Williams (1987). *Continuing to Learn: A Guidebook for Teacher Development*. Andover, Massachusetts: Regional Laboratory for Educational Improvement of the Northeast and Islands, and the National Staff Development Council.

McGreal, T. (1983). *Successful Teacher Evaluation*. Alexandria, Virginia: Association for Supervision and Curriculum Development.

Sparks, Dennis and Susan Loucks-Horsley, (1989). "Five Models of Staff Development for Teachers," *Journal of Staff Development*, 10(4): 40–57.

CHAPTER 4

Student Environment

A consistent body of research points to the significance of establishing and maintaining a student climate conducive to learning and well-being. Students' perceptions of school climate tend to have a direct impact on their functioning within the school. Moreover, evidence exists that the learning environment is a critical element that can be either conducive or detrimental to student success.

"Unfriendly schools" tend to promote student disengagement by establishing real or perceived obstacles to student success. These obstacles lead to feelings of isolation, alienation, and ultimately, feelings of failure. "Friendly schools" provide students with a climate that values involvement in school decisions, systematically develops students' interest in learning, and creates opportunities for students to build sustained relationships with teachers and other adults.

There is a strong relationship between school environment and students' feelings and behavior within them (Strother, 1983). An effective educational program for students does not require a change in the entire educational system; it does, however, take the vision of a committed professional staff to examine the environment that has been created for its students. It takes the dedicated leadership of the principal and school staff to analyze current school practices in terms of their impact on student learning and well-being. Finally, it takes the courage and sustained effort on the part of the entire school community to modify existing school norms and teaching strategies to help ensure the success for all children.

This chapter will examine the characteristics of a productive student environment in America's Best Schools. Additionally, examples of best practices will be highlighted for use as a practical guide toward the development of a student climate that fosters learning and well-being.

Specifically, this chapter will address the following questions:

- What are the elements and practices associated with a productive environment?
- What classroom practices tend to enhance student learning and well-being?
- How do the Best Schools ensure that children who are entering school are prepared to participate successfully in formal schooling?
- What programs, procedures, and strategies are utilized in the Best Schools to develop students' interest in learning and to motivate them to study?
- What opportunities do the Best Schools create to build sustained relationships with teachers and other adults?
- What programs and practices are initiated in the Best Schools to identify and assist at-risk students?
- What extracurricular activities are available for students in the Best Schools?
- What discipline strategies and policies exist in the Best Schools?
- How do the Best Schools prevent the sale, possession, and use of drugs, alcohol, and tobacco?

- What opportunities exist in the Best Schools for students to influence classroom and school policy?
- How do the Best Schools prepare students to live effectively in a culturally diverse society?

THE PRODUCTIVE SCHOOL ENVIRONMENT

The trials and tribulations of all young children during the early school years, as they try to formulate their piece of the world, are difficult. All children experience risks that can limit learning. Most young people make it and, as a result of their experiences, emerge as the people they are satisfied to be and meet with the approval and pride of family and friends.

Students who achieve in school and feel successful as a result of that achievement have positive attitudes toward school and themselves. Teachers, principals, and parents have major responsibilities in establishing a climate for learning. Learning in the school goes beyond the content areas such as reading and math and includes learning to live effectively in society. A significant portion of the young child's "society" is the school. What the teachers and principal do enhances or limits the child's ability to function in that society, to build a base for future interactions in society, and to succeed as a learner.

In addition to the direct effect on individual children of the learning climate, there are significant effects of such instruction on the total school society of students, teachers, administrators, and parents. Teachers in orderly task-oriented schools experience less stress, students are not intimidated by the actions of other students, and principals have time to focus on instruction rather than discipline.

The literature on effective schools consistently stresses the need for high expectations in schools. Teachers and principals in successful schools believe students (*all* students) can learn. In some ways, it is a paradoxical situation. Does the staff believe the students can learn and, therefore, they do learn? Or do the students learn and, therefore, the staff believes they can learn? It is probably more of the former: staff positive beliefs come first. However, success takes more than a belief that students can learn; it takes a commitment that all students "will" learn. Expectations always exist in schools, whether they are implied or formally stated. In order to have a maximum impact on learning, expectations need to be agreed upon by staff, stated in understandable terms, and used as the base for learning and for the interactions of the society within the school.

CREATING A CLASSROOM ENVIRONMENT FOR LEARNING

It is relatively easy to identify classrooms where a positive feeling or tone exists. These feelings are typically associated with a warm, supportive environment in which students are more likely to raise their hands, take an active part in the learning process, and feel more confident about the responses they anticipate receiving from the teacher when they make mistakes or need assistance in learning activities.

Recent studies have begun to identify specific climate factors that are linked in both correlational and experimental studies to increases in student learning and feelings of self-worth. Teachers must systematically analyze their behaviors as they relate to the concepts discussed below to help ensure that their behaviors and routines actively promote success for all students.

Students are likely to work better and achieve at higher levels in an atmosphere that assures that they can and will succeed in the tasks established by the teacher. This *success orientation* is especially important for the at-risk student since there is a clear relationship between achievement gains in average and below average students and the number of successful responses they give in a classroom. Thus, teachers must plan strategies and events that are designed to provide opportunities for students to get the "right answers" and, thus, earn the praise and reinforcement associated with high achievement. In a practical sense, teachers should look for opportunities to provide a successful experience each day for students. Although difficult, the success a student achieves in the classroom may be the only positive reinforcement he/she receives during a typical day.

Significant evidence exists (Good, 1982) to support the contention that typical elementary classrooms do not provide equal opportunity for student involvement and success. Most teachers tend to call on those students who can be consistently depended upon to provide a correct answer. This is primarily done so that (1) a student not expected to know the answer does not get embarrassed, (2) the students in the class hear a correct and thoughtful reply, and (3) a certain degree of teacher reward becomes associated with high-quality student performances (Kerman and Martin, 1980). This phenomenon produces an interesting paradox. Students will soon realize that they are less likely to be called on; consequently, because they are not actually engaged in classroom interaction, they become less able. Knowing that they probably will not be called upon, many students are likely to seek attention and success through dysfunctional means, or they unresponsively drift through school.

If this pattern is permitted to exist, students become increasingly less likely to gain the benefits of praise and recognition associated with success and higher levels of achievement. Interestingly, many students may become so disengaged from active learning that they actually forget how to participate. A technique to help these students is to use paired or small group learning opportunities so that the reluctant learner can begin to model successful response strategies.

As the teacher systematically increases the learners' response opportunities, it is very important for the teacher to analyze the amount and quality of feedback those students receive. Frequently, the majority of feedback consists of short praise, routine comment, or corrections. The ongoing stream of one-liners such as "good," "okay," "no," or "wrong," adds little to a student's feeling of well-being in the classroom. Feedback has proved to be a powerful tool in motivating students and ensuring the correctness of original learning (Hunter, 1986). Praise can and should be used to extend *pupil-teacher contact* and to encourage and reinforce desired behaviors. Yet there is significant evidence to support the idea that less able students actually receive less praise than higher achieving students (Good and Brophy, 1984). This was true even when less able students provided correct answers.

Hunter (1986) has provided a vehicle to help ensure that students receive appropriate and intended feedback to their responses. She suggests that each student comment/response should be "dignified" so that the student feels he/she has made an important contribution to the class. Secondly, the teachers should "probe" for the correct answer so that the students in the class will receive appropriate information. Finally, regardless of correctness of student response, he/she should be held "accountable" for providing information relative to the topic at a future time during the lesson.

Thus, an incorrect student response should be followed by a clarifying statement emphasizing the correct and/or thoughtful parts of a student's comments; then, through a series of direct questions, the teacher should help "draw out" the correct response, and finally, regardless of the success achieved by the student, he/she should be given credit for his/her contributions and told that he/she will again be asked to share his/her thoughts at a later time in the lesson.

Teachers must actively seek opportunities to provide personal contact and regard for their students. Thus, teachers should plan personal encounters with children. Comments related to positive feelings about a child's school work, athletic or aesthetic skills, class playground or cafeteria behavior, personal grooming, or dress, may provide the sense of security and worth needed to integrate the child into the mainstream of school life.

Effectively teaching and supporting the efforts of elementary students is a difficult task. Yet it becomes critical that all educators continue to review the large body of knowledge embodied in effective schools and teacher effectiveness research to guide school and classroom practices. Moreover, they must go about this task with a high degree of *commitment and enthusiasm.* This enthusiasm in the classroom can manifest itself through the high energy level an individual teacher can generate, as well as by the personal, genuine, valuable sincerity and encouragement a teacher shares with a child. Thus, concepts related to a teacher's inherent personality and/or "style" may have little to do with a child's perception of which teachers genuinely care about their profession, school, or most importantly, their students. Instead, it is more important that each teacher behave in a manner that clearly sends a message of enthusiasm and support.

The remainder of this chapter will examine specific school and classroom practices that enrich the learning environment for students. A wide range of topics linked to student success and well-being will be reviewed with illustrations from selected Best Schools as a vehicle to provide an application of theory into practice.

ENSURING SUCCESS FOR CHILDREN ENTERING SCHOOL

In the fall of 1989, President George Bush and the governors of the fifty states framed the six "National Educational Goals." Education goal #1 provides that *by the year 2000, all children in America will start school ready to learn.*

Children's readiness to engage actively in learning is crucial if the student is to benefit from instruction at school, yet assessing this readiness is quite complex. In some cases, a child's full potential to learn is threatened by poor health, inadequate nutrition, emotional instability, stress, cultural deprivation, and/or developmental delays. The issue is further clouded by the vast difference, from school to school, in the expectations and delivery of kindergarten programs.

Although kindergarten attendance is exceedingly valuable for every child in the United States, the experience itself is far from consistent. Full-day programs, half-day programs, developmental programs, differences in the age for kindergarten entrance, and vast differences in curriculum approaches all add to the difficulty in determining what programs will help ensure a successful initial learning experience for each child.

In recent publications from the U. S. Department of Health and Human Services (1993), several concepts related to a child's readiness to learn were identified:

- For children to make full use of the schooling they are offered, they must be in good health. Although prevention of prenatal and childhood health problems are primarily the responsibility of the parents, increasingly, schools and social service agencies are being called upon to educate parents and, at times, provide direct intervention to ensure the emotional and physical well-being for children.
- Of all the elements of a child's environment, the family has the most far-reaching and pervasive impact on his/her well-being and readiness to learn. Although the dynamics of the family and the availability of quality time with children may be a problem, often, inadequate parenting skills leave parents with many misconceptions regarding

effective child-rearing practices. Increasingly, schools have engaged in systematic parent education programs.
- Children learn best in early childhood school settings in which developmentally appropriate teaching strategies are used. Schools serve a very diverse population of children and families; to meet this challenge, schools must be responsive to individual differences in children and their families to ensure that instructional methods correspond to the varied ways that children learn.

Enormous variance exists in the timing of individual development that is within normal range. Developmentally appropriate schools implement strategies to assess the nature of learning readiness and are flexible in their expectations about when and how children will acquire certain competencies. Additionally, quality early childhood programs view the child in terms of the family and seek to provide comprehensive services working with other organizations in the community to serve students' overall needs.

A wide variety of strategies have been utilized to meet the school readiness needs of children and their families. Typically, these include a comprehensive screening process aimed at assessing child's physical and developmental factors that may affect school success. These assessments should never be used for exclusion from a program. Instead, they are most successful when used as diagnostic tools to assist teachers in the development of appropriate teaching and learning strategies. Additionally, data collected through formal screenings can help identify physical, learning, or other developmental disabilities that may require specific remedial intervention. Frequently, successful schools have established parent education and orientation sessions. During these sessions, parents are made aware of the learning nuances and developmental expectations for young children. Handbooks are typically provided which contain strategies that parents can use at home to enrich the child's language and cultural frame of reference. Finally, schools often provide a list of referral agencies where parents can go to deal with a wide variety of practices that may assist the family in dealing with issues that may limit a family's ability to successfully foster a healthy and productive home environment.

The Best Schools—Ensuring Success for Children Entering Schools

The Best Schools throughout the country have accepted the challenges associated with our national goal to ensure that our children entering school are prepared to successfully participate in formal schooling. The schools illustrated below provide comprehensive mechanisms to help children and their parents benefit from their first formal schooling experience.

ADLER PARK SCHOOL, LIBERTYVILLE, IL

The Adler Park School is located approximately thirty-five miles north of Chicago. Its student population comes from families who range from the highest to the lowest socioeconomic backgrounds within the Libertyville Elementary School District. The school serves an ethnically diverse student population, with a higher enrollment in English as a Second Language classes than any other school in the district.

To help ensure that children come to school ready to learn, the school provides extensive preschool and kindergarten screenings, a district early childhood program, kindergarten orientation programs, and parent education and support opportunities.

Preschool screening is encouraged, beginning at age three, to identify students with special needs. These children are referred to a district early childhood program. The kindergarten screening assesses student readiness and provides specific information about strengths and deficiencies. These programs are provided at no cost to district families. At both the preschool and kindergarten screenings, the children are tested for language and motor and concept development; parents share their concerns about their child and receive specific feedback from the school psychologist and special education coordinator.

At kindergarten orientation each spring, incoming kindergarten students and their parents are introduced to the Adler school family. "New" students have an opportunity to explore their room, meet their new teacher, tour the school with student council members, and enjoy cookies. During this time, parents meet with the principal, staff, and the Adler Family Association President to learn about curriculum and discuss school policies, programs and schedules; this is followed by a question and answer period. Following kindergarten orientation, Adler parents can bring their child for "A Day in Kindergarten" or to visit and participate in a kindergarten class in progress. This helps prepare both students and parents for the beginning of school.

When school begins, there are two "first days" for kindergartners. With half of the kindergarten class attending each day, the teacher can give extra attention to each child as he/she gets acquainted with the new environment. To ease their fears and familiarize them with bus rules, a counselor accompanies students on the kindergarten bus route for the first week of school.

The school supports parental efforts to help children come to school ready to learn. The district's early childhood staff provides community workshops and inservices on a variety of readiness topics. The school principal, kindergarten teacher, and members of the Student-Based Assistance Team designed a parent and student packet, which is distributed districtwide at kindergarten screening and orientation. The packet includes fun activities to promote enthusiasm for starting school. Over the summer, the kindergarten teacher sends a personal letter to each student and information to parents. The school psychologist and special education coordinator communicate with local preschools to identify children who require special services. In addition, the school has established a partnership with the Libertyville Cooperative Nursery School. Their staff observes kindergarten classes and meets with the principal, kindergarten teacher, and Student-Based Assistance Team to exchange information and coordinate programs in order to promote a smooth transition of preschoolers to kindergarten.

Janet H. Brownlie, *Principal, K – 5, 260 Students*

BELLERIVE ELEMENTARY SCHOOL, CREVE COEUR, MS

The Bellerive School is one of eighteen public elementary schools of the Parkway School District, located in suburban St. Louis County. The school serves a diverse student population made up of 72% Caucasian, 18% African-American, 19% Asian-American, and 1% Hispanic. Approximately 5% of the student population has limited English proficiency.

Parents of school children are characterized as professional and well-educated and are very active in supporting a quality education for their children.

Bellerive School has sixty-three parents enrolled in the Parents-as-Teachers Project sponsored by the district. Parents may receive services such as monthly visits to the home by parent educators trained in child development, monthly group discussion meetings with other parents, and a parent resource center (Early Childhood Center) for learning materials and developmental and language screening. Parents have the opportunity to attend a choice of twenty-one workshop topics on parenting the young child from birth to five years old. They may also join the Early Childhood Organization, which provides special events and programs for parents of the young child. Records of students participating in the Early Childhood Programs are hand-delivered to the school. Those that are at-risk are identified early, and the records become a part of their permanent record. Four teachers monitor three and four year olds and provide at-risk staffing in language, vision, and hearing, and may contact the Early Childhood Center for further evaluation. Alternative intervention strategies are implemented with parents, and they learn to document their child's progress.

Bellerive kindergarten teachers work closely with the area day-care organizations and willingly share the curriculum and expectations of their kindergarten program. Five different day-care vans drop children off or pick them up at Bellerive each day.

Registration is held in the spring for fall kindergarten classes. It includes screening, parent education, and a general orientation process to make the initial contact with school a positive one for parent and child. Information on day-care services, health, school procedures, parenting, a school tour, and a small gift is given to each parent and child. Parents and children from the St. Louis Voluntary Desegregation Program also attend this registration.

The screening instrument Kindergarten Inventory of Developmental Skills is used as a guide to the students' capabilities and maturity. Bellerive personnel also work closely with the St. Louis City Head Start Program when a child is making the transition to the Bellerive kindergarten.

In August, another orientation is held for kindergarten students and parents. Bus safety, healthy snacks, records, and other information are given to provide for a safe and smooth transition into kindergarten.

Dr. Kenneth Russell, *Principal, K – 6, 564 Students*

MARSHALL ELEMENTARY SCHOOL, FORT CAMPBELL, KY

Marshall Elementary School was officially opened May 14, 1961. Centrally located at the main entrance of Fort Campbell on 14.7 acres, this school serves students of noncommissioned officers residing in on-post housing. Approximately 17% of all students are on the free and reduced lunch program. A fourth of the students are new to Fort Campbell at the start of each school year. Before the year's end, another third will move, requiring the staff to constantly assess educational gaps in each child's program. Marshall Elementary serves a very diverse student population; 57% of its students are Caucasian, 28% African-American, 10% Hispanic, 4% Asian-American, and 1% Native American.

Marshall has implemented a new Early Childhood Program (ECP). While the state of Kentucky mandates offering preschool for at-risk students, this school educates all of its four-year-old population. This decision was based on many factors, including intensive research, site visits to outside programs, and inservice training. The staff supports the National Association for the Education of Young Children's belief that a high-quality early childhood program provides a safe and nurturing environment. The ECP promotes the physical, social, emotional, and cognitive development of young children while responding to the overall needs of their families.

Four and five year olds are intermingled to ease the transition into the school environment. Four year olds visit ECP in the spring prior to entry. Kindergarten students get an opportunity to visit in the first grade classroom and "shadow" an older student. ECP's positive classroom climate encourages learning through supervised active exploration of materials and interaction with other children. Children are viewed as unique individuals with different ability levels and learning styles. Developmentally appropriate activities are designed to meet these differences. Interest areas such as blockbuilding, science and art projects, dramatic play, manipulatives, music, and storytelling are the organizational focus of these activities. Rich teacher-directed language development opportunities highlight the program.

ECP strives to promote continuity between home and school. Family-style settings are promoted with two group meals. Family outreach and education include two fall parent orientations, spring visitation day for new students, monthly Parent Involvement Seminars, fall open house, regular scheduled conferences, personal notes, phone calls, and school newsletters. Since parents are considered vital to the success of early childhood development, they serve as guest readers, help with mealtime, share areas of expertise, and chaperone field trips. The systemwide Early Childhood Council includes a parent and two Marshall ECP teachers.

Assessment of the children relies heavily on developmental observations and descriptive data. More specific assessment is provided by counselor, psychologist, or specialized personnel as needed. Because it is an environment where children experiment and try new ideas without fear of failure, ECP nurtures a love of learning.

John P. Hunt, Principal, Pre-K – 5, 816 Students

MOTIVATING STUDENTS TO LEARN

Why are some students eager to learn, ready to work, and willing to make a personal commitment to do well in school? Why do others become disinterested and disengaged and show little desire to succeed? Ability, of course, may account for part of the answer, but another significant factor is motivation.

Student motivation to learn can be conceptualized as either a general trait or as a situation-specific state (Brophy, 1987). The trait of motivation to learn is an enduring disposition to strive for content knowledge and skill mastery in learning situations. The state of motivation to learn exists when student engagement in a particular activity is guided by the intention of acquiring the knowledge or mastering the skill that the activity is designed to teach (Brophy, 1987).

Waxman and Walberg (1991) have identified five kinds of motivational knowledge. In performing tasks, all five kinds are involved in shaping a student's temperament, attitude toward the task, and persistence to accomplish the task:

(1) An *attribution* is an inference made that identifies a reason for why an event has the outcome that it does. A major dimension of attribution theory include concerns of control, attempting to explain the cause of an event's outcome as either internal (e.g., one's inherent ability) or external (teacher's help and support). Stability addresses the consistency by which the cause of an outcome can be determined (e.g., ability is considered stable because it does not vary if the same task is reattempted, whereas luck and effort are considered unstable because they fluctuate over time). Finally, control-lability deals with whether the cause is governed by oneself or is beyond one's influence (e.g., studying vs. being ill).

(2) *Efficacy* is a belief about one's competency and ability to achieve; typically, when approaching a task, students develop an expectation about being able to perform the task.

(3) *Incentive* provides the value that a goal has if it can be achieved. It is personally what the students want from their efforts but do not yet have.

(4) All tasks have *outcomes,* which define the results of individual effort. Clear, unam-biguous goals help students determine what a finished task should look like.

(5) *Utility* establishes alternatives, causes of action, and parameters for judging the value of each relative to the others. Thus, students can choose or not choose to participate in a learning activity after having assessed the value of each course of action.

Understanding the various factors that shape an individual student's proclivity to be motivated or unmotivated in a particular situation has value. Yet, given the complexity of the issues related to motivation, it is highly unlikely that any single programmatic approach can serve as a panacea for motivating students.

Brophy (1987) believes that no motivational strategies can succeed with students unless certain preconditions are in effect. These include the establishment of a supportive learning environment where learning activities are organized and classroom practices are well managed. Also included are appropriate management of students, parent support of their learning efforts, and provision of an atmosphere where students feel comfortable taking intellectual risks.

Additionally, teachers must provide an appropriate level of challenge, ensuring that students can achieve high levels of success when they apply reasonable effort. Clearly, teachers must provide meaningful learning activities that are considered worth learning, either in their own rights or as steps toward a higher objective. Finally, motivational strategies must be moderated for optimal effectiveness. Motivational attempts can be overdone, and any particular strategy can lose its effectiveness if it is used too often or too routinely.

Successful schools recognize the need to understand the importance of motivating students as an essential element in developing students' interest in learning and study. Although many specific strategies, initiatives, and programs are utilized to meet the unique needs of individual students, classrooms, and schools, many common elements exist that may serve as a foundation for establishing a framework for student motivation and success:

- a relevant, interesting curriculum and learning activities
- the maintenance of higher expectations clearly communicated through a positive sentiment that students can and will learn
- the utilization of well-conceived opportunities for both intrinsic and extrinsic motivations
- the effective use of rewards and positive reinforcement
- the development of a supportive environment that invites student success
- the spirit of mastery that embraces the need for students to feel competent and in control of their learning outcomes
- the teaching of cooperation that does not allow students to criticize themselves or allow others to criticize them
- the recognition that students need a sense of belonging, actively integrating them into the mainstream of school life
- the acceptance of the interdependence among students, parents, teachers, and the principals in shaping a positive school climate directed toward student success

The Best Schools—Motivating Students to Learn

The Best Schools demonstrate the capacity to understand the nature and importance of motivating students and have translated that knowledge into unique, meaningful school programs and learning opportunities. The illustrations provided below attempt to describe how several highly successful schools actually plan and employ instructional strategies that develop students' interest in learning and motivate them to study.

NELSON ELEMENTARY SCHOOL, PINEDALE, CA

Nelson Elementary School serves a unique and diverse population. It is a suburban school located in North Fresno in the Clovis Unified School District. Serving approximately 714 students, the ethnic composition includes 2% Native American, 17% Asian, 26% Hispanic, 4% African-American, and 50% Caucasian. Nelson's socioeconomic range is representative of the following: 50% skilled trade or craft, unskilled employee, or unemployed; 15% semi-professional, clerical, salesworker, or technician; and 35% executive, professional, or manager. Over 24% of the population served has a primary language other than English. There are over eleven languages spoken on the Nelson campus, but the three most predominant languages are English, Spanish, and Hmong.

The Nelson school has student awards that provide incentives for students and serves as a means of acknowledging their efforts and accomplishments. More importantly, the goals, expectations, and values of the school and community are communicated through the criteria for student recognition. In an effort to promote curricular and co-curricular goals and to recognize student effort and achievement in the goal areas, Nelson provides many opportunities for individual students, classes, groups, and teams to receive recognition. The criteria for student recognition at Nelson School reflect achievement, participation, improvement, and/or effort.

Nelson has been a leader in developing innovative programs to best meet all students' needs and motivate students to learn:

- Beginning with a positive, family-like atmosphere, all Nelson staff reward effort, hard work, and appropriate behavior with "WOW" cards and "Happy Grams."
- Individual classrooms have a system of reward activities appropriate to their grade level and classroom goals. Through the Personal Accountability Program, all students are held personally accountable and are rewarded with a quarterly field trip or special activity.
- Through the Virtue of the Month Program, specific qualities such as responsibility, perseverance, cooperation, and others are highlighted for the whole school. Each classroom selects a "Roadrunner of the Week" who exemplifies the virtue of the month and is awarded by the principal with a certificate and pencil.
- An Exemplary Roadrunner—"Block N" Award recognizes students in grades 4–6 who have exemplified the meaning of the "Sparthenian Concept" —being the best you can be in mind, body, and spirit. This program acknowledges students who have actively and enthusiastically participated in all aspects of school life and engaged in the pursuit of excellence by meeting certain standards of achievement and performance. The principal and teachers encourage and assist all upper grade students to apply for Exemplary Roadrunner. Each student is given a detailed booklet outlining the requirements and rewards for this program. A special dinner served by the Nelson staff is given twice a year for all students who achieve this award.
- Nelson holds academic and co-curricular awards assemblies each quarter to celebrate the achievements of all students who reach high academic goals, improve their grade point averages, and participate in co-curricular activities.
- Cooperative learning, peer-tutoring, thematic teaching, whole-language techniques, hands-on science and math programs, field trips, and other strategies are widely used to promote love of learning.
- Weekly Nelson "rallies" exhibit the pride and spirit of Nelson school.
- In an effort to ensure school success, Nelson has implemented a schoolwide organizational and learning strategies program. Students, parents, staff, and business leaders are very positive and supportive of the program. Students are proud of their notebooks and responsibly organize and record all assignments in their daily planner.
- The extended reading program, Roadrunners Are Readers, is another incentive for learning. All grades have set goals for independent student reading with a system of rewards for the number of minutes read and variety of projects completed. Many classrooms implement the "Book It Club."

Linda Hauser, *Principal, K–6, 714 Students*

SANDPIPER ELEMENTARY SCHOOL, SCOTTSDALE, AZ

Sandpiper Elementary School was founded in 1979 to serve the families of the Paradise Valley School District's most eastern boundaries. The school is nestled in the desert some twenty miles south of Carefree and ten miles north of Old Scottsdale. The number of students has grown dramatically in the past four years. The influx of students has brought several portable classrooms to the facility and has created a challenge in meeting the needs of this large population. Socioeconomic conditions have also seen a significant change. For the most part, the school services middle- to upper middle-class families who have lived in the community for a number of years. However, recent trends have shown an increase in lower middle-class families with the introduction of apartments to the area, increasing the degree of transiency. All of this has brought about greater demands on the staff, facility use, and budget allocations, as well as a need to closely evaluate programs of instruction.

Sandpiper utilizes an integrated, relevant curriculum that emphasizes the need to peak students' interests. Two such programs include: The Star Cruiser and S.P.A.C.E. (Students Simulating, Predicting, Analyzing, Creating, and Evaluation Program), which began with the building of a twenty-six−foot mock space shuttle and which provides integrated activities that promote higher order thinking skills through computer-generated student simulations.

Another unique instructional strategy at Sandpiper is the use of a Schoolwide Theme developed each year to integrate experiences. Through the implementation of activities, students are motivated to connect learning with life. Over 92% of staff and parents feel that the theme approved is successful. Program effectiveness is also measured by the variety of integrative activities that occur annually and the number of Principal's Challenge ribbons distributed (approximately 65−75% annually). Following is a list of the yearly themes and a sampling of unique, motivational activities that develop student interest in learning:

1990−1991: "WE ARE THE WORLD"

Principal's Challenge−Collecting 100 aluminum cans per family and/or logging individual and
   family efforts to learn more about world cultures
Schoolwide Activities−Quarterly "Global Citizen" Certificates to over 100 students, two
   related Artist-in-Residence Programs (Kawambe African Dance and Mei Kuei Chinese
   culture), Student Council recycling, Geography Awareness Week and Geography Bee,
   Folklorico Assembly, and Earth Day Ceremony.

1991−1992: "DISCOVERY!: WHERE WE'VE BEEN AND WHERE WE'RE GOING"

Principal's Challenge−Choosing a topic of personal interest and logging personal and family
   "discovery" learning activities
Schoolwide Activities−Quarterly Certificates to over 100 students for demonstration of a thirst
   for knowledge, Geography/History Awareness Week, and Family Evenings with Columbus
   and Lincoln (other activities being planned)
Humanities Forum Exhibits−Hispanic Culture; Native American Culture; "Discovery;
   1492−1992"

Other instructional procedures used to motivate student learning and actively involve students in higher order thinking are the integration of basic skills with high-interest thematic units and literature; the use of cooperative learning, where student motivation and participation are increased because of the feeling of cooperation and mutual responsibility; and the use of simulations, actually bringing learning to life through integrated, cooperative experiences (i.e., Westward Ho!, with students encountering real-life difficulties in their wagon trains as they move west).

Other programs to spark student interest in learning at Sandpiper include field trip experiences, such as the Arts Experience Program, Catalina/Astrocamp, and Outdoor Education each year (students in grades 3 and 5 journey to Sky-Y, Prescott), and the involvement of families in learning, with programs such as Family Learning Nights, Family Math/Science, and Family Learning Trunks.

The Sandpiper staff has noted that attendance and attitude is consistently high when integrative, motivational, active learning experiences are planned. The internalized reward is evidenced when students comment, "I like Sandpiper because learning is fun!"

Besides making learning fun, students are recognized for outstanding efforts. Teachers write positive notes and comments on papers, send home Happy Grams, and constantly reinforce quality work. Quarterly Awards Assemblies provide a structured time for students to be recognized in the following areas: Perfect Attendance (35−40% average), Outstanding Citizenship (80−90% average), Honor Roll (40−50% average), three Special Recognition Awards per class, one Most Improved Award per class, one Theme-Related Award per class, and one Academic Goal-Related Award per class. The goal is to provide each child with some sort of recognition during the school year. The outstanding efforts of students are published in the school newspaper and announced on the intercom. The principal follows up with personal commendation letters to students and parents (580 sent during 1990−91).

Tacy Ashby, Principal, K − 6, 862 Students

SHERIDAN SCHOOL, LAKE FOREST, IL

The Sheridan School is located in the northeast corner of Illinois. It is one of six schools that comprise the Lake Forest School District 67. This small suburban school serves a student population that is 95% Caucasian and 5% African-American, Asian, and Hispanic. The staff at Sheridan recognizes that student well-being is a precondition to success and has developed ongoing strategies to motivate its students.

Sheridan's major focus is to build children's self-esteem so that they can develop a strong self-concept about their ability to learn. The teacher's role is to develop a variety of techniques, procedures, and instructional strategies that develop a student's interest in learning. The children's involvement in the learning process is of primary importance.

The instructional approach used at Sheridan is based on Bloom's Taxonomy, with an emphasis on the teaching of higher level thinking skills. Teachers also present material through a "multi-sensory" approach incorporating visual, auditory, and kinesthetic activities to all students. What is evident, but not found in any guidebook, is the high degree of creativity and commitment present within the teaching staff. Because of their commitment, enthusiasm, and sense of humor, love of learning is radiated daily throughout the building to each student.

Specific programs that have been implemented at the school:

- Read a book to the principal and receive an "I Read to the Principal" button.
- Keep a reading log of books read individually or as a class and receive public recognition for this success.
- The "Science Olympiad" and "Invention Convention" encourage students to use the scientific method to find the answers to problems or to "invent" and create new ideas in order to solve everyday problems.
- "Odyssey of the Mind" allows students to work in small groups to find creative solutions to problems through their production of plays that they have written, produced, and performed in a presentation to the entire school body.

Many instructional strategies focus on promoting self-directed learning. For example, the use of curriculum-related centers in the classroom that incorporate choices made by the student; the use of tape recorders, language masters, overheads, records, books, songs, drama-movement, and "message boards" (message centers where students can write notes to one another); storytelling through acting, and puppets; flannel boards; games related to specific skills; finger plays; posters; literature sharing (presenting an original piece of writing); and arts and crafts in various "hands-on" activities in the Discovery Center where students can actively participate in various experiments or discoveries are all incorporated to encourage an interest in learning. Ongoing positive praise and encouragement through both verbal (comments) and nonverbal (hugs, pats on the backs) channels are all used to promote and sustain the student's interest in learning.

Computers are another integral part in motivating students to learn. Each classroom has at least one computer, and the school's media center is equipped with twelve computers for whole class, small group, or individual student use.

James W. Walton, Principal, K − 3, 197 Students

STUDENTS BUILDING SUSTAINED RELATIONSHIPS WITH COUNSELORS, TEACHERS, AND OTHER ADULTS

A primary indicator of a student's sense of belonging in a school is the quality of interactions and relationships he/she has with the adults in that school. It is those adults who help model the world for the child. It is those adults upon whom the child relies for security, support, and recognition. Through the development of trust between students and those adults around them, fear and apprehension are managed. Thus, students are far more likely to take more intellectual risks in classrooms, feel more free to engage in activities throughout the school, and be more likely to seek adult assistance when confronted with a school or life problem.

To be successful, students need to view their school as a special place where teachers are caring, the principal is nice, others are friends, and learning takes place. In an environment that conveys a sense of community or a feeling of family, there are many opportunities for children to meet and learn from adults.

THE BEST SCHOOLS—BUILDING SUSTAINED RELATIONSHIPS WITH ADULTS

The Best Schools throughout the country maximize the opportunities to personalize the school experience for their students by providing a wide variety of planned strategies to enrich the relationships between students and school staff. Several illustrations are provided below.

PIONEER ELEMENTARY SCHOOL, COLORADO SPRINGS, CO

Pioneer Elementary School is located in the north end of Colorado Springs in the Academy District #20. The surrounding community consists primarily of white-collar workers, serving a diverse student population made up of 86% Caucasian, 7% Hispanic, 5% African-American, 3% Asian-American, and 1% Native American.

The school has established as its highest priority a commitment to provide an environment where children can experience success and feel comfortable, both in their academic work and their relationships with other children and adults. Because the staff recognizes the importance of adult-child relationships to the learning process, a vast number of opportunities for students to build sustained, supportive relationships with staff members have been developed.

A task force charged with researching elementary schools organized, designed, and implemented a "school within a school" program entitled "Moving Ahead Together" (MAT). In this program, two (team) teachers plan and deliver instruction to the same students for a minimum of two years. This program is particularly beneficial for those students whose success has been predicated on the unique relationship they have developed with specific teachers.

The MAT program provides a particularly outstanding example of the commitment to build sustained relationships between teachers and students. Teachers work toward this goal in a myriad of ways. Some teachers serve as mentors to students while others serve as sponsors of numerous after-school organizations such as Choir, Odyssey of the Mind, Future Problem Solving, the Geography Club, and the Math Club. Through Potential Unlimited, children learn skills that increase their personal effectiveness in relationships with both peers and adults. All teachers work with students on an ongoing, personal basis in their progress toward the goals they set during annual goal conferences. Teachers also interact with students before and after school, and many choose to have lunch with their students on a regular basis. Several staff members extend the opportunity for students to have continuing relationships by holding reunions of previous classes.

Children have numerous opportunities to develop a relationship with the school counselor, and many avail themselves of this service. The counselor visits every classroom during the first week of school for the purpose of introductions and discussing her role in the school with the students. At that time, the process is described by which students may refer themselves to counseling via the use of "Bear Hug Coupons." Individual and small-group counseling sessions are provided to students following these self-referrals. The counselor continues to follow up and maintain a close relationship with these students even after direct counseling services have been terminated. In addition to these activities, the schoolwide, comprehensive developmental guidance program provides all students with the opportunity to develop a comfortable, long-term relationship with the counselor during weekly guidance lessons.

Heidi Pace, Principal (Suzanne Loughran, Principal at time of recognition),
K – 5, 688 Students

NORTH DADE CENTER FOR MODERN LANGUAGES, MIAMI, FL

The North Dade Center for Modern Languages (CML) is an elementary international studies magnet school where every student is a participant in the magnet curriculum. The school began in 1988 – 89 and offered an international studies curriculum to interested students in grades 3 through 5. The school's goal is to provide the opportunity for students to become bilingual, biliterate, and multicultural.

The school serves a very diverse student population consisting of 41 % Caucasian, 32 % African-American, 23 % Hispanic, and 6 % Asian-American. Students choose to come to CML and very few choose to leave. In addition to its unique curriculum, CML provides a stable sense of community for its students.

Opportunities to build sustained relationships with counselors, teachers, and other adults are varied and readily available. Programs are in place to provide counseling and advisement, and these approaches are systematically reviewed for effectiveness. A significant number of students take advantage of these opportunities. The school prides itself on its affective education program. In addition to biweekly classroom visits by the school counselor, the following programs are in place: developmental group counseling, small group counseling, drop-out prevention, children of divorced parents counseling, and group and individual counseling.

Student/teacher relationships are optimal as a result of the very effective advisor-advisee program. Using the acronym of RRR Time (Reflect, Relax, Relate), teachers meet with a regular group of students weekly for one-half hour to discuss feelings, concerns, and potential problems. The program enhances a new theme yearly with this year's emphasis on the cultivation of peacemakers. An end-of-the-year evaluation by the students guides the curriculum.

Student interests are further served by very popular monthly club meetings that take place on campus. Activities include Adopt-a-Grandparent, environment club, and French and Spanish culture clubs; teachers and students alike enjoy this opportunity to share common interests.

Dr. Maria Anyela Castaigne, Principal (Lois Lindahl, Principal at time of recognition),
Grades 1 – 6, 537 Students

ARNOLD J. TYLER SCHOOL, NEW LENOX, IL

The Tyler School is located in an area that is rapidly changing from a rural community to a suburb of Chicago. The school serves a predominantly Caucasian student population, with 45 % of its population made up of students from Hispanic or Asian ethnic groups.

With the advent of the educational reform movements in the mid-1980's, a School Improvement Team was instituted to guide school improvement. One foundation of the school's success revolves around the quality relationships between students and staff. Knowing that the well-being of students is a primary concern, the staff at Arnold J. Tyler School works together to form a closely knit bond. They know that, in order to meet the children's needs academically, they must address the whole child: physically, socially, and emotionally. Therefore, the faculty is available to assist children before and after school, during lunch or recess, or when needed. Many students take advantage of this personal time, often seeking out teachers or other caring personnel in order to share their experiences.

The school's guidance counselor is a highly respected resource for both parents and teachers who are seeking advice about students' special needs. She counsels students individually or in small groups, as needed. Students can sign up to be a member of the "Lunch Bunch," or teachers and parents can suggest a student in need of improved study skill strategies. The "Lunch Bunch," a small group (ten to twelve students), is composed of both those who need study skills help and some students who are successful in this area. The students meet weekly at lunch to discuss ways of studying and organizing their work. The group remains fluid, and students join and leave throughout the year. With parental permission, the counselor takes students bowling and to dinner for achieving or maintaining specific social and academic goals. The guidance counselor also facilitates classroom discussions on a regular basis in order to promote students' self-confidence, good study skills, and social interactions. In the lower grades, she has implemented a "Warm Fuzzy" program in which social interactions, along with self-image, are addressed. In the upper grades, the counselor has implemented a mentoring program to promote drug awareness. The children are actively involved in discussions as they pertain to their life surroundings.

The school nurse, counselor, and principal also conduct a growing up seminar with all fourth graders entitled "A New You Coming." Students have the opportunity to view a filmstrip and ask questions about physical, social, and emotional topics encountered in the growing up process. Since parents are the child's most important resource, a separate parents' seminar is conducted.

Edward A. Tatro, *Principal, 1 – 4, 568 Students*

PROGRAMS AND STRATEGIES TO ASSIST AT-RISK STUDENTS

All children are, at times, at risk of failure. Yet most can effectively utilize the standard resources and support systems established at home or school to deal with the trials and tribulations of growing up. As a result of their positive developmental experiences, they emerge as young adults satisfied with who they are and pleased with the approval and pride from their families and friends. Similarly, children who achieve in school experience success and, typically, develop positive attitudes toward school and themselves.

Unfortunately, there is a portion of every school population that consistently shows a lack of necessary intellectual, emotional, and/or social skills to take full advantage of the educational opportunities available to them. Often, these students become disenchanted and, ultimately, passively or openly reject school. It is these students who are at high risk of failure.

The At-Risk Child

There is no prototype closely related to the at risk elementary school student. Students who do not succeed in our schools come from all social, ethnic, and racial groups; still, various key demographic characteristics tend to place certain students at a potentially higher risk for school failure.

Pallas, Natriello, and McDill (1989) characterize the educationally disadvantaged child as one who has been exposed to certain background factors or experiences in formal schooling, family, or community. Although not a categorical model to predict at-risk status, these authors have determined that particular combinations of risk factors have been shown to be particularly detrimental to success. Examples of these are single-parent homes with low incomes, and parents with limited English proficiency who have no high school diploma. Similarly, a study conducted by the National Center for Education Statistics (U. S. Center of Educational Statistics, 1989) identifies indicators of at-risk status. These include (among others), living in a single-parent family, low parental income and/or education, limited English proficiency, having a brother or sister who dropped out of high school, and being at home alone without an adult for a period greater than three hours on weekdays.

Although helpful in a general sense, demographic characteristics, in and of themselves, cannot consistently identify those elementary school students destined for school failure.

Research has shown that the characteristics and school behaviors listed below are closely associated with school failure:

- attendance problems
- previous school retention
- prior school suspensions
- working two or more years below grade level
- lack of participation in extracurricular activities
- special program placement

From both an empirical and common sense perspective, these behaviors can accurately identify those students who, for whatever reason, will not meet with success. Yet these characteristics tend to manifest themselves long after a student has begun to develop attitude and behavioral patterns that lead to school failure. Instead, it may be more beneficial to examine general descriptors of a student's profile to establish parameters for determining the nature of risk. A review of the research can help synthesize this profile by analyzing four basic conditions: self-concept, alienation, lack of school success, and student learning style.

Student Self-Concept

Self-concept has been found to be related to students' grades, test scores, and other significant educational outcomes (Coleman et al., 1966). Teachers instinctively know that, when students feel better about themselves, they tend to do better in school. It becomes critical that school personnel actively seek ways to promote self-esteem in the classroom and to promote a school climate that conscientiously attempts to foster students' feelings of pride in themselves and their schools.

Alienation

For at-risk students, lack of success in school both contributes to and results from an increased sense of alienation from school as an institution. Newman (1981) associates alienation in schools with disruptive student behaviors and poor achievement. He suggests that student disengagement generally goes unrecognized as the source of many school problems. He insists that reducing student alienation is key to engaging students in the positive benefits in their schooling.

Thus, schools need to identify and revise school and classroom practices that send negative messages about school membership and belonging. Common practices associated with class grouping patterns, discipline and attendance policies, school regulations, school curriculum, and special class placement may be rooted in good intentions, yet they may, in fact, lead to increased feelings of isolation and lack of belonging.

Level of School Success

Success in early years is a critical prerequisite to success in later schooling and, ultimately, in life. Third graders who are reading a year or more below grade level or who have been retained one or more times are particularly at risk; and when these students are from low socioeconomic backgrounds and attend school with many other poor children, their chances of eventually graduating from high school approach zero (McPartland and Slavin, 1990).

School failure leads to messages of rejection and a poor sense of self. Without basic academic and social skills, children face failure every day and may quickly reach the conclusion that they are incapable and that schools don't care about their learning.

Success, however, can come from a variety of aspects of school life. Achievement, not only in academics, but in areas related to athletics or aesthetics can lead to increased feelings of self with a greater sense of belonging to the mainstream of the school. It becomes imperative that schools continue to examine how they incorporate a success orientation in daily practices. Clearly, teachers have the greatest impact on the sense of success a student may encounter. Yet the principal, coach, play director, custodian, and bus driver also provide significant contributions to the at-risk student's feeling of belonging and worth.

Learning Style

Every student has a preferred learning style. While most students can learn through a variety of sensory stimuli and within different learning environments, enough research is available to support the notion that teaching through learning styles can improve student learning (Dunn and Dunn, et al., 1978).

There is some evidence to suggest that at-risk students may have measurably different learning styles. In fact, at-risk students may have predominant learning modalities that differ significantly from traditional teaching styles. In a recent study, at-risk learners were identified as having poor to fair auditory and visual learning capabilities. However, a very large percentage of these students demonstrated high preference for tactical and kinesthetic learning experiences. It becomes important, then, that we begin to train teachers to utilize a more multi-sensory approach with identified at-risk students. It seems logical that providing variability in instructional delivery systems would ultimately help all learners.

Program Rationale

Schools have an expressed obligation to educate all students. This responsibility is most typically met through direct instruction in the traditional curriculum areas. However, schools must now embrace the responsibility of successfully educating those students who, for whatever reason, come to school unable to maximize their learning potential. No longer can schools afford to disregard the role that society has placed upon them.

There are a variety of factors that compel our schools to engage in early prevention and intervention initiatives to help ensure the success of our elementary school students.

The first is that a variety of societal problems are, at least in part, the result of a poor education. Early success in school correlates with high school graduation. More than 80% of prison inmates are high school dropouts (U.S. Department of Education, 1990). The best way to reduce crime is to increase education, because the chances are greater that a high school dropout will go to prison than that a smoker will contract cancer (Hodgehenson, 1990).

The second concern is the question of equity in access to educational opportunity. State and federal laws have been enacted to help educate learning disabled children, non-English speaking children, gifted children, etc.; so it may be argued that the disaffected students, the majority of whom have normal intelligence, require specialized learning experiences and support systems to truly maximize their learning potential.

A third reason is linked to changing societal expectations for our schools. The world has become increasingly complex for elementary school students. Confronted with increased pressure from familial, environmental, and social stresses, today's children may have greater difficulty determining their places in the world. Increasingly, parents will look to the school for help. Schools have now been asked to assume a more direct role in teaching the essential life skills that were traditionally within the domain of family and church.

Finally, schools have the awesome responsibility of preparing students for the roles they will be asked to play in our ever-complex society. It is through our efforts that a significant foundation can be established to ensure success for a generation of young Americans.

Components of a Comprehensive Program

Because the factors that place a student at risk are numerous and complex, successful programming for at-risk students must address multiple needs and be carefully tailored to meet the individuals they serve. Nonetheless, general parameters of effective programs emerge and can be identified.

THE BEST SCHOOLS – PROGRAMS AND STRATEGIES TO ASSIST THE AT-RISK STUDENT

Successful programs in elementary schools are comprehensive and intensive. They start with a viable mechanism to identify at-risk students and provide the systematic application of instructional strategies and school programs that help students succeed in school; help students overcome feelings of isolation and alienation; and optimally, create an environment that formulates self-motivation and student interest in continued learning.

Specifically, successful programs:

- *Develop a curriculum basis for school improvement initiatives* – Teachers are best trained to teach. Programs that are rooted in counseling or the dynamics of the family are best suited for psychologists and social workers. Schools must capitalize on the staff's ability to improve student learning and self-esteem as the most primary of all at-risk prevention vehicles. Providing a success orientation for elementary school students will significantly increase the chances of life-long success.
- *Stress intimacy and individual attention* – Virtually all successful programs provide for strong personal attention to each student. They strive to create a feeling of nurturing and belonging that is often absent from the home and school experience of at-risk students.
- *Deal with the child as part of the family and the family as part of the neighborhood* – Research clearly shows that student attitudes and performance are better when parents are supportive and involved in the school environment (National School Boards Association, 1988). Special care should be given to accommodate access to the school for the parents of at-risk students. Parenting classes, home visits, and a recognition of parental responsibilities in educating their children are examples of bringing parents into the mainstream of school life.
- *Utilize a team approach to programming for the at-risk student* – The responsibility cannot fall on the counselor, child psychologist, nurse, or special education teacher. The entire school community must learn to embrace its responsibility to assist in the education of at-risk students.
- *Possess caring, dedicated staff members who have the time and the skills to build relationships of trust and respect with at-risk children and their families* – Thus, the

school must make a commitment to training the staff as to the nature of risk and in strategies that facilitate the learning of the at-risk student.

- *Monitor program* — Very few programs fail because of lack of initial enthusiasm or the utility of purpose. Instead, many programs fail because they are either not implemented as designed, or they are not periodically assessed for their impact on the intended outcome.
- *Have administrative and school board support* — Through the development of policies or commitment to provide needed resources and, most importantly, effective leadership, programs aimed at providing success for at-risk students (like all other programs) will prove beneficial.
- *Evaluate program* — Once implemented, monitoring must be initiated to ensure that activities are being conducted according to plan. Evaluation mechanisms must be put into place to determine if expectations/objectives are being met.

Many of America's Best Schools have developed systematic programs that effectively identify and provide interventions to assist the at-risk student. Although different in their approaches, the schools illustrated below provide a sample of how successful programs operate.

GEORGE C. BAKER SCHOOL, MOORESTOWN, NJ

Moorestown is a suburban community of almost 20,000 residents, located in the southwestern part of New Jersey, approximately twenty miles from center city Philadelphia. The population is largely upper middle-class with a significant low-moderate income group. This school district has had several nationally recognized schools.

While the school maintains high expectations for academic achievement, it has developed a student assistance program specifically aimed at providing a support system for at-risk students. This program utilizes a team approach and provides specific intervention strategies to foster success for identified students. The goal of the Student Assistance Resource Committee is to assist teachers with strategies for dealing with students whose behavior interferes with the learning process. The committee consists of a Student Assistance Coordinator, the building principal, a learning disabilities teacher consultant (member of the district's Child Study Team), the school nurse, and a member of the faculty. The committee handles referrals from teachers and administrators.

Parents are notified that a referral is being made. The committee collects information, develops and maintains an individual student file, meets with the referring individual to decide on a course of action, and establishes a time line for ongoing feedback, monitoring, and assessment. To ensure appropriate support, the team carefully matches identified students with one of the many intervention strategies listed below:

- modifying the student's program so that the child meets with more academic and/or personal success
- providing group activities, such as in-common reading, so that students in the low reading groups work regularly with the total class, allowing the opportunity to interact with positive peer models
- changing the physical arrangement of the class so that certain students can be separated or encouraged to work together
- avoiding classroom activities that emphasize competition, which may lead to consistent feelings of failure
- providing an ongoing system for teachers to explore problem-solving techniques
- providing individual counseling with principals
- using cooperative learning groups in the classroom
- employing behavior modification strategies

- instituting a peer tutoring/buddy system
- assigning an instructional aide to the student
- making available in-house support services (physical education, reading specialist, nurse, art, music, speech, and language) to the student on a short-term basis
- offering mentorships
- ensuring referral to a special education team for consultation or comprehensive evaluation
- referring to outside agencies
- referring to volunteer student assistance support services, e.g., grandparents, psychological counseling, and Adopt-a-School
- maintaining contact with home (daily or weekly monitoring)
- ensuring referral to Basic Skills Improvement Program
- providing group and/or individual support services if deemed applicable by the primary prevention counselor

Richard L. Bucko, *Principal, K–4, 225 Students*

INDIAN CREEK ELEMENTARY SCHOOL, OLATHE, KS

Olathe is a mid-size city located twenty miles south of Kansas City. The community is a mixture of single-family dwellings, apartments, and duplexes. The median income for families could be stated as a combination of low to low-middle and middle income. Approximately 4% of the students are receiving federal assistance for the lunch program. The student population is predominantly white, with a high level of transiency by families; approximately 15% of the student population changes each year.

The entire school community believes that emotional and physical well-being are essential for becoming a productive citizen. In order to deal with the kinds of problems that face our society, the school creates a systematic analysis of students who may be classified at-risk. The school screens the student population according to the symptoms of at-risk students: poverty, low achievement, high absenteeism, disruptive behavior, atypical behavior, victim of abuse, physical or emotional health problems, and dysfunctional home. According to this screening process, 119 students have one or more symptoms.

Absences, grade cards, study hall referrals, and disruptive behavior are monitored regularly by the principal. At-risk or underachieving students are also identified through the CARE team, which is comprised of the principal, counselor, speech pathologist, learning disabilities facilitator, social worker, school nurse, school psychologist, and other classroom teachers. The team meets bimonthly to discuss referrals made by staff, parents, and other social agencies that have contact with children. The total number of students served in 1988–89 was thirty-six; sixty-four were served in 1989–90 and seventy-four in 1990–91. The team's primary responsibilities are to identify, assess, propose intervention strategies, monitor, and provide support for at-risk students, their families and the teachers who serve them. Students identified by the CARE team are given individual guidance by a counselor. Counseling is also given at the request of students and parents. All staff evaluate the effectiveness of the CARE team and intervention practices on a yearly basis.

At present, fifteen students are receiving counseling every week, and approximately forty weekly self-referrals are made. The counselor provides small group guidance on the topics of social skills, self-esteem, divorce, bereavement, and living with alcoholic parents. At present, ninety-two students are involved in these groups. The goal of the CARE team and guidance program is to maximize student learning and promote physical and emotional well-being.

Several programs assist the at-risk or underachieving student. The S.O.S. (Save One Student) program matches a staff volunteer to an at-risk student. Daily contact is encouraged, and the staff person is given suggestions for ways to help the student. Also, the school has implemented the D.A.R.E. program for prevention of drug abuse. The staff at Indian Creek believes that one of the most effective ways to promote a positive change in a child's life is to help the parents see their role as change agents. Workshops and parenting classes are offered in both day and evening sessions by counselors and social workers at building and district levels.

The staff at Indian Creek believes that the entire staff must be knowledgeable of strategies to assist at-risk students. All teachers have been trained in cooperative learning, which fosters a child's sense of belonging. Direct instruction and active teaching are used to increase academic achievement and student accountability. Teachers have been trained in whole-language programs and critical thinking skills, two strategies proven effective in making a positive impact on the at-risk student. The school is noted for its intensive academic and behavior intervention program. Individual behavior plans, curriculum modifications, small class size, and tutors also help the at-risk and low-achieving student. The school's atmosphere promotes safety, stability, and caring to enable a child to view school as a place in which to grow and develop to the best of his/her ability.

Donna M. Dunne, *Principal, K – 6, 528 Students*

BIDDEFORD MIDDLE SCHOOL, BIDDEFORD, ME

The city of Biddeford is located in southern Maine. It can be characterized as a working class community struggling to cope with the extraction of blue-collar employment. The city has a high unemployment rate and more low income housing than the combined total of its county. Two out of five students live in single-parent homes. One-half meet the guidelines for the subsidized lunch program. Biddeford has the highest percentage of welfare recipients and the second highest rate of child abuse in Maine. More than 40% of the adults in this community did not complete high school.

Despite this profile, this small city has a sense of community and pride in its schools. Biddeford's success is no accident. It plans for student success and provides a variety of strategies for its identified at-risk population.

The HARBOR Project has identified and is following fifteen students for three years using a case management mode with parent contact and adult mentoring used for keeping kids on track.

REACH (Realizing Esteem and Aspirations through Community Help), a mentoring project, pairs underachievers with high school students and adult mentors. The program is funded by a $7500 grant from the Maine Aspirations Foundation. The focus is to expose students to opportunities and occupations available with post-secondary training. Twenty-four eighth graders participate yearly.

The Student Assistance Team, SAT, is comprised of teachers, special educators, administrators, nurse, social worker, guidance counselors, and other specialists that meet once a week after the school day. This group has received special training in how to assist students who are at risk for any reason: behavior, attendance, low achievement, social and emotional difficulty, or poor peer relations. The SAT harnesses the expertise of school professionals to define possible intervention strategies; these professionals also serve as individual case managers. Students are referred by team teachers or parents. Interventions include contracts for behavior, attendance, and work production; special education evaluation; referral to services in the school setting; and referral to outside community services. Biddeford Middle School has been selected by the department of education to serve as an evaluation site for this process over the next three years.

A full-time social worker and a part-time substance abuse counselor are available on premises. Social work is also available to families in an off-site clinical setting. The substance abuse counselor works with individuals and small groups each week and assists in planning awareness programs.

BEAT (Biddeford's Educational Alternative to Truancy) is an alternative education program located at the high school. Designed for individual attention and academic skill building, the program provides a bridge to high school for students who are not succeeding in a traditional setting. Project Adventure, community service, social work, and a 1:4 teacher-student ratio are part of the BEAT program.

Work Plus identifies underachieving gifted and talented students and brings them together in an attempt to build self-esteem and provide challenging activities outside the regular classroom.

Suzanne B. Lukas, Principal, 6 – 8, 534 Students

EXTRACURRICULAR SCHOOL ACTIVITIES

Successful schools consistently look for ways to enrich the learning environment for their students. Additionally, successful schools extend the opportunity for students to learn beyond the parameters of the academic day. The most common way this is accomplished is through a comprehensive extracurricular program. Successful schools plan these activities as carefully as they plan daily lessons. Special care is given to promote optimum participation while deemphasizing winning and losing. It is through a cooperative spirit of teamwork that many important life skills are developed and nurtured.

Regardless of the availability of resources, successful schools recognize the importance of extending learning opportunities. Often, teachers and administrators volunteer their time and energy to help foster a sense of community for their students. The ultimate benefactors of these efforts are the students who learn and mature physically, emotionally, and intellectually under the watchful eye of a caring professional.

THE BEST SCHOOLS – EXTRACURRICULAR ACTIVITIES

The Best Schools capitalize on every opportunity to extend student learning and well-being. To this end, many fine extracurricular programs have spawned exciting learning situations for their students. While all Best Schools have recognized the importance of extracurricular programs, several specific strategies are illustrated next.

FREEDOM ELEMENTARY SCHOOL, WEST CHESTER, OH

Freedom Elementary is located within a middle/upper middle-class planned community twenty-five miles north of Cincinnati, Ohio. One of seven schools in the Lakota School District, Freedom serves a mobile, diverse population ranging from families living in poverty to those of upper middle class professionals. Freedom serves a predominantly Caucasian student population with 5% African-American and Asian-American students.

Extracurricular activities available for students include a physical education program involving third through sixth grade students. The intramural program at Freedom is an extension of classroom activities and provides an outlet for instructional activity at a higher level with increased interest and participation. Instruction and recreation are offered at no cost and without interfering with community programs. The school participates in community and church athletic programs, however, by disseminating information and offering facilities and staff support.

Sixth grade students serve as officials, umpires, and coaches for many activities. Teachers and parents aid in supervision, officiating, and coaching. Many students with special needs participate in the regular program or with bowling and track intramurals conducted by adaptive physical education instructors.

Field Day, held every spring, culminates the year's physical education program and includes 100% participation of staff, administrators, and students. Incorporated into this day is a wide variety of individual and team activities. The day is filled with healthy competition and activity while encouraging a coming together for friendship, sportsmanship, and team spirit. Videorecording of the day's activities allows the community to view this day of unity.

Freedom supports the American Heart Association with a Jump-for-Heart-athon involving second through sixth grade students. Students are encouraged to participate as an extension of the classroom jump rope curriculum. Last year, $5600.00 was raised for the Association from this two-hour effort. The program is in conjunction with the P.T.A. Health Week.

All activities are announced by newsletter, the school newspaper, and closed circuit TV. Freedom's music program offers fifth and sixth grade chorus. All fifth grade students participate in chorus, which performs several times each year. Sixth grade has 60−70% participation in two concerts. Students are encouraged to take part in public performances, learn advanced vocal skills, and perform on an instrument. Select small groups often stay after school for ensemble work with choir chimes. Also, band at Freedom for fifth and sixth grade students includes 60−70% of the fifth grade class and 25% of the sixth grade class. Fifth and sixth grade band performs in two public concerts.

Leadership Council stimulates students in sixth grade to serve as role models for Freedom's student population. Membership is by teacher selection. Students who have served as positive role models are approached by their teachers for membership on the council. Participants assume necessary jobs and responsibilities including serving as peer tutors, art aides, library aides, and assembly role models. Students are encouraged to set a good example and to respect and remain loyal to their leadership commitment.

David R. Tobergate, *Principal, K−6, 904 Students*

GLENN E. MURDOCK ELEMENTARY SCHOOL, LA MESA, CA

Murdock Elementary School is one of seventeen elementary schools in the La Mesa-Spring Valley School District. Located within the boundaries of a mid-size city, Murdock serves a diverse student population that includes 85% Caucasian, 7% Hispanic, 4% African-American, and 4% Asian-American.

The school is situated around an open setting of three large "lofts," each containing four to five classrooms. This setting has proven to be very successful, providing opportunities for team teaching and shared revenues. Murdock has supplemented its school program with a wide variety of outstanding extracurricular student activities that are available to the entire student population, both during the school day and after school. In-school programs stimulate interest in a broad range of curricular areas. Student Council involves grades 4 and 5 and sponsors many events that build school spirit and unity. This year, forty students ran for the four school wide offices and four class representatives; many others were involved in the related activities of voter registration or campaigning. The media center teacher coordinates the schoolwide Reading Incentive Program where students receive "Bonus Bucks" for reading. This generated over 1 million pages of reading and a 95% participation rate. The Accelerated Reader, a computerized comprehension program, attracted eighty-seven students in 1990−91. In this program, students read books from a recommended list of highly acclaimed children's literature and take tests using correlated software. Band is an elective for fourth grade students. Last year, twenty-five students went to the adjoining Middle School for an hour each week, learning to play an instrument. Know Your States Program is an exciting schoolwide activity; classes compete to collect postcards from all fifty states, and parent volunteers award certificates to students who can locate all states on a map. The culminating celebration for this event included a giant American flag made of hundreds of red, white, and blue cupcakes. Math Field Day offers fourth and fifth grade math lovers a chance to test their skills. Students can then compete at the district and county level; Murdock had twelve students competing at the district level in 1990−91 and two winners in the county. Science enthusiasts participate in Invent America (K−5) and Science Olympiad (4−5). These activities involve a significant amount of home-school collaboration, and attracted sixty-seven students last year. Parent leaders and Resource Teachers publicize the program objectives and standards, and the outstanding parent volunteers become consultants to interested students. Students must work independently to create original inventions to solve real-life problems or do research necessary to develop knowledge and skills for the Olympic Events such as Science Bowl and Mystery Powders. They proudly display their Science Olympiad trophy in the school office.

After the school day ends, Murdock continues to hum with activity. Students have the choice of a number of after-school clubs, many of which build on academic foundations. The Voyage of the Mimi Club carries students beyond the pages of the science book into a seven-week whale-watching adventure with a specific science lesson each week. Investormania worked with their Adopt-a-School Partner Bank in buying and selling stocks and bonds. Students can also choose from Computer Club, Spanish Club, and Garden Club. Fine Arts are addressed by the Music Club, Movie Makers Club, Clown College, Drama Production Club, Shakespeare Club, Ceramics Club, and Printmaking Club. Approximately 80% of the students participated in the After-School Program.

The activities described above are open to all students, restricted only by grade level interests. They provide a climate of enthusiasm and encouragement that fosters participation. A school-sponsored Celebration of Success assembly is held annually to reward students who participate and to encourage future participation in extracurricular events.

Kathie W. Dobberteen, *Principal, K—5, 410 Students*

GROSSE POINTE ACADEMY, GROSSE POINT FARMS, MI

The Grosse Pointe Academy is an independent day school enrolling boys and girls in a Montessori Early School (ages 2-1/2—5) through grade 8. Grosse Pointe Farms is a suburb located six miles northeast of downtown Detroit and is the central community of the five Grosse Pointes. The school makes extensive use of museums and other cultural resources of Detroit.

The Academy is a nonprofit organization with financial support coming from tuitions and an involved alumni. The student population consists of 82% Caucasian, 15% African-American, 1% Hispanic, and 1% Asian-American. To meet the interests of the diverse student body, a wide range of extracurricular activities is offered.

For those with an interest in the arts, the selections include band, modern dance, piano, community architectural analysis and awareness, jewelry making, Show Choir, Honors Bell Choir, and Forensics. For those with athletic interests, choices are boys/girls tennis, soccer, volleyball, basketball, softball, cross-country, baseball, and track. For those with a less definite area of interest, cooking, crafts, and an elective program are offered. The elective classes meet weekly on Wednesday morning. Chess, fishing, computer typing, mural, tutoring, and documentary video are a sampling of this quarter's offerings.

Although participation in at least one sport each year is mandatory for all Middle School students, many opt to participate in all three sport seasons. Electives are mandatory as well, with new offerings added every quarter to replace those that are not possible due to personnel or weather constraints.

In total, well over 85% of the students take part in one or more of the activities offered. New additions to the extracurricular activities since the 1987—88 school year are band, Show Choir, French Choir, modern dance, geography bee, intramurals for grade 3 in soccer, basketball and softball, service opportunity, and eighth grade leadership camp.

Dr. Sidney F. DuPont, *Principal, K—8, 414 Students*

SCHOOL DISCIPLINE POLICIES AND PROCEDURES

Much research supports the notion of effective classroom/school discipline as primarily a by-product of effective instruction and classroom management. Yet managing student behavior is a very complex task. There is a delicate balance between meeting the needs of the group by maintaining social order and meeting the unique needs of each student. Few choices work for all teachers and all students (Curwin and Mendler, 1988). Classroom and school discipline has continued to be a concern for children, educators, and the public for many years. For children, concerns range from loss of opportunity for learning to simple physical danger. For teachers, discipline problems are a serious threat to their ability to do their jobs and, in some cases, provide fear of physical harm. For the public at large, as evidenced in most public opinion polls (e.g., Gallup, 1992), discipline in schools continues to be viewed as the most significant problem confronting schools today.

Promoting effective discipline in the school requires a comprehensive program supported by everyone in the entire school community. As with all other aspects in successful schools, discipline programs are based on sound research and development. They are characterized by high expectations for teachers to systematically apply agreed-upon strategies and consistently administer the discipline code. Moreover, successful schools take the initiative to appropriately sensitize and train staff as to the nature of effective discipline in the classroom and throughout the school.

Curwin and Mendler (1988) speak to three integrated dimensions of discipline that should be established as the cornerstone of the school's discipline program:

(1) *The Prevention Dimension:* What the teacher can do to actively prevent problems. To a large degree, these strategies are aimed at attacking problems long before they arise, through intensive organization and planning. In the classroom, they include (but are not limited to) the establishing and reinforcement of clear expectations for appropriate behavior; the maintenance of a positive classroom climate; provision for interesting, relevant, instructional activities; the development and communication of classroom routines; the monitoring of students within small groups and during other nondirected times; and involvement of parents in the development and implementation of classroom procedures.

From a schoolwide perspective, the selection of a schoolwide program is often difficult. Yet consistent, uniform, total school discipline programs can have a positive effect on student behavior and performance. Often, successful schools have embraced a system to help systematize expectations for student behavior. A popular example is the use of Assertive Discipline (Canter and Canter, 1976), which emphasizes systematic reinforcement of clearly communicated classroom requirements. Assertive discipline requires teachers to take the following steps (MacNaughton and Johns, 1991):
   — Make clear that they will not tolerate anyone preventing them from teaching, stopping learning, or doing anything else that is not in the best interest of the class, the individual, or the teacher.
   — Instruct students clearly and in specific terms about what behaviors are desired and what behaviors are not tolerated.
   — Plan positive and negative consequences for predetermined acceptable or unacceptable behaviors.
   — Plan positive reinforcement for compliance. Reinforcements include verbal acknowledgment, notes, free time for talking, and, of course, tokens that can be exchanged for appropriate rewards.
   — Plan a sequence of steps to punish noncompliance. These range from writing a youngster's name on the board to sending the student to the principal's office.

(2) *The Action Dimension:* What actions the teacher can take when, in spite of all the steps taken to prevent discipline problems, they still occur. There are many approaches that can be utilized to stop minor discipline problems before they escalate into situations that increase loss of instructional time and precipitate the need for direct (often negative) teacher intervention. Cummings (1983) provides an approach to dealing with minor classroom disturbances that fills the gap between simply ignoring the student's inappropriate behavior and forceful, negative intervention. This approach organizes teacher response on a continuum using behaviors that take relatively little time and little interruption to the learning environment (i.e., eye contact, physical closeness, etc.).

The goals of this continuum of choices are:

— to maintain a positive feeling tone in the classroom
— to maximize time-on-task
— to present the teacher as a positive role model
— to avoid students' generalized negative feelings toward teacher, school and district

Palandy (1993) has identified seven intervention strategies that he believes should be in every teacher's repertoire:

— Nonverbal techniques, particularly at the beginning stages of misbehavior, can be an effective way of letting students know that one (or all) of them had better settle down. Eye contact, body posture, facial expressions, etc., are typical examples of effective nonverbal strategies.
— Proximity control is used by walking up to and simply standing beside (and possibly putting your hand on a shoulder) of the misbehaving student.
— Remove the source of a disturbance by either taking away the items (such as rubber bands, food, etc.) that may be involved in the misbehavior or allow the misbehavior to "run its course" by permitting a brief period of indulgence.
— Point out the consequences of misbehavior. Clearly, this is most effective when the "right" consequence can be matched with the student(s).
— Behavior modification techniques using systematized reinforcement (as described earlier) can be an effective intervention strategy.
— Isolation of misbehaving students by asking them to leave the room or to go to the "time-out corner" can be effective in providing an angry student a chance to "cool off."
— Punishment can be a necessary and, at times, effective intervention strategy. But when punishment is considered, certain principles must be kept in mind:
  - Punishment should be used sparingly; the more often it is used, the less effective it becomes.
  - Punishment should never constitute the following: subject matter should never be used as punishment; "mass punishment" is almost always ineffective; corporal punishment should *never* be used.

The principal has a most significant role in ensuring a safe, orderly, and productive learning environment. His/her primary role is to mobilize the students, parents, and teachers toward the establishment of high expectations, appropriate reinforcements, and, of course, a discipline code that clearly communicates consequences of student misbehavior. Additionally, the principal must insist that students learn to understand that they must assume responsibility for their actions and, hopefully, learn the importance of the relationship between appropriate behavior and success in school.

The principal, parents or guardians, and teachers must collaboratively demonstrate to the students that adults at home and at school share the same expectations. The simple belief that deference, civility, courtesy, accountability, and respect are mutual behaviors to be reinforced in the home and school is the common ground on which conflicts are resolved and the teacher-learning process is elevated. The principal's responsibility includes working with misbehaving students and with their parents to teach both, if necessary, that authority, civility, courtesy, and accountability are critical to everyone's interests (Hartzell and Petrie, 1992).

(3) *The Resolution Dimension:* What the teacher can do to resolve problems with chronic rule breakers and the extreme, "out-of-control" student. Reaching these students

requires a great deal of effort with no real guarantee that there will be a truly effective resolution. General strategies can be characterized as in-house interventions and outside referral.

In-house strategies, like those described in the previous sections related to at-risk students, can, if systematically applied, have significant impact on modifying the behavior of chronic disciplinary problems. Common strategies include individual counseling, mentorships, and customized classroom strategies, such as modified assignments, peer tutors, or cooperative learning.

Unfortunately, in-house strategies are not always adequate to meet the complex school and, often, family needs of the student. Thus, referral to the district Child Study (Special Education) Team and, at times, referral to outside social service agencies may be required. It is important, if a referral strategy is pursued, that the parent is involved in all stages of the resolution process. This is increasingly important since many times a child's behavioral problems in school are (at least in part) a function of family dynamics.

THE BEST SCHOOLS – SCHOOL DISCIPLINE

The Best Schools have planned, organized, and implemented effective discipline standards and procedures. They have committed to effective pupil management as a cornerstone to student learning and school effectiveness. Additionally, they have taken the time to provide the necessary training to the staff to optimize staff involvement, develop common goals, and establish uniform behavioral expectations for all students. Examples from the Best School's disciplinary strategies and programs that reflect the concepts and practices reviewed above are illustrated next.

LAWRENCE BROOK SCHOOL, EAST BRUNSWICK, N.J.

The Lawrence Brook School is one of eight elementary schools in the East Brunswick School District. The district is a suburban K – 12 district with a total enrollment of 6791 students.

The Lawrence Brook School serves an interestingly diverse student population; 68% Caucasian, 24% Asian-American, 4% African-American and 4% Hispanic. The East Brunswick School District has had a longstanding reputation for excellence, with several of its schools being honored as National Blue Ribbon Award winners.

The entire staff is committed to establishing and maintaining a positive atmosphere in which children feel safe, secure, and happy. All teachers establish their own classroom discipline plan or cooperatively write a classroom discipline plan as part of a grade-level team. The plan is sent home to each parent to be signed on the first day of school. The plan is also clearly posted in the front of each classroom.

The school's approach to discipline is based upon the concept that, once students understand the classroom rules and rationale, they need to learn to make decisions that are in their best interest. Should a child choose to break a classroom rule, the disciplinary consequences are implemented on a consistent basis. Students, both on an individual and classwide basis, are also provided with a variety of positive consequences when they behave appropriately. Both disciplinary consequences and positive consequences are part of each teacher's classroom discipline plan. All staff, including lunchroom aides, have been trained by the principal in assertive discipline techniques. A great deal of positive reinforcement in the form of verbal praise ("I like the way Johnny is taking out his materials." "Table 3 is really working cooperatively to clean up.") can be heard throughout the school. Positive notes are sent home and class rewards that serve to acknowledge and reinforce positive behavior are provided.

Michael J. LaRaus, Principal, K – 5, 367 Students

EASTOVER ELEMENTARY SCHOOL, BLOOMFIELD HILLS, MI

Eastover Elementary School is located in a predominantly residential neighborhood located in an upper middle-class suburban community. The school considers itself a melting pot of diverse races, religions, ethnic heritages, and socioeconomic levels. A strong tradition of parent participation and support helps to promote highly effective programs. The school community values the importance of an orderly, nurturing, learning environment.

One of the continuing objectives of Eastover School is the development of students who exhibit pride in themselves and their school and who show respect for the rights and property of others. Eastover School believes that it is the right of every student to have access to an environment that provides academic excellence, self-discipline, and positive social development. With this right comes the responsibility to respect the rights of other people.

Eastover staff members stress discipline through positive interactions with students via adult role modeling and rewarding of good behaviors. Because of this, discipline problems are typically minor in nature and few in number. Realizing, however, the need for specific discipline procedures, the Eastover staff has formulated four simple rules that encompass behaviors in the school, on the playground, and on the bus: 1) follow directions; 2) keep your hands and feet to yourself; 3) use proper language in the proper tone of voice; and 4) walk inside the school. Additional rules for the playground are 1) do not play in the woods; 2) no snowball throwing; and 3) no tackle football.

Students choosing to repeatedly break those rules through irresponsible behaviors lose privileges, see the principal, and have their parents contacted. A highly serious infraction may warrant an in-school suspension. Students who repeatedly demonstrate irresponsible behaviors on the bus receive a warning, written notifications sent home, and temporary loss of bus privileges. The discipline policy is reviewed annually and shared with parents through the parent handbook.

All Eastover teachers have received three hours of training in conflict resolution, and some have chosen to further develop their involvement in this technique. Upper grade students have been trained as well and have assumed the responsibility for mediating playground disputes.

Adrienne Jones Crockett, Principal, K – 5, 447 Students

LAKE BLUFF JUNIOR HIGH SCHOOL, LAKE BLUFF, IL

Lake Bluff Junior High School (LBJH) is located in a suburban community on the border of Lake Michigan and is situated approximately thirty miles north of Chicago. The school serves a student population represented by 94% Caucasian, 3% Asian-American, 2% Hispanic, and 1% African-American. The school has a long tradition of scholastic excellence with well-established criteria for student behavior.

The framework for the school's discipline policy is the Code of Conduct. This is a choices-consequences system meant to foster mature and appropriate choices. The Code of Conduct is a staff-designed tool that included parent and student input and that outlines expected behaviors for students.

Each fall, the Code of Conduct is reviewed during the homeroom period. Students are given the opportunity to voice their opinions in a small group setting, and discussions help to present both sides of the discipline issue. After students have reviewed this, they are asked to share the Code of Conduct at home with their parents. To assure that everyone is clear on the consequences for inappropriate behavior, both parents and students sign a contract from the Code agreeing that they understand what has been outlined.

The Code of Conduct is a preventative system. When staff observes a pattern of inappropriate behaviors developing, there are built-in measures to correct it. The Code of Conduct is built on a ladder system. When students make inappropriate choices, a warning or a detention is issued. Three warnings result in a detention. All detention notices must be signed by the parent, and the detention is served the next day for a forty-five minute period after school. When a student has accumulated five detentions due to inappropriate behavior, a letter is sent home to the parents informing them of the situation and that a sixth detention will result in suspension from extracurricular school activities for one month. If a sixth detention is issued, a principal-counselor-student-parent meeting is arranged and all parties meet to discuss possible resolutions. The counselor is in charge of keeping records of the detentions and is in constant contact with students discussing the student's choices, alternatives, and consequences. Last year, fewer than 2% of the students received more than six detentions in any one semester.

The Code of Conduct is the foundation for discipline at LBJH. Teachers are encouraged to deal with inappropriate behavior in a manner that is appropriate to their class. A concerted effort has been made to use warnings and detentions as a last resort. Staff are committed to issuing appropriate consequences for chosen actions. Teachers' explanation of rules with students, alternative consequences such as scrubbing desks, scraping gum off of surfaces, essays, apology notes, and other options have helped to reduce discipline problems and have created an atmosphere more conducive to learning.

Kathleen O'Hara, Principal, Grades 6–8, 247 Students

THE PREVENTION OF ALCOHOL AND DRUG ABUSE

The use of alcohol and drugs continues to be a major societal problem that impacts on our youth at an alarming rate with alarming consequences:

- Two-thirds of all teenagers will use drugs before they graduate from high school (University of Michigan, 1986).
- While it may take adults years to become truly addicted to drugs/alcohol, teenagers can become addicted in less than six months (Horton, 1985).
- Most teenage unwanted pregnancies began when one or both of the partners were under the influence of drugs/alcohol (Pennsylvania Department of Education, 1986).
- Drugs/alcohol are involved in two out of three suicides (Bolton, 1986).
- Drugs/alcohol use are major contributors to school failure and dropping out of school (U. S. Department of Education, 1986).
- Drugs/alcohol dependency is a major contributor to crimes such as stealing and violence (U. S. Department of Education, 1986).

Schools alone cannot prevent drug and alcohol abuse or cure the abuse when it occurs. Substance abuse is a complex and long-term problem. Patterns of behavior and attitudes developed at a very early age may determine, to a great degree, the level of risk of addiction experienced by the student. A study by Sheppard Kellman (1987) found that antisocial first-graders were more likely than other students to be involved in drug abuse ten years later. Society at large also gives contradictory messages concerning the use of drugs and alcohol, particularly in the case of smoking and alcohol. Advertisements, media programs, and frequently, parents, associate the use of alcohol and cigarettes with a "good time." In the case of smoking, the evidence of health risks is overwhelming. In the case of alcohol, there is little evidence that a drink or two will have long-term negative health effects on adults, except when combined with driving. However, research consistently shows that some people are more genetically and environmentally at risk of becoming substance abusers than are others.

The Role of Schools

While controlling student drug and alcohol use is difficult, schools can play a significant and positive role. Because the problem is complex, only a multifaceted program will be effective. Expectations for the program must recognize limitations, since no school program will prevent all substance abuse. The basic strategies available to the school include:

- effective teaching of decision-making skills, negative peer resistance skills, and facts concerning the dangers of drugs/alcohol
- setting tough policies, guidelines, and procedures, which make it clear to students, staff, and parents that drug/alcohol use will not be tolerated
- training staff to recognize and act upon signs of drug/alcohol use
- providing opportunities for students to seek help for themselves or others
- establishing a proactive plan and procedures for identifying students with problems and assisting them to get help
- developing a plan for working with parents as a group and with parents of individual students
- establishing procedures and plans for working with community groups
- establishing a procedure for confrontation, complete with penalties, to get help for students who resist assistance or whose parents resist assistance
- enforcing the penalties for drug/alcohol use or sale established by the school board and law
- establishing procedures for working with the police
- building strong working relationships with outside agencies that provide therapy and support programs for addicted students
- providing group and individual support for school-related problems for students returning from treatment
- providing as much support as possible to all students so they will succeed academically and socially in the school environment (Ogden and Germinario, 1988)

Successful schools do not ignore the problem of drug/alcohol use and abuse among students (or among staff members). The problem is there, it is a progressive disease, it will continue to be there, and it will get worse if it is ignored, thus affecting the ability of the school to complete its mission of educating students. Successful drug prevention programs in elementary schools are rooted in systematic curriculum that addresses issues related to it. These include:

- information about drugs and their effects
- decision-making and drug resistance skills
- coping skills
- positive peer relationships
- positive alternatives to drugs (Ogden and Germinario, 1988)

Curriculum

The content of the curriculum must take into account the age of the children. The kindergarten program should include, for example, a simple definition of "What is a drug?" learning that pills are not candy, that there are poisons in the home, and why we have rules. By fourth grade, the program should include the study of the effects of the two drugs they will encounter first: alcohol and nicotine. Developing skills in saying "No" to people who pressure them to try drugs must be emphasized. Additionally, social interaction skills must be taught to help students make and keep friends without using drugs as a vehicle for group acceptance. A good drug prevention curriculum, while aimed at preventing drug use, must also focus on developing positive self-image, developing friendships, coping with problems, and developing decision-making skills that will ultimately contribute to maximizing learning throughout a student's school experience.

The drug prevention curriculum can be taught by a health teacher, nurse, or the classroom teacher. It is important that the curriculum be coordinated throughout grades K−4 and that all children do, in fact, receive instruction. Specific activities can be altered to better meet the needs or interests of the students or the knowledge of the teacher. Yet all objectives identified for a grade must be covered. As in all school programs, effectiveness should be assessed annually. Finally, there should be definite plans for communicating with parents concerning the need, purpose, and content of the program. This will help parents understand the importance of such a curriculum and develop a support base for implementation.

The drug prevention curriculum can be developed locally if time, resources, and knowledge are available. Another approach is the adoption of a program that has evidence of being successful. The program "Here's Looking At You, 2000," developed by Roberts, Fitzmahan and Associates, the Educational Service District #121, in Seattle, Washington (revised 1986), and "Growing Healthy" (NDN), developed by the National Defusion Network, are the types of programs that should, at least, be reviewed before attempting to develop a new program. The NDN program is sequenced K−12, but the K−4 section can be used alone. It has been extensively field-tested in schools throughout the country. It includes all the activities and materials needed for implementation of the program, and it is sufficiently detailed that extensive training of teachers may not be needed.

Policy

Essential to the development and implementation of a drug/alcohol prevention, intervention, and treatment program are the formulation and adoption by the board of education of a policy on drug and alcohol use. The policy protects the staff by making it clear who is to do what, under what conditions. The policy makes it clear to students that drug and alcohol use will not be tolerated and what the consequences will be if they break the rules. The very existence of a clear policy is an initial step in assisting students to resist negative peer pressure. In schools in which it is recognized that penalties will be imposed for drug/alcohol use, it gives students another valid excuse for saying "No."

Policy needs to be built on federal and state law and precedent cases. In general, all boards of education have the responsibility for the health and safety of students. All states have laws concerning the use and distribution of controlled substances. Cases heard by the Supreme Court have also clarified the rights of schools, for example, to conduct searches when there are "reasonable grounds" for suspicion that a student has violated the law or school rules. The Comprehensive Crime Control Act of 1984 makes it a federal crime to sell drugs in or near a school. Before developing a policy and procedures, state laws should be reviewed. In many states, the department of education has gathered the pertinent laws together and made them available to school districts. Some states have mandated that districts adopt a policy concerning the use of controlled substances and have developed model policies. Whether a district starts from scratch or adapts/adopts a state sample policy, the district solicitor should review the policy before it is adopted by the board of education. The policy should make explicit:

- that drug/alcohol use will not be tolerated
- that it is the staff's responsibility to act on information concerning drug/alcohol use by students
- that the staff will be "held harmless" for reporting information concerning the use or distribution of drugs/alcohol
- to whom and when information on drug/alcohol use or distribution is to be reported
- what procedures the school will follow to confirm the use or distribution of drugs
- if and how drug testing will be required and under what conditions
- drug/alcohol prevention curriculum requirements, grades K−12
- when and by whom the police will be informed in cases of suspected distribution or sale
- that the use of drugs/alcohol by students constitutes a physical and mental risk to students and that information cannot be kept confidential and must be reported
- that not only do parents have the right to know that their child is suspected or known to be using a controlled substance, but they have the primary responsibility for treatment
- that lockers and personal possessions will be searched when there are "reasonable grounds" to suspect violations of school rules or laws
- what the school penalties will be for using, possessing, distributing, or selling drugs/alcohol
- what requirements the board will make concerning assessment and treatment as a condition of re-entry into the school
- what assistance the school will make available to students concerned with drug/alcohol issues and for assistance during and after treatment
- what the roles of the Student Assistance Team, counselors, administrators, and nurses will be in confirming suspected drug/alcohol use, abuse, distribution, or sale
- what medical procedures should be followed if a student appears to be physically at risk
- what the relationship is between the schools and public and private agencies, treatment centers, and hospitals (Ogden and Germinario, 1988)

Finally, as with all other school programs, drug/alcohol prevention initiatives must be formulated with the staff and community. Additionally, systematic training for staff is critical in areas related to implementation of the drug prevention curriculum, identification of drug-related risk behavior, the standards and procedures set forth in board policy, and knowledge of appropriate referral services for those students (and/or families) that may be drug involved.

THE BEST SCHOOLS—PREVENTION OF ALCOHOL AND DRUG ABUSE

The illustrations of Best Schools practices that successfully integrate school and community resources are provided.

VILLAGE ELEMENTARY SCHOOL, SANTA ROSA, CA

Village School is located in the eastern part of Santa Rosa, a town that now has a population of 96,000. The school's attendance areas include a middle-class suburban area, pockets of low socioeconomic areas and a small, highly affluent area. The overall socioeconomic status of the parents is lower than the district average and the school also has a high degree of student mobility; there is an annual 33% turnover. Twenty-seven percent of students live in a single-parent home, and 38% qualify for either free or reduced price lunch.

Although Village School has had no campus drug-related problems, much effort has gone into developing drug education programs that are informative and preventative. The district health program, developed by a committee of nurses, teachers, and parents and piloted by Village for two years, helps to educate the students concerning the hazards of substance abuse. Beginning in kindergarten, yearly presentations are made concerning smoking, alcohol, and chemical dependencies and abuses, presentations which address problems that many students face in their homes. Outside speakers, from pharmacists to drug rehabilitation center participants, are brought into the classrooms to reinforce a "Just Say No" approach to drugs. A police person is on campus twice a week during lunch hour to become acquainted with the students and offer them a positive feeling toward law enforcement and the relationship of police officers to the community.

The Stanford DECIDE program is used in grades kindergarten through six. As the students focus on problem-solving activities that allow each individual to make smart decisions free from peer, social, or personal pressures, problems are Defined, Explored, and Considered, outside advice is Invited, a Decision is made, and that decision is Evaluated. Students discuss freely and openly their concerns and feelings about their own experiences. These activities enable them to make responsible choices about their lives, concerning not only drug and alcohol use but other issues as well. Working with local organizations and Parents' Club, Village staff and students engage in a week of activities each year that focus on developing an awareness of the many problems that individuals, communities, and country face concerning drugs. This program has grown from a single "Red Ribbon Day" to a week-long focus on a major problem within our society.

Thomas E. Crawford, *Principal, K - 6, 393 Students*

CAROLINE BENTLEY SCHOOL, NEW LENOX, IL

The Caroline Bentley School is located in New Lenox, a middle-class community with a strong sense of family and pride in their schools. It serves a predominantly Caucasian population, with a 2% Hispanic population and less than 1% African-American and Asian-American population.

Caroline Bentley has a multifaceted drug prevention and awareness program. At the fifth grade level, it employs the nationally recognized D.A.R.E. Program (Drug Abuse Resistance Education). In the second semester of each year, the Will County Sheriff's Department assigns a D.A.R.E. Officer to the school. This officer becomes an integral part of the school, working with each homeroom forty-five minutes weekly. The teacher remains in the room and works with the officer in a team approach. The officer's full-dress appearance adds a touch of significance to the drug education program. The D.A.R.E. officer is visible throughout the building during all times of the day, on the playground and in the lunchroom.

At the sixth grade level, the school uses the internationally recognized QUEST Program. All sixth grade teachers are required to take three days of QUEST training before teaching the program. Students are explicitly taught that drugs are harmful; they are shown techniques to help them make healthy decisions and are taught how to handle peer pressure.

Parents gain guidance from Parenting Plus nights, which are held each year. Large group presentations provide parenting suggestions; parents contribute to small group discussions that are chaired by staff. Each year both fifth and sixth grade students take a field trip to Robert Crown Health Museum where they attend a professional presentation on Drug Education and AIDS Awareness.

The Just Say No Club organizes Red Ribbon Week in October along with a community-wide Just Say No week during April of each year. The Chamber of Commerce, the New Lenox Lions, and the Police Department cosponsor and provide awards for the annual essay and slogan contest. The winning slogan last year was LET'S ALL AGREE TO BE DRUG FREE. Over 1500 bumper stickers with this slogan were distributed throughout the community. Since the implementation of these programs five years ago, the school has had only one student involved in a substance abuse incident.

Robert Gaines, *Principal, Grades 5 – 6, 645 Students*

DOROTHEA H. SIMMONS SCHOOL, HORSHAM, PA

The Simmons School is located approximately twenty miles north of Philadelphia in the suburban community of Horsham. Horsham is predominantly a middle-, upper-middle-class community with about a third of the community holding college degrees. The student population is composed of 91% Caucasian, 4% Asian-American, 3% African-American and 1% Hispanic.

The staff at Simmons has worked diligently to develop an outstanding drug prevention program. Students in kindergarten, first, and second grades receive drug and alcohol education as part of the health curriculum. Simmons piloted the "Here's Looking at You 2000" drug and alcohol program with the principal acting as the district trainer. Students in third, fourth, and fifth grades receive eight weeks of lessons taught by the health and classroom teachers and the guidance counselor. This program includes drug and alcohol information, self-esteem, decision making, and development of refusal skills.

The effectiveness of the "Here's Looking at You 2000" curriculum was evident in reviewing the pre- and post-tests given to third, fourth, and fifth graders. These tests showed a marked improvement in students' knowledge of drug- and alcohol-related information. The effectiveness of the refusal skills segment of the program was seen in the videotape on refusal skills, which fourth grade students prepared. Parents were invited to see the tape, and 85% of the fourth grade parents attended the presentation along with their children. Parents expressed positive feelings about the program, recommending its continuation. They documented increased communication in the home about this subject. High school students visited the school and talked with fourth and fifth grade students about the "natural highs" available in a teen's life. A counselor from a local drug and alcohol agency was present at the three parent meetings held prior to the start of the "Here's Looking at You 2000" curriculum.

Tobacco, as well as all drugs, is prohibited in Hatboro-Horsham, and possession or sale of these substances results in suspension, as well as police notification and a hearing before the superintendent. The school has administrative and parent representation on the Hatters' Commitment Committee, a district group that coordinates the efforts of elementary, middle, and high school programs. This group has planned two evening programs on drug and alcohol prevention and has brought the program "Quiet Riot" into each elementary school. This program has a strong refusal message and was received positively by elementary students.

Rita M. Klein, *Principal, K – 5, 367 Students*

INVOLVEMENT OF STUDENTS IN THE DEVELOPMENT OF SCHOOL POLICY

Educators' decisions affect the lives of students, and it is for this reason that input from students about their school life is important. A major concern of educators is that students will make irresponsible decisions, but experience shows that they will make excellent decisions when guided in the decision-making process by caring and open adults. To establish an environment that encourages students to value their school experience, schools must increasingly involve them in important decision-making efforts. There are many benefits to be derived from student involvement in decision making. For example, the concept helps develop social skills, promotes an appreciation of democratic action, and promotes creativity and independent thought and action.

Decision making should be viewed as a deliberate process that can be taught as a basic classroom skill. Typically, six steps are embodied in systematic decision making: 1) identifying the problem or issue, 2) exploring the many alternatives available to resolve the problem/issue, 3) evaluating the plausibility of each solution, 4) making the decision/choice, 5) defending (justifying) the decision, and 6) acting and evaluating.

The school's primary function in teaching decision-making skills is to encourage and help the students to use their abilities and insights effectively in making their own decisions. This means that the school staff must approach the teaching of decision-making skills without any preconceptions or ready-made answers (Stewart, 1989). Thus, to successfully involve students in school decision making, teachers and administrators must:

- be willing to let the pupils share in making decisions and to have a ''piece of the action''
- see themselves as members of the group rather than the final authority on all topics
- free themselves of any feelings that the pupils will ''run the class''
- be a helper and guide, rather than merely a transmitter of facts
- create a relaxed classroom atmosphere in which the pupils feel secure in being themselves
- be accepting of all the pupils' responses and recognize that each response has legitimacy and worth (Stewart, 1989)

The Best Schools have created opportunities for students to actively influence school policy. Through the systematic learning of decision-making skills, students have been able to effectively access their school's improvement efforts. With these efforts, students have achieved greater ownership in goals of their schools, developed a greater sense of trust in the adults around them, and obtained and practiced an extremely important life skill.

The Best Schools—Involvement of Students with Development of School Policy

A wide range of strategies have been utilized by the Best Schools to increase student decisional involvement. Several examples are illustrated here.

VEGAS VERDES ELEMENTARY SCHOOL, LAS VEGAS, NV

Vegas Verdes Elementary, once located in the outskirts of Las Vegas, now finds itself surrounded by a large metropolitan city. The campus, serving as a neighborhood park, rests among homes that have changed from being occupied by middle-income home owners to one of lower income renters surrounded by businesses and apartment buildings. In its thirty-two years of tradition, the school has expanded from twenty classrooms to thirty-seven classrooms. With this expansion has come a dramatic increase in enrollment of 18% in the last four years. The student composition of Vegas Verdes has changed significantly in the last three years. The number of students receiving free and reduced lunch has increased from 15% to 23%. The racial/ethnic composition has grown from 22% to 30% with the number of Hispanic students increasing from 6% to 10% of the student body. With the increase in racial/ethnic minorities, the number of nonproficient English-speaking students has also increased.

The staff feels strongly that students should play an active role in the formation of school and classroom policy. To that end, the Parent Teacher Association (PTA) was changed to a Parent Teacher Student Association (PTSA) to emphasize this belief. The general commissioner of the student government is a member of the PTSA Executive Board. Each year, the student government officers suggest and coordinate activities for student and staff participation. This year, a new Homework Club is being instituted as a result of student government input. Recently, a lunchroom problem was addressed following student initiation and input leading to a change in lunch count procedures and the implementation of a new procedure for ensuring a selection of lunches for classes eating at the end of the scheduled lunch periods.

Within the classroom, students are actively involved in the formation of classroom rules, allowing them to feel ownership and respect toward rules. Classroom meetings are often held to resolve conflicts and brainstorm solutions. Even some instructional decisions are made by students, e.g., students self-select some reading materials, choose the order in which they will complete learning center activities, select the assignment they want to complete toward a given instructional goal, write contracts for work completion, and at times determine the direction of classroom study projects.

Jeffrey N. Lobel, Principal (Carla J. Steinforth, Principal at time of recognition),
K – 5, 752 Students

ASSETS SCHOOL, PEARL HARBOR, HI

The Assets School is an independent, nonprofit agency that provides highly specialized service to a unique student population. Student composition can be divided into approximate thirds for 1) dyslexics (average IQ with lack of expected achievement in reading, spelling, writing), 2) gifted/high-potential (placed for curriculum acceleration/enrichment, motivation, and/or under-achievement), and 3) others including the gifted/dyslexic (high IQ with lack of expected achievement). Those with inattention-hyperactivity (e.g., Attention Deficit Hyperactivity Disorder) are distributed among the three categories. First contact with Assets for nearly all students is through a recommendation from an outside professional due to educational and/or social-emotional failure in the past setting. Therefore, for most, Assets is "a last resort," wherein nothing in the mainstream has "worked." Student population originates from well over seventy different (approximately half public, half private) schools per year.

Assets attempts to teach students lifelong skills that will allow them to be successful and contributing citizens. A major component in fulfilling this goal is the heavy emphasis on having students voice their opinions appropriately, seek possible solutions, and select and implement one of these solutions. In this regard, student input is extremely valued and nurtured, and a problem-solving approach is utilized. For example, class council provides an opportunity for students to solve classroom problems and to affect policies. This counseling format is held weekly, and students are allowed to address individual concerns. After classmates brainstorm solutions, students raising concerns commit to a peer-suggested strategy. In the next session, students report on successes or failures with the latter, resulting in a continuation of the problem-solving process. In addition, student council is another avenue for pupil input. Members meet once per week with two representatives per class in the elementary and intermediate divisions and a student-buddy representative per class for primary levels.

Examples of student-initiated change range from relatively straightforward actions such as a petition for more recess balls (which was immediately granted) to more substantive changes such as creating a lunch-period social room and giving responsibility to upper level students to transition between classes without teacher monitoring. These opportunities promote growth of problem-solving skills, give students "ownership," and emphasize the assumption of responsibility.

Ron Yoshimoto, Principal, K – 8, 275 Students

FRANCONE ELEMENTARY SCHOOL, HOUSTON, TX

The Francone School is located in northwest Harris County, approximately twenty miles from downtown Houston. Originally a rich farmland, in the past twenty years it has become part of a rapidly developing residential area. The school serves a very diverse ethnic and socioeconomic student population. Nine different languages are spoken within the school. Specifically, the student population is made up of 55% Caucasian students, 26% Hispanic, 13% African-American and 6% Asian-American. Student involvement and influence in school policy are fostered through a variety of strategies.

Each year, teachers meet with students to discuss classroom rules, policies, and procedures. They solicit students' opinions and incorporate them into the school rules and post them in each classroom area. Classes meet throughout the year, at all grade levels, to discuss specific concerns. Students express opinions, ask questions, and make suggestions.

When students are interested in changing a school policy, they are encouraged to use positive strategies such as writing persuasive letters to the principal and assistant principals. An informal committee of students (from all grade levels) attends cultural arts previews sponsored by Young Audiences and the Childrens' Theatre of Houston. The children's opinions and evaluations of performances are given great weight when the PTO Cultural Arts committee chooses performances to bring to Francone.

The Francone Student Council works to solve problems related to the restrooms, cafeteria, and safety. They help supervise younger students as they work together to see that school grounds are kept free of litter. Council members also meet with each grade level to discuss students' concerns. The student council leader then channels those concerns to the appropriate adult. Third grade social studies students hold mock elections. As candidates, they write and present speeches outlining issues for change. Students present school problems and propose solutions in a practical experiment in democracy.

From time to time, many of the teachers, counselors, and administrators eat lunch with students. This is a time when students tend to open up and offer insights into what they need. This enjoyable method of communicating with the children in a nonacademic setting builds a better rapport between students and adults.

Through the activities mentioned here, the school offers all students the opportunity to have a voice in school decisions. In this way, they build the foundation for these students to be active participants in our democratic society.

Sue Romanowsky, *Principal (Arlene Robison, Principal at time of recognition),*
Pre-K – 5, 1085 Students

PREPARATION FOR LIFE IN A CULTURALLY AND ETHNICALLY DIVERSE SOCIETY

Often, teachers and students take their culture for granted, giving it little thought or having little influence on their attitude or behavior. As educators, we are challenged to help students to first become conscious of their own cultures and, secondly, to understand that any individual culture does not prescribe the only way of doing things.

Education within a pluralistic society should affirm and help students understand their home and community cultures. However, it should also help free them from their cultural boundaries (Banks, 1992). In spite of the country's rich ethnic and cultural diversity, the curriculum continues to focus on a very narrow portion of our past and present. In a very real sense, all students need to be more culturally literate: to gain a broader view of the real world that includes people of many colors and traditions and with two genders. This awareness does not only affect an appreciation of others, but helps students prepare for an economy that is now clearly globally competitive.

A school that is truly committed to teaching about diversity reinforces the curriculum with ongoing interdisciplinary opportunities for students to learn about culture, develop cultural sensitivity, examine their own biases (and the biases of others), and develop skills necessary to communicate effectively with all types of people and to survive in a multicultural world. Specific objectives common to multicultural programs include:

- knowing about and feeling proud of one's own culture and ethnic identity
- knowing about and appreciating cultures different from one's own
- recognizing contributions that all types of people — women and men, young and old, rich and poor, including those from minority and nontypical cultures — have made to the school, community, nation, and world
- developing skills for communicating effectively with people from different backgrounds

- recognizing and refusing to accept any behavior based on stereotypes, prejudice, or discrimination
- recognizing the economic interdependence among nations

An analysis of the current literature reveals several identifiable levels and approaches to the integration of diverse ethnic content into curriculum (Banks, 1987). These are:

- *The Contributions Approach* — the addition of ethnic heroes into the curriculum
- *The Ethnic Additive Approach* — the addition of a book, a unit, or a course to the existing curriculum
- *The Transformation Approach* — changes the basic assumptions of the curriculum and enables students to view concepts, issues, themes, and problems from several ethnic perspectives and points of view
- *The Decision-Making and Social Action Approach* — includes all of the elements of the Transformation Approach, but adds components that require students to make decisions and to take actions related to the concept, issue, or problem studied in the unit

The demographics of America are changing, and nowhere are the shifts better reflected than in the nation's public schools. From 1976 to 1986, white, non-Hispanic student enrollment declined by nearly 13% while total minority enrollment increased by more than 16%. By 2020, demographers predict minorities will comprise nearly one-third of the United States population and nearly half of the school-age youth.

To an increasing degree, the task of erasing ethnic and racial stereotypes and prejudice has become the responsibility of America's public schools. Sociologists and policymakers see education as the key to overcoming bias and discrimination and fostering an appreciation for cultural and ethnic diversity. Developing K−12 multicultural programs that promote diverse ethnic and cultural perspectives has challenged educators. Multicultural content is still emerging and constantly changing.

The Best Schools — Preparing Students for Life in a Culturally and Ethnically Diverse Society

The Best Schools have committed to develop programs and provide activities that foster a curriculum that promotes understanding and appreciation for differences in culture and people. Several examples of such programs are illustrated here.

FOOTHILL ELEMENTARY SCHOOL, SARATOGA, CA

Foothill Elementary School is located in Saratoga, California, an affluent community southwest of San Jose. The population consists mostly of professionals, many working in computer-related fields in Silicon Valley. The ethnic makeup of the area consists mainly of Caucasians, with an Asian population that has steadily increased over the past decade. To meet the needs of the diverse student population, a major school and district goal for 1991−92 was providing multicultural education that will equip students with the skills and experiences that will enable them to live in a culturally diverse society. Foothill's high standards and expectations and strong integrated curriculum provide the foundation for developing knowledge, sensitivity, acceptance of others, and self-confidence. The literature-based language arts program links literature with cultural heritage. For example, after fifth graders studied the Japanese story "Sasdako and the Thousand Paper Cranes," several students folded 1000 origami paper cranes, which were displayed in the school library. Recently, the Foothill staff evaluated the social studies curriculum to ensure that cultural diversity of past and present is emphasized at each grade level through historical, ethnic, cultural, geographic, and economic literacy.

Throughout the year, students are exposed to the diverse cultures and ethnic groups that make up the Foothill community. Parents speak to classes about their cultural, ethnic, and religious backgrounds. Assemblies bring performing arts to students through music and dance. Ethnic celebrations, such as Chinese New Year, Cinco de Mayo, May Day, and United Nations Day involve all students in building cultural awareness and acceptance. Other special events, such as Martin Luther King, Jr., Day, Women's History Month, and Black History Month, are spotlighted in the classroom and library. The health curriculum and drug-abuse prevention programs develop students' self-esteem and pride in their cultural heritage.

Recently, Foothill participated in an exchange program through the Association of French-American Classes (AFAC). For three weeks this spring, twenty French students, their teacher, and counselor attended Foothill School and stayed with host families. Twelve fourth and fifth grade Foothill students, accompanied by a teacher and bilingual parent, spent three weeks at a French school. This program is part of a year-long project in which the French and Foothill students learn about their hosting countries and make intensive preparations to present various aspects of their culture to the hosting school community. To prepare primary students for this experience, a multicultural French center is incorporated in the Back-to-Back program. French Center activities expose students to the geography, literature, music, art, food and language of France. Through this exchange, the Foothill community is reaching across the Atlantic to develop bonds with another community in another nation.

Louise Klayman, *Principal, K – 5, 297 Students*

GRAYSVILLE ELEMENTARY SCHOOL, GRAYSVILLE, GA

Graysville Elementary School is located in a rural portion of North Georgia. The community of Graysville is primarily inhabited by lower- to middle-class families. In the past five years, they have seen a decline in the socioeconomic level of the school district. The percentage of students eligible for free and reduced lunches (almost one-third of the student population) and student transient rate (an average of 18%) have steadily increased. Almost 40% of the members of the student body are from nontraditional families and are the product of a variety of lifestyles and home environments.

Because Graysville is a rural community, the staff recognized several years ago the need to expose students to a variety of cultural and ethnic groups to enlarge their understanding of the world in which they live. They have fostered an appreciation for their rich Appalachian culture and heritage, yet at the same time have attempted to open the doors of the world to their students. The emphasis on geography has heightened student awareness of lives and customs of peoples. Special activities such as "Christmas Around the World" enable each class to learn about the customs and culture of one specific country, then share what they learn with other classes by making a video. Spin-offs from this three-week, schoolwide activity last throughout the year. Recently, after studying Japan, one class had "Japanese Day." Students wore kimonos, took their shoes off before entering the room, sat on the floor around low tables, made Japanese lanterns, cooked fried rice, and ate with chopsticks! In the spring of 1992, a cultural ambassador from the Japanese School Internship Programs spent three months at the school, sharing the language, culture, and history of Japan.

Units on values and citizenship encourage students to live harmoniously with each other and to respect differences in race, age, and gender. The staff attempts to choose nonbiased literature that reflects a culturally diverse world. Children are placed in nontraditional roles when possible (girls raise flags, boys help in cooking activities). They read stories about women, such as Sally Ride who have nontraditional roles. Age is valued as a resource; several retired staff members volunteer on a regular basis and serve on school committees. Grandparent's Day last year brought almost 200 senior citizens to the school. Children interview their grandparents and other senior citizens to better understand their heritage.

Economics has become an increasingly important part of the math/social studies curriculum. "Business Day" is described in Math. Fourth graders operate a mini-society. This year, a collaboration with the University of Tennessee at Chattanooga provides economics education K−5.

Additionally, Graysville recognizes technology as critical to global awareness. All classrooms are equipped with computers, and a mini-lab is housed in the media center. Closed-circuit cable has increased awareness of how accessible the world is to Graysville via technology. Fifth graders are provided copies of *U.S.A. Today* to inform them of current world events. Gifted students participate in a stock market game. Students also access school and countywide resources through the Media Center's computer network. They take advantage of nearby urban resources in an attempt to eliminate prejudice and bias among students, which helps them to learn that we are all people living on this planet together and that we must learn to live and work in harmony if we are to survive.

Beth Kellerhals, *Principal, K − 5, 463 Students*

SEQUOYA ELEMENTARY SCHOOL, SCOTTSDALE, AZ

The Sequoya Community is predominantly a middle-class area with the majority of the 800 students living in homes where both parents are working professionals. Sequoya is one of fifteen elementary schools in the Scottsdale Unified School District #48. It has a relatively low student mobility rate and a student population made up of predominantly Caucasian, non-Hispanic origin students. Although the major part of the attendance area is composed of single-family homes, a number of condominium and apartment complexes also exist. There is also a significant business community, and each year the business support to the school continues to increase.

Sequoya has targeted the development of multicultural education as a major improvement goal. Since the school community lacks an ethnically and culturally diverse population, the school volunteered to be a site for a district English as a Second Language Program. The twenty students in the program speak five different languages. These children are mainstreamed into regular classrooms for most of the day and have truly enriched and expanded the lives of everyone. The celebration of "Cultural Diversity" has been selected as the school theme for this year. Ten representatives are on a school Cultural Diversity Team and plan special student programs and activities that include community speakers, an Olympic Celebration for open house that pairs two classrooms (one primary and one intermediate) to represent a country, an international banquet, and a cultural exchange with a school in Japan. Each grade level is also scheduled to attend a fine arts trip with the theme of cultural diversity. Two classrooms are also piloting a Spanish Program. The Community School (after-school) Spanish Program was the first class to fill!

To prepare for an economy that is globally competitive, the staff continuously evaluates and upgrades programs. Computer literacy begins as a formal part of the curriculum in grade 3 with the teaching of keyboarding and word processing. Students have access to a networked computer system in the library to link to all of the community libraries to expand their resources for research. Analysis of cultures is a focus of our basal reading series, as well as our literature program at all grade levels. A "Weekly News Quiz" that focuses on current events is the highlight of the week for many intermediate students as they discuss and compete in teams using their knowledge of global happenings. As the school continues to integrate the curriculum, less emphasis is placed on learning factual information in specific content areas, but children are taught to look at the global picture, analyze problems, evaluate alternatives, predict outcomes, and synthesize information. They learn problem solving, collaboration, and research skills that will help them in a society that is changing at a rapid pace. Career education programs are also sponsored cooperatively with local business people and parents.

Dr. Bobbie Sferra, *Principal, K − 6, 767 Students*

SUMMARY

The Best Schools throughout the country have made a strong commitment to the development and maintenance of an educational climate that promotes students' learning and well-being. Through curricular and extracurricular initiatives, the Best Schools take great care to ensure that their students come to school prepared to learn; are challenged through relevant, interesting instructional activities; and have the appropriate support systems necessary to assist underachieving and/or at-risk students. Within these efforts, several common themes become apparent: the Best Schools value students and create opportunities for them to influence school goals and processes; they are committed to involving the parents and community as valuable resources; and they provide ongoing staff and parent training in a wide variety of areas dealing with the nature of child development, current curricular and instructional trends, and the nature of risk in the complex world in which our children live.

Finally, with all their efforts, the school community shares a sense of pride, enthusiasm, and commitment to the successful education of the children they serve.

REFERENCES

Banks, James A. (1992). "Multicultural Education: For Freedom's Sake," *Educational Leadership*, 49(4):32–35.

Banks, James A. (1987). *Teaching Strategies for Ethnic Studies, Fourth Edition:* Boston: Allyn and Bacon.

Bolton, Iris. (1986). "Educated Suicide Program," *School Safety* (Spring).

Brophy, Jere. (1987). "Synthesis of Research on Strategies for Motivating Students to Learn," *Educational Leadership*, 45(2):40–48.

Canter, L. and M. Canter. (1976). *Assertive Discipline*. Low Angeles, CA: Canter and Associates.

Coleman, James S. *Equality of Educational Opportunity*, Washington: United States Department of Health, Education and Welfare, Office of Education, 1966.

Cummings, Carol. (1983). *Managing to Teach*. Edmonds, Washington: Teaching, Inc.

Curwin, Richard and Allen N. Mendler. (1988). *Discipline with Dignity*. Association for Supervision and Curriculum Development.

Dunn, R. and K. Dunn. (1978). *Teaching Students Through Their Individual Learning Styles: A Practical Approach*. Reston, VA: Reston Publishing Company.

Educational Service District No. 121. (1986). "Here's Looking at You 2000," Seattle, Washington.

Gallup, George F. (1992). "The 11th Annual Gallup Pool in Education," *Phi Delta Kappan*, 74:43–52.

Germinario, Vito, Janet Cervalli, and Evelyn H. Ogden. (1992). *All Children Successful: Real Answers for Helping At-Risk Elementary Students*. Lancaster, PA: Technomic Publishing Company, Inc.

Good, T. L. (1982). "How Teachers' Expectations Affect Results," *American Education*, 18(10):25–32.

Good, T. L. and J. E. Brophy. (1984). *Looking into Classrooms, Third Edition*. New York: Harper and Row.

Hartzell, Gary N. and Thomas A. Petrie. (1992). "The Principal and Discipline: Working with School Structures, Teachers and Students," *The Clearing House*, 65(6), 376–380.

Hodgehenson, H. (1990). Director of the Center for Demographic Policy, Remarks from *American Association of School Administrators—Twelfth Annual Educational Policy Conference*. Washington, D. C.

Horton, Lowell. (1985). "Adolescent Alcohol Abuse," Fastback 217, Bloomington, IN: Phi Delta Kappan Foundation.

Hunter, M. (1986). *Motivation Theory into Practice*. El Sequido, CA: TIP Publications.

Kellman, Sheppard. (1987). "Prevention Research on Early Risk Behaviors," Conference Paper, World Health Organization, 1986, in Association for Supervision and Curriculum Development Update.

Kerman, S. and M. Martin. (1980). *Teacher Expectations and Students' Achievement—TESA*. Bloomington, IN: Phi Delta Kappan.

MacNaughton, Robert H. and Frank A. Johns. (1991) "Developing a Successful Schoolwide Discipline Program," *NASSP Bulletin*, 75(536):47−57.

McPartland, J. M. and R. E. Slavin. (1990). *"Increasing Achievement of At-Risk Students at Each Grade Level*, Policy Perspective, Office of Educational Research and Information, United States Department of Education.

National School Boards Association. (1988). *First Teachers: Parental Involvement in Public Schools*. Alexandria, VA

Neuman, F. M. (1981). "Reducing Student Alienation in High Schools: Implications of Theory," *Harvard Educational Review*, 51(4):546−564.

Ogden, Evelyn H. and Vito Germinario. (1988). *The At-Risk Student: Answers for Educators*. Lancaster, PA: Technomic Publishing Company, Inc.

Palandy, J. Michael. (1993). "Classroom Discipline: The Diagnostic Approach," *Streamliner Seminar*. National Association of Elementary School Principals, 11(6):1−4.

Pallas, A., G. Natriello, and E. McDill. (1989). "The Changing Nature of the Disadvantaged Generation: Current Dimensions and Future Trends," *Educational Researcher*, 18:16−22.

Pennsylvania Department of Education. (1986). *Student Assistance Program Training Manual*, Harrisburg, PA

Stewart, William J. (1989). "Improving the Teaching of Decision-Making Skills," *The Clearing House*, (63):64−66.

Strother, D. B. (1983). "Practical Applications of Research: Mental Health Education," *Phi Delta Kappan*, 65(2):140−141.

U. S. Center of Educational Statistics. (1988). "Dropout Rates in the United States."

U. S. Center of Educational Statistics. (1989). "Dropout Rates in the United States."

U. S. Department of Education. (1990). *A Profile of the American Eighth Grader*. Office of Educational Research and Improvement. National Longitudinal Study of 1988, Washington, D. C.

U. S. Department of Education. (1986). *What Works—Schools Without Drugs*. Washington, D. C.

U. S. Department of Health and Human Services. (1993). *Learning Readiness: Promising Strategies*. Washington, D. C.

University of Michigan Institute for Social Research. (1986). Survey reported by Bianca Gonzales in "Delusions of Grandeur," *School Safety* (Spring).

Waxman, Hersholt C. and Herbert Jed Walberg. (1991). *Effective Teaching: Current Research*. Berkeley, CA: McCutchan Publishing Company.

CHAPTER 5

Parent and Community Support

SINCE the 1960s, increasing recognition has been given to enhance student achievement and parent involvement. Education and policymakers have tried, by means of various federal and state legislative mandates, to foster low-income families' involvement in schools. The main purpose of including parent involvement in regulations governing a variety of federal initiatives, including Head Start (1965), the Bilingual Education Act (1965), Follow Through (1967), the Elementary and Secondary Education Act (1965), and the Education for All Handicapped Children Act (1975), was to improve student achievement in school (Chrispeels, 1991).

Research strongly supports parent involvement in schools. When parents are meaningfully involved in their child's education, children achieve at a higher level and have more positive attitudes toward school (Jones, 1991). Yet meaningful parent involvement is only achieved when the school creates an environment that makes parents feel welcome, reaches out in a wide variety of ways, connects parents to needed resources, and provides systematic opportunities for participation. Epstein (1988) suggests that a comprehensive program of parent involvement should include: 1) techniques to help parents create home environments conducive to learning, 2) frequent and clear communications from teachers to parents about pupil progress, 3) the use of parents as resources in school (i.e., volunteers), 4) teacher assistance with educational activities in the home, and 5) involvement in school governance, through such vehicles as the PTA and school planning committees.

Although approaches and strategies may vary, in schools focused on excellence the principal and staff realize that parents and the school are linked by the common goal of providing the best for the child. To facilitate this relationship, successful schools have developed partnerships with parents to ensure that:

- Parents have a real voice in shaping the schools' educational program.
- Parents are helped to increase their effectiveness in working with their children both in school and at home.
- Parents are given, through both formal and informal vehicles, specific information regarding their child's performance and progress in school.
- Parents' concerns regarding their role in parenting is facilitated through parent training opportunities.
- Parents are provided with the necessary resources and networks to ensure greater control over their own lives and their child's future.

When a trusting, nurturing climate has been developed by a school which actually seeks and values parental involvement, everyone within the school community benefits.

For children, substantial evidence exists to show that children whose parents are involved in their schooling demonstrate advanced academic achievement and cooperative development (Henderson, 1988). The parent-child relationship is improved, and parents become better teachers of their children at home and use more positive forms of reinforcement (Henderson, 1988).

Liontos (1992) summarizes the positive outcomes for children as a result of their parent involvement in their schooling:

- improved achievement
- improved student behavior
- greater student motivation
- more regular attendance
- lower student dropout rates
- a more positive attitude toward homework
- increased parent and community support

Research also indicates that parents benefit from involvement in their children's education. These parents tend to develop positive attitudes about themselves, increase self-confidence, and often enroll in programs to enhance their own personal development (Becker, 1986). They are also more positive about school, help to gather community support for educational programs, and become more active in community activities (Becker, 1986). In a very real sense, parents not only become more effective as parents, but they become more effective as people, with their increased knowledge and participation fostering positive outcomes for the entire family.

Dauber and Epstein (1989) report that teachers have strong positive attitudes and perceive direct classroom benefits from parental involvement. In many respects, teachers discovered that their classroom lives got easier when they received help from parents. Additionally, involved parents tend to rate teachers' interpersonal skills higher, appreciate teachers' efforts more, and rate teachers' overall ability higher (Liontos, 1992).

This chapter will examine the characteristics of parental involvement in America's Best Schools. Additionally, examples of best practices will be highlighted for use as a practical guide for improving school-home relationships.

Specifically, this chapter will address the following questions:

- How do Best Schools encourage parental involvement in schools?
- How do Best Schools communicate student progress and overall school performance to parents and the broader community?
- What strategies do Best Schools use to encourage parents to provide supportive learning environments in the home?
- How do Best Schools support the needs of families?
- What types of opportunities do Best Schools provide for meaningful collaboration with other educational and community groups?

ENCOURAGEMENT OF PARENTAL INVOLVEMENT

All too often, schools fail to involve parents effectively as meaningful partners in their child's education. Teachers may only contact parents when there is a problem with the child; administrators may not give parents an opportunity for a meaningful role in school governance. Additionally, demographic changes, such as increased numbers of teenaged parents and increased numbers of working parents, are sometimes seen as barriers to involvement. Yet, as previously cited, the benefits of parental involvement in schools are enormous! Families provide the first educational involvement and strongly influence the child's intellectual growth, achievement, and attitude about schooling. Thus, schools must consistently develop structured opportunities to involve parents, and to a large degree, other community members in most all aspects of school life.

The strongest and most consistent predictors of parent involvement at school and at home are the specific school programs and teacher practices that encourage and guide parent involvement. Parent programs are more likely to be successful when they are designed with high expectations for parent involvement, when they provide a variety of ways for parents to be involved, when they accommodate the needs of particular families to be involved, and when they are comprehensive.

The Best Schools—Parental Involvement

The Best Schools recognize the powerful influence parents have in their children's success and the positive effect they can have on school effectiveness. Although research has not identified the "best" form of parental involvement, these schools have created the appropriate climate and meaningful ways to involve parents as partners in their schools. The following illustrations provide specific examples of the Best School practices.

DR. JAMES H. ELDREDGE ELEMENTARY SCHOOL, EAST GREENWICH, RI

Eldredge is one of four elementary schools located in the small town of East Greenwich, Rhode Island. Its student population is relatively homogeneous, with minority groups comprising approximately 4% of the student population. A strong bond exists among teachers, students, parents, and community. The Eldredge community works diligently to help students and families in time of need. Parental involvement and community support are considered an important component of school success. Eldredge parents are most welcome in school at all times to meet with the principal and teachers or to make classroom visits. The parent-teacher group is very active in providing volunteers to aid in school activities and for monetary support for a wide range of school programs.

Eldredge's parent-teacher group (PTG) is the primary vehicle of communication between parents, teachers, and community—sponsoring many activities to allow for parent and teacher involvement. This includes a staff luncheon at the beginning of the year to acquaint parents and teachers. In mid-September, there is an open house that provides an overview of the goals and objectives of both the PTG and the school staff. At this time, the PTG presents teachers with gift certificates to be used for classroom materials of their choice and parent handbooks outlining the school's philosophy and goals; rules and disciplinary actions are distributed along with classroom curricula. Parents then proceed to their children's classroom where the teachers share their goals, objectives, and expectations. This is not the only time, however, that parents may interact. In addition to the PTG holding monthly meetings where parents may seek information, dialogue forums are held monthly. Parents are invited to attend these small discussion groups with the principal to voice any concern or constructive criticism regarding the overall operation of the school. Teachers are aware of all the PTG undertakings through the faculty liaison who is present at all meetings.

The School Committee meets every month with the presidents of all the PTG groups in the town to share concerns, questions, and objectives of each school. The presidents meet with one another on a monthly basis to share with each other what each PTG is doing and also to help put together a districtwide calendar, which aids in improving communications among schools.

The Principal's Advisory Committee is yet another vehicle of communication that has been established at Eldredge. A small group of parents and teachers meet monthly with the principal and act as advocates for education. Any issue or concern may be brought up for discussion. Philosophy and goals of the school, fiscal input, safety equipment, and necessary repairs are but a few of the issues discussed.

Parents also have had a strong teaching impact on Eldredge. The volunteer program, which runs districtwide, implements programs such as Art Appreciation, Suitcase Museum, Centers for Growth, Kids and Kritters, and the Parent Resource Center. In the 1990−91 school year, Eldredge accrued 1500 volunteer hours representing both parent and community involvement. In addition, parents have been lecturers in the classroom; have taught a six-week program called Invent America to students; and have tutored individual students before, during, and after school. Parents and community members have also been resourceful in providing demonstrations on career opportunities and have served as excellent role models to students. A reading program instituted last year, Million Minutes of Reading, brought a local newscaster to speak to students emphasizing the need and importance of reading in all walks of life.

Another facet of learning opportunity provided by parents and community members at large involves an after-school enrichment program. Programs of student interest are established for a six-week period for time after school. They have included such topics as Red Cross, Certified Baby-Sitting, Animal and Environment Discoveries, Computer, Word-Processing, Cartooning as a Profession, Cheerleading, Rocketry, and French and Spanish as conversational languages.

Parents and community people have been supporters of Eldredge for many years. Besides the many field trips parents themselves attend, they volunteer for the daily Breakfast Program, as well as the book fair and book swaps.

Dr. Frances Gallo, *Principal, Grades 4 − 6, 263 Students*

MOORESTOWN FRIENDS SCHOOL, MOORESTOWN, NJ

The Moorestown Friends School is located in suburban Moorestown, New Jersey, approximately twenty miles from downtown Philadelphia. The school's main purpose is to provide a quality education with spiritual values in a Quaker context. It strives for a balance in the school's population so as to include social, economic, and cultural divergence. The school has operated under the care of the Religious Society of Friends of the Moorestown Monthly Meeting since the school's inception 206 years ago.

Parents are well represented on the school committee level; therefore, they have a central role in policy decisions. The parent organization is called the Parent Council. Parents are actively involved in fund-raising through the Thrift Shop, Annual Sustaining Fund, Phon-a-thon, and other functions that come out of the Development Office. In addition, they serve as advocates for the school by volunteering as tour guides for visiting families during open house. They also help host major school events such as Grandparents? Day, May Day, Alumni Day, and sporting events.

Parents are encouraged to be actively involved in their children's classrooms. These opportunities emerge from the relationship between the teacher and parent:

- Parents feel that the school reinforces their own view that they are an integral part of their child's educational process. Parents welcome the classroom newsletters and update sheets.
- Each class (Pre-K−4) has Parent Council representatives (usually two, sometimes four) who are parent volunteers that assist in school activities, parties, family gatherings, and in disseminating information to and from Parent Council. Often, Parent Council representatives bring questions from the larger parent body to the attention of the administrator/teacher for further clarification.
- Parents are often encouraged to share their expertise or personal interests in the classroom.
- Twelve percent of the school's parents serve on the Parent Council Executive Committee.

Larue Evans, *Principal, Pre-K − 4, 192 Students*

CREST HILL ELEMENTARY SCHOOL, CASPER, WY

Crest Hill is centrally located in Casper, Wyoming, and is one of thirty-two schools in the

Nortrona County School District #1. A strong parent group is responsible for many of Crest Hill's traditions and school improvement initiatives.

There are multiple opportunities for parents to be involved with school activities. At the beginning of the year, a survey form is sent out to parents wishing to volunteer at Crest Hill. Many parents send the form back stating they would like to assist with one of the thirteen committees currently operating. These committees include: co-curricular clubs, library assistants, writing center assistants, coaching volleyball and basketball, and fund-raising to purchase state-of-the-art equipment for Crest Hill's students. This is in addition to room parents who help with classroom information on their career or a special interest. From this a resource sheet for teachers is developed, and parents are called upon to give a demonstration or help with an enrichment project. Within individual classrooms, parents assist during computer time or large group activities, help put up bulletin boards, or listen while a student needing extra attention reads to them. The parents of Crest Hill were instrumental in the designing of the "Freedom Trail" and the restoration of the library. The art seen throughout the building is a result of parental efforts to make the school more appealing aesthetically.

Parents are encouraged to become involved in the Building Leadership Team formed in 1990. This group has also directly contributed to the addition of more physical education time in the week, the writing of grants for the writing center, and the United Way YES Program.

Recently, a parent/student committee was formed that will together develop several newsletters that may supplant individual classroom newsletters. This effort has resulted in the abandonment of the traditional class newsletters.

Finally, a Parents' Involved in Education Group has been formed for the sixth grade. They meet twice a month to discuss communicating with adolescents, study skills, and other topics of interest.

William Owen Jones, *Principal, K – 6, 493 Students*

REPORTING STUDENT PROGRESS AND PERFORMANCE

Parents have long sought accurate measures of their childrens' performance in school. Although, at one time, information relative to grades (e.g., A, B, C, etc.) was the only readily understandable vehicle for parents to assess their child's performance, most parents now expect information regarding a much broader spectrum of student performance and behavior. The essential ingredient of effective school/parent communication is embodied in the frequent, warm, respectful, and honest dialogue between the school and the home.

With increased parental sophistication regarding the nature of student performance, as well as the heightened interest of community members in the results produced by their local schools, educators must develop meaningful ways to share these outcomes with their constituencies.

Communicating student progress is a critical component of the parental and community involvement process. Not only does it provide unique information about a child, it serves as a mechanism by which comparisons are made among schools and school districts. It is exceedingly important that outcome data is addressed in relation to local student/school/district performance, since all too often raw test data is used to make faulty judgments about a child or school.

The Best Schools—Reporting Student Progress and Performance

Thus, successful schools have developed a wide variety of strategies that provide parents and community members with meaningful information about their children and their schools.

Warner (1991) describes several strategies that have been employed in the Indianapolis Public Schools:

- parent/teacher conferences
- Dial-a-Teacher program designed to give students and parents assistance and information about homework
- homework hotline — a live call-in television program produced by the school district to help parents help their children accurately complete assignments
- parent line/communicator or computerized telephone system that gives callers access to 140 prerecorded messages on a variety of school topics
- parent Focus Series — a parent education and information program offering ninety parent-oriented workshops
- work-site seminars offered throughout the community for parents who cannot come to the school for seminars
- Teachers Involve Parents in Schoolwork (TIPS) developed by Joyce Epstein at Johns Hopkins University, which structures communication from home to school regarding homework and student progress

Additionally, strategies from successful schools are illustrated next.

ROBERT D. JOHNSON ELEMENTARY SCHOOL, FT. THOMAS, KY

Johnson School is located in the northern end of the city of Ft. Thomas, Kentucky. Ft. Thomas has a rich heritage dating back to the Civil War. Beginning as a farming area south of Cincinnati, Ohio, Ft. Thomas has developed primarily into a residential community with no industry and only limited pockets of business and commerce. Ft. Thomas is predominately Caucasian with a middle- to upper middle-class economic population.

Formal means of communicating with parents include Campus Days, standardized test results, and biweekly computer reports on their child's progress in basic skills. The broader community is informed through the annual "School Facts," a comprehensive report to citizens; "The Johnson Journal," a quarterly newsletter; and a semi-annual "Report to Citizens." Because of the collaborative spirit in the Johnson School family, feedback from parents is frequent. Campus Days are especially effective; parents spend a half-day at school observing all aspects of the school program. The principal conducts an orientation before classroom visitations and a feedback session at the closing luncheon. This first-hand program has met with much parental support and enthusiasm for the school's staff and program.

In addition to report cards, Johnson teachers communicate with parents through individual conferences, prompt phone response, plan books (two-way communications between teacher and parent), Awards Day, standardized test results, and computer-generated management reports to parents on their child's basic skills development. For at-risk students, staffings are conducted with parents to identify specific needs and strategies to improve student achievement. Individual cards and notes ("Something good happened to your child . . . "), and sharing student portfolios provide positive parent/teacher contacts.

The school receives feedback from the community through the "Superintendent's Community Coffees," Campus Day, School Council, and the PTA. The administration encourages frequent contact by phone, notes, and conferences to discuss children's needs and/or achievement.

Henry Clay Beekley, *Principal, K – 6, 504 Students*

LEWIS H. POWELL GIFTED AND TALENTED MAGNET ELEMENTARY SCHOOL, RALEIGH, NC

Powell Gifted and Talented Magnet School is an urban K – 5 school located in the city of Raleigh. Powell GT Magnet School believes that all children have gifts and talents, which should be identified, valued, nurtured, and rewarded. As a result, no special performance standards or test scores are required for admission. Acceptance into the program is based on the availability of magnet spaces, transportation patterns, and racial equity considerations. Therefore, the school serves a diverse student population of varying abilities and socioeconomic levels. Specifically, the school serves a student population consisting of 53% Caucasian, 44% African-American, 2% Hispanic, and 1% Asian American. To serve this unique population, Powell provides a wide variety of vehicles to communicate student progress.

Communication with parents is excellent at Powell. Each week, students take home Monday Folders containing papers, grades, a weekly behavior checklist, and newsletters. A teacher and parent comment section is also a part of the folder. Parents review the folder with students and return it signed on Tuesday.

Parent conferences are held regularly to communicate student progress and to exchange valuable information. Two parent/teacher conferences are required each year. Evening hours are provided to accommodate parents.

Progress reports are issued each quarter, along with elective report cards. Interim reports are also available to inform parents mid-quarter. Information is sent home and to the local news media regarding the Panther Honor Roll and the Climber's Program. Achievement test information is shared with parents in person and results are published in local newspapers. Additionally, Powell gains valuable information from parents through surveys, conferences, and phone calls.

> Joyce Faulkner, *Principal, (Patrick C. Kinlaw, Principal at time of recognition),*
> *K – 5, 497 Students*

GRANT WOOD ELEMENTARY SCHOOL, CEDAR RAPIDS, IA

Grant Wood is one of twenty-two elementary schools in the Cedar Rapids Community School District. Cedar Rapids can be characterized as a mid-size city with a diverse student population. A boundary change at Grant Wood has created a school with a very diverse population and provides a setting for students to experience and appreciate cultural customs, traditions, and values other than their own. Examples of the extent of the changes are an increase of students on free/reduced lunch (17% to 43%), an increase in minority students (1% to 26.7%), an increase of nontraditional families (15 to 65%), a decrease of high-income professional families (75% to 10%), and over one-third bus riders versus all being walkers.

Parents and the community are informed of student progress in a number of ways. Regularly scheduled conferences with parents are held in fall and spring to review the child's academic progress. At the fall conference, results of the Iowa Test of Basic Skills are discussed, and a handout is given to help parents interpret scores. Ideas are suggested on how those at home can help with the child's academic growth. To accommodate differing schedules, evening conferences, as well as daytime conferences, are held. Transportation is provided for parents who desire it; staff members may also make home visits. Almost 99% of the parents participate in fall and spring conferences. During conference days, Grant Wood provides a warm, caring atmosphere for visitors by providing doughnuts and coffee. Videos of students participating in musicals, plays, and other student events are shown in the foyer. Photo albums containing snapshots of students involved in activities are displayed.

Report cards based on curriculum objectives have been developed by a committee of teachers. Report cards are issued each quarter and are shared with parents at fall and spring conferences. Students may attend these conferences with parents; often, teachers share the report card individually with the child before the parent conference. Chapter 1 and learning disabled students have an additional report card. Parents also confer with special teachers during parent/teacher conferences.

"The Grant Wood Scene," a weekly newsletter, is used to inform parents of student successes. Also included are expectations for students. Some individual classrooms have their own newsletters to inform parents of student progress and activities.

Local newspaper, radio, and TV are encouraged to display the achievements of students, volunteers, and staff. Recently, national TV has begun featuring a segment of the Grant Wood "Art Presenter" program.

Grant Wood school has opened its hallways for walkers from the neighborhood between 6:15 and 8:15 A.M. As neighbors exercise, they read school bulletins, examine student work that is displayed in the halls, and visit with teachers. Some have volunteered to work with students.

The staff promotes the "open door" policy. Visitors are always welcome anytime during the school day. The Grant Wood staff is committed to a team effort—school, home, and community supporting each others' goals.

Sheila Billington, *Principal, Pre-K – 5, 421 Students*

STRATEGIES TO ENCOURAGE PARENTS TO PROVIDE SUPPORTIVE LEARNING ENVIRONMENTS

Efforts to strengthen the home learning environment and to promote parent education are increasingly viewed as a way to enrich the learning potential of all students. By acknowledging the learning environment of the home and developing strategies to build and extend family influence on children, educators have discovered a viable mechanism to enhance student learning. As the child's first teacher, parents have a significant role in influencing achievement and attitudes about school. When one considers that, from birth to age eighteen, a child spends approximately 12% of his/her life in school, the need to promote a productive learning environment in the home becomes very significant. Parents can create a curriculum at home that teaches children skills and the importance of school.

Yet a study of American families (U.S. Dept. of Education, 1986) indicated that many parents are not actively involved in promoting school success for their children. For example, American women, on average, spend less than half an hour a day talking, explaining, or reading with their children. Fathers spend less than fifteen minutes.

Successful schools provide parents with the necessary skills and opportunities that foster the value of hard work, the importance of personal responsibility, and the importance of education as a significant contributor to greater success for their children. Several strategies parents can use at home that are directly linked to student success are discussed below (Source: U. S. Department of Education, 1986).

Conversation is important. Children learn to read, reason, and understand things better when their parents:

- read, talk, and listen to them
- tell them stories, play games, and share hobbies
- discuss news, TV programs, and special events

In order to enrich the "curriculum of the home," some parents:

- provide books, supplies, and a special place for studying
- observe routine for meals, bedtime, and homework
- monitor the amount of time spent watching TV and doing after-school jobs

Parents stay aware of their children's lives at school when they:

- discuss school events
- help children meet deadlines
- talk with their children about school problems and successes

Successful schools promote parent education by offering courses on and (at times) off the school campus. They conduct home visits, distribute handbooks and other materials such as ''Tips for Parents,'' and disseminate the names of organizations that may serve as resources to parents (see Appendix A). Parent seminars, workshops, and support groups provide valuable opportunities for enriched involvement with their children and their schools. As parents increase their understanding of child development, parenting skills, and the nature of teaching and learning, students reap the benefits in terms of motivation, achievement, and success. Jones (1991) provides a brief list and description of seven parent workshops or activities that schools may utilize to help parents create a productive learning environment in the home. Some are for parents only; others are for parents and children:

(1) ''Make It–Take It'' Workshops–These are designed for parents to construct home learning materials. Parents may be asked to bring special materials, or the school can provide ready-to-assemble materials.

(2) Family Learning Center–The school is open two or more evenings per week with learning activities provided for all ages. When feasible, access to the computer lab and library is available to both adults and students.

(3) ''Learning Fairs''–Single-session workshops are held in the evening on a variety of topics, such as study skills, memory techniques, concentration, etc. Students, parents, and teachers are invited to attend.

(4) Parent-Support Groups–These are organized and run by parents with meetings held in homes or at school.

(5) Family Room–This is a room at school containing educational books, toys, and games for loan to parents. Parents are welcome to drop in and participate in informal activities. Parents share with each other and learn ways of helping their children.

(6) Child and Adolescent Development Series–These programs provide parents with a better understanding of their children's physical, social, and intellectual development. Series on the middle school child are especially popular.

(7) Special Topic Workshops–These focus on helping children learn and succeed in school. Popular topics include reading, math, study skills, self-esteem, motivation, alternatives to television, and creating a learning environment in the home.

The Best Schools–Parent Support for Learning

The Best Schools have capitalized on the potential for increased student success through parental involvement. Through the creation of a trusting parent-school climate, parent education programs and activities significantly extend the learning opportunities for children. Following are illustrations from selected Best Schools.

BOYCE MIDDLE SCHOOL, UPPER ST. CLAIR, PA

Upper St. Clair's Boyce School is located in a suburban area of Pittsburgh, Pennsylvania. It is primarily a transient, upper middle-class professional community characterized by high expectations and high achievement. The transient nature of the community contributes to Boyce's uniqueness. Although a small number of residents are moving from communities within the Pittsburgh metropolitan area, the majority are moving there from places across the nation and the world. As a result, during the 1990–91 school year, there has been an increase in the cultural diversity in the Boyce population, with 12% of the students born in foreign countries.

Teachers meet with most of their students' parents during the school year. During these individual conferences, the teachers share strategies and procedures they use to create a supportive learning environment. In addition, there are a variety of initiatives that facilitate the involvement of parents in their children's learning at home:

- Each student receives a "Binder Reminder," which is an organizer with assignment sheets, calendar, tips for getting organized, and a parent/teacher communications section. The Binder Reminder is an attempt to help students get organized and to insure that parents know what their children are doing and what is expected of them.
- A monthly, commercially prepared newsletter, "Parent News," is sent to all parents. It contains a myriad of ideas on how parents can help their children with the learning process.
- The principal writes a monthly column for the PTA newsletter, "Voice of Boyce," in which he gives parents professional advice on how to work with their young learners in the home.
- The developmental guidance program includes a comprehensive study unit for the student and provides parents with guidelines as to what they can do at home to promote good study habits. The counselors also contact the parents to inform them of the special needs their children have and to suggest intervention strategies.
- The counselors meet with the parents from each teaching team during the first weeks of the school year to discuss the characteristics of this age group and to facilitate the development of a parent network for the sharing of common parenting problems.
- The principal encourages the parents to become involved in the activities of the districtwide TIP (Together in Parenting) program. This group offers training and informational sessions for parents throughout the school year.
- The principal addresses age characteristics, learning patterns, teaching strategies, self-esteem needs, etc., at the fall open house, as well as during the "Open Mikes," which are held throughout the school year.
- For the past four years, the principal and teachers have held a Middle Level Learner Conference at a nearby hotel the week after school is over in June. The topics are designed for teachers and parents of middle school students, and many parents attend the conference.

Dr. Robert L. Furman, *Principal, 5 – 6, 561 Students*

W.H.L. WELLS ELEMENTARY, PLANO, TX

W.H.L. Wells Elementary is a neighborhood school in Plano, Texas, serving students in pre-kindergarten through fifth grades. The city of Plano continues to be one of the most rapidly growing communities in our nation. Wells' student body consists largely of children from upper and middle socioeconomic levels, whose parents value education and have high expectations. In addition to single-family homes, the neighborhood also has duplexes and one large apartment complex. Rental housing and professional career pursuits of these families contribute to the 35% student mobility factor. With a growing minority population of 9%, Wells is increasingly responsive to multiple cultures. The school is enriched by the diverse ethnic and religious backgrounds of its students. With a long tradition of excellence in education, the Plano Independent School District has had several of its schools awarded national recognition.

Wells Elementary seeks a commitment from each family to partnership with the school in the education of its children. Communication folders, homework calendars, and study skills programs provide a structure for learning in the home. At grade level back-to-school meetings, expectations for homework are explained. Parents are urged to provide guidance, gradually decreasing their involvement as children gain independence. The Wells' Parent Handbook suggests that parents expect daily assignment folders, select a place in the home most conducive to study, and monitor homework. All students keep homework calendars. Fifteen percent of Wells' students who need additional help with organization set study skill goals. These students use a daily check-out system in which teachers verify that assignments are written on student calendars to insure that the necessary materials are in their backpacks. Parents of these children initial calendars each night when work is done. As good study habits are established, the check-out system is discontinued. Study guides for tests are provided to focus review on important learning objectives. Parents conference with teachers on how students learn best and set collaborative goals to advance learning. Parents encourage children as they review graded work in Thursday's "Go-Folders" each week.

Parents are urged to model reading and to select library books at their children's reading level; incentive programs have parents and children spend 100 minutes a week reading for pleasure. Homework assignments encourage students to use newspapers and periodicals for information on current events.

Wells' parents benefit from PTA speakers on the partnership of home and education. Brown bag lunches and evening programs address such topics as computer literacy, sports and competition, and responsibility. Thursday communications folders carry fliers from the school counselor on parenting. Teachers send a newsletter with summaries of units of study so that learning may be extended to the home. Community opportunities for learning are also publicized through these folders.

Teachers throughout the school help parents to see their valuable contributions to learning. The speech therapist gives parents a summer calendar of daily language activities. When special education test results are explained, parents learn ways to assist in remediation. The counselor teaches parenting classes that convey expectations and build responsibility in the child for his/her own learning. Consistent schoolwide procedures and clear expectations enable parents to be true partners in education. Wells Elementary believes that the home must be a place of learning.

Lanecia Nell Pearce, *Principal, Pre-K – 5, 685 Students*

LAURA B. SPRAGUE SCHOOL, LINCOLNSHIRE, IL

The Laura B. Sprague School is located in the town of Lincolnshire, Illinois, a suburban community of approximately 5000 residents located forty miles north of Chicago. The school serves several communities and maintains a student population of 91% Caucasian, 4% Hispanic, 4% Asian-American, and 1% African-American.

Throughout its history, Sprague has maintained a close partnership with its community. Parents are highly supportive and involved, both in directly enhancing the education of their children and in enriching the school programs in general. The level of parent volunteering at Sprague exemplifies this partnership with an estimated 11,000 hours of parent time last year in formal volunteer activities.

The school provides a variety of strategies in assisting parents to create a positive home learning environment and support their child's learning experience. Weekly notes are sent by teachers to parents and the "Weekly Bulletin" communicates concerns, ideas, and strategies for parents in reinforcing messages about effective learning. The "Weekly Bulletin" often includes articles for parents about effective parenting.

The school offers parent information sessions and formal parenting classes throughout the year on such topics as "Helping Children Learn to Learn," "Encouraging Reading at Home," "Emergent Writing," "Parents as Encouragers and Not as Discouragers," and "Understanding Developmental Issues for Primary Aged Children." "STEP" (Systematic Training for Effective Parenting) is a highly regarded parenting course.

At the end of each school year, the school sends home summer materials to assist parents in encouraging their children to make the summer a valuable learning time. This information includes reading, writing and math activities, field trips, and story letters.

A Parent Advisory Committee created an Enrichment Resource Center in the library, which includes articles, books, and other information about programs for children.

Richard L. Best, *Principal, K – 4, 648 Students*

SUPPORTING THE NEEDS OF FAMILIES

Most schools are structured to accommodate the (now) atypical family composed of a husband who works and a wife that stays at home. Today, the time of the school day, scheduling for parent-teacher conferences, special events and programs, procedures for dealing with sick children, and other opportunities for meaningful parental involvement are, all too often, best suited for the family with a full-time "stay-at-home" parent. Increasingly, schools have acknowledged this phenomenon and have initiated more flexible scheduling for important school events and activities. Yet merely changing schedules may not be enough to meet the diverse needs of today's parents. One way to gain information about the needs of parents as it relates to the education of their children is to conduct an in-school survey. Such surveys are relatively simple to construct and may provide the school with pertinent information regarding the needs of specific families (the National School Boards Association and the National School Public Relations Association are excellent sources for sample surveys).

Each survey should outline several vital areas of possible school assistance. For example:

- What specific aspects of classroom procedures are you most interested in (e.g., homework, building student self-esteem, testing, reading skills, etc.)?
- What special parenting sessions are you interested in (e.g., single parenting, child development, teaching your child about sex, drugs, or disease, etc.)?
- What is the best time to hold such meetings/workshops?
- Where would you like these meetings/workshops held?
- Do you need transportation for you (and/or your child) to attend a meeting/workshop?
- Would you like to speak directly to the teacher, principal, counselor, or the substance abuse coordinator?

The surveys should be tailored to the unique needs of the school community. Often the school can serve as a resource by providing the names of community agencies and outreach programs that may help troubled or dysfunctional families. Other resources could include school/town library hours, car pooling opportunities, parent support groups, and state and national advocacy groups. Regardless of what format is utilized, it is important to assess the needs of families first, as family needs relate to their ability to help their children learn and grow. Secondly, a variety of vehicles to disseminate appropriate information and give appropriate support must be provided.

Davies (1991) cites the need for a new and broader definition of parent involvement, which goes beyond the term *parent* and which more closely describes today's reality:

- *Family* is a more encompassing term that includes other significant adults who have some involvement in child care.
- Involvement should go beyond parent or family and include all agencies and institutions that serve children.
- Involvement should go beyond having family members come to school; services should be available at home or in the neighborhood setting.
- Involvement should not only include the readily available parent, but those who are "hard to reach."
- Involvement should go beyond the agendas and priorities of teachers and school administrators to include priorities of the families.
- Involvement in urban schools should replace the old "deficit" views of pathologies,

traumas, and troubles with a new mindset that emphasizes the inherent strengths of families.

The Best Schools—Supporting the Needs of Families

The illustrations of Best Schools practices, highlighted here, can serve as a guide to help promote active family involvement in schools. It is important, however, that individual school practices closely match the unique needs of individual families and communities.

JOHN MUIR ELEMENTARY SCHOOL, MADISON, WI

Once a largely white, homogeneous upper middle class school, John Muir Elementary now has a very diversified student population. After the construction in 1976 of a subsidized housing development of 248 units, the number of Muir students from African-American, Hispanic, Asian refugee and low-income white families grew to nearly 35% by the mid-1980s. Currently, these groups represent 25−30% of families.

In order to meet the needs of all students at Muir, the staff recognized that change was necessary. In the mid-1980s, a two-year diversity study was undertaken by a committee of staff, parents, community members, university faculty, and central office personnel. Muir's educational goals, instructional program, policies and procedures, staff development, and parent/community interaction were examined through extensive surveys of teachers, parents, and students. The results were tabulated and evaluated by the committee at a summer workshop.

The results of the study capitalized on existing staff, program, and community strengths to delineate a course of future action that would reinforce the areas of early intervention, primary team development of whole language, cognitively guided math instruction and writing labs, multicultural education, interdisciplinary curriculum, higher order thinking skills, authentic assessment, parent and community involvement, and shared decision making. Since that point, school wide goals, staff development opportunities, and resource distribution have all reflected these priorities.

Muir recognizes that family well-being is central to a child's academic and emotional success. For that reason, the school attempts to view each student as an extension of a family unit that belongs to our learning community:

- In keeping with their emphasis on early intervention, Muir's full-day kindergarten, low primary class sizes, and heightened contact with the home through goal-setting and parent involvement efforts are cornerstones to meeting parent needs.
- In response to family needs, Muir offers a daily breakfast program and serves as a site for a city after-school day-care program.
- Muir has designated half of its English as a Second Language allocation to be used for home-school coordination. This time has resulted in many grants and projects.
- There are many connections to community agencies that meet families' educational needs. In addition, the social worker, home-school coordinator, bilingual resource specialist, and nurse maintain close ties to agencies and community programs that serve families' financial, emotional, parenting, health, and legal needs. Assistance is provided in making referrals, arranging appointments and payments, offering translators/interpreters, transporting parents and students to appointments/meetings, obtaining prescriptions/eyeglasses, and following up to see that the intervention has been carried out successfully. Support staff and classroom teachers are also frequently in contact with agency and medical personnel when consultation is required.
- Parents may choose to initiate in-house or more formal testing, counseling or support through the Building Consultant Team.
- Translators, interpreters, and written translations are provided when necessary and possible. Muir has two Hispanic staff members; two more are fluent in Spanish.

District bilingual specialists are called in for conferences with Hmong, Lao, and Cambodian families.

• Muir regularly offers transportation and child care for parents attending school functions, conferences, and parent involvement programs.

Dr. David Bray, *Principal, K – 5, 467 Students*

HIGH LAWN ELEMENTARY SCHOOL, ST. ALBANS, WV

High Lawn Elementary School is one of sixty-nine elementary schools in the very large town of St. Albans, West Virginia. Interestingly, the three-story brick building first opened in 1870. The present building, finished in 1921, is scheduled to close its doors in 1997. Throughout its honored history, High Lawn has maintained excellence in education and a commitment to the families it serves.

The community has an extended day program in another school. Attending students from High Lawn are bused there. The physical education teacher has conducted games and exercise programs with all students who go to the center. Parent workshops support the needs of families.

Keep-a-Child-in-School has worked with the principal to provide Big Brothers/Sisters for some of the students. This agency also provided scholarships for two sixth grade students to help with expenses of the sixth grade trip in June 1991.

Students are transported by a dental hygienist to the Kanawha County Dental Clinic, and the school nurse secures eyeglasses for low S.E.S. students when there is a need. The school social worker collaborates with community agencies to provide jackets and shoes for needy students. High Lawn has its own school clothes closet to help with other clothing needs.

Students and parents are referred to family counseling agencies. A few years ago when one student died unexpectedly, the principal worked with the family and the director of district guidance and counseling department to secure counseling help for family members. The staff also stayed in close contact with the family through notes and visits to give support. The family still visits and remains close to the school.

Clara M. Jett, *Principal (Judith M. Reed, Principal at time of recognition), K – 6, 319 Students*

ST. MARY'S ELEMENTARY SCHOOL, ST. MARY'S, GA

St. Mary's is one of five elementary schools located in Camden County, the fastest growing county in Georgia. The population of this previously rural county has grown from 13,000 in 1980 to over 30,000 in 1991. The town of St. Mary's has grown from 3600 in 1980 to over 8500 in 1991. This phenomenal growth is a result of the construction and opening of Kings Bay Naval Base, a Trident nuclear submarine port. During the last decade, the Camden County School System has progressed from one of the smallest rural districts in Georgia to the fastest growing one, increasing now by 500 students per year. The impact of this growth on St. Mary's Elementary has been tremendous. This growth has prompted diversity among the student population which includes 76% Caucasian, 21% African-American, 2% Asian-American, and 1% Hispanic.

According to parent and community feedback, an attribute of St. Mary's Elementary that clearly distinguishes the school from other schools is its program of comprehensive services for children. Staff is said to be sensitive to what is in a child's heart, as well as what's in his head. Because they deal with cultural, demographic, and economic realities, they must serve as a "hub," integrating and focusing multiple community resources on young children. The school identifies and coordinates the social networks necessary for children to become healthy, motivated, and productive:

• Special child/family needs are identified through staff observation, conferences with students and parents, and through referrals by the guidance counselor or other staff members.

• Various agencies and organizations are utilized to provide support or intervention for children and training for staff. School staff work closely with Cumberland Health Services, Psychiatric Health Services, and Charter Hospital. Counselors and therapists from these agencies collaborate with teachers on strategies for working with children. They sometimes participate in the Student Study Team process and in special education placement meetings.

- The school district has a full-time licensed social worker who works with children and their families and serves as a liaison to the Department of Family and Children Services. She also refers families to the county mental health agency and Camden House, a refuge for abused women and children.
- The school makes every attempt to meet the physical and social needs of children. They provide a breakfast program as part of the school nutrition program. An after-school day-care program provides a nurturing environment for students who might otherwise become "latchkey" children.
- The school district employs a full-time, registered nurse. She provides counseling and referral services for parents concerning such problems as head lice and hygiene and makes home visits when needed. She conducts hearing and vision tests for students experiencing problems. She provides parent education opportunities throughout the year.
- The school had a local pediatrician speak on child abuse and a health counselor present a session entitled "AIDS and Your Child."
- The school system operates an adult literacy program and frequently serves as a referral agent for this program.
- Other local resources that are utilized to serve students are: Lions Club—provides eyeglasses for students with visual impairments; First Baptist Church—sponsors a community clothes closet for needy families; Social Sororities—prepare and donate holiday meals and gifts of clothing and toys for students and their families; PTA—conducts several fund-raisers and other school-related activities to provide both financial and volunteer support for students and their families; Kiwanis Club—coordinated a county-wide Christmas for Kids program for needy children; Salvation Army—provides clothing and other services for needy families; DFACS (Dept. of Family and Children Services)—offers numerous services including supplemental financial support and child abuse/neglect intervention; United Way—supplies a variety of special services for both children and adults residing within Camden County; and Coastal Area Public Health Services—offers many public health services.

Barbara Howard Christmas, Principal, K – 5, 746 Students

The school serves special needs students and their families as a resource center by functioning as an information disseminator for both community organizations and locally operated state/federal agencies. Essentially, the school is a starting point for children and families with special needs seeking help. By providing parents with information about existing resources, groups, and agencies, the school links families with services and later provides follow-up activities to ensure that children and their families receive necessary assistance. A local community resource file is housed at the Camden County Board of Education office to which faculty and staff members have access.

COLLABORATION WITH EDUCATIONAL INSTITUTIONS AND COMMUNITY GROUPS

There is an old African saying that "it takes a whole village to educate a child." The potential of a parent involvement program will be enhanced if it is treated as an integrated strategy with three distinct features: a means of attracting family members to the school; a means of reaching families at home; and a clearly supported, school-controlled way of engaging teachers in creating new kinds of connections with parents and other community resources (Davies, 1991). It is often that link to other educational institutions and community services that can truly fulfill the school's outreach strategy. The school may be limited in its potential to meet the divergent educational needs of its communities. Similarly, it is likely that it cannot meet most complex family-oriented social, financial, or mental health needs. To this end, successful schools have increasingly developed access to support networks for their children and their families.

Successful schools also understand the benefits of working relationships with colleges and universities. Those schools fortunate enough to have such institutions in reasonable proximity have a ready source for active research, consultation, and staff development.

Additionally, the financial impact of quality schooling continues to establish barriers to school improvement. To meet the ever-increasing demands of educating today's youth, many schools have formed active partnerships with local and regional businesses and corporations. These partnerships often provide reciprocal benefits. In return for financial or capital resource donations by corporations, schools may provide basic skills instruction for low achieving corporate members, computer training, or have its band or chorus perform at special activities. In any event, many schools have found a valuable resource through these partnerships.

The Best Schools—Collaboration With Educational Institutions And Community Groups

Several illustrations of how the Best Schools have utilized educational and community resources are provided next.

COMO PARK ELEMENTARY SCHOOL, LANCASTER, NY

Como Park Elementary School is located in suburban Buffalo, New York, in the village of Lancaster. Como Park serves approximately 500 students who come from middle socioeconomic households. Most of the students live in single-family dwellings in the immediate attendance area of the school. Parents of the students are blue- and white-collar workers who highly value education and the role it plays in the lives of their children.

Como Park has begun a major effort with CitiBank, which through a competitive grant process, has provided a $20,000 grant for reading materials, AV equipment, and funds for a writers' festival that was held for students in Lancaster and two other adjoining school districts. Volunteers are provided to read to children on a regular basis. This is proven to be a most beneficial partnership because it is ongoing. Not only do they provide initial funds, but their workers will provide assistance. It is anticipated that this is just the beginning of a long relationship between the school and CitiBank.

The school also received a $35,000 grant from the village of Lancaster to install playground equipment for children at the school. This furthers the goal of being a major educational and social force in the community by having the school available in the evening and on weekends.

In addition, contact has been made with Ecology and Environment, Inc., a large corporation that deals with ecological issues. A committee met with them to discuss their role in the community, and its vice president came to speak to the fourth and fifth grade students. The school is hoping to facilitate further partnerships with this corporation in the future.

Como Park has been a member of the Northeast Regional Lab for two years and has made application to become part of its restructuring consortium for elementary schools. Como Park also acts as a training site for area colleges and universities and has hosted over thirty student teachers during these past two years from Buffalo State College, Damien College, D'Youville College, and Houghton College. They also worked closely with the area Teacher Center and on two different occasions has requested workshops to be established for the staff, which has helped train teachers in whole language and cooperative learning. The positive effects of this program can be seen in the classroom on a daily basis. The school has volunteered and been accepted as a site for the Lancaster Recreation Department for the summer recreation program.

Como Park has taken advantage of area business programs that stimulate and motivate children. This includes the "McDonald Tree Program," which enabled every child to receive a free tree from McDonald's. The "Pizza Hut Book-It Program" has motivated children to read many books. The "Ponderosa Attendance Certificate Program" has been helpful in encouraging better attendance in school.

The school also avails itself of the many educational opportunities that abound in the community. Schools visit the Lancaster Historical Museum, Opera House, Post Office, Fire and Sheriff Departments, and the Village Hall. Students are encouraged to take advantage of the Lancaster Youth Bureau remedial program, drug awareness program, summer recreation program, and summer musical program.

Como Park has been actively involved in the Institute for the Arts in Education program. This unique program makes it possible for teachers, students, and professional performers to work together and participate in the various arts.

Dr. Andrea Stein, *Principal, K – 5, 498 Students*

SANIBEL ELEMENTARY SCHOOL, SANIBEL, FLORIDA

Sanibel Elementary School has the unique privilege of being a cornerstone in an environmentally concerned community. The school is located on Sanibel, a barrier island in Lee County, Florida. It is surrounded on three sides by J.N. "Ding" Darling National Wildlife Refuge. This unique environmental feature, as well as the support of many community resources, has helped Sanibel develop its fine educational program.

The school works together with community groups and educational institutions to provide enrichment for children. Volunteers from the N.J. "Ding" Darling National Wildlife Refuge and teachers at Sanibel help students to become "environmental experts" through The Junior Naturalist Program.

The Citizens Responsibility in a Democratic Society (CRIDS) program prepares children to sit in the chairs of city government officials (mayor, city council, fire chief, police chief, etc.) and run Sanibel for a day. On Student Government Day in May, the "elected" officials hold a mock council meeting at Sanibel City Hall. The city of Sanibel provides plaques and a special banquet for all fifth graders and their parents.

The City of Sanibel Recreation Department cooperates with the school by testing each child's swimming ability through the Little Red Schoolhouse Swim Program.

At Edison Community College, the Young Authors' Conference is held in the spring. Young authors write and publish bound books and have the opportunity to meet with nationally known authors of children's literature. Also on campus, "College for Kids" is a series of programs developed especially for children, such as computer literacy, art, and music.

Children participating in the Marine Biology Program begin the study of shells with a visit from a conchologist. Members of the Sanibel Shell Club instruct the fifth graders in the study of marine biology. Fifth graders man the Live Shell Exhibit at the Sanibel Shell Fair, an annual event attended by over 10,000 people.

New to the school is the C&S Banking Program. The manager of the island branch is teaching fourth grade students how to set up and operate a bank. The bank is open for schoolwide use. Members of the Library Kids Club serve as volunteers at the local library. Children shelve books, read to young children, and make visual displays. Recently, the Sanibel Library provided the opportunity for children to produce a shadow puppet show. The Lee County School Board sponsors enrichment and remedial classes in the summer. Also, children can participate in the local swim team Sanibel Water Attack Team (SWAT), at the recreation complex. Children can take after-school art classes at the Big Arts gallery. The ultimate community/school collaboration is KIDSPLAY. The workforce for this playground included members of civic organizations, city officials, winter visitors, local island residents, teachers, parents, and children. The playground was constructed in five days in the fall of 1989 through the generosity of the community, which provided money, materials, and time. Volunteer workers continue to provide maintenance for the upkeep of the playground. Finally, students are involved in community service including UNICEF, Salvation Army Food Drive, and Goodwill Clothing Drive.

Barbara T. Ward, *Principal, K – 5, 255 Students*

HAVRE MIDDLE SCHOOL, HAVRE, MONTANA

Havre Middle School is a rural school serving approximately 631 students in grades six through eight. Approximately 18% of the students are Native American, with 1% from other minorities. Twenty-five percent of the student population qualifies for free or reduced lunch. Student mobility rates vary, but usually range between 24% to 28% of the student population.

The school runs as if there are six separate schools under one roof. Each one is coordinated by a teaching team charged with teaching skill levels using varied methods deemed appropriate by the team. These six schools are tied together through a traditional department head structure that assures that subject area content and skill development are met regardless of the methods employed by the teams. This environment encourages extensive experimentation and risk-taking due to the fact that measurement of objectives is assured regardless of how students attain the information.

The Community Education Program in the schools offers a wide variety of programs and educational assistance for all ages. Community Education works with the local Montana State University Extension office to put together various workshops, including, but not limited to, health, parenting skills, historical programs, financial programs, and a continuing series of free lunch-hour programs on a variety of topics. Community Education also has access to many local and state resources. These people and agencies present programs on specific areas to school students, volunteer to work as mentors with gifted and talented students or at-risk students, and teach various after-school enrichment classes. Every summer, Community Education offers a two week computer camp for third to sixth grade students, using the middle school's computer lab. The Jaycees use the schools for various student programs. The community uses the gyms for dance clubs and sporting events. Specific examples of partnership with Northern Montana College, a four-year branch of the State University system, include a 2 + 2 program for vocational education, which is an articulated four-year curriculum that includes the last two years of high school and two years of college; advanced placement courses at the college gifted high school for juniors and seniors; utilization of college staff to conduct professional development for teachers; sharing facilities and technology; placement of college teaching cadets in the public schools; and college students serving as volunteer tutors. The public schools and college have formalized their linkages through an agreement called "Project Havre" in which administrative staff from the college and school district explore new ways to collaborate and strengthen existing linkages. The District is entering formalized agreements with Montana Power and Burlington Northern for Adopt-a-School programs in which the businesses will commit their resources and manpower to one of the district schools. Athletic clinics are held at Havre Middle School and sponsored jointly by Northern Montana College and the District.

D. Jeff Pratt, *Principal, Grades 6 – 8, 631 Students*

SUMMARY

The accumulated evidence overwhelmingly supports the importance of parent involvement in children's education. Some parents have the skills and the motivation to foster both cooperative opportunities and achievement motivation. More importantly, parents who do not have these skills can readily acquire them if the school makes a concerted effort to reach out and facilitate the training of parents. This can be most successful if the school: 1) takes a proactive, positive role in creating a trusting, responsive climate; 2) seeks parent input in determining the needs appropriate to the involvement initiatives, 3) is willing to be flexible in meeting those needs by taking the program to homes, neighborhoods, and workplaces; 4) provides resources beyond the school to assist parents with complex family issues; and 5) inherently respects the values and cultures of the family.

The research shows that when teachers and administrators are strongly committed to drawing parents into their children's education, the outcomes for the child, family, teacher, and school are almost exclusively positive.

REFERENCES

Becher, Rhoda. (1986). "Parents and Schools," *ERIC Digest, ERIC Clearinghouse on Elementary and Early Childhood Education*. Urbana, IL

Chrispeels, Janet H. (1991). "District Leadership in Parent Involvement," *Phi Delta Kappan* (January):367–371.

Dauber, Susan L. and Joyce L. Epstein. (1989). "Parent Attitudes and Practices of Parent Involvement in Inner-City Elementary and Middle Schools," Johns Hopkins Center for Research in Elementary and Middle Schools, Report No. 33, Baltimore, MD.

Davies, Don. (1991). "Schools Reaching Out: Family, School, and Community Partnerships for Student Success," *Phi Delta Kappan* (January):376–382.

Epstein, Joyce. (1988). "How Do We Improve Programs for Parent Involvement?" *Educational Horizons* (66):58–59.

Henderson, A. (1988). "Parents are a School's Best Friend," *Phi Delta Kappan* (October):148–153.

Jones, Linda T. (1991). *Strategies for Involving Parents in Their Children's Education*, Fastback, No. 315, Bloomington, Indiana: Phi Delta Kappan Educational Foundation.

Liontos, Lynn Balster. (1992). *At-Risk Families and Schools Becoming Partners*: Eugene, OR: ERIC Clearinghouse on Educational Management.

U. S. Department of Education. (1986). *What Works: Research about Teaching and Learning*. Washington, D. C.

Warner, Izona. (1991). "Parents in Touch: District Leadership for Parent Involvement," *Phi Delta Kappan* (January):372–375.

PART TWO

8500 INSTRUCTIONAL HOURS—THE ELEMENTARY CURRICULUM

CHAPTER 6

The Language Arts

LANGUAGE arts instruction occupies as much as 40% of a child's instructional day, 3400 hours of a child's journey from kindergarten through grade 8. This chapter looks at the following questions concerning how this time is best spent in preparing children for their lives now and for life in the 21st century:

- What does theory say about what children should learn and how they should be taught in language arts classrooms?
- How have the Best Schools successfully translated theory into practice in language arts?
- How do the Best Schools assess what children know and what they can do?
- How have the effective programs been developed and implemented; what were the resources needed for development and support?
- What do case studies of Best Schools show about highly successful language arts instruction in four very different community contexts?
- Finally, what are some of the practices, programs and resources used by the Best Schools, which are widely available to other program developers?

WHAT CHILDREN SHOULD LEARN

According to the National Goals of Education,

By the year 2000, every adult American will be literate and will possess the knowledge and skills necessary to compete in a global economy and exercise the rights and responsibilities of citizenship.

The goal of language instruction has always been to develop literate citizens; however, what constitutes the literacy needs for every adult in the 1990s or the year 2000 is far different than it was 100 or 50 years ago. Over the past ten years, educational organizations such as the International Reading Association (IRA), the National Council of Teachers of English (NCTE), and the Modern Language Association have developed expectations for what children should know and be able to do. Currently, the bipartisan National Standards Task Force on Standards and Testing is working to develop national standards for English for grades 4, 8, and 12. In addition to national efforts to define what children should know, numerous states and thousands of teachers and experts in the field of communication and learning have worked to develop outcome objectives or proficiencies to serve as a basis for language arts instruction in states, schools, and classrooms. The results of these efforts have been definitions of literacy that require very high levels of comprehension, fluency, transference, interpretation, analysis, and appreciation in reading, writing, and speaking. Based on the published guidelines developed by the professional associations and a review of curriculum frameworks from states, the Council for Basic Education has published content and performance standards applicable to elementary/middle school students. These standards are representative of the growing consensus of what children should know and, more importantly what children should be able to do; they are typical of the standards already central to instruction in the Best Schools:

STANDARDS: A VISION FOR LEARNING ENGLISH

Grade 4

- Use prior knowledge to comprehend unfamiliar oral or written texts.
- Employ a variety of strategies for dealing with unfamiliar words and meanings in texts.
- Respond personally to texts, including poems, essays, stories, and expository texts in both print and electronic media.
- Use other readers' experiences with, responses to, and interpretations of texts to strengthen or change interpretation.
- Listen to literature, appreciating its sounds and cadences.
- Read and write; find pleasure and satisfaction in reading and writing.

Grade 8

- Read daily and accurately, making valid inferences; judge literature critically on the basis of personal response and literary quality.
- Write in different styles and for different purposes—personal experience narrative, story, report, communication, poem, summary, and research paper.
- Generate ideas for writing, select and arrange them, find appropriate modes for expressing them, and evaluate and revise what has been written.
- Speak clearly and expressively about ideas and concerns; adapt words and strategies to situations and audiences. (Council for Basic Education, 1991)

HOW CHILDREN LEARN—HOW CHILDREN ARE TAUGHT

For many years, educators worked within a paradigm that held that children learn primarily "part-to-whole." This view of how children acquire knowledge had profound effects on the decisions made in schools concerning curriculum, lesson objectives, instructional methods, materials selected for classroom use, organization of children for instruction, use of time, and assessment practices. The dominant belief that children learn "part-to-whole" led to a curriculum based on the sequential acquisition of discrete skills and instruction organized to maximize the effectiveness of learning the parts. Grammar, handwriting, reading, literature, and spelling were treated as separate entities with separate time slots, separate basal texts, and separate activities. In turn, each content area was divided into finite subskills taught in a given sequence. Two learning assumptions supported this instructional model. The first was that learning is linear; that is, it is necessary to master skills in an identified sequence. Each individual skill, therefore, must be learned before the subsequent skill. As a result, remedial programs focused on reteaching specific skills identified as deficient through testing. A second assumption of this model was that the student who mastered each discrete skill would automatically, or with little direct instruction, be able to put the skills together, emerging as a critical reader, a fluent writer.

Consistent with this view of learning, students were ability grouped to reduce variability within the class or between classes, particularly in reading. These "homogeneous groupings," usually three per grade—high, middle, and low—were thought to facilitate individual learning. Groups rotated, with each working through a separate basal directly with the teacher for twenty to forty minutes per day, while the other two groups did seatwork, usually in workbooks correlated with the basal. This view of learning reached its extreme in the late 1960s and early 1970s, with the advent of "programmed learning," which envisioned each student working alone on an individualized program geared to meet a set of sequenced objectives at his/her own pace.

The emphasis on the acquisition of discreet skills, close monitoring of these skills, and remediation of skills was credited with increasing standardized test scores in the late 1970s and early 1980s, especially in disadvantaged educational settings. The commercial standardized tests and state-developed minimal proficiency tests of the era paralleled the prevalent view of learning, instructional objectives, and the content of textbooks; in other words, the tests assessed the acquisition of discreet skills.

A different type of test, the National Assessment of Educational Progress (NAEP), confirmed that there were slight gains in lower level skills and concepts between 1971 and 1988 (NAEP, 1990). However, the NAEP also assessed higher level applications and concepts, such as the synthesizing of information from specialized reading materials and the understanding of material read. For these higher order skills, the NAEP found that there were almost no gains during the same period. The apparent differences in evaluation results between commercial standardized tests and the NAEP and their concomitant impact on a district's educational program rests with the decisions about what is important for students to learn as well as what and how they learn. The NAEP is much more aligned with emerging national and state standards.

Over the past twenty years, research on how students learn has challenged the assumptions on which the discreet/linear skill model was based. Numerous studies have shown that the acquisition of isolated skills is not positively related to fluency in reading, writing, or speaking (Goodman, 1964). For example, learning grammar out of the context of writing does not improve writing ability (Mellon, 1969; Sherwin, 1969; Hillocks 1986). Studies of ability grouping of students have shown that, rather than helping lower ability students to overcome deficits, homogeneous grouping increases the learning gap and undermines self-esteem (Oakes, 1985; Slaven, 1987). By April of first grade, significant differences in self-esteem and the child's perception of him/herself as a learner can be seen between high and low reading groups within classes (Ogden, 1992). Effective school studies have shown the importance of time-on-task and the negative effects of unsupervised seatwork (Fisher et al., 1978; Brophy and Good, 1985). In the typical rotating group reading program, the teacher works with one group for a third of the instructional time, and each child works independently for two-thirds of the instructional time, the inverse of effective practice.

During the late 1970s and 1980s, research on learning and brain development began to lead to a revised view of what is important for students to learn, how children learn, and how instruction should be organized to maximize learning. "Optimizing the use of the human brain means using the brain's infinite capacity to make connections and understanding what conditions maximize this process" (Caine and Caine, 1991, p. 9).

As part of the reassessment of how students learn, research distinguished between *surface knowledge*, i.e., the memorization of facts, procedures, and applications, and *meaningful knowledge*, connected learning that makes sense to the learner. This expanded view of what children should learn and the research on how children learn meaningful knowledge led to the development of a whole or integrated approach to teaching language. Five assumptions underlie the integrated language arts (ILA) model. The first is that teaching must provide a student with experiences that enable him/her to develop connections among content and skills, i.e., to perceive patterns and to make connections cumulatively and over time. For example, vocabulary and grammar are best learned when they are integrated into a total reading/writing experience.

A second assumption is that learning is natural and motivational; thus, the classroom should be organized around natural approaches to learning. For example, children have learned to speak and have developed an average vocabulary of 10,000 words by the time they enter school (ASCD, 1992). They accomplish this without memorizing rules of grammar, lists of spelling words, or rules of phonics. The model holds that to learn how to read, write and speak, students should engage actively in reading, writing, speaking, and listening activities, much more so than the discrete/linear model suggested.

A third assumption is that, rather than fragmenting content, blocks of time should be set aside for the integration of the strands of language arts with instructional emphasis on making connections among writing, reading, speaking, and listening. Individual skills continue to be taught; however, they should be taught in meaningful contexts that emphasize higher order thinking skills.

A fourth assumption is that students learn best when they are not placed in ability groups. Lower and average ability students benefit most from whole class, interest groups, and flexible and changing skill support groups; however, high ability students are not negatively impacted (Slaven, 1987). In fact, the integrated curriculum brings to all students an instructional approach that has traditionally been advocated and reserved for gifted students. The flexibility of the integrated language program provides challenges and opportunities for all students.

The fifth assumption is that assessment is best embedded in the instructional process; in other words, it is part of the instructional process rather than an add-on to instruction. Assessment should provide evidence of not only what a student knows but also what a student can do. As much as possible, it should be performance-based.

THE BEST SCHOOLS—LANGUAGE ARTS: THEORY INTO PRACTICE

The Best Schools, whether suburban, inner-city urban, or rural, teach their students in integrated language arts (ILA) programs that focus on making meaning and connections among the strands of the language arts. They are committed to achieving verifiable outcomes for all students in reading, writing, and speaking. Their curricula are based on the theory and research on learning that support integrated teaching and learning of reading, writing, and speaking. They are using and developing various forms of more authentic assessment, which are aligned with their curriculum and local, state, and/or national standards. In practice, the integrated language arts programs in the Best Schools have many characteristics in common. However, integrated language arts or whole language is an approach to curriculum, teaching, and assessment. It does not come packaged as a series of textbooks. Therefore, the ILA program must be developed to fit within the context of each school.

The Best Schools—Four Case Studies in Language Arts: The Contexts

MIRABEAU B. LAMAR ELEMENTARY, CORPUS CHRISTI, TX

Mirabeau B. Lamar School, a two-story brick structure built in 1941, is set in a neighborhood struggling with urban blight. The neighborhood residents are the constant victims of drugs and violence. Most students live in two- to five-room rented houses. There is a 31% turnover of students each year. Ninety-eight percent of the students are Hispanic. Ninety-six percent of the students qualify for free or reduced price lunch. However, Lamar is a "haven" for children, a school community totally focused on making every child a winner and a school where all children learn. Students, principal, staff, parents, and the business community are all members of the learning partnership. The school motto is, "Lamar is a great place to learn." Children and staff have an "I Can" attitude. In reading, 81% and, in math, 97% score above the 50th percentile on the California Achievement Test (CAT), 100% of the third graders meet the reading mastery level, and 100% of the fifth graders meet the writing standard on the Texas Assessment of Academic Skills. The average daily student attendance rate is 99%. In addition to Mirabeau B. Lamar, five other schools have been recognized as Blue Ribbon Schools in Corpus Christi.

Faye Webb, *Principal, Pre-K – 5, 331 Students*

UNION SCHOOL, UNIONVILLE, CT

Union School is one of four elementary schools in a suburban community of Farmington. The school serves an economically mixed area, with about 10% receiving free lunch and two affluent housing developments. Four percent of the students are bused from elementary schools in the city of Hartford. ILA is used districtwide. The over-arching goal is for every student to use language to create meaning, acquire knowledge, and foster a lifelong love of reading. The board, the central administration, principal, and school staff will never be satisfied until every child meets the goal; therefore, the language arts program is always evolving. The median national percentile on the CAT in language arts is 87. The middle school in the district is also a Blue Ribbon School.

Roberta Kurlantzick, *Principal, Pre-K – 5, 410 Students*

CAL ELEMENTARY SCHOOL, LATIMER, IA

In 1979, *Phi Delta Kappan* magazine called CAL "small, rural and good"; in 1993, CAL is "small, rural and excellent." CAL really is small! The district's 346 children attend school in one building from age three until they graduate from high school. Within the building, CAL Elementary serves a growing population in grades Pre-K to 6. More than a quarter of the students come from low-income families, and there have been many economic obstacles to developing and maintaining programs of excellence. However, there is a strong belief in the value of small schools. The motto of the school is "A Small School with Big Ideas." CAL High School was recognized as a School of Excellence in 1987; therefore, CAL is one of the few districts in the country where every student Pre-K through twelfth grade attends a Blue Ribbon School. The median I.T.B.S. score for sixth grade is 90 for language and 79 for reading.

Cynthia Martinek, *Principal, Pre-K – 6, 222 Students*

GREENBROOK SCHOOL, KENDALL PARK, NJ

Greenbrook School draws its students from seven distinct suburban lower to upper middle-income neighborhoods. The racial breakdown is 76% Caucasian, 6% African-American and 17% Asian. More than a dozen different languages are spoken in the homes of the students. The school community has built a program for children, which recognizes the importance of children's expressions of their own ideas and experiences. Ninety-three percent of the students score above the 50th percentile in reading on the CTBS test. Greenbrook's Early Childhood Program was featured in the Newsweek magazine cover story entitled "How Kids Learn" in 1989. Greenbrook is one of three schools in the South Brunswick School District to be recognized as a Blue Ribbon School.

Stephanie Craib, *Principal, K – 6, 349 Students*

CLASS ORGANIZATION AND INSTRUCTIONAL TIME

ILA in the Best Schools is block scheduled for approximately 600 minutes per week. Class sections are heterogeneously assigned. Within the class, children are not divided into ability-based reading groups; instead, teachers work with the class as a whole for many activities and form temporary groups based on interest in a particular book or the need to introduce or reinforce a particular set of skills. Frequently, students also work in cooperative groups, pairs, and individually. Class projects may involve cross-age groups, with some schools being nongraded or multi-aged grouped (Richmond, VT; Greenbrook, NJ; Loma Heights, NM; Ashley River Creative Arts, SC; Craycroft, AZ).

The Best Schools—Class Organization Illustrations

MIRABEAU B. LAMAR, TX

All students in kindergarten through grade five receive approximately three hours of heterogeneously grouped integrated language arts instruction per day. Class sizes are at the state-mandated limit of twenty-two. Some grouping is done within the class based on learning style or need. Typically, small groups of students who might experience difficulty with new material are *pre-taught* for five to ten minutes before the material is introduced to the whole class the next day. These same students may also receive *post-teaching* in small groups during independent reading or writing time to reinforce the learning of new material. The focus is on *accelerating learning* and preventing the need for remediation.

CAL, IA

Language arts is taught in 40-minute blocks for kindergarten, 150-minute blocks for Grades 1–4 and 120 minutes for Grades 5–6. There is a single section of twenty-six to thirty children per grade level. Each class through grade 6 has a part-time aide. Within classes, students are divided into flexible groups for skill development and literature for part of the instructional block; however, there are no blue birds, red birds, or green birds in CAL. A team (teacher/teacher or teacher/aide) plans the activities for each group and the class as a whole. Cooperative learning tactics are used extensively within the classroom and across grade levels to offer students opportunities to share reading, writing, speaking, and dramatic experiences. For example, the presence of high school students in the building allows them to work with fifth graders on writing projects. Cross-age groupings of grades 1, 2, 3 and 4, 5, 6 have been piloted.

GREENBROOK, NJ

All students are heterogeneously grouped. Every year, the school is reorganized by staff to determine what combinations of mixed grades and straight grades will best serve the needs of the students.

CURRICULUM

The goal of instruction is for students to become fluent and self-motivated writers, readers, and speakers. In most of the Best Schools, the curriculum is organized around themes (i. e., "people around the world," "discovery") determined by individual teachers and/or school or district committees. Frequently, the chosen themes correlate with social studies and/or science curricula at the given grade level. Every opportunity is taken to make explicit connections among content areas.

The Best Schools—Curriculum Illustrations

UNION, CT

The faculty and principal establish annual instructional school goals. Teachers are required to write one performance goal to reasonably improve student learning and one professional growth goal each year. Within the language arts curriculum framework, each teacher develops an overall plan for implementing the ILA program in their class for the year. The plan is then discussed and mutually agreed upon by the teacher and the principal. Grade level teachers use common planning time to share ideas and to review student progress. The language arts teacher-leaders from the four schools in the district, with input from grade level teachers, meet with the reading consultant to determine titles by grade level and to develop guides for each book.

CAL, IA

The integrated language program is organized around thematic units that emphasize reading skills, literature, writing, and speaking. Skill development is balanced with a more holistic approach to instruction. The teacher and aide plan the activities for each group. The ILA program is articulated K−12.

GREENBROOK, NJ

The school's academic program is based on a district-wide framework that defines the core of the program and those skills and concepts children are expected to achieve. Beyond the core, each teacher or team has autonomy to design projects, select textbooks and materials, and use strategies and techniques they think are appropriate. Teachers use a whole-language approach to reading, writing, and oral communications. Classrooms provide language-rich environments. Children keep journals from day one of school; they rewrite books and charts that they read or that are read to them; they turn their ideas into murals and playlets; they write reports on subjects of interest. Teachers keep track of language proficiency, retaining reading samples, writing samples, and story retelling in portfolios that follow a student from kindergarten through second grade.

READING

The reading strand of language arts is taught as a process that actively involves students with print. Since students learn to read by reading, students must want to read and must develop a love of literature. To aid in this process, students are usually read to every day. Research confirms that children who are read to early and often in life become the best and most motivated readers. The Best Schools take full advantage of this knowledge. For example, in Tiskelwah, West Virginia, it is required that all children be read to thirty minutes every day. The schools also use many strategies to encourage parents to read to their children on a regular basis at home. They orient parents to the need for this activity and facilitate the process by sending books home, which may be ones selected by the teacher or child or even books written by the children. The Best Schools are very successful in getting this kind of parent involvement, whether the school is inner-city, suburban, or rural. The "Reading at Home" program in Candelwood, Maryland is an example of such a program. In cases where parents are unavailable to read to a child, it is not uncommon for school volunteers, secretaries, custodians, teachers, older students, and/or the principal to read regularly with a child.

Since the whole is emphasized first in ILA classrooms, whole books are read starting in kindergarten. In the early grades, books are read and re-read several times; students read core books related to the specific themes as a whole class or in interest groups, read them again in pairs, and again independently. These core books are usually the ones that lead to major theme-related projects. Comprehension is enhanced through such activities as webbing, story maps, and pair-share. Groups of students select and read books based on interest. In addition, each student also selects and reads books from the class and/or school library, choosing to read a wide variety of materials including fiction, nonfiction, literature, original source materials, news articles, and materials from other courses.

LITERATURE

A comprehensive literature program is an important component of ILA. Through assigned and self-selected books, students become familiar with literary genres, authors, style, and cultural traditions. Some schools use literature anthologies in addition to class and group sets of books. The Junior Great Books (NDN) program is used in some of the schools (Gulliver Academy, FL; Pearl, NY; Wantagh, NY). The Best Schools use a host of strategies to motivate students to read. Time is set aside every day for silent reading. In some cases, the entire school, including the teachers and principal, read at the same time. Two examples of this approach are the "Excited about Reading" schoolwide silent reading program developed in Brookmeade, Tennessee, and the "Drop Everything And Read" (DEAR), used in such schools as Irwin, New Jersey and Wantagh, New York. Individual teachers also build time within the school day for children to read. It is common for an individual student to be reading three different books at the same time—a core book, a group interest book, and an individual selection. Teachers model reading by actually reading with and then sharing their reading experiences with the class. Also, contests and reading logs are used to motivate and monitor children's reading. Some of the contests are local in nature; others, such as Book-It (Baker's Chapel, SC; Brookmead, TE; John Grasse, PA) sponsored by Pizza Hut, are national. The "Children's Choice Program" is a national program that involves children in critiquing new books (Wantagh, NY). Booklists encourage children to read during the summer recess.

It is not just the quantity of books that children read that is central to an ILA approach. Children are taught to reflect on what they read in conferences with the teacher and other students and through their writing. The focus is on comprehension, meaning, and making connections. They are taught to read the lines, to read between the lines, and to read beyond the lines. Students engage in prereading activities, active reading, review activities, and a wide spectrum of response strategies. They read for various purposes. Some of what they read connects across the curriculum with math, science, social studies, health, and the arts. Meaning, connections, and transference are emphasized throughout the day.

In most of the Best Schools, basal reading texts are still used, but not as the center of instruction. The basal texts are used for introducing and reinforcing specific skills within a broader context of instruction and are also used as a source of literature. Usually, when the basal is used, all students use the same level book. Phonics are still taught in lower grades, but more often in the context of stories and without emphasis on memorization of phonic rules. Teachers plan lessons that recognize the variations in learning styles within the classroom.

The Best Schools—Reading/Literature Strand Illustrations

MIRABEAU B. LAMAR, TX

An extensive array of classical literature, as well as informational articles and stories relating to science, math, and social studies, are used to expand and enrich student experiences while developing and reinforcing skills such as summarizing and outlining. Students participate in many motivational reading projects such as Reading Rally, Reading Superbowl, Bluebonnet Award Promotion, V.I.P., Reader Week, and Newberry Mania. The Open Court Reading program is used along with the literature. All students within the same grade use the same book. Each lesson includes review and enrichment activities.

UNION, CT

Students read a wide range of materials for a variety of purposes—fiction, nonfiction, biography, drama, folk tales, and poetry. Instruction emphasizes the student's ability to self-monitor comprehension through flexible use of reading strategies. Essential reading subskills are taught within the context of reading and writing. Students begin with predictable text in primary grades and move to more complex texts in upper grades. Criterion-referenced tests, which are part of the basal textbook series, are used to benchmark acquisition of specific skills and to determine areas needing concentration. Only a single grade level—appropriate basal reader is used in the classroom. It is used with flexible groups to teach or reinforce specific skills. Some teachers and many students do not use the basal at all in a given year. Literature is the heart of the reading strand of the curriculum. Many of the literature selections are linked to social studies and science topics to facilitate reading across the curriculum. Children are surrounded with books, at some grade levels, using several dozen titles available in sets of ten to twelve copies each. Instruction focuses on the strategies good readers use.

WRITING

Writing in an ILA program is taught as a process and includes pre-writing, drafting, revising, editing, and publishing. This approach to the teaching of writing gained wide acceptance through the Bay Area Writing Project and the New Jersey Writing Project (NDN) almost twenty years ago. Students begin to write in kindergarten using picture writing, inventive spelling, and dictation. Conventional spelling is introduced gradually and in the context of reading and writing. Writing is frequently linked to what the children are reading. Students learn to write in order to inform, persuade, narrate, describe, and entertain; they learn to consider the audience in their writing. They work in large, small, or cooperative groups or alone to review, critique, and edit work in progress prior to publication. Students write every day; they keep individual journals, share their writing with others, conference with the teacher, and reflect on their own writing. For example, Saigling, California, begins each day with three minutes of fluency writing. Brainstorming, drafting, critiquing, redrafting, and editing all lead to the "publishing" of the final work. The published work is what is displayed and formally assessed by the teacher and/or the student. Young authors' conferences are often held (Loma Heights, NM) to share the students' published works.

The Best Schools use many strategies to develop and recognize the published products of students. Most of the Best Schools use word processing and simple publishing programs to enable children to prepare work for publication. Elementary keyboarding and word processing skills are introduced as early as kindergarten and are enhanced throughout the elementary school years (Knowlton, UT; Birmingham, TX; Candlewood, MD; Mirabeau, TX; Ashley River Creative Arts, SC). Some of the software these elementary schools use include Word Processing for Kids, Bankstreet Writer III, Primary Editor and Primary Editor Plus, Children's Writing and Publishing, Apple Works, and Microsoft Works. Computers used for publishing include single stand-alone computers in classrooms, separate computer labs, and/or a cluster of computers in the library. In schools serving disadvantaged populations computers may be available for students to take home (Mirabeau, TX; Loma Heights, NM). The use of computers as tools also supports the development of technological literacy. Many of the Best Schools have established "publishing companies," which involve media specialists, children, and parent volunteers in laminating, collating, binding, and, in some cases, typing the final written work of individual students, groups, or classes. It is not unusual for hundreds of books a year to be published and added to the library. In some schools, every child adds a book to the library each year. When he/she moves on to middle school or high school, the child is given all of the books he/she has published, a longitudinal record of his/her achievement.   The published works are displayed in the classroom, shared with other grades, sent home to share with parents, combined into class books, and/or placed in the school library (Salanter Akiba Riverdale Academy, NY; Chaparral, CA; Bowdoin, NY; River Bend, MO; Wantagh, NY; Craycroft, AZ).

The Best Schools—Writing Strand Illustrations

MIRABEAU B. LAMAR, TX

Teachers work to develop and nurture a rich oral language that children use for their writing experience. Young children dictate to teachers, parents, and older students. Process writing begins with pictorial compositions and is extended to narrative, description, information narrative, informative, classification, and persuasive descriptive modes. Stories and literature are springboards for creative writing. Students write science journals, personal journals, learning logs, and letters to business and to pen pals.

Students are motivated to improve their writing through the use of computers; parents have joined with teachers to make students computer literate. All third graders learn keyboarding, using the pre-computer tutorial "Type-Right." The PTA has provided a computer for every classroom. In addition, a computer take-home project for the third to fifth grades allow students to borrow an Apple IIe computer and software for six weeks to compose at home.

UNION, CT

Reading and writing are integrated to support literacy and language development. Response journals and learning logs are used extensively. Grammar and usage are taught as part of the writing process, which includes the generating of ideas, drafting, discussing, revising, editing, publishing, and reflecting. Temporary spelling is utilized in the lower grades. The Daily Oral Language Program is used in each grade to teach editing skills in the context of writing. Instruction in speaking, listening, and viewing are also included. The student-teacher conference is considered central to improving writing. Children in grades 4 and 5 are taught word processing using Bank Street Writer III; they use the schools' twelve computers to produce drafts and final work. A parent-run publishing center types, binds, and publishes student books; in one year, over 700 books from all grade levels were produced.

CAL, IA

There is an articulated objective-based approach to writing at each grade level K–12. Assessments and examples of writing are taken routinely and shared with parents at conferences. Journal writing, creative writing, and pen pal letters augment the curriculum. The Great Mailrace encourages students to correspond with students across the nation. The "Read a Million Minutes" program provides motivation for reading. Lower and upper elementary students pair for "Book Buddy" and writing activities. Creative dramatics are integrated throughout the language arts program. The five-minute per day, Daily Oral Language Program, is used to support editing, thinking, and oral skills. A computer lab and individual classroom computers are used for publishing and to support skill development.

SPEAKING AND LISTENING

Speaking and listening are two important strands of the ILA program, for each helps students to develop self-confidence, to expand their understanding by questioning and responding, to problem solve, to clarify their ideas, and to develop social skills necessary for successful participation in the school and work community. Informal activities for speaking and listening include small and large group sharing, task-related talk, impromptu talks, dialogues, improvised dramatics, and reading aloud. Formal activities for speaking and listening include opportunities for formal presentations, panel discussions, note-taking, and demonstrations.

SUPPORT SKILLS AND STRATEGIES

Support skills and strategies underlie the ILA program. Specific skills may be taught prior to, during, or after a more holistic activity. For example, the five minute a day ''Daily Oral Language Program'' is used in a number of schools to reinforce editing skills and foster good grammar (Union, CT; CAL, IA; Tiskelwah, WV; Skyline, WA). Strategies, processes for doing something, are generally taught prior to an activity and reinforced subsequent to an activity. Thus, a reading skill might be to identify fact and fantasy in a story, whereas a reading strategy might be to create a story-map of that story to determine if the fact and fantasy remain consistent. A literature skill might be to discuss a character in a story. A literature strategy might focus on comparison and contrasting of two characters via a chart or graphic organizer. Writing skills might include editing one's own or another's paper for standard English spelling; a writing strategy might be to use webbing as a pre-writing activity in order to discover and to narrow down a topic. ''Talents Unlimited'' (NDN) is used in a number of schools to increase productive thinking and communication skills (Norfeldt, CT; Pearl, NY; Rawls Byrd, VA). ''Tactics for Thinking'' (Marzano and Paynter) is another set of strategies used to develop higher order thinking skills (T. F. Birmingham, TX; Baker's Chapel, SC; Saigling, TX).

Actively involving parents in the education and support for their children is a high priority of the Best Schools. Volunteers are used extensively in many of the schools. However, the importance of involving parents with their own child is also emphasized and specific strategies used to gain active parent support. Community organizations, business, and industry are also frequently involved with supporting learning. Pre-school programs focus on getting children ready for kindergarten.

The Best Schools—Support Skills and Strategy Illustrations

MIRABEAU B. LAMAR, TX

If you want to understand why children are so successful in learning to read, write, and speak at Lamar, you must also look beyond the curriculum to the practices that support all learning at the school. Every effort has been made to maximize learning. It is recognized that parents need to be involved in their children's learning. Because most of the children do not come from homes with phones, the principal, teachers, and aides go to the homes. In one typical six-week period, there were 170 parent conferences, and more than a third were home visits. The principal averages five to ten home visits a week. Every child who is absent for two days receives a visit from staff. The principal works personally with each new child and his/her parents and monitors the child's transition into the learning community. The result is a 99% attendance rate. Parents also come to school. In the same six-week period, there were 499 parent volunteer hours logged. Parent involvement and support is actively sought and highly valued at Lamar. Each six weeks, the principal and teachers hold conferences with parents by note, phone, or in person. The principal makes a practice of calling or visiting parents to congratulate them on their children's Honor Roll or other achievements. Parent letters are sent home explaining upcoming units and offering suggestions for at-home activities. Parents are provided with guidance and support, as well as a place to sharpen parenting skills. Ten foster grandparents work every day in the school.

Five businesses have adopted the school. They provide expertise, a career focus, and resources. They see their role as being directly involved with their future employees. Lamar is not a 9 A.M. to 3 P.M. school; there are before- and after-school activities. Lamar is obsessed with not letting any child ''fall through the cracks'' and holds the belief that every child will succeed.

CAL, IA

A public preschool has been maintained in the district for three to four year olds for more than twenty years. Combined with a two-day KinderKamp prior to entering kindergarten, these pre-school programs are considered important in a rural setting with few social contacts for children. Parenting classes are also held in conjunction with the PTA and community organizations.

SPECIAL NEED STUDENT

The focus in the Best Schools is clearly on development and on prevention of the need for *remediation*; however, there are still children who experience a lag in language-related development. Reading Recovery (NDN) is a frequently used program for the lowest achieving first grade children. In this nationally validated program, which is based on the research of Marie Clay from New Zealand, a highly and specifically trained teacher works one-on-one with each child thirty minutes per day for approximately sixteen weeks. The aim of the program is to correct the reading problem once and for all and return the child to the mainstream program (Twiskelwah, WV; Saigling, TX; Rawls Byrd, VA). Another program, H.O.T.S. – Higher Order Thinking (NDN), used in the upper grades, takes an alternative approach to reading remediation, which consists solely of higher order thinking activities. The aim of the program is to equip students with the conceptual skills needed to learn content in the regular class the first time it is taught (Greenbrook, NJ). IBM's Writing to Read, a computer-based lab program that links reading and writing, is used in some schools at the kindergarten and/or first grade level for remediation or language development support (Mirabeau, TX; T.F. Birmingham, TX; Baker's Chapel, SC; Craycroft, AZ; Saigling, TX). Schools that have developed their own remedial pull-out programs usually continue to use a whole-language approach in these classes and coordinate the activities with the regular classroom. Instead of pull-out programs, increased developmental support is being provided within the regular classroom in many of the Best Schools (Union, CT; Loma Heights, NM; Ashley River Creative Arts, SC). Another means of avoiding pulling students out from class is the use of before- and/or after-school programs (Skyline, WA; Loma Heights, NM). The Best Schools use combinations of strategies to decrease or eliminate the need for remediation. When extra assistance is needed, multiple strategies are used to eliminate learning problems as quickly as possible and so eliminate the need for further remediation.

The Best Schools – Special Need Student Illustrations

MIRABEAU B. LAMAR, TX

All learning modalities are incorporated into the regular instructional program. Attention is given to preferred learning style in assigning children to classes, and in some cases, students are flexibly grouped by learning style within class. However, instruction is not limited to one or two modalities. The majority of lessons include activities geared to the visual, auditory, and tactile kinesthetic learner. Higher order thinking skills, synthesis, and evaluation are emphasized, all of which facilitate the placement of most special education students in the regular classroom. Non-English speaking students are also accommodated in the classroom with in-class support from bilingual teachers. However, ESL students also receive intensive ESL instruction in small groups. All children at Lamar are eligible for Chapter 1 support. In addition to in-class instruction, kindergarten students use the IBM Writing to Read program. For grades 1–5, a Computer Assisted Instruction Laboratory is provided for children who need extra help on skill development. However, the focus of instruction is on prevention of learning problems and the provision of extra assistance in the classroom when needed. Achievement is reviewed every six weeks, and if a child begins to slip, immediate action is taken to provide additional help.

UNION, CT

The aim of the remedial program is to solve language problems in first grade. The Chapter 1 program allows first grade teachers to provide extended learning time to low functioning students within the classroom through the provision of aides who monitor and assist regular students during this time. In addition, the lowest functioning Chapter 1 students receive one-on-one instruction thirty minutes per day in the Program for Early Intervention and Literacy, a program developed locally by staff who have been trained in the *Reading Recovery* program. The program resulted last year in five out of every six students in the program reaching grade level.

CAL, IA

Special education students are not labeled and are mainstreamed into regular classes with the special education teacher and regular teacher team teaching. Developmental assistance is provided for Chapter 1 eligible students within the regular classroom.

GREENBROOK, NJ

First grade students who are at-risk in reading work individually outside the class in Reading Discovery (a variation on Reading Recovery). Older at-risk children work in small groups in the Higher Order Thinking Skills (H.O.T.S); this computer-based instruction develops fundamental thinking skills that underlie all learning (H.O.T.S. is a nationally validated program in the NDN).

ASSESSING WHAT STUDENTS KNOW AND CAN DO

Consistent with the emergence of new and higher standards for literacy, states have been actively involved in developing assessment processes that provide for higher order and more authentic measurement of reading and writing achievement. Many states now include writing samples that are holistically scored based on rubrics that are shared with schools and that can be used by teachers in the classroom to enhance instruction. State reading tests are beginning to include long passages or complete stories or narratives and require higher level narrative responses rather than multiple choice answer selection. Different forms of reading are assessed. State tests in New Jersey, for example, assess the student's ability to "read the lines," "read between the lines," and "read beyond the lines." Vermont is supplementing more traditional forms of assessment with portfolios of actual class work, which are scored according to established standards. A number of the Best Schools cite new state testing programs as much more in line with the goals of their ILA programs than traditional standardized tests. Some of the Best Schools are working with state and private agencies to develop valid alternative forms of assessment.

The Best Schools give high priority to assessment and are evolving new assessment approaches that provide better information about student learning. Most of the schools continue to give nationally normed standardized tests at least at some grade levels. The more recent editions of the popular standardized tests have attempted to place more emphasis on higher order assessment. However, the schools still consider these tests of limited validity in terms of current literacy standards and the ILA curriculum. They give the commercial standardized tests because of state regulations and federal and state program requirements and to assure school boards and parents that students are acquiring reading and writing skills and because there are few alternatives available to assess the higher standards for learning at the school or district level.

Assessment within the classroom and school is undergoing the greatest change. Rejected is the bell curve view of assessment designed to rank students and sort them into excellent, above average, average, below average, and failed groups. The goal is to determine what the student knows and can do in terms of criterion standards. It is expected that all children will meet the standards. For example, only the final product of writing, after drafts and editing, is assessed, frequently using teacher-, school-, district- or even state-developed rubrics. In addition, students learn to assess their own writing and reading as a significant component of the instructional process. Reading ability is evaluated through oral reading, writing, and individual teacher/student reading conferences. Writing portfolios of students' work are assessed over time to show individual growth and level of achievement, as well as overall class and school achievement. Acquisition of traditional skills is also monitored, through criterion-referenced tests, checklists, and reading and writing assignments. A most important feature of assessment in conjunction with ILA is the continuous use of data to plan instruction for the class, groups, and individual students.

The Best Schools—Assessment Illustrations

MIRABEAU B. LAMAR, TX

Assessment is an integral part of the total ILA program. Students are taught to edit their own work and model and critique for their classmates. Students learn to evaluate their own writing through a structured composition cycle. Portfolios, language acquisition, and development checklists and achievement test results are used regularly to assess and plan programs. The principal and teachers monitor grade sheets and individual student learning indicators every three- and six-week period.

UNION, CT

Reflection and self-assessment are integral parts of the language arts program. Samples of students' beginning and end-of-year writing are assessed and holistically scored in grades 3 and 5 according to the Connecticut Mastery Test (CMT) criteria with two teachers scoring each piece of writing. The principal frequently volunteers to serve as second reader. The CMT is given in grade 4 and is considered a valid measure of language arts. A multi-strand literacy assessment, which includes writing samples, dictation tests, running records, basal criterion tests, and word recognition is used in grades 1 and 2. In addition, at the end of the year, 94% of the students test to mastery level on basal criterion-referenced tests and Farmington Strategic Reading Assessment. Two forms of assessment that are used to provide teachers with insights on the learning process are the Metacognitive Strategy Index and the Temple Features Developmental Stages of Spelling Test.

CAL, IA

The school has been involved in the State Curriculum-Based Measurement norming project for four years. The assessment provides data from reading, math, and spelling for individual and class performance, which is consistent with the CAL curriculum in grades 2−6. Writing portfolios for assessment have been initiated.

GREENBROOK, NJ

The progress of all children, K−2, is monitored through a literacy portfolio, which includes four types of data: 1) criterion-referenced measures such as test of word construction or sight reading, 2) norm-referenced measures such as Concepts about Print from New Zealand, 3) samples of children's work including reading and writing samples and self-portraits, and 4) observational information including behavior checklists and child parent interviews. With researchers from Educational Testing Service (ETS), teachers have built a literacy scale that allows for ascertaining progress from grades K−2. Portfolios are shared with parents at conferences. As a measure of the degree to which a child enjoys reading, every child in grades 2−6 logs his or her self-selected reading selections.

THE BEST SCHOOLS: PROGRAM DEVELOPMENT AND SUPPORT OF LANGUAGE ARTS

The ILA Implementation Process

The Best Schools began the implementation of their ILA programs three to ten years ago and have agendas for further development of the program extending over the next three to five years. In many cases, the process writing component of ILA has been used in the Best Schools for ten to twenty years. It is important to note that implementing an ILA program is very different than the process used to adopt a new basal reading or English textbook series. Integration of the language arts requires administrative, teacher, and parent understanding and commitment to new and higher standards and to the theory of learning, which supports integrated instruction. Therefore, extensive and ongoing staff development and parent orientation is required. While ILA programs have many features in common, implementation at the local level among schools, and even classrooms, can vary substantially; in most schools the move from a skill-sequenced basal-dominated approach to a significant ILA program has taken from three to seven years.

Districts and schools vary in how ILA was implemented. In some schools, ILA was started at the kindergarten level and was moved up through the grades at a rate of one or two a year. In other schools, the process was started at the upper grade levels and worked down through the grades. In many schools, individual or small groups of teachers who had an early interest in ILA were encouraged to and supported in making the transition to the approach, with other teachers joining in subsequent years as they ''saw the results'' and had opportunities for training.

The Best Schools—Implementation Illustrations

MIRABEAU B. LAMAR, TX

The language arts program has been evolving over the past ten years. Essential to the development of ILA and other programs is involvement of the principal, teachers, and parents in decision making and staff development. Every year, the entire faculty returns three days before other teachers in the district to develop goals and plans for the year.

CAL, IA

The district has viewed itself for a long time as being on the cutting edge of improvements in education. The superintendent, board of education, community, and principal have high standards for instruction and support risk taking and innovation. The evolution of the language arts program began five years ago when visitors from a school in Canada, where the whole-language program was used, visited CAL and shared the approach. This led to development of objectives, program plans, and training for staff at CAL. The principal encouraged and supported teachers who piloted the integrated approach, for example, when teachers asked that funds for workbooks be redirected into the purchase of novels. Teachers were given and continue to be given flexibility in planning and implementing the language arts program; however, there are very high standards of accountability for student learning. The language arts program has been articulated Pre-K−12. This was facilitated by the fact that the elementary principal is also the curriculum coordinator for the elementary and high school. Over the years, teachers, parents, and students have been involved in the development and articulation of curriculum that continues to evolve. Among the objectives for the next few years are the further development of technical and creative writing and portfolio assessment.

UNION SCHOOL, CT

The school began the evolution of the language arts program from a skill-centered curriculum to one focusing on process, strategies, and connections more than twenty years ago, with implementation of the process approach to writing. In the area of writing, they became one of the lead districts in piloting holistic assessment with the state of Connecticut. The research on learning and reading led, eight years ago, to the initial development of a process literature−based approach to reading and finally, to a totally integrated language program. The initial decision that was made was that all children in all classes would experience some whole texts. Supporting the evolution of programs have been the superintendent, assistant superintendent, and board of education who have had a strong and sustained interest in instruction and the assessment of student learning and who have encouraged risk-taking and innovation. The Connecticut initiatives in assessment for all schools and the establishment by the state of very high standards also support ILA program development.

GREENBROOK, NJ

More than fifteen years ago, the ''process'' approach to writing was developed in the South Brunswick School District as part of the New Jersey Writing Project (NDN). The writing process approach is a cornerstone of the integrated language program. The current program also has as its roots the Early Childhood Program initiated in 1983. The program began with a one-year study, which asked the question, ''How do little children learn?'' Based on the study of brain development and learning, three assumptions were adopted to guide program development:

- Children learn through approximation.
- Little children want to learn.
- Schools will be ready for the children, not children ready for the school.

During year two some goals were written. Some materials were found. Teachers ''played'' with the use of big books. Data was examined that confirmed a fear that self-selection of books was low. Given choice, too many children did not like to read. The already implemented writing process was based on the notion that children should like to write. Parents were involved in workshops on early childhood learning, using outside speakers.

In year three, themes and concepts were developed in the curriculum. During the summer, a two-week Early Childhood Lab School for 150 children was established to pilot program and train teachers. (The Lab School continues as a teacher training program and as a site to pilot developments in program.)

Year four brought the realization that assessment was out-of-sink with the instructional goals of the program. A common means was needed to track children progress. A long checklist was developed by the teachers. A year's experience showed that it was a total failure. It was too time consuming. The effort was more than the product was worth. A new much shorter checklist was developed and more detailed analyses of progress was made only when an area showed weakness.

In year five, the program began to flow up into the upper grades and the literature-based approach used in the upper grades began to flow down into the primary grades. A new portfolio assessment was based on the answer to three questions: 1) What do we need to know? 2) What do we need it for? and 3) What effects does the assessment have on the program? Decisions were made to guide the ILA program, such as, "Nothing is sent home or displayed which is not edited."

In year 6, a set of K − 12 language development objectives was established. A "best works portfolio" assessment process was initiated. Working with Educational Testing Service (ETS), assessment rubrics were developed and the assessment process began what has become a year six through year ten program of field-testing, revision, and development.

Materials used

A wide variety of fiction and nonfiction reading material is required to implement a literature-based approach. In most cases, these books are paperbacks or Perma-bound editions. For core books read by the entire class, a copy is needed for each student; however, these class sets are usually circulated among sections at a grade level to reduce costs. In some cases, books included in the "reading library" of some social studies programs, i.e., Houghton Mifflin, are among the core books used at a grade level. Six to eight copies of interest group books are needed, while class libraries and the school library provide for individual selections. Some schools are using literature anthologies in addition to paperbacks; existing basal readers are also used as sources for reading material.

The "publishing" of children's work is an important part of ILA. To facilitate this process, computers are widely used in classrooms or in labs for word processing and for preparing final work for publication. Simple laminating and binding machines are used in many schools to enhance the published work.

STAFF DEVELOPMENT

Staff development is an essential factor in ILA program implementation; teachers need to understand the theory and research undergirding ILA. In addition, there are many specific strategies that require comprehensive training of teachers and principals, such as training in reading strategies, the writing process, and assessment approaches. ILA cannot be adopted like a new textbook with just a publisher's representative providing an orientation to the new textbook and teacher's edition. This is one of the major reasons why ILA has been implemented over a course of years. Training usually requires release time to observe other schools or classrooms where ILA is in use, as well as involvement in specific workshops in ILA theory and research, reading strategies, writing process strategies, and assessment approaches such as holistic scoring.

The training required for implementing ILA is provided by district supervisory staff, state and regional agencies, National Diffusion Network programs, educational consultants, and/or highly skilled principals and teachers within the school or district. Early program adopters are frequently used as turnkey trainers for colleagues. Principals provide some of the direct training for their staff and provide an essential support role for the program in the school and classrooms. Training takes place after school, on release time, during the summer recess, and regularly at faculty meetings. Books and articles concerning ILA strategies are circulated to staff to support the program. In a number of cases, schools have linked themselves into networks or joined regional or national networks (ASCD Whole Language Network), which include schools that have already implemented ILA. Schools using an ILA approach serve as models for staff from other schools who are considering changing to ILA or who are in the initial stages of the change process. "Seeing" ILA in practice seems to be an essential first step in making a commitment to the approach.

In addition, curriculum development is a key factor in implementing ILA. Developing the grade level proficiencies and curriculum structure should be considered a part of the staff development process. In many schools teachers form whole language or ILA support groups which meet to exchange information and reflect on classroom instruction. Many schools schedule common planning time for grade level teachers to facilitate planning.

The Best Schools—Staff Development Illustrations

MIRABEAU B. LAMAR, TX

Texas requires 20 hours of teacher inservice per year; however, the staff of Lamar far exceed this amount. For example, 100% of the teachers have attended each of the twelve hour on-campus inservice programs for Process Writing, Cooperative Learning and Open Court Reading Instruction, as well as eight hours of the Teacher Utility Computer Program. Twenty-six teachers have completed the twenty-one hour Teacher Expectation Student Achievement (TESA) course. Most inservice trainers are district supervisors. Lamar teachers also serve as trainers both within the school and throughout the district. Teachers spend a great deal of time outside of the classroom on professional activities. This year each teacher has a goal to attend one out-of-district inservice. The principal/teacher team which interviews and recommends new teachers for hiring makes willingness to commit beyond the classroom a priority in hiring. Assessment plays a major role in program development; data concerning achievement is constantly scrutinized not only to signal the need for assistance to individual children but to determine strengths and weaknesses in practices and program.

UNION, CT

On-going staff training is an essential component of an ILA program. Both the principal and the district reading specialist provide training and serve as "cheerleaders" for the continually evolving ILA program. Consultants from out of the district are also used for training; usually a full-day or half-day workshop is followed by a series of short workshops given after school throughout the year. Teachers provide training for other teachers in the district and are asked to provide training in other districts, while staff meetings are usually used for inservice training. The greatest emphasis has been on training in reading strategies.

CAL, IA

Much of the initial training was provided through the Area Educational Agency. Once trained, the teachers turnkeyed the training within the school. Training of staff took place on release time and after school hours. The process approach to writing was already well established prior to the introduction of ILA.

FUNDING DEVELOPMENT

Language arts instruction, whether the discreet/linear model with separate time scheduled for reading, English and spelling, or an ILA instructional approach, occupies at least a third of the instructional school day. Since the purpose of schools is learning, it can be argued that all school-related costs should be calculated in terms of actual instructional time. With a national average cost per pupil of $5243, language instruction averages at least $1748 per pupil at the elementary level (National Center for Educational Statistics, 1992). In other words, language instruction is expensive, regardless of the approach used.

Staff development, curriculum development, books, and assessment are the major expenditure in initiating and maintaining an ILA program. Class sets of core books have usually been purchased at a rate of three to four titles a year for each grade level. In some cases, ''reading libraries'' that accompany reading basal and social studies texts have been assembled by title from among classes at a particular grade level to create class sets. Interest books (six to twelve copies per title) have been added for each grade level over a period of years. Funds previously allocated for the purchase of workbooks have been redirected to the purchase of these books. Class, as well as school, libraries have grown over time through purchase, book donations, and PTA projects. Because paperback books have a shorter life span than hardcover texts, they need to be replaced more often than hardback books. However, traditional basals used to support skills or as sources of literature are being replaced less frequently by schools.

It must be stressed that effective staff development requires, first and foremost, time. The Best Schools invest heavily in staff development. The two to four inservice days built into most school calendars provide some time for ILA development; however, release time to observe and to receive training is also needed. Courses are offered after school either on a voluntary basis or for continuing education credits. Summer workshops for staff development and curriculum development are planned and implemented. In some states, requirements for continuing education of staff facilitate involvement in professional development. Costs for inservice training usually involve the costs for substitutes for release time, travel to training sessions and to model ILA programs, summer workshop pay for teachers, inservice credits that may effect movement on salary guides, workshop registration fees, professional literature, and training consultant fees.

The Best Schools—Program Cost Illustrations

MIRABEAU B. LAMAR, TX

The school receives $8300, just over $25 per student, for basic instructional supplies; from this amount, each teacher receives $50 for special materials for his/her class. Textbooks are provided through the central district budget. The school receives about $2300 for library books, which also covers the purchase of paperback novels and software for in class use. Lamar is considered a total Chapter 1 school, so considerable funding and program flexibility is provided through the Chapter 1 grant. For example, each teacher receives $200 from Chapter 1 funds for support of classroom projects. While the school makes extensive use of volunteers, there are also nine paid paraprofessionals, including two aides who work with children in the library and the aides who work with the Writing to Read and CAI programs. Most of the staff training is done after school hours on a voluntary basis. The exception to this are the three days of planning and development activities prior to the opening of school. On these days, staff receives $10 per hour. The PTA has been very active in raising funds, and it was through their efforts that computers for home use were purchased. Cooperative arrangements with five business partners also provide human resources and some small incentives to students for achievement and attendance.

UNION, CT

Funding for education in Farmington is considered average for the area; however, more is spent on nonsalary instruction than is typical. There is a strong belief that, ''If you are going to have a community of life-long readers, you must have great libraries.'' The annual school budget of over $10,000 for the library (about $7000 spent on books and $3000 on magazines, journals, professional materials, and audiovisuals) reflects this belief. Funds are available for the extensive purchase and replacement of trade books for the classrooms; some grades have ten to twelve copies each of many different titles. Approximately $18,000 of the school's budget is spent on language arts. A limited number of computers have also been purchased, which are used extensively by students to publish their work. Funds have been made available for out-of-district trainers and for summer stipends for curriculum and staff development. Some savings have been realized in instructional materials since the district no longer purchases workbooks, and basal texts are replaced less frequently. The PTO has assisted with the purchase of computers and classroom libraries.

CAL, IA

The cost for education in CAL approximates the average for similar districts. Most of the costs for materials in the language arts program have come from the regular school budget. Funds that used to be spent on workbooks are now spent on developing collections of literature and novels. The availability of aides to reduce the ratio of adults to students not only facilitates the language arts program, but all areas of the curriculum. Grant funds provided under special legislation in Iowa have provided for the salary of the aides. While continuing staff development has very high priority, the actual costs have been modest through the use of Area Educational Agency workshops, grant funding, and the use of CAL staff for turnkey training.

GREENBROOK, NJ

South Brunswick Township is a middle spending district in New Jersey; however, it places a high priority on program and staff development. The annual budget for staff development for the district's seven schools is approximately $250,000. An aggressive and effective grant writing approach also supports programs like the R. J. Nabisco Grant. The summer Early Childhood Lab School is supported through tuition paid by parents. Partnerships, for example, with ETS, provide expertise to the district.

SUMMARY

The Best Schools have adopted standards for literacy, which include not only what students know but what they can do. They use integrated language arts (ILA) programs that are reflective of current theory and research. Language-rich environments are created in integrated language arts programs. Instruction emphasizes the connections among reading, writing, and speaking. Development of a love of reading and writing is considered essential to successful learning. Students are grouped heterogeneously, and regrouping occurs within the class based on interest or to introduce or reinforce skills. Gone are the fixed reading groups, each with a separate basal and the accompanying workbooks and black-line masters. New forms of more authentic assessment are being introduced. The Best Schools, urban, suburban, and rural, have developed their ILA programs over a period of years and have plans to continue program development. Extensive and ongoing staff development is characteristic of the Best Schools. Essential to their success is an unwavering belief that all children in the school will read, write, and speak fluently.

REFERENCES

Anderson, R. et al. (1985). *Becoming a Nation of Readers: The Report of the Commission in Reading*. The National Institute of Education.

ASCD. (1992). *Making Meaning: Integrated Language Arts*. Alexandria, VA.

Brophy, J. and T. Good. (1985). ''Teacher Behaviors and Student Achievement,'' in *Handbook of Research on Teaching, 3rd Edition*, Wittrock, ed., New York: McMillan Publishing Co.

Caine, R. and G. Caine. (1991). ''Understanding a Brain Approach to Learning and Teaching,'' *Educational Leadership* (October).

Council for Basic Education. (1991). ''Standards: A Vision for Learning,'' *Perspective*, 4(1).

(1993). *Educational Programs That Work: The Catalogue of the National Diffusion Network (NDN), 19th Edition*. Longmont, CO: Sopis West Inc.

Fisher, C. W., et al. (1978). ''Teaching Behaviors, Academic Learning Time and Student Achievement,'' Final Report of the Beginning Teacher Evaluation Study, San Francisco: Far West Laboratory.

Goodman, K. S. (1964). ''A Linguistic Study of Cues and Miscues in Reading,'' *Elementary English*. National Council of Teachers of English.

Hillocks, George. (1986). *Research on Written Composition*. Urbana, IL: ERIC Clearinghouse on Reading and Communication Skills.

McDougal, Littel and Company. (1993). *Daily Oral Language*. Evanston, IL.

Mellon, John. (1969). ''Transformational Sentence-Combining,'' Research Report #10, National Council of Teachers of English, Urbana, IL.

National Assessment of Educational Progress (NAEP). 1990. *America's Challenge: Accelerating Academic Achievement*. Educational Testing Service, Princeton, NJ.

National Center for Educational Statistics. (1992). ''Digest of Educational Statistics for 1992,'' Washington, D.C.: U. S. Department of Education.

Oakes, J. (1985). *Keeping Track: How Schools Structure Inequality*. CT: Yale University Press.

Ogen, Evelyn. (1992). ''Profile of High Challenge Students,'' East Brunswick.

Sherwin, Stephen. (1969). *Four Problems in Teaching English: A Critique of Research*. New York: International Textbook Co.

Slaven, R. E. ''Ability Grouping and Student Achievement in Elementary Schools: A Best Evidence Synthesis.'' *Review of Educational Research*, 57, 293–336. 1987.

CHAPTER 7

Mathematics

MATHEMATICS instruction usually accounts for approximately 18% of a child's instructional day, 1500 hours of instruction from kindergarten through eighth grade. This chapter looks at the following questions concerning the development of world-class competency in mathematics for children who will spend their adult years in the 21st Century:

- What does theory and research say about what children should learn and how they should be taught?
- How do the Best Schools successfully translate theory into practice in teaching mathematics?
- How do the Best Schools assess what children know and what they can do?
- What do case studies of Best Schools reveal about how highly successful mathematics instruction is carried out in four very different community contexts?
- Finally, what are some of the specific practices, programs, and resources used by the Best Schools that are widely available to other program developers?

WHAT CHILDREN SHOULD LEARN

According to the National Goals of Education,

By the year 2000, American students will leave grades four, eight and twelve having demonstrated competency in challenging subject matter including . . . mathematics . . . ; and every school in America will ensure that all students learn to use their minds well, so they may be prepared for responsible citizenship, further learning, and productive employment in our modern economy.

By the year 2000, U.S. students will be first in the world in . . . mathematics achievement.

Schools have always had as a goal the development of mathematical literacy. While literacy has not in the past been specifically defined in practice, it has generally meant the development of basic competence in mathematical operations such as adding, subtracting, multiplying, and dividing, with some attention to the use of mathematics in solving relatively simple problems for all students. In addition, for college-bound students, mathematical literacy has traditionally included some level of competence in algebra and geometry, with the study of calculus limited to a highly motivated few. The National Goals set forth much higher expectations for defining mathematical literacy for children of the year 2000. Key words and phrases within the goals include "*demonstrated competency,*" "*challenging subject matter,*" "*all students,*" "*prepared for responsible citizenship,*" "*prepared for further learning,*" "*prepared for productive employment in our modern economy.*" These statements imply the setting of standards for *all students* far beyond the traditional standards for mathematic learning implicit in the instruction aims of mathematics in the past.

In 1986, the National Council of Teachers of Mathematics (NCTM) established the

Commission on Standards for School Mathematics as a means for improving the quality of school mathematics. The resulting *Curriculum and Evaluation Standards for Teaching Mathematics* (1989) and *Professional Standards for Teaching Mathematics* (1991) represent a broadly held professional consensus about the fundamental content of school mathematics, outcomes of instruction, student and program evaluation and attitudes toward instruction. The NCTM standards provide the operational framework for these national goals. Inherent in the standards is "a consensus that all students need to learn more, and often different, mathematics and that instruction in mathematics must be significantly revised" (NCTM, 1989, p. 1). The NCTM standards have been endorsed by virtually all of the mathematical and scientific organizations nationwide and by the National Standards Task Force coordinated by the Office of Educational Research and Instruction (OERI).

The need for new goals and standards is embedded in the changes of the society in which we live. The industrial society has been replaced with the information society. The availability of calculators, computers, and other technology has dramatically changed the nature of the physical, life, and social sciences; business; industry; and government. Electronic communication has supplemented and, in some cases, supplanted the voice and printed page. Information is shared almost instantly from desk to desk or across the world. "Information is the new capital and the new material, and communication is the new means of production" (NCTM, 1989, p. 3). New societal goals have replaced goals based on the development of most citizens to become workers in fields and factories, with advanced education for the few who would be the managers, the professionals, and the leaders. Today, mathematically literate workers must understand the complexities and technologies of communication, assimilate new information, generate questions and propose solutions, work in cooperative teams, adjust rapidly to changes in roles and functions within jobs, and totally change jobs four or five times during their careers. Mathematical knowledge has become a significant filter for employment and full participation in society. All students must have the opportunity to become mathematically literate, as equity is an economic necessity. Finally, mathematics itself is rapidly growing and being applied to continually expanding and diverse fields. The concept of the person as a life-long mathematics learner has become a necessary reality.

In line with the need to develop students who can function effectively in mathematics, the NCTM standards include what should be taught and what students should be able to do as a result of instruction for students K−4, 5−8, and 9−12. In addition, standards have been established for student assessment and program evaluation. There are thirteen standards each for grades K−4 and 5−8, and each standard is further delineated by descriptions of what students should be able to do as a result of instruction. The length of the NCTM standards precludes a listing in this chapter of all of them; however, following is an example of a K−4 and a 5−8 NCTM standard (NCTM, pp. 26 and 94):

GRADES K−4

Standard 2: Mathematics as Communication

In grades K−4, the study of mathematics should include numerous opportunities for communication so that students can—

- relate physical materials, pictures, and diagrams to mathematical ideas;
- reflect on and clarify their thinking about mathematical ideas and situations;
- relate their everyday language to mathematical language and symbols;
- realize that representing, discussing, reading, writing and listening to mathematics are a vital part of learning and using mathematics.

GRADES 5−8

Standard 7: Computation and Estimation

In grades 5 − 8, the mathematics curriculum should develop the concepts underlying computation and estimation in various contexts so that students can −

- compute with whole numbers, fractions, decimals, integers, and rational numbers;
- develop, analyze, and explain procedures for computation and techniques for estimation;
- develop, analyze, and explain methods for solving proportions;
- select and use an appropriate method for computing from among mental arithmetic, paper-and-pencil, calculator, and computer methods;
- use computation, estimation, and proportions to solve problems;
- use estimation to check the reasonableness of results.

HOW CHILDREN LEARN−HOW CHILDREN ARE TAUGHT

What children are taught and how they are taught has changed little in mathematics in the past 100 years in most of the nation's schools. The mission has been to develop minimal competency in calculation and knowledge of facts and formulas for the majority of students and advanced mathematics for the few. For those who did not reach minimal proficiency levels, remedial instruction focused on the reteaching of missing skills. For those students expected to go beyond minimal or practical everyday mathematics, each successive course was designed to prepare the student for the next higher level course.

The students in our schools today live and will work in a very different world than the students of 1900. The world of now and the future relies on computers and calculators. New mathematical concepts and applications are emerging, mathematics is recognized as a means of communication, and the workplace requires complex and creative problem solving. As a result, the mission of schools preparing students for the 21st Century is for *all students* to develop broad-based mathematical power and mathematical confidence. The need for change in preparation of students in mathematics is confirmed by the results of the National Test of Educational Progress. Between 1978 and 1986, students at grades 4, 8, and 12 showed some improvement in basic operations; however, no gains were recorded in student ability to handle even moderately complex procedures or to complete multistep problems (NAEP, 1990). In the second International Assessment of Mathematical Study, the United States ranked in the lower third quartile for overall math achievement worldwide (McKnight et al., 1987). American students compete favorably only with third-world countries, and not with the industrialized world (Lockwood, 1991).

The curriculum implemented in most of the schools of today is totally inadequate to prepare students to meet the national goals, the NCTM standards, the needs of the workplace and society of the 21st Century. Thomas Romberg, who chaired the panel that developed the NCTM standards, notes that we are still teaching "shopkeeper arithmetic" and that our elementary textbooks do not look much different than 15th Century accounting text. No other country teaches eight years of arithmetic, followed by a year of algebra, followed by a year of geometry. Other countries organize mathematics instruction differently (Lockwood, 1991). Based on the NAEP and IAEP assessments, the current curriculum is also inadequate to achieve even the older arithmetic standards.

The National Council of Teachers of Mathematics (NCTM) and the Mathematical Sciences Education Board (MSEB) are providing leadership in the restructuring of the mathematics curriculum and instructional approaches. In *Everybody Counts: A Report to the Nation on the Future of Mathematics Education* (1989), the MSEB put forth some tenets for mathematics education:

(a) mathematics is for everyone;

(b) mathematics is the science of patterns, a broad field with myriad applications rather than routines of arithmetic with limited "right answers"; and

(c) teaching means engaging students in solving real problems and inventing mathematics for themselves rather than lecturing and testing for low-level skills."

The NCTM has, in the development of curriculum standards, shifted the focus of mathematics from simply knowing and being a competent calculator to mathematics as doing. Five general goals guide the development of the standards for curriculum for all students:

(1) that they learn to value mathematics,

(2) that they become confident in their ability to do mathematics,

(3) that they become mathematical problem solvers,

(4) that they learn to communicate mathematically, and

(5) that they learn to reason mathematically.

In the NCTM Curriculum Standards, mathematics is viewed as much more than a collection of skills and concepts. Instruction includes methods for investigating and reasoning, communicating about math, exploring properties, solving real problems, and exploring important mathematical ideas. Problem solving is central in the mathematics classroom; exploration, conjecture, and experimentation are the standard approaches to problem solving. Technology broadens areas in which mathematics is applied and has changed the discipline itself by changing the nature of problems and the methods for solving them. "It is now possible to execute almost all of the mathematical techniques taught from kindergarten through the first two years of college on hand-held calculators" (Steen, 1992, p. 4.18). Because technology is changing mathematics and its uses, NCTM believes that

- appropriate calculators should be available to all students at all times;
- a computer should be available in every classroom for demonstration purposes;
- every student should have access to a computer for individual and group work;
- students should learn to use the computer as a tool for processing information and performing calculations to investigate and solve problems. (NCTM, 1989, p. 8).

The availability of calculators does not eliminate the needs for students to gain some proficiency with paper-and-pencil calculations. However, students should be aware of and choose the appropriate procedure in a given context. Research has shown that the use of calculators and computers does not diminish the student's ability to do mental or paper-and-pencil calculations; however, the use of technology allows for greater indepth exploration of important mathematical concepts and applications.

The curriculum standards also recognize changes in the understanding of how children learn. Children do not passively absorb information in retrievable fragments as a result of repeated practice. Children approach new tasks with some prior knowledge, assimilate new information, and construct their own meaning; therefore, instruction needs to involve reflection (Resnick, 1987). There is also recognition that there isn't a fixed linear order to the teaching and learning of mathematics. In the past, great emphasis has been placed on ensuring that each identified skill in the curriculum was mastered before progressing to skills identified as of a higher order. This led to many students being stuck in drill and practice

Table 2. *Summary of Changes in Mathematics Instruction.*

Move From	Move Toward
Instructional Practice	Instructional Practice
Lecture, memorization of rules/formulas/procedures; worksheets; one method – one answer	Discussion of mathematics; problemsolving; use of manipulatives, calculators, computers; justification of thinking
Reasoning	Reasoning
Reliance on the teacher or answer-key	Reasoning from spatial contexts, proportions, graphs; inductive and deductive reasoning.
Communication	Communications
Doing fill-in-the-blank worksheets.	Discussing, writing, reading, and listening about mathematical ideas; journals; reflections.
Connections	Connections
Learning isolated topics and development of skills out of context.	Problems related to real-life situations, other subjects, and other topics in math.
Content	Content
Textbook and workbook centered; memorization of formulas/rules/algorithms/procedures.	Multiple resources; greater emphasis on using patterns/relationships/statistics/probability/geometry to solve problems.
Tracking	Tracking
Students grouped by ability; differentiated content based on assignment to group.	Heterogeneous and flexible grouping; higher level curriculum for all students
Assessment	Assessment
True/false; multiple choice; solving one-step problems	Answering open-ended problems; extended problem-solving projects; development of portfolios; representation of situations verbally, numerically, graphically, geometrically and symbolically.

Adapted from NCTM *Curriculum and Evaluation Standards for School Mathematics.*

modes while higher achieving students were involved in problem solving or more advanced skills. The assumption of the fixed linearity of mathematics also provided the focus for remediation and served as the basis for tracking students in mathematics. As a result of this approach, the gap between lower achieving students and higher achieving students grew rather than narrowed over time. The new mathematical curriculum paradigm does not accept that there is a fixed order to learning.

Communicating about mathematics is another important tenet of the curriculum standards. Students should learn to communicate mathematically in problem-solving situations where they have the opportunity to read, write, and discuss ideas that use the language of mathematics. In addition, students should reason mathematically by making conjectures, gathering evidence, and building arguments to support notions. Good reasoning should be valued more than the ability to find the right answer. In the workplace, most complex problems demand the talents of teams of people. Learning in the classroom should frequently take place in working groups where students can argue strategy, learn from each other, and communicate approach and solutions in writing.

The curriculum standards also provide for significant shifts in the content of mathematics for grades K−4 and 5−8. Changes in content and emphasis are summarized as shown in Table 2.

The NCTM standards were adopted in 1989 after several years of development and review. It will take a number of years before the practices in most of the classrooms nationwide are congruent with the standards. Textbooks appearing since 1991 have begun to reflect aspects of the standards; however, it is anticipated that it will not be until 1994 that textbooks will be aligned with the curriculum standards.

HOW LEARNING SHOULD BE ASSESSED

Assessment in mathematics should become an integral part of learning. Assessment should be multidimensional and include not only assessment of what students know, but also what they can do. Furthermore, assessment should not be dominated by standardized multiple choice tests; more valid assessment practices are emerging. The framework for the NAEP for 1994 follows the NCTM standards closely. The *Report on Educational Research* paraphrases the NAEP proficient or middle-level assessment standards:

Fourth Grade: Students should consistently integrate procedures and concepts in solving problems. Using whole numbers, they should be able to estimate, compute and assess their results. They should understand fractions and decimals and know how to use calculators and geometric shapes. They also should explain in writing how they arrive at answers.

Eighth Grade: Proficient students should apply concepts and procedures consistently to complex problems. They should make conjectures and defend their ideas. They should be able to relate connections among fractions, percentages and decimals, as well as topics such as algebra and functions.

They should be familiar with quantity and spatial relationships in problem-solving and reasoning, and be able to convey underlying reasoning skills beyond arithmetic.

Students should make inferences from data and graphs; understand how to gather and organize data; calculate; and evaluate and communicate results in statistics and probability. They should also be able to apply the properties of informal geometry. (Report on Educational Research, 1992, p. 3)

The state of Vermont has implemented a portfolio assessment, which is aligned with the NCTM standards. Other states are also modifying their testing approaches to assess the higher levels of mathematics.

In summary, as part of the reassessment of how children learn, research distinguishes between surface knowledge (i.e., the memorization of facts, procedures, and applications) and *meaningful knowledge*, connected learning that makes sense to the learner. This expanded view of how children learn and what they should learn is reflected in the new standards for mathematics instruction. Six assumptions underlie the standards-based model.

- The first is that teaching must provide a student with experiences that enable him/her to develop connections among content and skills, i.e., to perceive patterns and to make connections cumulatively and over time.
- A second assumption is that learning is natural and motivational; classrooms should be organized around real-life problems that build on previous experience and knowledge.
- A third assumption is that children should be engaged in doing real math; children should learn to choose and apply appropriate procedures from among mental math, pencil-and-paper, calculator, and computer in solving problems, and they should be proficient in using each approach.
- Fourth is that children should write and speak about mathematics; they should learn to prepare data visually through graphs and models; they should appreciate mathematics as a language.
- A fifth assumption is that the availability of technology allows for the expansion and revision of mathematical content for all children; indepth knowledge of topics, patterns, and relationships should take prescience over surface knowledge and rote memorization of discrete facts and procedures; curriculum development should be guided by the concept that ''less is more.''
- Sixth is that assessment is best embedded in the instructional process; in other words, it is part of the instructional process rather than an add-on to instruction. Assessment

should provide evidence of not only what a student knows, but also what a student can do. As much as possible, it should be performance-based. Assessment should not be dominated by multiple choice items, which simply ask the student to select from a fixed list of solutions.

THE BEST SCHOOLS—MATHEMATICS: THEORY INTO PRACTICE

The Best Schools have implemented mathematics programs aligned with the NCTM standards for instruction. It would probably be difficult to find a school in which mathematics is taught where the staff does not verbalize support for the NCTM standards. However, at this point in time, most school mathematics programs show little real change in practice. All too often, one hears teachers and administrators make the statement, "We are using the NCTM standards; we use manipulatives in math class." The new goals, content, instructional approaches, assessment and professional standards represent a whole new paradigm for mathematics instruction. In the new paradigm, the use of manipulatives as an instructional tool plays a part; however, to equate their use with implementation of a program aligned with the standards is to miss the point of the new paradigm. A mathematics program that is consistent with the new goals, content, and assessment does not come packaged in a textbook. Newer texts reflect some of the standards, and books due out in 1994 will be much more closely aligned with the objectives; however, programs that prepare students to meet the standards require major changes in how children are taught and will always rely on much more than a textbook.

The Best Schools have adopted the new paradigm for mathematics instruction. Based on the theory and research on learning, which supports the NCTM standards, they have made major changes in how mathematics is taught, in curriculum, and in assessment. They have accomplished their mission with diverse social, economic and physical contexts.

The Best Schools—Four Case Studies in Mathematics: The Contexts

BAKER'S CHAPEL ELEMENTARY SCHOOL, GREENVILLE, SC

Baker's Chapel Elementary is a rural school located along a railroad track in the impoverished portion of Greenville County. Students are bused from various rural communities. Fifty percent of the students qualify for free or reduced price lunch, 50% are minority, 15% receive special education services, 45% of the parents did not complete high school, and there is a high mobility rate. The student profile at Baker's Chapel has not been used as an excuse for mediocre performance, but as a welcome opportunity to prove that excellence among at-risk students can take place. The median mathematics CTBS score rose from the 35th percentile in 1983 to the 95th percentile in 1990 for fourth grade students. In the spring of 1991, the school won South Carolina's most prestigious school award, Palmetto's Finest. The school district of Greenville County has three other Blue Ribbon Schools of Excellence.

Nancy Farnsworth, *Principal, K – 5, 316 Students*

CHAPARRAL ELEMENTARY SCHOOL, POWAY, CA

Chaparral has a tradition of excellence. It has been named in the "Top 100 California Schools" for three of the past four years and is one of thirteen schools that is part of the State of California Math Leadership Project. The school serves two suburban middle- and upper-class "bedroom communities" in the Poway Unified School District. Success is based on four elements that combine to make the school special: first, establishment of a values-driven organization; second, research-based instruction; third, shared decision making, which includes staff, students, and parents; and fourth, commitment to community service. In mathematics, 88% of the students score above the 50th percentile on the Metropolitan Achievement Test. The Poway Unified

School District's two high schools, two middle schools and another elementary school are also designated Blue Ribbon Schools.

Raymon Wilson, Principal, K – 5, 737 Students

CHAMBERLIN SCHOOL, SOUTH BURLINGTON, VT

Chamberlin is a small school serving a middle and lower socioeconomic suburban community. The school is actively involved in devising new connections and inventing new combinations consistent with AMERICA 2000 and Vermont's Green Mountain Challenge. At Chamberlin, "Everybody becomes SOMEBODY; No exceptions, no excuses." In mathematics, 77% of the students in grades 3 and 5 score above the 50th percentile on the Metropolitan Achievement Test. Grade 4 students participate in the statewide Vermont's formal portfolio assessment in mathematics designed to assess the NCTM standards. The South Burlington School District's middle school and high school are also Blue Ribbon Schools.

Roderick Marcotte, Principal, Pre-K – 5, 286 Students

WESTCHESTER ELEMENTARY SCHOOL, CORAL SPRINGS, FL

Westchester Elementary School serves the large central city of Coral Springs, in the Broward County School District, Florida. It has an abundance of single-family and multi-family housing and is rapidly becoming a multicultural community. At present, over twenty languages are spoken by the children and their parents. There has been more than a 40% turnover of students in the past three years. The mission of Westchester is "Excellence and Innovation." As one of the 120-member schools of the Coalition of Essential Schools, they have adopted the nine principles that provide a framework that envisions the "New Generation of American Schools," a basic shared belief that schools should promote the student as thinker, worker, leader, manager, and responsible citizen. In 1991, 79% of the students scored above the 50th percentile on the IOWA Test of Basic Skills in mathematics.

Sharon Shaulis, Principal, K – 5, 1132 Students

CLASS ORGANIZATION AND INSTRUCTIONAL TIME

The NCTM recommends that a minimum of one hour per day be devoted to mathematics instruction at the elementary level. The Best Schools frequently exceed this time commitment. Time for mathematics comes in three ways. First is the regularly scheduled math period, usually forty-five to sixty minutes. Second is time scheduled into mathematics labs. Third is time children are involved in integrated learning units, which include mathematics applications and problems. The integrated units include those developed locally, as well as the frequently used AIMS (Activities that Integrate Math and Science) materials, which integrate science and mathematics (AIMS Education Foundation, 1989).

The Best Schools are cognizant of the negative effects of grouping or tracking on student learning. There is an accepted assumption that all children will learn mathematics. There is a rejection of the prevalent and accepted view in America that some students are just naturally good at math and some are not. A number of studies have shown that this perception of math ability, as something you have or don't have and, therefore, an acceptance that achievement in math is pre-ordained by genetics may be at the heart of the lower achievement in math in the United States. It is not uncommon to hear American parents "brag" that they were not good at math and, thus, expect their sons/daughters also to have limited success. In contrast to the American perception, Asian cultures view math as something everyone can learn with proper instruction and diligence. Further, they see no need to track students in math, either on some estimate of ability or on past achievement (Stevenson et al., 1990). The curriculum and instructional approaches used in the Best Schools facilitate heterogeneous grouping of children in mathematics. Moreover, some of the schools use no grouping at all, with even Chapter 1 remedial and special education resources provided by in-class support.

The Best Schools — Class Organization Illustrations

CHAPARRAL, CA

Every student in grades 1–5 receives 250 minutes of math per week. Kindergarten children spend 180 minutes in exploring math/science skills and concepts. Students in grades 1–5 enjoy integrated, thematic units each week. All classes are heterogeneously grouped. Teachers have developed series of lessons on common themes, and students rotate among the teachers at specific grade levels. Simulation projects are employed at the third to fifth grade levels; for example, a fifth grade created an entire economic system for a town.

In addition to classroom instruction, students receive eighty minutes per month in the math lab, where groups of thirteen to sixteen students work individually or cooperatively to solve logic and spatial reasoning problems. Approximately ninety trained parent volunteers and a math lab aide/coordinator assist students in groups of three or four by asking questions, prompting, and providing encouragement. The emphasis is on authentic experiences such as weighing and measuring and on development of skills in orally explaining math strategies. Students are also scheduled for an average of eighty minutes per month in the computer labs (1 Apple IIe/GS and 1 Mac labs) where they explore mathematical concepts using such software as The Factory.

BAKER'S CHAPEL, SC

Instruction in math is planned for 300 minutes per week in grades 1–5. Students are grouped homogeneously for math after grade 1. The student-to-teacher ratio is 21:1 in grades 1–3, 28:1 in grades 4–5. One day a week the children go to the Discovery Room to do hands-on experiments that often integrate math and science. The Discovery Room Program is taught by a classroom teacher who is released in the afternoon from regular classroom activities to provide service to the entire school.

CHAMBERLIN, VT

Math is taught in flexible groupings (heterogeneous, homogeneous, large and small, individual and cooperative) three to five hours per week. In addition to classroom math instruction, students have two forty-five minute periods a week of instruction in the computer lab (12 Mac's) and one period a week of math portfolio problem solving.

CURRICULUM

The Best Schools have restructured their curriculum to align it with the NCTM curriculum standards. Less time is devoted to the number strand of the curriculum, and more time is spent on such topics as statistics, probability, and geometry. The focus is on indepth study rather than coverage of the program. In order to gain time to cover topics in depth, decisions have been made to eliminate sections and/or whole chapters of textbooks. The traditional "spiral curriculum" is repetitious with much of the content not thoroughly learned but merely reviewed year after year at the same level. It is estimated that, in grades 2–8 in America, only 30% of the material presented in math textbooks each year is new (Flanders, 1989). This is not true of other countries with higher math achievement. Many of the Best Schools estimate that 50% or less of math instruction is based on a textbook. They also gain time for significant study of content by using tools such as calculators and computers to do calculations that are time-consuming and have little learning value when done with pencil and paper.

Instruction in math classrooms in the Best Schools is based on helping children make connections — connections to previously learned material, connections to real-life situations, connections to other subject areas. Students are actively engaged in learning by collecting and analyzing data and participating in simulations. Math instruction is frequently integrated with other subject matter. For example, The AIMS integrated math and science program is used in many of the schools. Students learn what approaches to solving mathematics problems are most appropriate and efficient. Mathematics is taught as a means of communication; therefore, students reflect, keep math journals, write, and discuss mathematics on a daily basis. Selecting the best approach for a problem and explaining and justifying the process used is central to instruction. Cooperative learning groups are used frequently to simulate real-life math applications, foster math communication, and increase problem-solving ability. Manipulatives of all kinds are used in the instructional process at all grade levels. *Math Their Way,* a program that uses a conceptual manipulative approach, is used in many schools at the kindergarten and primary levels. Calculators and computers are used extensively. Research has demonstrated that fears are unfounded that the use of calculators and computers at the elementary grades will result in the decrease in learning of basic arithmetic skills. For example, students in grade 3 who used calculators outscored peers who did not use calculators by 20% on the NAEP even though calculators were not used in testing (National Assessment of Educational Progress, 1988). Computer software enables students to create and use data bases, spread sheets, and graphing capabilities of computers to solve complex problems. Software such as the Math Factory and How the West Was Won, designed to foster problem solving, are also used extensively. As a result, rote memorization, workbooks, skill, and drill computer software and worksheets are de-emphasized.

Regular classroom instruction in math in the Best Schools is frequently supplemented by learning centers within the class or math problem-solving labs. Some labs make use of computers; others use volunteers to present and discuss problems with small groups of students; still others are organized to make use of teacher and student interest within a grade level. Labs help students understand mathematics by using instructional activities in which students can apply their mathematical skills to real-life situations and can communicate mathematically. While the use of lab activities is common in the Best Schools, fewer than 25% of students nationally report ever being involved in such activities (NAEP, 1988).

The Best Schools — Curriculum Illustrations

BAKER'S CHAPEL, SC

The goal of mathematics education at Baker's Chapel is for students to become life-long, literate mathematical problem solvers. The K−5 program, based on a district curriculum guide and the NCTM standards, focuses on problem solving, mathematical communication, reasoning, mathematical connections, estimation, number sense and numeration, concepts of whole number operations, geometry and spatial sense, measurement, statistics and probability, fractions, and patterns. Mathematical content is investigated by students in countless problem-solving approaches related to the real world, such as measuring classrooms and other spaces in metric and English to determine area and volume, designing toys with pattern blocks, estimating the costs of original toys, using fractions in recipes, solving geometric problems with toothpicks, comparing the weight of top soil to sand and clay, calculating the size of a dinosaur, and drawing it on the playground.

Teachers place special emphasis on mathematical discourse in order to analyze the reasoning patterns of students, most of whom are at-risk with few opportunities outside of the classroom for formal learning experiences. In teacher-directed instruction on word problems, for example, children work out the process(es) by which they will solve the problem to reinforce their understanding; then after the solution, they discuss alternative ways to solve the problem. All grades emphasize word problem discussion; in primary grades, students draw the word problem. There is also a heavy emphasis on graphing and measurement, such as plotting students' favorite ice cream, pets, percentage of PTA membership over months, or measuring the distance Paul Bunyon traveled from Maine to California. The content-rich program gives children many opportunities to make connections to other curriculum areas such as science and social studies.

Instructional resources are wide and varied; each teacher has a manipulative kit correlated to the *Merrill Mathematics* textbook and an additional manipulative kit developed by Educational Testing Service. All classes have calculators. Other resources include additional manipulatives, such as coins, blocks, and base ten sets; Math Their Way materials; games; South Carolina's ETV instructional programs such as Multiplication Rock and School House Rock; and guest speakers from the world of work where math is used. In addition, nineteen Apple IIe computers in one computer lab and twenty-seven IBM computers in another lab, plus three to four computers in each classroom, support the program.

CHAPARRAL, CA

The curriculum is based on the NCTM standards and California Mathematics Framework. There has been a decrease in the amount of time devoted to the number strand of the curriculum, particularly computation/algorithms. This instructional time has been replaced with greater emphasis on problem solving, statistics, geometry and measurement, mental math, and estimation. In the area of curriculum, the school subscribes to the theory "less is more." It is estimated that about 50% of instruction involves the use of the district adopted *Addison Wesley Mathematics* textbook series in grades 2−5, and less time in grades K−1. Chapters, particularly those from the end of each text, are eliminated in order to provide room for other essential parts of the curriculum. The balance of the program is experiential based. In the primary grades, instruction now focuses more on pattern and number concepts and less on rote memorization and computation. Looking for patterns and building models or diagrams foster critical thinking. Students are presented with real, complex problems and required to explain their thinking. The focus of much of the instruction is on the "essential learnings" outlined in the Mathematics−Model Curriculum Guide (California State Department of Education, 1987).

Every classroom teacher employs math warm-ups or problem-solving activities on a daily basis using materials such as Math Their Way, Explorations, or Randy Charles Problem Solving. Every opportunity is taken to integrate math across the curriculum. The school strives for a balance of teacher-oriented lesson presentations, and student-oriented learning experiences include simulations, cooperative group projects and Math Menu activities. Math Menu activities (*The Math Solution,* Marilyn Burns) provide flexibility and a range of stimulating activities in learning centers for all of the heterogeneously grouped students in the classroom. Every classroom is equipped with calculators, and calculators can also be borrowed from the library.

CHAMBERLIN, VT

The entire K−5 curriculum stresses application, real-world experience, writing about math, conducting investigations, and technology. Manipulatives, computers, and calculator activities are built around life problem simulations at all grade levels. Trips to the "pumpkin patch" to estimate seed content, Scholastic Reader, and newspapers are some of the sources used to relate math to life problems. The curriculum covers the thirty types of problems included in Vermont's mathematics program evaluation criteria. Content areas stress those recommended by NCTM: estimation of ratio and proportion, statistics and probability, problem solving, and geometry and basic algebra. The 1991 *Addison Wesley* is used because of its relationship to NCTM. *Math Their Way,* a conceptual, manipulative approach, is used at the primary level. *Creative Problem Solving* is also used at each grade level. Integration of math content with other subject areas is encouraged. Cooperative learning is used extensively. Computer skills are taught in primary grades weekly by classroom teachers in the lab.

Student communication about mathematical ideas and situations occur routinely. Oral and written communications are required under the "Portfolio Process" and "Writing about Math Strategies;" investigations and data presentation are an essential part of the program. An appreciation of the importance of math is emphasized through peer tutoring and such special activities as Technology Day, which provides connections between the school and the real world.

WESTCHESTER ELEMENTARY, FL

Focusing on the Coalition of Essential School's principles of "Less Is More" and "Demonstration of Mastery," Westchester's approach is simply to teach students to think, not merely compute. Basic math skills and functions are explored and taught in conjunction with Bloom's Taxonomy. Each grade covers the areas of whole numbers; the functions of addition, subtraction, multiplication, and division; fractions; decimals; probability; estimation; algebra; geometry; percents; graphing; time; and measurement. Students apply skills to real-world situations across every discipline. For example, students average their daily/weekly grades, estimate the cumulative weight of students in their class, and predict how many footprints would be needed to reach the front door. Higher level thinking skills are developed through activities such as "Circus Math," "Counting Kitters," "Number Munchers," "Adventures in Math," "Speedway Math" and "Conquering Decimals." "Mental Gymnastics" is used to begin classes, and this encourages the recall of math facts and foster terminology becoming incorporated into everyday conversation. Instructional strategies are based on concrete experiences, which serve as a foundation for representational and abstract reasoning. Concrete materials used in all classrooms include such manipulatives as Attribute Blocks, Base 10 Blocks, Pattern Blocks, Color Tiles, Cuisenaire Rods, Geoboards, and Chip Trading. Teachers also use *Math Their Way* and *Explorations.*

Writing about math, both stories and strategies; writing test questions, strategizing; patterning; making charts, tables, and graphs; and validating findings by proof and reasonableness are other tools of instruction. There is integration of math and science through AIMS activities. Students use calculators to find number patterns, perform simple algorithms, and manipulate higher numbers while focusing on process and reasonableness of answers. Models are shared using an overhead calculator. A computer lab is used to further support the program.

A myriad of learning centers in every class allows for individuality and enrichment. Centers include self-corrected packets in every mathematical function; materials include "Fantastic Fabrication" where students construct problems from scientific and historical perspectives and "Florida Word Problem Packets."

SPECIAL NEED STUDENTS

The focus in the Best Schools is clearly on development in class and prevention of the need for remediation, separate enrichment, or separate programs. In some of the schools, all services are provided within the regular classroom, through flexible programming, and through in-class special instruction support. Other schools do pull out students with special needs. However, in the case of remediation, the emphasis is on providing needed supplementary instruction quickly and indepth and elimination of the need for special services. This instruction is provided in small groups by remedial specialists and/or through one-on-one tutoring by volunteers or peers.

The Best Schools—Special Needs Students Illustrations

CHAPARRAL, CA

A resource room program meets the needs of special education students using instructional strategies that are multi-sensory with a high degree of student participation and engagement in learning tasks using math manipulatives, exploration, problem solving, and cooperation. Students develop problem-solving and critical thinking skills, study/organizational skills, and academic skills. Instruction is provided in a resource center, by the resource specialist in the regular classroom, and through curriculum modification by the regular classroom teacher and reverse mainstreaming using peer tutors. All regular classrooms that have special education students use the *Circle of Friends* curriculum. The program builds acceptance and shared responsibility for special need students. In some cases, classmates of special education students attend IEP meetings. Very few classified students spend more than one hour per day out of the regular classroom. Severely handicapped students, estimated at 2% of the handicapped students, may spend up to 50% of their time in self-contained classes.

The need for remediation and enrichment is met within the classroom through menu activities and through the lab activities.

BAKER'S CHAPEL, SC

Students in need of basic skills remediation are served by a specially trained teacher as required by the state-mandated compensatory mathematics program. Gifted children are identified through a number of processes. One means is the use of the Raven Matrix Pattern Test, a visually based test that adjusts for eleven socioeconomic factors. Identified children receive supplemental instruction in the "Challenge Program," 200 minutes per week in grades 4 and 5.

CHAMBERLIN, VT

The mainstreaming of special education students into the regular classroom is the norm in South Burlington. Individual, small group, and cooperative group learning approaches are used. Computers are used extensively with special education and Chapter 1 students. Peer tutoring is used when appropriate. A half-time teacher serves the Chapter 1 eligible students; in most cases, instruction takes place in the classroom; however, students are also pulled out of class for some instruction. An enrichment teacher works with all students in class, in small groups, and in the school as a whole.

WESTCHESTER, FL

The IEPs of special education students focus on skills necessary to enable the students to succeed in regular classes. The strategy of all remediation of at-risk students is to identify, instruct, bring up to grade level, and return to the regular classroom. Special volunteers work weekly on a one-to-one basis with students who need to develop skills.

ASSESSING WHAT STUDENTS KNOW AND CAN DO

Most of the standardized norm-referenced commercial tests available to schools today measure only a small portion of the national goals for mathematics instruction or the more specific outcomes envisioned in the NCTM standards. The National Assessment of Educational Progress (NAEP) has, in the past, attempted to measure higher level skills and has adopted the NCTM standards as the framework for future math assessments. Some states, most notably Vermont, have introduced new forms of criterion-based assessments, which provide for more direct measurement of not only what students know, but what they can do. Open-ended questions require students to consider alternative approaches to complex problems, describe the process they used, justify their approach, and provide one or more answers. In some ways, it is at the assessment stage that the magnitude of the needed change in the curriculum and instruction in mathematics is most clearly focused. Now and for the future, it has become clear that the ever-expanding users of complex math will not be in situations that require them to select solution a, b, c, or d. They will be in situations where the problem itself will frequently have to be identified, alternative approaches considered, and solutions justified.

The Vermont Portfolio Mathematics Assessment provides good insight into the type of assessment emerging in conjunction with the new standards in mathematics. In the Vermont fourth and eighth grades, model assessment is embedded in the instructional process. Throughout the year, students keep portfolios of their problem-solving work in mathematics. In the spring, students, in collaboration with their teachers, select five to seven pieces of their best work in mathematics. Students also include mathematics-related writing such as essays and journals. Portfolios are assessed, based on the criteria, by teachers within the district. A sample of portfolios from each school are then assessed at the state level by a second assessor; an additional sample is then independently assessed at the state level to check for reliability in application of the criterion standards. The student's work is assessed based on the following criteria (Vermont Department of Education, 1991).

Problem Solving

- Understanding of the task.
- How the student approached the task: The approach(es), procedure(s) and/or strategies adopted to attack the task.
- Why the student made the choices along the way; The reflections, justification, analysis, rational, verification that influenced decisions.
- What findings, conclusions, observations, connections, generalizations the student reached.

Communication Criteria

- Language of mathematics
- Mathematical representations
- Clarity of presentation

Vermont also uses the mathematics portfolios to assess the mathematics instructional opportunities provided in the schools. Samples of portfolios from each school are assessed in terms of their reflection of instructional opportunities considered critical elements of effective mathematics programs, variety of content, and student disposition/empowerment in mathematics (Vermont Department of Education, 1991):

Instructional Opportunities Criteria

Portfolios reflect evidence of:

- Group work
- Interdisciplinary work
- Construction of mathematical understanding through manipulation of concrete objects
- The real-world nature of the problems and generalizability of skills to other contexts
- Assignments and products show the use of calculators and computers

Content Criteria

Portfolios reflect:

Grade 4

- Number sense—Whole No./Fractions
- Operations/place value
- Estimation

- Patterns/relationships
- Geometry/spatial sense
- Measurement
- Statistics/probability
- Logic

Grade 8

- Number relationships/number theory
- Operations/estimation
- Patterns/functions
- Algebra
- Geometry/spatial sense
- Measurement
- Statistics/probability
- Logic

Disposition/Empowerment Criteria

Narratives accompanying problem solving entries reflect some evidence of:

- Curiosity
- Flexibility
- Perserverence
- Risk-taking
- Reflection

Vermont has organized schools into networks. Extensive teacher training in the development of mathematics programs and assessment is provided within each network.

The Best Schools—Assessment Illustrations

BAKER'S CHAPEL, SC

Because of the record of high scores on standardized tests, Baker's Chapel has been exempt from administering the state-mandated nationally normed reference tests in grades 4 and 5 and state-developed criterion reference grades 1, 2, and 3 for the past two years. Baker's Chapel is one of four elementary schools in the state that was selected to participate in the 12-Schools Project. The project involves the development of authentic assessment in mathematics. One day per month, teachers in the school write student performance tasks, which are then field-tested. The performance tasks are embedded in the curriculum and involve both group and individual activities. A scoring rubric is developed for each task and the results reported to the state. The school has found that the complex authentic performance activities are particularly suited to low-ability students. Math cards are used within the classroom to track the acquisition of skills and strategies.

CHAPARRAL, CA

Students are required to demonstrate their understanding by building models—producing charts, diagrams, maps, and conceptual representations—and by explaining their thinking orally or in written form. There is an expanding use of portfolio assessment based on units of instruction. Tests include oral and written activities, as well as independent and small group tasks. Question types include open-ended, enhanced multiple choice, investigations, and portfolios. The school has been influenced by the Kentucky assessment and holistic goals projects, as well as the California enhanced math portfolio assessment currently in the pilot stage.

CHAMBERLIN, VT

Critical thinking skills are enhanced by the structure of the Vermont Portfolio Assessment procedure. State assessment occurs at grade 4; however, at Chamberlin, all grades develop portfolios. The Mathematic Portfolio contains five to seven pieces of each student's best pieces in four categories. An example of a portfolio might include

(1) The solution to a math puzzle with an explanation concerning the strategy
(2) A problem requiring the use of technology to develop a table and a paragraph explaining the approach
(3) A graph that shows the data from a survey investigation conducted in the school
(4) A real-world experience with math, such as a series of estimations of the number of seeds in a pumpkin, with written observations concerning estimation

The fourth grade portfolios are holistically scored by the state based on developed rubrics. In addition, Vermont State Department evaluates the school program by reviewing the portfolios from each school in terms of instructional opportunities considered essential to the development of mathematical proficiency. Portfolios for grades 1−3 and 5 are evaluated by the teachers within the school.

THE BEST SCHOOLS—PROGRAM DEVELOPMENT AND SUPPORT IN MATHEMATICS

The NCTM curriculum standards and the related instructional approaches are rooted in the same research on how children learn as the whole-language or integrated language arts (ILA) approach. In most cases, Best Schools had already been successfully involved for many years with the ILA approach prior to adopting the new paradigm for mathematics. Therefore, many principles of the NCTM mathematics were already ingrained in the instructional practices of the school. For example,

- Learning is natural and motivational.
- Children learn by making connections to previously acquired knowledge.
- Learning involves making connections with real-life situations.
- Rather than fragmented skill sequenced curriculum, children learn better when instruction emphasizes connections among content areas.
- Learning of surface knowledge, i.e., memorization of facts, formulas, and procedures, does not automatically result in the learning of meaningful knowledge.
- Students learn best when not placed in ability groups.
- Assessment should be embedded in instruction and assess what students can do, as well as what they know.

Many of the Best Schools began to transform mathematics education a number of years ago, prior to the release of the NCTM standards. Emerging state standards for assessment, more consistent with NCTM standards, also served to stimulate reform. Also, many of the Best Schools served as pilot sites for state initiatives. What all the Best Schools have in common was a recognition that *all* students needed to learn meaningful mathematics and that both the curriculum and mode of instruction would have to be aligned to the principles of how children learn based on research.

The transformation of mathematics instruction in the Best Schools was a planned change. Those that began the process in the late 1980s had to rely almost totally on materials they developed and on supplemental programs developed by others. For example, *Math Their Way,* a conceptual manipulative-based program, used extensively in kindergarten and primary grades. Starting in 1991, new textbooks began to reflect the NCTM standards. "Drill and skill" computer programs were replaced by problem-centered software and easy-to-use integrated packages that include data base, spread sheet, and word processing. Calculators became inexpensive and more user friendly for elementary use. However, a program that meets the NCTM standards is far more than textbooks, software packages, supplemental materials, calculators, and computers. The program requires major changes in curriculum and modes of instruction. The Best Schools are committed to ongoing curriculum development; each year, the program is reviewed and the curriculum refined based on student outcomes and available resources. Each school continues to design connections to other subject areas and to incorporate real-life problems relevant to their own context.

The Best Schools—Implementation Illustrations

BAKER'S CHAPEL, SC

The roots of the dynamic mathematics program at Baker's Chapel can be traced back seven years to the placement of a new principal in the school and a new atmosphere of staff commitment and involvement. Part of the commitment was to replace the teacher-centered, basal-driven, pencil-and-paper learning strategies with a hands-on, cooperative learning, technology supported, experience-based program with high expectations for all students.

CHAPARRAL, CA

In 1989, student improvement in math was the school goal. Teachers elected to participate in the California Mathematics Leadership Project, which included a commitment to participate in approximately 100 hours of staff development and to engage in experimentation with instructional strategies in their classrooms over a three-year period.

CHAMBERLIN, VT

Vermont began the development of the writing portfolio assessment program more than twelve years ago. The development of a mathematics portfolio built around the NCTM standards was anticipated by the district several years ago. The district has embraced the new approach to mathematics instruction and has been involved in piloting materials and approaches.

WESTCHESTER, FL

In order to prepare students for life in the 21st Century, the school has undertaken a "change strategy" that has shaped goals and priorities. An elected Shared Decision-Making Council, with input from staff, parents, students, community, and administration, has identified three goals for an action plan: to establish alternative assessment techniques in the classroom; to implement an interdisciplinary, outcome-based curriculum focusing on the student as worker; and to promote an atmosphere of collegiality throughout the school. The school has received waivers from the district regarding use of the adopted textbooks and waivers from local and state policies. Because the school is a member of the Coalition of Essential Schools, staff from Brown University and other coalition centers are available for workshops and conferencing. In addition, Westchester is working with Nova University on the development of its mathematics program.

MATERIALS

A wide variety of programs, materials, and equipment are used in the teaching of mathematics in the Best Schools. *Math Their Way,* a conceptual based program using manipulatives, is used in most schools (Chaparral, CA; Chamberlin, VT; Baker's Chapel, SC; Westchester, FL; Spring Glen, WA; Howard C. Reich Community School, ME; Craycroft, AZ; Mine Hill, NJ). The *Addison Wesley Mathematics* (1991) is a widely used textbook series. AIMS (Activities that Integrate Math and Science) is also used by a number of schools (Westchester, FL; Chaparral, CA; Craycroft, AZ; Rawls Byrd, VA). STAMM (Systematic Teaching and Measurement Mathematics) (NDN) is a program that focuses on the application of mathematics skills to daily life experiences and links problem solving and critical thinking skills to other school subjects (Rawls Byrd, VA).

A number of problem solving centered programs are used extensively by the Best Schools: *Math Solutions I and II* (Chaparral, CA; Spring Glen, WA; Craycroft, AZ, Laura B. Sprague, IL); *Creative Problem Solving* (Chamberlin, VT; Westchester, FL); *Randy Charles Problem Solving* (Chaparral, CA); *Explorations* (Westchester, FL; Chaparral, CA); Edward deBono's CoRT Thinking Skills and Six Thinking Hats (Westchester, FL); and Fantastic Fabrications (Westchester, FL).

Classroom sets of calculators are available in the Best Schools. In addition, many schools have calculators in the library, which can be checked out. Computers are also used in the Best Schools; most of the schools have computers in the classrooms and in one or more laboratories. For example, Westchester, Florida, has ninety-seven computers spread throughout the school, plus a computer lab. Baker's Chapel has twenty-seven computers in a lab, plus others in classrooms. Chaparral has three computer labs. Schools use Apple IIe's, GS's and Mac's and IBM PC's and PC compatibles. Some of the most popular software allow students to create data bases, spread sheets, and visual representations of data, such as ClarisWorks and Microsoft Works. Among the many other software programs used are The Factory, Math Mall, Lego Logo, and How the West Was Won.

Manipulatives are used extensively by the Best Schools at all grade levels. Some of the manipulatives used include Attribute Blocks, Base 10 Blocks, Pattern Blocks, Color Tiles, Cuisenaire Rods, and Geoboards.

The value of family support of the learning process is recognized by the Best Schools. Family Math, a program that instructs parents in how to work with their children in mathematics, is used by many of the schools (Lawrence Brook, NJ; Irwin School, NJ; Lake Seneca, MD; Howard C. Reich Community School, ME; Craycroft, AZ).

STAFF DEVELOPMENT

Staff development is an essential factor in implementing a mathematics program to meet national goals and the NCTM *Professional Standards for Teaching Mathematics* (1991); teachers and principals need to understand the theory and research undergirding the approach to learning. In addition, there are many specific strategies that require comprehensive training of teachers and principals. For example, teachers need to learn how to select the appropriate tools of learning and also how to use such tools as computers, calculators, and manipulatives to support a problem-solving mode of instruction. Even with the emergence of new textbooks anticipated to be more fully aligned with the standards, the new curriculum and approach to teaching mathematics cannot be implemented with a short inservice conducted by a textbook representative. The Best Schools have been willing to make an extensive commitment over time to staff development.

Training in the Best Schools has been provided by district supervisors, teachers, principals, state department staff, university staff, and network and coalition partners who are dedicated to the new paradigm of instruction. Schools have provided release time for teachers, used scheduled inservice, built on continuing education requirements, and provided programs and voluntary professional development time. What the Best Schools have in common is the recognition of the need for comprehensive and ongoing staff development.

The Best Schools—Staff Development Illustrations

BAKER'S CHAPEL, SC

Staff development is continuous and extensive. All teachers are required to attend five workshops per year. Visits to other schools to observe programs and activities are frequent. Many staff members take graduate courses. Seventy-five percent of the faculty attended the district summer seminar on mathematics topics. All teachers are involved in the 12-Schools Project, which provides for assessment training and hands-on involvement in development of the math framework and alternative assessment methods. All teachers write thematic units to restructure the curriculum. Specific workshops held after school for one to two hours have included Manipulative in Mathematics, New Standards in Mathematics, Math Superstars, Polyhedrons, Project Hands-on, and Teaching Problem Solving. In addition, Baker's Chapel hosts at least one workshop per month with all teachers attending. Other optional workshops are held in the district and region of the state. Teachers have been trained in Math Their Way, computer and calculator use, cooperative learning, and assessment. Training is conducted by staff members, the principal, district staff, regional and state department personnel, and hired consultants.

CHAPARRAL, CA

At Chaparral, every teacher has received at least forty hours of training in mathematics via Marilyn Burn's *Math Solutions I* and 60 hours of site-based training in Teaching Number Concepts Using Unifix Cubes, by K. Richardson; *Math Solutions II*; Activities Integrating Math and Science (AIMS); *Math Their Way;* and California State Replacement Units. Time for professional development is provided in part by "time banking." In addition to the one hour and fifteen minutes provided after student dismissal each day, twenty minutes is added to the instructional day four days a week; on the fifth day, students leave one and one-half hours early. One-fourth of the noninstructional time is used for staff development and the rest for individual staff planning and preparation. In the case of training in *Math Solutions I,* staff received stipends for participation in a one-week summer program. New teachers receive a week of basic training.

CHAMBERLIN, VT

All teachers and support staff participate in planned staff development programs. Nine inservice days are provided by the district—four in August, three during the school year, and two determined at the discretion of the teacher. Offerings are held on-site or in a central district location. Professional growth is a priority. Some of the courses during the past three years have included *Math Their Way,* Guiding Children Through Math, Connecting Reading and Math, Cooperative Learning, Multimedia and Computers in Education, and Mac Academy. Training is provided by district and school staff, as well as out-of-district consultants. The Vermont State Department of Education also maintains seventeen training networks, which provide eighteen hours of mathematics portfolio training to fourth grade teachers in the school. The school media director has provided teachers with training before school on the use of the Mac's in the lab. Inservice training is directly related to the classroom program; for example in 1991–92, each teacher chose a cooperative education objective as part of their Professional Improvement Plan.

FUNDING DEVELOPMENT

Mathematics instruction, whether the discreet/linear approach or the NCTM problem-solving approach, occupies approximately 20% of the instructional day. Based on the national average cost per pupil of $5243, mathematics instruction costs, on the average, at least $1048 per pupil per year at the elementary level (National Center for Educational Statistics, 1992). In other words, no matter what approach to mathematics is used, instruction is expensive.

Staff development, curriculum development, textbooks, supplementary materials, computers, calculators, manipulatives, and software are the major expenditures associated with initiating and maintaining an effective mathematics program. An extensive array of manipulatives are needed for each classroom. Class sets, library sets, and individually assigned calculators need to be available to insure that all students have access to calculators. Sufficient computers need to be available to make them a viable tool for problem solving. The Best Schools have as a goal placement of four to six computers per classroom, plus computer laboratories. Technology has been purchased by the Best Schools through reallocation of district funds and grants. The PTAs and PTOs have been major fund-raisers to support the acquisition of technology for the schools. Business partnerships have also been effective sources of technology and expertise. For example, in at least one case, a business provided the expertise and the wire, and volunteer parents installed the computer network. Few schools have been able to purchase all of the support materials and technology at one time, rather, they have developed plans to ensure that they will have the needed resources and technology in a fixed period of years. They also recognize that technology will change over the years and will have to be supplemented, enhanced, or replaced.

In general, there has been little or no increase in staffing resulting from the transformation of the mathematics program. In schools where there are mathematics or exploration labs, the classroom teacher accompanies the class to the lab and conducts the lab experience. In some cases, a trained instructional aide has been added to assist in the labs' experience. Other schools have made use of volunteers.

Effective staff and curriculum development requires time. The Best Schools invest heavily in development. The two to four inservice days built into most school calendars provide some time for focused staff development; however, release time to observe and to receive training is also needed. Courses are also offered after school on either a voluntary basis or for continuing education credits. Summer workshops for staff development and curriculum writing are planned and implemented. A number of states have requirements for continuing education, which facilitate professional development. Because of the need to work with technology, most schools encourage faculty to take computers home during holidays. In many schools the goal is that, eventually, every teacher will have a computer. Costs for inservice training usually involve the costs for substitutes for release time, travel to training sessions and to observe model programs, summer workshop pay for teachers, inservice credits that may affect movement on salary guides, workshop registration fees, professional literature, and training consultants' fees. In addition to district funds, many schools use their Education for Economic Security Dwight D. Eisenhower Mathematics and Science Education Act funds for inservice. Most of the Best Schools have found business partners who provide technical assistance and, in some cases, financial resources. University partners are also sources of technical assistance and training. The Best Schools, because of their commitment to staff and program development, have managed to find the resources for development, regardless of their economic status.

The Best Schools—Funding Illustrations

BAKER'S CHAPEL, SC

District funding is average for the region. The school receives basic funds for materials, supplies, and equipment from the district. The district budget is supplemented through grants and partnerships. The state of South Carolina's 12-Schools Project provides $15,000 per year to the school. Every teacher is required to apply for a $400 teacher grant provided by the district. Finally, the high level of student achievement has earned the school a $10,000 bonus grant from the state. These funds provide flexibility and the opportunity to transform programs, partnerships with business are also important. The new twenty-seven—IBM computer lab was donated by its business partner IBM. Baker's Chapel has been designated as a demonstration site by IBM for new equipment. McDonald's, Pepsi, Little Ceasars, Quincy's, Shoney's, TCBY, and Pizza Hut are also partners who provide limited support for student incentives and programs.

CHAPARRAL, CA

Decisions concerning school funding is sitebased. The school receives an allocation that includes salary units based on population. In 1991, approximately $9600 was directed toward the school goal-related on-site staff development activities, and $4500 was allocated for pursuit of individual professional goals. In the past three years, teachers have participated in over 2500 hours of training in mathematics, conducted primarily on the school site. The school has also applied to the district for grants for special projects. A Technology Fair is held to interest business in supporting technology. Chaparral has a corporate partnership with Downey Savings and Loan and a higher education partnership with San Diego State University.

CHAMBERLIN, VT

Time for inservice (9 days each year) is provided for within the staff contract and the school calendar. Much of the training is provided by school or district staff or through the state of Vermont training network. However, the district also provides funds for out-of-district trainers.

Funds for math manipulatives, calculators, and computers have come from district funds. The PTO has been active in redeeming grocery coupons for computers and calculators. Small grants have also provided support.

SUMMARY

The Best Schools have adopted the NCTM Curriculum and Evaluation Standards and the NCTM Professional Standards for Teaching Mathematics, which focus on not only what students know, but what they can do. They have developed mathematics programs that are reflective of current theory and research. They are committed to the belief that all children can learn and develop an appreciation for a high level of mathematics achievement. Instruction is centered on problem solving and making connections with real-life situations. Mathematics instruction is frequently integrated with other subjects. A rich environment of materials, computers, calculators, and manipulatives support higher level programs for all students. New forms of more authentic assessment are being introduced. Gone are tracked/basal/workbook/select-the-right answer based math classes. The Best Schools, urban, suburban, and rural, have developed their mathematics programs over a period of years and have plans to continue program development. In addition, there has been and will continue to be extensive staff development in the Best Schools. The Best Schools reach out to the community, business, state departments, parents and networks of schools for aid in developing programs.

REFERENCES

AIMS Education Foundation. (1989). "Project AIMS Update," Fresno, CA.

Association for Supervision and Curriculum Development. (1992). *ASCD Curriculum Handbook: A Resource for Curriculum Administrators*, Alexandria, VA.

Association for Supervision and Curriculum Development. (1989). *Toward the Thinking Curriculum: Current Cognitive Research,* L. B. Resnick and L. E. Klopher, eds., Alexandria, VA.

Bennett, William J. (1986). *First Lessons: A Report on Elementary Education in America.* Washington, D.C.: U. S. Government Printing Office.

Bennett, William J. (1988). *James Madison Elementary School.* Washington, D. C.: U. S. Government Printing Office.

Burns, Marilyn. *The Math Solution I and II,* 11707 Cooksey Rd., Adkins, TX 78801.

California State Department of Education. (1987). *Mathematics Model Curriculum Guide.* Sacramento, CA.

de Bono, Edward. *The CoRT Thinking Program.* San Diego, CA: Pergamon Press, Dormac Inc.

Educational Testing Service, Center for the Assessment of Educational Progress. (1991). *The 1991 IAEP Assessment: Objectives for Mathematics, Science, and Geography.* Princeton, NJ.

Flanders, J. R. (1987). "How Much Of the Content in Mathematics Textbooks Is New?" *Arithmetic Teacher,* 35:18–23.

Lockwood, Anne T. (1991). "Mathematics for the Information Age," *Focus in Change,* The National Center for Effective Research and Development, Madison, WI, Winter(5).

Mathematical Sciences Education Board. *Everybody Counts: A Report to the Nation on the Future of Mathematics Education.* National Academy Press, Washington, D. C., 1989.

McKnight, C. C. et al. (1987). *The Underachieving Curriculum: Assessing U. S. School Mathematics from an International Perspective.* Champaign, IL: Stipes Publishing Co.

National Assessment of Educational Progress (NAEP). (1990). *America's Challenge: Accelerating Academic Achievement.* Princeton, NJ: Educational Testing Service.

National Assessment of Educational Progress (NAEP). (1988). *The Mathematics Report Card: Are We Measuring Up?* Princeton, NJ: Educational Testing Service.

National Assessment of Educational Progress (NAEP). (1987). *Learning by Doing: A Manual for Teaching and Assessing Higher-Order Thinking in Science and Mathematics.* Princeton, NJ: Educational Testing Service.

National Center for Educational Statistics. *The Condition of Education 1992.* U. S. Department of Education, Office of Educational Research, U. S. Government Printing Office, 1992.

National Council of Teachers of Mathematics. (1989). *Curriculum and Evaluation Standards for School Mathematics* Reston, VA: NCTM.

National Council of Teachers of Mathematics. (1991). *Professional Standards for Teaching Mathematics.* Reston, VA: NCTM.

National Council of Teachers of Mathematics. (1992). "The Road to Reform in Mathematics Education: How Far Have We Traveled," Reston, VA: NCTM.

Oakes, J. et al. (1990). "Multiplying Inequalities: The Effects of Race, Social Class, and Tracking on Opportunities to Learn Mathematics and Science," Report No. R-3928-NSF, Rand Co., Santa Monica, CA.

Phi Delta Kappa, Center on Evaluation, Development, Research. (1987). *Exemplary Practice Series: Mathematics.* Bloomington, IN.

Report on Educational Research. (1992). "NAEP Board Approves New Math Standard," Alexandria, VA: Capitol Publications.

Resnick, L. B. *Education and Learning to Think.* Committee on Mathematics, Science and Social Sciences and Education, National Research Council, National Academy Press, Washington, D. C. 1987.

Steen, Lynn A. (1992). "Mathematics," In *Curriculum Handbook,* Alexandria, VA: Association for Supervision and Curriculum Development.

Stevenson. H. W. et al. (1990), *Making the Grade in Mathematics.* Reston, VA: National Council of Teachers of Mathematics.

U. S. Department of Education. (1991). *America 2000: An Educational Strategy.* Washington, D. C.

Vermont Department of Education. (1991). *Vermont Mathematics Portfolio Project: Teacher's Guide.* Vermont Department of Education, VT.

Willoughby, Stephen S. (1990). *Mathematics Education for a Changing World.* Alexandria, VA: Association for Supervision and Curriculum Development.

CHAPTER 8

Social Studies

IT has been estimated that on the average instruction in history, geography and civics accounts for only about twenty-eight minutes of a student's day and only 750 hours of a child's journey from kindergarten through grade 8. This chapter looks at the following questions concerning the development of world-class competencies in social studies for children who will spend their adult years in the 21st Century:

- What does theory and research say about what children should learn and how they should be taught?
- How do the Best Schools successfully translate theory into practice in teaching social studies?
- How do the Best Schools assess what children know and what they can do?
- What do case studies of Best Schools reveal about how highly successful social studies instruction is carried out in three very different community contexts?
- Finally, what are some of the specific practices, programs, and resources used by the Best Schools, which are widely available to other program developers?

WHAT CHILDREN SHOULD LEARN

According to the National Goals of Education,

By the year 2000, American students will leave grades four, eight and twelve having demonstrated competency in challenging subject matter including . . . history, and geography; and every school in America will ensure that all students learn to use their minds well, so they may be prepared for responsible citizenship, further learning, and productive employment in our modern economy.

By the year 2000, every adult American will be literate and will possess the knowledge and skills necessary to compete in a global economy and exercise the rights and responsibilities of citizenship.

Instruction in social studies has traditionally been part of the elementary school curriculum. However, unlike "readin, riting, and rithmetic," social studies has frequently been relegated, along with science, the arts, physical education, and health, to whatever time is left over after instruction in reading, English, and mathematics has taken place. While most schools have a social studies curriculum and social studies texts, the amount of time and the quality of time spent on instruction in the social studies content areas has varied greatly from district to district and classroom to classroom. Five major reports can be credited with refocusing the nation and the schools on social studies. These include 1) the results of the National Assessment of Educational Progress (NAEP); 2) the establishment of the National Goals for Education, explicitly including history, geography and civics and including those knowledges and abilities included in the umbrella of the social sciences; 3) the issuance of a geography curriculum framework by the Joint Committee of the National Council for Geography

Education/Association of American Geographers; 4) the issuance of nine recommendations concerning the teaching of history by the Bradley Commission on History in the Schools; and 5) the report of the forty-five member commission established by the American Historical Society, the Carnegie Foundation for the Advancement of Teaching, the National Council for Social Studies, and the Organization of American Historians.

The National Assessment of Educational Progress reports concerning the achievement of students in history, civics, and geography are consistent with their findings about other subjects, in that children in the United States have a high level of ''knowledge of simple facts'' but low achievement in ''understanding basic terms and relationships'' and almost no competence to ''interpret information and ideas.'' These results have been reported in *The Civics Report Card* (Anderson, et al., 1990), *The U.S. History Report Card* (Hammack et al., 1990), and *The Geography Learning of High School Seniors* (Allen et al., 1990).

The National Goals of Education include achievement in history and geography as two of the five subject areas in which students must demonstrate competency. The supporting objectives recognize the ever-increasing diversity of the nation (by the year 2000, one in three students will be a minority) and the need for students to have knowledge of our diverse cultural heritage and about the world community; the need for all students to increase achievement in subject areas and demonstrate ability to ''reason, solve problems, apply knowledge, and write and communicate effectively''; and the need for ''all students to be involved in activities which promote and demonstrate good citizenship, community service and personal responsibility.'' The results of the NAEP indicate that the current social studies programs in most schools are not effectively preparing students to meet these goals and objectives.

Guidelines for Geographic Education: Elementary and Secondary Schools (Natoli et al., 1984) was the first report to propose a change in the social studies framework prevalent in schools. The report focused on geography as a separate subject organized around five themes:

- location (e.g., the absolute and relative position of people and physical objects)
- place (e.g., the distinguishing physical and human characteristics of locations)
- human-environmental interaction (e.g., human sustainability and environments; responses and adaptations to physical attributes in each place)
- movement (e.g., transportation of materials and communication by people between places)
- region (e.g., the study of political, governmental, linguistic, physical, and democratic areas unifying features).

The Bradley Commission report, *Building a History Curriculum: Guidelines for Teaching History in the Schools* (1988), focused on the teaching of history as the core of social studies instruction in schools and recommended how practices could be improved, starting with history. The Commission argues that ''History is the discipline that can best help [students] to understand and deal with change, and at the same time to identify the deep continuities that link the past and present.''

''What children should know and be able to do in the field of social studies if they are to lead effective public and personal lives in the century ahead'' was the subject of the National Commission on Social Studies in the Schools (NCSSS, 1989). The final report recommended that

- Social studies should be taught every year, grades K – 12.
- Coursework is to be based on a matrix of history and geography, but each course should be infused with information and methodologies from the other social sciences.
- The curriculum must provide a sound grounding in United States history and

government but devote equal time to other regions of the world so that students will understand the economic and cultural connections between nations.

- Coursework should incorporate and act as a bridge between the humanities and sciences.
- Teaching materials and teaching strategies are to be chosen to help students become both independent and cooperative learners.
- Emphasis must be on a selective and coherent core knowledge that promotes depth of understanding, rather than superficial coverage.
- Community service be an element of the curriculum.

In 1991, Congress established the National Council on Educational Standards and Testing, a bipartisan panel that recommended the establishment of voluntary national standards and voluntary national assessment. The U.S. Department of Education has made grants to major professional and scholarly organizations to develop standards in the different subject areas, including standards for history, civics, and geography. The standards communicate what is important and relevant to teach and what performance standards students should achieve by grades 4, 8, and 12.

HOW CHILDREN LEARN—HOW CHILDREN ARE TAUGHT

A review of elementary textbooks for social studies over the past years confirms that a consistent scope and sequence, commonly referred to as the ''expanding horizons curriculum,'' has endured for more than fifty years (Bennett, 1988). Starting in kindergarten, children learn about those things closest to them—home, school, and community. These subjects are then covered in more depth in first, second, and third grades. This is then followed in grade 4 by the study of their state and region and in grades 5−8 with United States history, world history, and geography and a second year of United States history. This scope and sequence has been criticized for its failure to include ''real content,'' particularly history and geography in the lower grades and its shallow coverage of topics in the upper grades. The Bradley Commission suggested an alternative scope and sequence with history as the central focus; however, this has also been criticized for its single-minded emphasis on history. The NCSSS has recommended three alternatives for organizing curriculum, one much like the existing expanding horizons or environments and two that focus on themes or essential elements, one of which emphasizes global education and the other emphasizing democratic citizenship within the global context.

In 1987, the California State Department of Education issued the History-Social Studies Framework. This framework is divided into three broad categories that are constant at every grade level:

Knowledge and Cultural Understanding—incorporating learnings from history and the other humanities, geography and the social sciences;

Democratic Understanding and Civic Values—incorporating an understanding of our national identity, constitutional heritage, civic values, and rights and responsibilities; and

Skill Attainment and Social Participation—including basic skills, critical thinking skills, and participation skills essential for effective citizenship. (History-Social Science Curriculum Framework and Criteria Committee, 1987, p. 10)

California is a state that adopts textbooks at the state level for use in the schools. The issuance of the state-adopted framework for social studies not only has an impact on textbooks to be used in California, but also the textbooks available nationwide. While the framework includes changes in content, the course titles for grades K − 8 are reminiscent of the expanding horizons scope and sequence. However, the most important changes lie below the surface course titles and affect how social studies is taught and what students should be able to do as a result of instruction. The curriculum is organized to emphasize the development of higher level critical thinking skills and understandings. The need for students to learn some facts and information is recognized, but it is not the central focus of the program. The California Framework has been a major influence on curriculum development throughout the country since its release.

C. Frederick Risinger, past president of the National Council for the Social Studies and a member of the coordinating committee for the New National History Standards, has identified ten trends in social studies that are recognizable in the new curriculum patterns and in significant changes in subject content and teaching methods (Risinger, 1992):

- more history and different history
- more geography and different geography
- use of literature to enrich social studies themes
- focus on the multicultural nature of American society
- renewed attention to western ideas in American society
- renewed attention to ethics and values
- increased attention to the role of religion in the study of history
- attention to contemporary and controversial issues
- covering issues in depth
- writing, writing, and more writing

Allocation of time to the social studies curriculum is an essential ingredient in effective instruction. Particularly at the primary level in the elementary program, too often social studies has been relegated to a "catch as catch can" status, a subject to be taught from a textbook when the "important" language arts and mathematics instruction is done. Even in districts with well-articulated curriculum, there have often been widespread variances between the curriculum printed and the curriculum taught. Assessment practices that emphasize achievement of reading, language, and mathematics skills on standardized tests have also contributed to the view of social studies as a less important subject. Even in districts where social studies is included in the annual testing, little importance has been attached to the results. In order to implement the new social studies effectively, increased and consistent time must be allocated to the subject. Some of the time can be found through integration of at least some of the social studies curriculum with instruction in language arts, mathematics, science, and the arts.

Students need to become excited about social studies and see the relevance of study to their lives now and in the future. Too often, children consider social studies their least favorite and most uninteresting subject. All too often, particularly at the lower grades, teachers also are less than excited about the subject matter in the social studies curriculum. This may be because of their own limited indepth knowledge and training in the subject and/or because of the competing priorities of other subject areas. In order for both children and teachers to become actively interested in social studies, instructional methods must change. Without sacrificing content, students can become activity-engaged in social studies at all grade levels. Rote memorization of historical facts and place names and read-the-chapter/answer the-questions-at-the-end-of-the-chapter methods must be replaced with indepth study of concepts by discussion, writing, and oral discourse. The skills of effective social studies teachers are no different than the skills required to teach other subjects effectively.

In addition, because the social studies curriculum deals extensively with issues of diversity and the goals of the program include development of understanding and appreciation of similarity and differences, tracking or grouping of students by ability flies in the face of basic aims of the program. From a learning point view, tracking has also been shown to be ineffective. However, while tracking is an undesirable practice, flexible groupings and cooperative groups have immediate benefits in terms of learning content and for learning to function as part of a team.

HOW LEARNING SHOULD BE ASSESSED

While many schools do not use commercial standardized tests in the assessment of social studies, most book tests and teacher-developed tests have been of the short-answer or select-the-right-answer variety, similar to common standardized testing formats. Assessment in social studies should provide the opportunity for students to read and interpret maps, graphs, diagrams, pictures, and charts; to retrieve and analyze information from books, data bases, documents, newspapers, and periodicals; and to organize and express ideas orally and in writing. This type of assessment, individually and as part of a group, requires formats for assessment that include essays, oral reports, and project products. These forms of assessment require time for student preparation and are best developed as part of the instructional process.

In summary, as part of the reassessment of how children learn, the distinction needs to be made between surface knowledge (i.e., the memorization of facts, procedures and application) and meaningful knowledge, connected learning that makes sense to the learner and prepares the student for further learning. The goals and emerging standards for social studies are grounded in at least seven assumptions:

- Social studies is an essential subject that should be a regular part of every child's educational program.
- There is a need for more significant study of content, particularly from the disciplines of history and geography; however, the instructional emphasis needs to be on indepth study, not coverage of surface facts and information.
- Learning is natural and motivational; instruction should be organized to make connections among strands of the social studies curriculum, events, and real-life experiences of children.
- Children should be actively engaged in learning, rather than passively receiving teacher recitations or textbook readings.
- Children should write about, speak of, and discuss social studies; they should learn to critique sources and develop cogent arguments to support positions.
- The availability of technology allows for the expansion of resources available to children and teachers in accomplishing the aims of the social studies curriculum.
- Finally, assessment is best embedded in the instructional process, rather than being an add-on. Assessment should provide evidence of not only what a child knows, but what a student can do. As much as possible, it should be performance- and product-based.

THE BEST SCHOOLS—THEORY INTO PRACTICE IN SOCIAL STUDIES

In the Best Schools, social studies is an important subject that is seriously attended to. Programs reflect the recommendations of the many studies and reports that make recommendations concerning the social studies curriculum and methods of instruction. Social studies is frequently integrated with other subjects; however, individual integrity of the disciplines of history and geography are maintained. How social studies is taught in the Best Schools is consistent with how students are taught in all subject areas. The emphasis is on the development of higher order thinking skills and indepth knowledge and understanding of historical events rather than on the rote memorization of dates, names and events. The consistent underlying acceptance of how children learn and how they should be taught acts as facilitators for integration of content, field experiences, research studies, and activities related to broad themes. The Best Schools have accomplished their mission with diverse social, economic, and physical resources.

The Best Schools—Three Case Studies in Social Studies: The Contexts

ETON SCHOOL, BELLEVUE, WA

Eton is a Montessori school serving students from the communities on the eastern shore of Lake Washington. While located in and drawing students from an affluent socioeconomic area, the school has recognized since its inception the importance of diversity in its student population. Tuition has been kept to a minimum, scholarships are offered, and the school contracts with the Department of Social Services for the education of disadvantaged students. Students are drawn to the school by its unique program. Eton School received special recognition for history as part of the Blue Ribbon School Program.

Dr. Patricia Feltin, *Principal, Pre-K – 8, 248 Students*

HOPEWELL ELEMENTARY SCHOOL, WEST CHESTER, OH

With an enrollment of over eleven hundred students, Hopewell is the third largest elementary school in Ohio. The school serves a diverse student population in a suburban setting and is the focal point of the community. While the school is large, it has as an ongoing theme, ''Hopewell has a heart,'' and a dedication to challenging students in all academic areas and learning processes. Two other schools in West Chester have been recognized as Blue Ribbon Schools.

Thomas I. Hayden, *Principal, K – 6, 1162 Students*

HIGHLAND PARK ELEMENTARY SCHOOL, AUSTIN TX

Highland Park Elementary School is actively involved in the preparation of today's students for the 21st Century. The school is located in a middle- to upper middle-class neighborhood, which is being revitalized by young families and a resulting growth in the student population. Because of its population, the school is not eligible for special funding from local, state, or federal sources. However, through resourcefulness, the school's operating expenses are consistently lower than the local district average. Highland Park is one of twenty-nine schools worldwide selected by Apple Computer to participate in the Christopher Columbus Consortium and work with the University of Texas and other members of the consortium on research and development designed to demonstrate how technology can significantly improve learning and creativity. Highland Park School received special recognition for history as part of the Blue Ribbon School Program. Eleven other Austin schools have been recognized as Blue Ribbon Schools.

Claudia Tousek, *Principal, K – 5, 561 Students*

CLASS ORGANIZATION AND INSTRUCTIONAL TIME

The Best Schools teach social studies in heterogeneous classes. Whole-class, small group, and cooperative learning groups are used based on the purposes and structure of lessons. The schools schedule between 150 minutes and 250 minutes per week for social studies classes;

however, integration of social studies content into other areas of the curriculum provides for considerable extended study, in some cases doubling the scheduled social studies time block. Most of the schools use the literature strand of the language arts curriculum to have children read fiction and nonfiction related to history. The writing strand of language arts is also used for joint social studies/English research and writing experiences. Science is also often integrated with social studies. For example, in *PEARL Elementary School #32*, in Yonkers, New York, students are engaged in an integrated unit on the Hudson River. Students learn about the physical geography and economic impact of the river, as well as river ecology and environmental problems.

The arts are also frequently integrated and correlated with social studies through themes and projects. Even mathematics finds its way into the curriculum through the study of the history of mathematics and through the collection, analysis, and representation of data in various forms.

The Best Schools—Class Organization Illustrations

ETON SCHOOL, WA

Students are clustered in classes that encompass three-year grade spans, grades 3−6, 6−9, and 9−12. There are no grade levels at Eton, no high or low reading groups, no separate special education or English-as-a-Second Language classes. Because the Montessori curriculum is completely individualized, students move through the program at their own pace determined by their own interests, abilities, and developmental clocks, learning to make choices and to use time constructively. Students contract with their teachers for what will be accomplished each week. It is estimated that 10% of instructional time is spent in the study of history and 10% in the study of geography.

HOPEWELL, OH

Classes of from twenty to twenty-nine are heterogeneously grouped. Emphasis is placed on providing the best educational environment for each student. Schoolwide activities are structured to minimize interruption of instructional time. Students with special needs are mainstreamed to the degree possible. The Hopewell Odyssey of the Mind Team exemplifies the school's success in achieving acceptance and integration of all of the student populations. Five students comprised the award-winning team: one student enrolled in the gifted program, one in the program for severe behavioral handicaps, one with learning disabilities, and two students who were not involved in a special program.

HIGHLAND PARK, TX

History concepts are integrated into a social studies block, which also includes geography, government, economics, sociology, character education, and social studies skills. This integrated approach allows teachers to incorporate Texas state objectives in comprehensive units that explore many features of a selected historical period. Grade level teams alternate social studies and science instruction or integrate the two subjects in cross-curricular units. Time spent each day on social studies varies from thirty to forty-five minutes of formal instruction.

CURRICULUM

The Best Schools provide a content-rich program in social studies, which includes history, geography, and other areas of social science. The curriculum follows the expanding horizon sequence, in that it begins with age appropriate studies, which are easy for young children to relate to and progresses through the grades to more abstract and remote concepts. Broad themes are used to organize the social studies program at each grade level. Students are engaged in a wide variety of instructional strategies that make the subject interesting. They read fiction and nonfiction, conduct research studies, work with computers, discuss issues, work on projects in cooperative groups, visit museums and historical sites, and participate in multi-media lessons. For example, sixth grade students in River Bend School, Chesterfield, Missouri, participate in a unit on acid rain. Students study their community indepth including population density, industry, and prevalent modes of transportation. Through Kidsnet (National Geographic Society) via telecommunications, they share data with schools across the nation and analyze the data to determine the relationship between human and environmental factors.

In the Best Schools, much of the literature used in the language arts program is correlated with the social studies curriculum. Students read both fiction and nonfiction related to periods of history, including biographies of historical figures. Writing assignments relate to both language arts and social studies curriculum.

Geography is considered part of the social studies curriculum and frequently parallels the history strand. Instruction includes the five themes of geography: location, place, relationships within place, movement, and region. Software such as Jenny's Journey, Where in the World Is Carmen Sandiego? and Oregon Trail are programs frequently used to reinforce geographical knowledge. Many different kinds of maps, globes, and multi-media sources are used to enhance understanding. Children make maps and graphs and collect data in the field. Classes are frequently organized into collaborative, mixed ability teams for activities and projects. The diverse cultural and ethnic nature of the class, school, region, and nation is used in the study of geographic areas. For example:

ASHLAWN ELEMENTARY SCHOOL, ARLINGTON, VA

The five themes of geography (location, place, relationships within places, movement, and region) are stressed throughout the curriculum.

- Kindergarten students explore the theme of location by using simple community maps and maps of the school; they learn about direction and the relationships between places.
- Grade 1 students begin to identify physical features such as mountains and bodies of water on their maps. They also learn about distances and are given simple map-related problems to solve that require them to plot routes and describe them in geographic terms.
- Grade 2 students begin to use map symbols and new geographic terms; they learn how to make their own maps. Discussions about other world traditions and cultures are introduced.
- Grade 3 students use more advanced symbols and legends related to bodies of water, vegetation, and elevation. The significance of map scales are also examined, and the students use tables and graphs to convey information about different countries.
- Grade 4 students explore the uses for different types of maps such as population density maps, natural resources maps, weather maps, and aerial maps. The features and characteristics of different regions of the world are also examined, along with the concepts of latitude, longitude, and time zones.
- Grade 5 students learn about early civilizations, and they examine differences between ancient and modern maps. Reasons for changes over time are discussed.

Throughout the social studies curriculum, the emphasis is on the development of higher order critical thinking skills. Instruction is organized to make connections among the strands of the social studies curriculum, events, and real-life experiences of children. The focus is on indepth study of "real content" and understanding, not on surface coverage of facts and information. Although textbooks are used in most schools, they are only one source of information in the program.

The Best Schools—Curriculum Illustrations

ETON SCHOOL, WA

The study of history begins with the concept of time and progresses through the curriculum centered around the fundamental needs of humans and the stages in the progress of civilization. The Montessori Time Line of Mankind is used to show the gradual development of humans and their contributions to the planet over 500,000 years. History permeates the curriculum. The study of history begins with reality and moves to abstraction. The youngest students begin with familiar measurement such as calendars, the seasons, the clock, and special celebrations and holidays. In the elementary years, students learn about the beginnings of the earth and where they fit into the progression of life on the planet. Indepth study of human history follows.

The "Fundamental Needs of Humans" are studied as the foundation for studying six periods of human history: pre-history, Egyptian, Greek, medieval, Renaissance and present day. Using a variety of books as resources, students label maps; research an event or personality of the time; and produce book reports, creative writing, and summaries. Projects to reinforce the concepts include art replication, dioramas, field trips, and play acting. For example, in the study of United States history, a classroom was converted in an early colonial town. Each student chose and researched a different occupation, dressed the part, and was interviewed by other students.

Primary classes study the history of the Northwest, intermediate classes study United States history, and middle schoolers study world history. Textbooks are only one resource used in instruction. The literature and cultural program enhances the curriculum. Myths and legends are investigated at all age levels. The ethnic diversity of the students inspires cross cultural celebrations and sharing. Young students study people of various continents and enjoy the stories of the cultures. At the elementary level, students read legends of early Americans among other selections. Older students read historically based literature, biographies, and current events materials. Field trips are planned to museums and hands-on historical settings. Relatives of students and other visitors share their histories and cultures with students.

Eton's geography program combines both physical and cultural studies to provide a clear picture of the ways in which we are compared to the world around us. The youngest preschoolers begin with the most general of all maps, the world map; learn the language of geography as they place the continents into the world map puzzle; trace the outlines of the seven continents; color them; and make their own maps. In the elementary years, this process is repeated for the United States, as well as for topographical details of the entire globe, and classes begin to talk about concepts of physical and political geography. An understanding develops about how the physical shapes the cultural. Diversity of cultures and the different ways in which each of us views the world emerges from cross-curricular discussions and readings. By middle school, students have become vocal advocates of responsible global decision making. Recycling and protection of natural resources are two important projects for which students assume leadership.

HOPEWELL, OH

The school follows the Lakota district graded course of study. The curriculum builds on the egocentric nature of kindergarten students and spirals throughout the grades to encompass the world. History, geography, and social behavior studies form an integrated social studies program. A common thread of personal values, citizenship, and fundamentals of democracy is reinforced at all grade levels. The curriculum is implemented through a widely varied program of thematic units, integrating all subject areas and involving the unified arts teams, as well as audiovisual, community, and field experiences.

- Kindergarten—Instruction in kindergarten begins with the identification of historical American figures. The people range from Johnny "Appleseed" Chapman to Dr. Martin Luther King, Jr. Teachers combine activities with audio lessons and active play to produce mentally stimulating and memorable units. Book-making, poetry, finger plays, music, dances, drama, songs, and read-aloud books on historical events combine to create the multifaceted curriculum.

- Grade 1 – The first grade curriculum spirals upward by repeating the study of some historical figures and adding studies of Chinese, Afro-American, and Native American cultures. These items are taught in thematic units of study that incorporate the visual and performing arts. The children use their new reading skills to discover historical times and places through personal reading and by listening to many biographies and historical fiction read to them. An example of a thematic unit is one on Chinese culture that ends with a unified arts and classroom-sponsored Chinese New Year Parade complete with dragons, lanterns, fans, and kites.

- Grade 2 – Comparing and contrasting yesterday to today is the headline of the second grade curriculum. Recognizing the multi-ethnic and diverse nature of our American populace is a main objective. The grade level accomplishes this objective through such units as "Everyone Counts," which focuses on physical and mental imitations using literature and drama to study historical figures such as Helen Keller, Annie Sullivan, and Louis Braille. The multicultural foundations laid in first grade are expanded through examining the literature of Arnold Lobel. This focuses on Asian cultures and culminates with a Chinese unit that integrates math, science, and language arts. Finally, in conjunction with Grandparent's Day, children prepare poems, books, and interviews with their grandparents to recognize their own multi-ethnic and individual diversity.

- Grade 3 – In grade three, students begin the serious historical studies. Literature is integrated into the lessons by creating a unit on pioneer culture around the Laura Ingalls Wilder books. The students recreate pioneer homes and crafts in a multi-media project and use a variety of creative writings to record their experiences. Local history is explored through slide "walk-through" of local landmarks and unfolding local history. The multi-ethnic nature of the North American people is shown by comparing and contrasting the literature, families, celebrations, and foods of Canada, Mexico, and the United States. The year culminates with a visit to a local camp specializing in pioneer handicrafts, cooking, culture, and historical reenactment.

- Grade 4 – Independent work and research begins in grade 4, with literature a basic component of the thematic units. Western and Eastern religious holidays are explained and their origins explored. The idea is stressed that differences in beliefs and customs make the world an interesting place. One activity that melds history and literature is the construction of a time line with historical quotations.

- Grade 5 – The fifth grade encounters pure history in the form of an intensive American history course, which takes the learner from prehistoric hunters and gatherers through westward expansion. Teachers focus on the reasons behind immigration and continental migration. The objectives of our diverse cultural heritage, multi-ethnic foundations, and democratic fundamentals are constantly reinforced. This is done through examination of such historical fiction as Johnny Tremain and biographies and fiction set against proper time periods. By meeting language arts objectives through history lessons, the teachers find more time for historical research, cooperative projects, multi-media presentations, and integrated study.

- Grade 6 – World history, from the rise of civilizations in Mesopotamia through the Renaissance, is the focus of the sixth grade. The students examine the development of religion from the polytheistic agrarian societies to the Judeo-Christian revolution to the rise of Islam. The literature of each period is discussed, and the students are constantly asked to research and write about their findings. Cooperative projects have included foods of the Greco-Roman Empire, heraldry, and architecture of the ages.

HIGHLAND PARK, TX

Highland Park teachers believe that even young children can grasp historical concepts in that children can develop a sense of time and are capable of a rich and full awareness of the past. As recommended by the National Council on Social Studies in the Schools, teachers have developed a cycle of learning approach, which builds on student understanding by teaching from what is familiar to what is new, and from the new to another familiar concept. Teachers pull from a variety of instructional strategies and resources to create units that stimulate student interest and build understanding. Students often construct classroom time lines to graphically illustrate sequence of events. Quality literature is incorporated by sharing historical novels, and enrichment is provided through music and art activities so that children develop an understanding that "real" people created history. Teachers use primary source materials such as letters, census records, journals, old photographs, and period maps to prove that significant people such as George Washington are not just characters in a story. People from the past serve as role models when they are portrayed as real people who used their talents and resources to achieve their goals.

Teachers also reach beyond American history through enrichment units. For example, fifth graders examine Greek culture and its contributions to modern society in a six-week unit that includes

- a vocabulary unit highlighting Greek roots of words
- comparison of ancient and modern systems of government
- art projects based on Greek myths read in class
- productions of teacher-written plays based on Greek myths
- independent research on specific elements of Greek culture

The culminating activity is a Greek Festival where students display the products of their studies.

The third grade students experience an indepth study of the Middle Ages. Teachers incorporate the Texas state objectives related to the concept of "community" into an overall study of the medieval period. Learning activities include

- displaying a time line that wraps around the room to illustrate the passage of time and sequence historical events
- comparing/contrasting modern maps of Europe with examples from medieval times
- viewing videotapes or films such as "Merrily Ever After: The Story of Two Medieval Weddings" and determining differences in the lives of lords and peasants
- creating medieval crafts such as stained glass designs, banners, coats of arms, and calligraphy products
- performing medieval dances and listening to period music
- role-playing a meeting of the Burwarmot, the borough court that dealt with the day-to-day management of medieval cities
- learning about inventors using "Inventions of the Renaissance," a teacher-developed HyperCard program for the computer lab

The culminating activity is a costume parade and Medieval Fair at which students participate in centers staffed by local members of the Society for Creative Anachronism.

Geography is integrated into the social studies program by having each grade study a unit relating geography to history and the economy. The most popular technological tool for teaching geography remains Where in the World Is Carmen Sandiego? computer software. However, individual teachers have also found creative ways to integrate geography and technology. For example, fourth graders use computer equipment to produce brochures on given states as if they were producing an advertisement for the Tourist Office.

ASSESSING WHAT STUDENTS KNOW AND CAN DO

Most of the Best Schools use some form of criterion-referenced testing rather than a commercial norm-referenced test to assess social studies progress. Products developed by individual students and/or groups, such as graphs, maps, research reports, dramas, reenactment of events, and oral reports are some of the means used in assessment. These are criterion-based approaches to assessment, where the work that children produce is compared to achievement criteria rather than to the performance of other children. Culminating projects that include written, visual, and oral work are frequently used for assessment. More traditional criterion-based tests are also used, as are checklists.

The Best Schools—Assessment Illustration

ETON SCHOOL, WA

Eton's teachers are trained observers. Every individual lesson a teacher does with a child is an assessment, comparing a child's performance of a task with a theoretically effective performance. Carefully maintained portfolio records are kept for each child, listing when the lesson was introduced, when practiced, and finally, when mastered. Written work is kept in subject matter notebooks yearlong. Progress is readily apparent, and parents are encouraged to view the notebooks and copies of the weekly contracts. The program is continually evaluated by comparison with current journals, new textbooks, and educational research findings.

THE BEST SCHOOLS—PROGRAM AND SUPPORT IN SOCIAL STUDIES

The Implementation Process

The Best Schools share a consistent view of how children learn, which includes the need for active engagement of learners, the need to make connections between content of real-life and other content, the importance of indepth knowledge versus surface acquisition of facts and information, the need to develop higher level thinking skills, and high expectations for all children. The development of curriculum in social studies has taken place over time and is grounded in learning research and meaningful content from the disciplines. There is a recognition that effective curriculum development does not mean just the periodic updating of textbooks.

STAFF DEVELOPMENT

Staff development is a major commitment in the Best Schools. It is recognized that teachers must continue to be learners if they are to work effectively with children. Staff development is related to the program objectives of the school, as well as the needs of individual staff; in addition, staff development is planned as part of every new or revised program. The aim is for indepth understanding of the concepts and themes underlying the curriculum, methods of instruction, and knowledge of content. These aims cannot be accomplished in single training sessions; they require time, practice, and follow-up. A good deal of staff development occurs as staff—teachers, principals, subject specialists, librarians—develop curriculum; current practices are assessed, research and theory reviewed, resources identified, and decisions made concerning scope and sequence and inclusion or exclusion of topics. Unifying themes are developed and assessment practices designed.

The Best Schools—Staff Development Illustrations

ETON SCHOOL, WA

Continuous staff development is a priority at Eton School. Prior to the start of school each fall, teachers devote two required weeks to inservice training and planning. Workshops vary according to the year's special emphasis and the areas of professional growth identified by teachers. During the school year, one afternoon meeting each month is devoted to sharing the expertise of faculty members. Teachers are encouraged to pursue individual goals by attending workshops, conferences, university courses, and seminars. Examples of workshops attended by staff include "Teaching World's Religions," "Christopher Columbus," "The History of Math," "Global Education," "Native American Culture and Spirituality," and "Dangerous Memories: America's Legacy of the European Encounter."

HOPEWELL, OH

Staff development is an important part of the Hopewell educational process. Staff are encouraged to attend workshops and conferences; the district supports inservice through release time and partial reimbursement for professional meetings. Two inservice days are part of the school calendar. Seventy-five percent of the staff holds master's degrees. New teachers receive basic orientation prior to the opening of school, meet with the elementary curriculum consultant bimonthly, meet periodically with the principal, and are part of a mentor program. Each mentor receives thirty hours of training provided by a local university. Duties of the mentor include orienting the entry-level teacher to the school district, building policies and procedures, classroom management, utilization of courses of study, and parent communication. Days are provided for observation between the entry-level teacher and mentor. County-wide inservices are also provided throughout the year.

HIGHLAND PARK, TX

The basic model for staff development is "teacher teaching teacher." All Highland Park teachers participate in faculty-planned programs at least twice a month after school or on district early release days when children go home early. For example, training was given in new word processing software to encourage writing through technology. In 1992, 70% of the teachers volunteered and participated in a week-long technology training session in the school's computer lab. Teachers in past years have developed history and geography curricula.

FUNDING DEVELOPMENT

Social studies instruction in all schools has associated costs. Based on the national average cost per pupil, a program that occupies 10% of instructional time would cost $524 per student and one that occupies 20% of instructional time, $1048 per student (National Center for Educational Statistics, 1992). In other words, no matter what approach to social studies is used, instruction is expensive.

In addition to staff salaries, expenses include staff development, curriculum development, maps, globes, fiction and nonfiction books, software, multi-media, news sources, field trips, computers, and general materials for projects. Basic books, resources, and supplies are purchased through district funds. Staff development is also an area in which districts and schools have made budget-related commitments. Field trips may be supported by the school, PTA and/or financed by students. Technology and multi-media may be purchased with district funds, through grants, or special fund-raising. In some cases where schools do not use textbooks, resources normally spent on these resources have been allocated to other resources that support the social studies program.

The Best Schools—Cost Illustrations

ETON SCHOOL, WA

The costs for development of the social studies program are primarily those associated with the purchase not only of textbooks but of other fiction and nonfiction books that support the program. Continuing staff development for social studies and for all program areas has related costs. Eton School spends about $700 per teacher each year on staff development. The school provides substitute coverage for attendance at workshops and underwrites one-half the registration fee for workshops and conferences.

HOPEWELL, OH

The library/media center plays an important part in the social studies program. The media center supports the classroom with closed circuit television. Resources available from the media center for circulation include abacuses, puppets, filmstrips, transparencies, study prints, records, audiocassettes, computer disks, and video discs. A teacher workroom is an extension of the media center. The collection of books has been enhanced through "Birthday Club" books. Several grants have enabled Hopewell to receive three video projection screens, a video camera, microphones, a sound mixer, a light kit, computer software, and a modem. Community support of a grocer promotion receipt redemption program provided seven computers and six printers.

SUMMARY

The Best Schools take instruction in social studies seriously, starting in kindergarten. They schedule from 150 to 250 minutes of instruction in social studies and increase the allocated time through integration of social studies with other subjects. The literature and writing strands of the language arts program are frequently correlated with social studies. Emphasis in the social studies program is on the development of higher order thinking skills, not on the acquisition of surface information. The social studies curriculum includes significant content in history and geography, as well as civics, current events, and other strands of the social sciences. Gone are tracked/basal/select-the-right-answer social studies classes. Students are actively engaged in activities that stimulate interest and promote indepth understanding. The Best Schools, urban, suburban, and rural, have developed their programs over time with programs grounded in theories of learning as well as content. In addition, there has been and continues to be a commitment to staff and curriculum development.

REFERENCES

Allen, R., et al. (1990). *The Geography Learning of High School Seniors.* Educational Testing Service, Princeton, NJ.

Anderson, L. et al. (1990). *The Civics Report Card.* Princeton, NJ: Educational Testing Service.

Bennett, William J. (1986). *First Lessons: A Report on Elementary Education in America.* Washington D.C.: United States Department of Education.

Bennett, William J. (1988). *James Madison Elementary School.* Washington D.C.: United States Department of Education.

Bradley Commission on History in the Schools. (1988). *Building a History Curriculum: Guidelines for Teaching History in the Schools.* Washington, D.C.: Educational Excellence Network.

Geography Educational Standards Project. (1993). "National Geography Standards: Draft June 30, 1993," Washington, D.C.: National Council for Geography Education.

Hammack, D. C. et al. (1990). *The U. S. History Report Card.* Princeton, NJ: Educational Testing Service.

History-Social Science Curriculum Framework and Criteria Committee. (1987). *History-Social Science Framework for California Public Schools Kindergarten Through Grade Twelve.* Sacramento, CA: California State Department of Education.

National Center for Educational Statistics. (1992). *The Condition of Education 1992.* U. S. Department of Education, Office of Educational Research, U. S. Government Printing Office.

National Center for History in the Schools. (1994). *National History Standards Project: Progress Report and Draft Standards.* University of California, Los Angeles, CA.

Natoli, S. and Joint Committee on Geography Education. (1984). *Guidelines for Geography Education: Elementary and Secondary Schools*. Washington D. C.: Association of American Geographers and the National Council for Geography Education.

Parker, Walter C. (1991). *Renewing the Social Studies Curriculum*. Alexandria, VA: Association for Supervision and Curriculum Development (ASCD).

Risinger, C. Frederick. (1992). *Current Directions in Social Studies*. Houghton Mifflin.

U. S. Department of Education. (1991). *America 2000: An Educational Strategy*. Washington, D. C.

CHAPTER 9

Science

IT has been estimated that science instruction in the average elementary school accounts for only twenty-eight minutes of a student's day and only 750 hours of a child's journey from kindergarten through grade 8. This chapter looks at the following questions concerning the development of science literacy in the 1990s:

- What does theory and research say about what children should learn and how they should be taught?
- How do the Best Schools successfully translate theory into practice in teaching science?
- How do the Best Schools assess what children know and what they can do?
- What do case studies of Best Schools reveal about how highly successful science instruction is implemented in five very different community contexts?
- Finally, what are some of the specific practices, programs, and resources used by the Best Schools which are widely available to other program developers?

WHAT CHILDREN SHOULD LEARN

According to the National Goals of Education,

By the year 2000, American students will leave grades four, eight and twelve having demonstrated competency in challenging subject matter including . . . science . . . and every school in America will ensure that all students learn to use their minds well, so they may be prepared for responsible citizenship, further learning, and productive employment in our modern economy.

By the year 2000, U.S. students will be first in the world in . . . science achievement.

Science has traditionally taken a backseat, at the elementary level, to the language arts and arithmetic. Among the reasons for this third-, fourth- or even fifth- rate status of science are low value placed on the development of science literacy for all students beginning at the elementary level; competing priorities for instructional time in a crowded academic day; the lack of training on the part of teachers, principals, board members, and parents in science; the perception that understanding science is for those who will become scientists and that instruction can be postponed until high school and beyond; prevalence of textbooks, materials, curriculum, and methods that focus on science as memorization of selected ''facts,'' which turn students and teachers off to science. Clearly, there is a need for change in time commitment, content, and methods of teaching science if the national goals are to be achieved and if students are going to function effectively in the 21st Century. The national goals set forth much higher expectations for defining science literacy for children of the year 2000 and beyond. Keywords and phrases within the goals include ''demonstrated competency,'' ''challenging subject matter,'' ''all students,'' and ''prepared for responsible citizenship," "prepared for further learning," and "prepared for productive employment in our modern economy." These statements imply the need for setting standards for *all students* far beyond the implicit low standards for scientific learning that is traditionally part of the elementary science program.

In 1990, the American Association for the Advancement of Science (AAAS) published *Science for All Americans,* (Rutherford and Ahlgren, 1990), which "consists of a set of recommendations on what understandings and ways of thinking are essential for all citizens in a world shaped by science and technology." The report and subsequent book was the result of a three-year collaboration involving several hundred scientists, mathematicians, engineers, physicians, philosophers, historians, and educators. The recommendations include mathematics and technology, as well as the natural and physical sciences and are applicable to all students. Recommendations concerning content are based both on scientific and human significance. Knowledge is doubling every five years, science has been fractioned into over 40,000 fields, and over any given two-day period, there may be as many as 3000 discoveries in chemistry alone. The framers of *Science for all Americans* recognized that schools cannot teach it all, and in fact, schools need to decrease content in order to teach it better. Curriculum developers need to focus more on what to eliminate than what to add to the curriculum. The recommendations for content included in the publication were selected based on what was judged as worth knowing now and for decades to come. Concepts were chosen that could serve as a lasting foundation on which further knowledge could be built. Choices for inclusion had to meet criteria having to do with human life and broad goals within a free society, including utility, social responsibility, intrinsic value of knowledge, philosophical value, and childhood enrichment. *Science for All Americans* is not a curriculum, nor does it make recommendations for learning outcomes at particular grade levels; rather, it defines what students should retain after graduation from high school, the cumulative effects of a K−12 education.

What students should learn, as put forth in *Science for All Americans*, has been presented in sets of related topics, which taken together, lay out a conceptual framework for understanding science and which can serve as a basis for further learning. The topics are not meant to be sequentially incorporated into a school curriculum nor dealt with as distinct topics. A major recommendation of the report is that the boundaries between the scientific disciplines be softened and that the connections between science and other disciplines be emphasized. The following list represents the recommended conceptual framework and the conceptual categories that all students should be familiar with, but not the specific content (Rutherford and Ahlgren, 1990, pp. xxiii−xxiv):

SCIENCE FRAMEWORK AND CONCEPTUAL CATEGORIES

(1) The nature of science—the scientific world view, scientific inquiry, and the scientific enterprise

(2) The nature of mathematics—some features of mathematics and mathematical processes;

(3) The nature of technology—science and technology, principles of technology, and technology and society

(4) The physical setting—The universe, the earth, forces that shape the earth, the structure of matter, transformations of energy, the motion of things, and the forces of nature;

(5) The living environment—diversity of life, heredity, cells, interdependence of life, flow of matter and energy, and evolution of life

(6) The human organism—human identity, life cycle, basic functions, learning, physical health, and mental health

(7) Human society – cultural effects on behavior, group organization and behavior, social change, social trade- offs, forms of political and economic organizations, social conflict, and worldwide social systems

(8) The designed world – the human presence, agriculture, materials, manufacturing, energy sources, energy use, communication, information processing, and health technology

(9) The mathematical world – numbers, symbolic relationships, shapes, uncertainty, summarizing data, sampling, and reasoning

(10) Historical perspectives – displacing the earth from the center of the universe, uniting the heavens and earth, uniting matter and energy, time and space, extending time, setting the earth's surface in motion, understanding fire, splitting the atom, explaining the diversity of life, discovering germs, and harnessing power

(11) Common themes – systems, models, constancy, patterns of change, evolution, and scale

(12) Habits of mind – values and attitudes and skills

Science for All Americans was part of the larger and ongoing Project 2061. *Benchmarks for Science Literacy* developed by Project 2061, details the progress students should make by the end of grades 2, 5, 8, and 12 (1994). The benchmarks were developed by six school district teams assisted by university faculty and extensively reviewed by teachers, curriculum specialists, and content supervisors. Following are three examples of elementary benchmarks. (In these statements, *know* is shorthand for understanding ideas well enough to use them in a variety of meaningful contexts.)

> *By the end of grade 2*, students should know that different plants and animals have external characteristics that help them thrive in different kinds of places.
>
> *By the end of grade 5*, students should know that individuals of the same kind differ in their characteristics, and sometimes the differences give individuals an advantage in surviving and producing.
>
> *By the end of grade 8*, students should know that individual organisms with certain traits are more likely to survive and have offspring. Changes in environmental conditions can affect the survival of individual organisms and entire species. [excerpted from the "Living Environment" chapter]

The National Science Education Standards and Assessment Project, commissioned in 1991, also has as its goal to develop national science education standards for grades K – 12 and to build consensus among a range of constituencies nationwide to adopt those standards. The science standards for curriculum, teaching, and assessment (grades 4, 8, and 12) are to be completed by summer 1994.

HOW CHILDREN LEARN – HOW CHILDREN ARE TAUGHT

Traditionally, the teaching of science at the elementary level has been based on the premise that science is solely knowing what science has already discovered, with a collection of identified facts for each grade level. Memorization has frequently been the major form of learning; little emphasis has been placed on science as doing. The limited nature of the science program has further been reinforced by the lack of science labs, science equipment, and the lack of science background of most elementary teachers. In the 1960s, there were several large-scale curriculum development efforts from which emerged science programs based on science as inquiry and science as doing, the most popular of which was SCIS (Science Curriculum Improvement Study). The lack of elementary labs and equipment was partly overcome in this program by the provision of "kits" that contained materials for experiments, as well as written materials for students and teachers. "Physical" and "life" science kits were developed for each grade level. However, while used effectively in some schools, lack of understanding and teacher training reduced the use of the kits, in many cases, to mere activities to be completed at scheduled times in the week. Other state and local projects developed curricula and materials that utilized hands-on approaches to science. During this period, the National Science Foundation and other groups sponsored institutes to provide training to teachers. Nevertheless, by the late 1970s, national level funding for training in science education had largely dried up, and funds for program development were also in short supply. Most schools returned to textbook science programs that were implemented by teachers with whatever knowledge they brought with them to the job. However, some schools continued to emphasize science, to actively engage students through hands-on activities, and to provide training for teachers at the local level.

The United States has paid a price for its lack of attention to meaningful science instruction. The National Assessment of Educational Progress (NAEP) describes "student's knowledge of science and their ability to use what they do know, as remarkably limited." By age nine, most students do "know everyday science facts," and by age thirteen more than half show "understanding of basic information from the life and physical sciences." However, less than 10% of the thirteen-year-olds "have some detailed scientific knowledge and can evaluate the appropriateness of scientific procedures," and less than 1% "can infer relationships and draw conclusions using detailed scientific knowledge" (NAEP, 1990). As in other subject areas assessed by NAEP, students knowledge of facts is far greater than their demonstrated ability to use higher order thinking skills.

If students are to achieve the goals of scientific literacy, dramatic changes must be made in what children are taught and how they are taught in most of the nation's schools. It is necessary that what is known about how children learn be applied in the classroom. Children construct their own meaning based on their previous knowledge and perceptions and new information or experiences encountered. Concepts are best learned and need to be taught using multiple contexts that build on previous knowledge and, at the same time, insure that previously held incorrect knowledge is replaced. Students learning must go beyond surface knowledge (i.e., the memorization of facts, procedures, and applications) to the development of meaningful knowledge (connected learning which makes sense to the learner), must be given time to explore concepts, apply ideas to novel situations, receive feedback, and reflect on what is learned. The need for time has at least two immediate implications for the elementary curriculum.

First, more time needs to be devoted to the teaching of science at the elementary level since the national average of twenty-eight minutes per week is clearly inadequate. Second, more time must be devoted to teaching important concepts and less time devoted to covering a vast array of facts and information. "Less is more" in the development of the elementary science curriculum. Those content areas that are included in the curriculum need to be covered and explored in the depth necessary to insure understanding. In AAAS's publication *Science For All Americans*, the following characteristics of effective science instructions are identified (Rutherford and Ahlgren, 1990, Chapter 13):

- Students should have experiences with the kinds of thought and action that are typical of science, mathematics, and technology.
- Students should be engaged with challenging subject matter and, at the same time, be provided with opportunities for success; understanding rather than vocabulary should be the main purpose of science teaching.

- Instruction should begin with questions and phenomena that are of interest to students; problems should be given that are appropriate to their developmental level and that require them to decide on the relevance of evidence and to offer their own interpretations.
- Students need to have opportunities to learn to use the tools of science, such as thermometers, hand lenses, cameras, microscopes, calculators, and computers, and to use the tools in various contexts.
- They need opportunities for observing, collecting, sorting, cataloging, surveying, interviewing, note taking, and sketching.
- Students need to have the time and opportunity to question, puzzle, and discuss findings; to collect, sort, and analyze evidence; and to build arguments based on evidence. Any topic that can be taught in a single lesson is probably not worth learning.
- Students should have opportunities to study scientific ideas in historical context in order to develop a sense of how science happens by learning about the growth of scientific ideas.
- A high priority needs to be placed on effective oral and written communication; emphasis should be on clear expression of procedures, findings, and ideas.
- "The collaborative nature of scientific and technological work should be strongly reinforced by frequent group activity in the classroom; . . . group approaches should be the norm in the science classroom; . . . competition among students for high grades can distort what should be the prime motivation for science: to find things out."
- The nature of inquiry is determined by what is being studied, and the method used determines what is learned; teaching scientific reasoning as a set of procedures separate from any particular substance is as futile as solely imparting accumulated knowledge of science to students; "science teachers should help students to acquire both scientific knowledge of the world and habits of mind at the same time."
- Teachers should value and foster creativity, imagination, and invention as distinct from academic achievement.
- "Teachers should make sure that students have some sense of success in learning science and mathematics, de-emphasizing getting all the right answers as being the main criteria of success." Students should be aware that, particularly in science, knowledge is not absolute; teachers should make students aware of their progress and encourage further study.
- Teachers should encourage all students in science and provide the opportunities for both boys and girls to gain proficiency in the use of scientific tools; teachers should "exploit the larger community and involve parents and other concerned adults in useful ways."

The California State Department of Education has developed a set of expectations for science programs, as a part of the *Science Framework for California Public Schools*. The science program expectations serve as a model and as a set of criteria for review of current curriculum and as a guide for curriculum development.

(1) The major themes underlying science, such as energy, evolution, patterns of change, scale and structure, stability, and systems and interactions, are developed and deepened through a thematic approach.

(2) The three basic scientific fields of study are addressed, ideally each year, and the connections among them are developed.

(3) The character of science is shown to be open to inquiry and controversy and free of dogmatism; the curriculum promotes student understanding of how we come to know what we know and how we test and revise our thinking.

(4) Science is presented in connection with its applications in technology and its implications for society.

(5) Science is presented in connection with the student's own experiences and interests, frequently using hands-on experiences that are integral to the instructional sequence.

(6) Students are given opportunities to construct the important ideas of science, which are then developed in depth, through inquiry and investigation.

(7) Instructional strategies and materials allow several levels and pathways of access so that all students can experience both challenge and success.

(8) Printed materials are written in an interesting and engaging narrative style; in particular, vocabulary is used to facilitate understanding rather than as an end in itself.

(9) Textbooks are not the sole source of the curriculum; everyday materials and laboratory equipment, videotapes and software, and other printed materials such as reference books provide a substantial part of the student experience.

(10) Assessment programs are aligned with the instructional program in both content and format; student performance and investigation play the same central role in assessment that they do in instruction. (California State Department of Education, 1990, pp. 8−9)

There are great similarities and reflected consensus among the work of Project 2061, the National Standards Committee, the California Science Framework and Criteria Committee, and other similar state initiatives. All of these projects have been influenced by national and international science achievement studies, the recommendations in *Science for All Americans*, and the National Goals for Education. In addition, many of the same individuals and professional associations are involved in more than one of these projects.

THE BEST SCHOOLS—THEORY INTO PRACTICE IN SCIENCE

The Best Schools have evolved their science programs over many years and the programs continue to evolve. The goals and objectives of these programs are congruent with national science literacy projects. Instruction is organized into units of instruction that allow all children to explore topics indepth and to be involved in hands-on activities that foster understanding of concepts. Programs have been developed to fit within the context and environment of each school.

The Best Schools—Five Case Studies in Science: The Contexts

SHEPARD ELEMENTARY SCHOOL, PLANO, TX

Shepard Elementary is in an aging neighborhood that consists of single-family homes and one large apartment complex. The community has high expectations for their children; many of the families have professional degrees. Traditionally, students have come from two-parent families; however, over the past five years, there has been a dramatic increase in children from single-parent homes and homes where both parents work. Shepard is a district site for children with autism and emotional disturbances, thus increasing the diversity of the student population. The school seeks to provide a warm, nurturing atmosphere in which learning is exciting, challenging, and rewarding. Shepard is one of thirteen Blue Ribbon designated schools in the Plano Independent School District.

Robert Sewell, *Principal, K – 5, 512 Students*

MILILANI-UKA ELEMENTARY SCHOOL, MILILANI, HI

Mililani-uka serves a burgeoning population in a "planned" suburban community in central Oahu. The school opened in 1974 in "houseshells" leased from the developer. While the campus now has permanent facilities, the "houseshell" campus is still used for instruction. The student population is comprised of thirteen different ethnic groups, predominantly Japanese and Caucasian. The transiency rates average 40% per year. Despite its size, Mililani-uka maintains a sense of "oneness." Mililani-uka is one of three elementary schools recognized from the district of Hawaii in 1993 and one of sixteen from the state recognized as Blue Ribbon Schools in the past ten years.

Shirley Hayashi, *Principal, (Betty Mow, Principal at time of nomination), K – 6, 1245 Students*

CRAYCROFT ELEMENTARY, TUCSON, AZ

Craycroft Elementary School is part of the Sunnyside Unified School District No. 12. The school is located in an economically depressed rural area, with 81% of the students receiving free or reduced price lunch. The ethnically diverse student population is 49% Caucasian, 43% Hispanic, 4% American Indian, 3% African-American, and 1% Asian. The staff is ethnically reflective of the student body. The school has averaged more than a 30% transient rate. By creating a stimulating, motivating learning environment that requires the commitment of students, staff, parents, and community, Craycroft has overcome past traditions and expectations for schooling. The 1991–92 attendance rate was 97%.

Franklin Narducci, *Principal, K – 5, 365 Students*

OUR LADY OF FATIMA, HUNTINGTON, WV

Our Lady of Fatima is a parish elementary school opened in 1954. It is located in the suburbs of the industrial city of Huntington. Decline of the city's economic base led to a decline in the student population; however, a vigorous funding strategy and strong educational program has led to a balanced budget and close to capacity enrollment. Education happens at the school because the instructional program moves outside the school for real-life experiences supported by community agencies and resource centers. Our Lady of Fatima is a combination of supportive parishioners, involved parents, dedicated staff, and motivated students.

Sister Carmella Campione, SSJ, *Principal, K – 8, 212 Students*

T. F. BIRMINGHAM ELEMENTARY, WYLIE, TX

Birmingham is a growing school that has experienced 23% growth in the student body in a given year and a student mobility rate of 37%. Despite the obstacles, the school has created a unified spirit based on a philosophy that all students *can* and *will* succeed.

Bettye Vickers, *Principal, (Joy Russell, Principal at time of nomination),*
Pre-K – 5, 521 Students

CLASS ORGANIZATION

Science is a priority in the Best Schools, and they devote from 100 to 300 minutes a week to science instruction. Time is extended through science activities integrated with other subject areas and field experiences. Classes are heterogeneously grouped for science. Special education students are mainstreamed to the degree possible within the classes. Some schools (Craycroft, AZ; Loma Heights, NM) use cross-age grouping. Cooperative learning groups are used extensively in science to enhance instruction and to model how scientists work in the real world.

The Best Schools — Class Organization Illustrations

SHEPARD, TX

Students are heterogeneously grouped for science, and this includes the special education classified students. The school uses a flexible time schedule for all subjects. Science might be the center of instruction for two or three hours a day at a grade level, as students work on experiments and projects. Much of the instruction at Shepard is organized around interdisciplinary themes that incorporate science activities, thereby extending time for science. Technology is incorporated at each grade level in all areas of the curriculum.

MILILANI-UKA, HI

Science is taught an average of twice a week. Classroom teachers have primary responsibility for science instruction; however, students and their teachers are also scheduled into the Science Discovery Room for a series of seven to eight lessons. The Discovery Room teacher works with the class and is assisted by the teacher. The Science Discovery Room is open to students during recess so that children can participate in activities in the various centers in the room.

BIRMINGHAM, TX

Time allocated for science is 150 minutes weekly in grade 3, 225 minutes weekly in grade 4, and 300 minutes weekly in grade 5. Additional time is realized in special projects as students plant gardens, produce science fair projects, and work in lab experience lessons.

CURRICULUM

Curriculum in the Best Schools is thematically based. Curriculum units may be drawn from programs such as Activities that Integrate Math and Science (AIMS), Science Curriculum Improvement Study (SCIS III), Developmental Approach to Science and Health (DASH) (NDN), Foundational Approaches in Science Teaching (FAST) (NDN), Voyage of the Mimi I and II, Project Jason, and/or others developed by states and locally by staff. In many cases, a combination of approaches is used. The emphasis is on indepth understanding of concepts rather than surface coverage of large quantities of information. In order to maximize understanding, many modes of instruction are used. Students read about science, hear about science, and most importantly, are actively engaged in doing science. Students learn to use the tools of science from simple measuring devices to microscopes and computers; they observe, collect, and record data; make hypotheses; analyze data; and communicate and support findings. Textbooks, if used at all, are used largely for reference. In order to "do science" and provide for hands-on activities, most of the schools have developed science labs or specialized science areas within their buildings or classrooms. Schools may also make use of nearby planetariums (Birmingham, TX) or use inflatable planetariums (Irwin and Lawrence Brook, NJ). In many cases, they have extended facilities outside of the building, including natural areas set aside for science and/or developed nature trails (Heights, FL).

Day field trips are a regular occurrence and overnight and even week-long experiences are incorporated into the program. Local resource people from industry, colleges, and museums serve as speakers or provide leadership for special science-related activities. Science fairs are regular events that focus children on science investigations and projects that demonstrate understanding of scientific concepts. Science fairs also provide the opportunity for parents and other children to see the outcomes of instruction. Some schools, for example, Heights Elementary, Florida, link home and school by providing take-home science kits on such topics as surface tension and paper chromatography.

Science activities are frequently integrated with technology and math activities. The tools used to study science are all forms of technology, from simple hand lenses to videomicroscopes and computers. Learning to use these tools is an essential part of instruction if students are to be involved in real science studies. Math and science are integrated in the real world, and it is logical to integrate them in the curriculum. If students are to learn the processes and attitudes of science, they need to be involved in activity-oriented investigations. This active learning increases understanding and retention. In addition, involvement in investigations stimulates children's curiosity and motivates children to explore and learn. A large number of the Best Schools use the integrated math/science investigations developed by the AIMS Education Foundation (Loma Heights, AZ; Birmingham, TX; Heights, FL; Brywood, CA). These hands-on activities are available for grades K−1, 3−4, and 5−9. Most of the investigations make use of simple, easy-to-use materials and tools. The Voyage of the Mimi I and II (Sunburst) are multi-media programs that actively involve students in scientific adventures through videotapes, books, and computer software (Loma Heights, AZ; Brywood, CA). KidsNet (National Geographic) units, which link children for research across the country and beyond, are also frequently used. Project Jason is a program that allows students to explore underwater via television and satellite technology (R. D. Head, GA). In addition, schools develop their own investigations, frequently related to their own environment. Students keep records of their investigations in science journals and logs and communicate findings through oral and written reports.

Texas broke with traditional textbook adoption when it approved a laser disc−based curriculum as a "science textbook" for the state. The program Windows on Science (Optical Data) uses laser disc technology combined with written support materials to present concepts in science in a highly visual and engaging manner. Schools outside of Texas are also using the program. The capability of the laser technology to hold large amounts of still and moving images and the ability to easily access and organize material for instruction are well suited to science education.

The Best Schools − Curriculum Illustrations

SHEPARD, TX

The schoolwide science curriculum goals are

- to increase students' conceptual base of scientific phenomena, which nurtures a sense of interrelatedness with the environment
- to promote abilities to think critically through the use of scientific investigations that focus on process skills and culminate in learning to make inferences
- to foster comfort with technological advances by providing access to and understanding of technological innovations and their scientific applications
- to develop awareness of career opportunities in science

Shepard teachers integrate science concepts into thematic units that appeal to students and make learning more relevant. It is not unusual to find science lessons being integrated with math, language arts, social studies, and fine arts. Shepard is committed to hands-on science instruction. Field trips to the Outdoor Learning Center, Living Materials Center, The Dallas Museum of Natural History, The Science Place, and nearby parks provide opportunities for students to experience science firsthand. A highlight of the fifth grade is a week-long environmental camp experience. The principal, teachers, and parents develop and teach exciting indoor and outdoor environment activities, which might not otherwise be available to the students, who return determined to make a difference in the world. Each grade level participates in a community service project each year as part of the school's commitment to developing responsible citizens.

Within each grade level complex is a science center that supports experimentation. Four IBM computer laboratories and classroom computers provide further support for science data analysis and projects. Classrooms house live animals, centers with science manipulatives, and bulletin boards displaying current events in science. Windows on Science (Optical Data), which makes use of an interactive videodisc system, is used in all grades. It is a series of lessons designed to provide a visual format for discussions and learning. Some parts of the program are still-life pictures, while other portions show a concept in action. The teachers use higher order thinking skill strategies to allow children to make observations and predictions throughout the video presentation. Written materials are also part of the program, and various textbooks are used for reference.

Recognition that students have to function in a highly technological world and be capable of higher order thinking skills focuses attention on developing these skills in science. Tactics for Thinking is used to help teach critical thinking skills. Students are encouraged to practice higher level thinking skills by developing projects for the annual science fair. Writing across the curriculum supports reflection and higher order thinking skills as students write about their observations, experiments, and science activities and conclusions.

MILILANI-UKA, HI

Science is presented as discovery and inquiry to the students at Mililani-uka. The goal is to nurture children's natural curiosity, to capitalize upon their interest in their environment, and to produce students who are scientifically literate. The focus is on doing science through a hands-on approach. The program is based on thematic units of study. These are developed locally, or units from the Elementary School Science (ESS) program, and for the lower grades, the Developmental Approach to Science and Health Technology (DASH), (NDN—University of Hawaii), materials are used. Units such as "Pattern Blocks" and "Tangrams" focus on general science, while physical science is explored through such units as "Light and Shadow" and biology is studied through units such as "Life of Beans and Peas."

Integration of science instruction into other content areas is practiced through programs like Activities for Integrating Math and Science (AIMS) and DASH. Environmental science instruction often encompasses other content areas such as the social sciences.

At Mililani-uka, science instruction has always been a high priority. A part of the library facility has been converted into a "Science Discovery Room." This well-equipped science classroom/laboratory houses many different science tools for instruction, including charts, models, instruments, equipment, live animals/plants, and preserved specimens. A science resource teacher supplements and supports classroom instruction. Her units of study on critical and higher order thinking skills encompasses seven to eight lessons per class. She also works with the staff on development of the curriculum based on the recommendations of Project 2061.

The Science Discovery Room is open to students during recess periods, when students are welcome to participate in activities in the various centers in the room. During the year, schoolwide science activities, such as "Science Is Fun" week and paper airplane contests, are organized. A very successful parent/child evening activity was held last year. Over 500 parents and children attended evening activities ranging from astronomy to measurement.

A social studies/science club has been organized. Activities such as the study of acid rain through the computer, participation in a project called "Marsville" (interplanetary travel), and various field trips are planned to motivate student interest in science. The school also participates in activities through the high school science learning center and activities sponsored by the district.

Every sixth grade child develops a science project that involves stating of a hypothesis, experimentation, and explanation of the outcome. Students are assessed in terms of the process they use to develop their project, as well as the final product.

CRAYCROFT, AZ

Students explore daily in science literate environments. All students are instructed in the science lab, utilizing hands-on activities integrating math, writing, reading, and science. A desert habitat provides students with understandings of the desert and its inhabitants; the environmental lab includes a mini-biosphere for students to explore global impacts of tropical rain, forests, grasslands, and marshlands. Data collected in the environmental lab is stored and communicated using computers. These "Biomes" are student-produced and include indigenous plants and insects. A garden center provides extensions in nutrition education. A weather station provides opportunities for students to collect data and relate these conditions to environmental impacts.

OUR LADY OF FATIMA, WV

The science program stresses learning science by doing science, emphasizing environmental responsibility, integrating math and science, and teaching an enriched program so that every student will succeed.

A garden was built in back of the school for students to plant herbs, watch them grow, and learn how to use them at home. There is also a sensory herb garden for primary students. Students have access to advanced equipment and modern technology to permit involvement in community action programs such as the Take Pride in America program and the West Virginia Save Our Streams program, both ecological projects outside of the school. Students use chemical testing kits, electronic meters, kick seines, and stereomicroscopes to monitor streams near the school and use the computer programs to record gathered data. Sixth grade students maintain an environmentally oriented computer bulletin board service, with entries of articles and television programs about the environment available to anyone with a modem. Commercial and public domain software teaches modeling of molecules, serves as planetariums, constructs topographic and three-dimensional maps, and creates a planet, all to reinforce learning of basic concepts. Middle school students also work with LEGO/LOGO programmable robots, coordinating science knowledge with computer programming. Computer technology is a powerful tool for developing critical thinking and problem-solving skills, for graphing and analyzing experimental data, and as support for demonstrations in class. At Science Day, students demonstrate their skills, understanding, and mastery of science concepts to parents and students.

BIRMINGHAM, TX

Science instructional strategies are based on formal scientific methods utilizing class experiments and inquiry skills in class activities. Students actually do what is studied—plant seeds, construct circuits, test magnets, and graph research data when testing hypotheses. The main thrust of instruction is done with hands-on activities using the Activities Integrating Math and Science (AIMS) curriculum, outdoor activities, and resource materials such as laser discs, science labs and informational textbooks. The spiral science curriculum is an integrated study of life science, earth science, and physical science, with all students emphasizing the environmental needs as part of their world future.

Higher order and critical thinking skills are stressed and applied in the Birmingham Science Fair. Students show the scientific method at work as they identify purpose, hypothesis, materials, procedures, results, and conclusions, demonstrating mastery of the project by presenting their findings to their classmates. Students are encouraged to experiment with enrichment activities after completion of a science lesson and then to share the information.

Curricular areas are easily integrated using the AIMS curriculum for activities in the areas of measurement, graphing, and decimals. Students also use their writing skills when composing "How To" and "Compare and Contrast" compositions in science exploration lessons. Social studies and geography are integrated in the study of the earth, maps, and geology.

Technology employed includes science software for Apple and IBM computers, microscopes, laser disc players, Windows on Science, films, and video programs. Guest speakers are used frequently. Enrichment activities include field trips at all grade levels.

SPECIAL NEED STUDENTS

In the Best Schools, emphasis is on mainstreaming special needs students. Activity-oriented programs using multiple teaching strategies facilitate the incorporation of all students into regular classrooms. Individual accommodations are made for students who need to learn at different paces or need to express what they have learned in different formats.

The Best Schools—Special Need Students Illustrations

SHEPARD, TX

Teachers maintain high expectations for each student. Differences in learning style and abilities are dealt with in a variety of ways; through the use of study guides, recycling, tutoring, and participation in science-related community service projects at every grade level, teachers are able to tailor the program to individual needs. The school has a commitment to inclusion. Autistic and emotionally disturbed and other handicapped students are mainstreamed in science, and modified testing is provided for children who qualify for special education or academic support programs.

ASSESSING WHAT STUDENTS KNOW AND CAN DO

Traditional standardized multiple choice science tests, as a means of assessing achievement in science, are rarely used in the Best Schools. These tests are considered invalid measures of the understandings, processes, and attitudes that are the heart of the science curriculum in these schools. In place of standardized tests, the schools are developing more performance-based assessments using projects, experiments, and observations of the processes used to determine progress of students. Individual writing and oral presentations of findings, teacher- or district-made tests, portfolios reflecting work over time, and products of cooperative groups are some of the means used. Some test publishers, such as Psychological Corporation, are developing performance-based tests with hands-on problems for children to investigate; some of the Best Schools are experimenting with these new forms of commercial assessment. In some states such as Texas, the state is introducing performance-based science testing as part of statewide assessment.

The Best Schools—Assessment Illustrations

SHEPARD, TX

The progress of kindergarten and first grade students is monitored through portfolios, with a checklist maintained for each student. Mastery of objectives is a cumulative process throughout the year. Teachers administer criterion-referenced tests at the end of each unit of instruction and also use reports and projects in assessment. In the spring of 1994, Texas will administer a new competency test, which includes hands-on activities as well as written questions, to grades 4, 8, and 10, in science, as well as other subjects.

BUNKER HILL ELEMENTARY, TX

Thinking skills are incorporated throughout science instruction. Students are required to use thinking strategies such as brainstorming and webbing. They are taught strategies to explain how they derive a conclusion, even to the point of expecting them to identify the level of complexity of their thinking. Test questions require students to use higher order and critical thinking skills; e.g., recently, during a test, students were required to design, create, and illustrate a balanced ecological system for a plant. The school has also been working with Psychological Corporation in field testing their new Science Performance Testing Program.

THE BEST SCHOOLS—PROGRAM DEVELOPMENT AND SUPPORT IN SCIENCE

Program development is a continuous process in the Best Schools. In the area of science, many of the programs have roots going back to hands-on approaches and environmental studies initiated in the 1960s. However, the programs in use in the schools today reflect the growth in knowledge of how children learn, the use of advanced technology, and a greater focus on standards of student performance.

Integration of science content with, for example, language arts has been facilitated by the change in the languages arts programs that focus on reading, writing, and speaking for a variety of purposes. Science can easily become the content for language arts instruction, and reading, writing, and speaking are recognized as essential parts of the science program. Also, the expanding view of mathematics as more than arithmetic has facilitated the integration of math and science. Recognition of the need for students to understand the role science has played in history and the impact of science on the modern world has led to greater integration of social studies and science. The congruence of views on how children best learn across all content areas; the work to establish meaningful standards for achievement at the national, state, and in the Best Schools at the local level; a well-entrenched "habit" in the Best Schools of continually assessing programs and developing curriculum; and interest in and, in many cases, participation in university, state, or nationally developed initiatives and networks aimed at improving instruction are among the reasons for development of their current science programs. The Best Schools also reach out to form partnerships with universities and businesses that have provided important support in the development and implementation of science programs.

The Best Schools—Science Development Illustrations

MILILANI-UKA, HI

The teachers, principal, and science resource teacher work continuously to improve the program. Much of the work during the past few years in the area of science has been in response to the work of the 2061 Project and has also been influenced by the *California Framework for Science*. Many of the outcomes proposed in *Science for All Americans* are already objectives of the school's science program. Themes that integrate science concepts with those from other disciplines, hands-on approaches that actively involve children in real science, and emphasis on higher order thinking skills are strategies consistent with achievement of the objectives. The science resource teacher is the school's representative to the district committee working to further develop the science program in light of 2061.

MATERIALS

Many of the Best Schools have science laboratories or "discovery rooms" within the school and outside areas designated or developed for scientific study. However, other schools have not had the space nor resources to establish full laboratories. These schools have devoted areas within the classroom or other parts of the school to science and have evolved the means for creative sharing of materials. Whether in a separate laboratory or part of a classroom, the Best Schools provide students with the "tools" of science, such as simple measuring devices, hand lenses, chemical testing kits, stereo microscopes, electronic meters, still and video cameras, calculators, and computers. In many schools, live animals, garden plots, and natural areas are maintained for study.

Science in the Best Schools is primarily based on thematic units with many hands-on activities. Most of the schools use a variety of university, foundation, commercial, and locally developed units that focus on development of indepth understanding of a limited topic. They may include written material for each student, problems and investigations, field experiments and observations, visuals, computer software, and multi-media. Textbooks, if purchased at all, are usually used mainly for reference.

The Best Schools — Materials Illustrations

SHEPARD, TX

The multi-media Windows on Science (Optical Data) program is the main resource in the classroom for instruction. A laser disc player is available in each grade level area. Science lab areas in each grade area also provide access to microscopes and science equipment. Over 150 IBM computers grouped in four labs and in individual classrooms support instruction. The computers are networked to several servers; software is varied and from a number of sources; a standard word processing, data base, graphing, and spread sheet program is available at all computer stations; and a variety of textbooks are available in classes for reference.

STAFF DEVELOPMENT

Staff development is of major importance in the development and implementation of elementary science programs. Typically, elementary teachers have had little formal background in science. Effective science programs cannot be implemented by purchasing a textbook and holding a half-day orientation on the use of the teacher's edition. The types of hands-on programs that focus on indepth understanding of science concepts require extensive staff development if the staff is to implement these science programs effectively. The Best Schools recognize this need. The growing consensus of how children learn across disciplines facilitates development in science. For example, teachers who use the whole-language or integrated language approach in the language arts classroom already should have a basic understanding of how children construct meaning. However, elementary teachers need to develop confidence in using the tools of science and in having students use these tools. They need to develop the indepth understanding of concepts and methods that they want their students to understand. The Best Schools accomplish this through a commitment to inservice focused on their school objectives and programs and by encouraging indepth study by teachers through summer institutes and courses. In some cases, the Best Schools have hired resource teachers who have extensive training in science and curriculum. These resource specialists work directly with children but also provide ongoing demonstration lessons, assistance, and direct training for classroom teachers. Partnerships can also be a source of staff development; for example, teachers at Lawrence Brook School, New Jersey, received training through their partnership with BellCore scientists and follow-up assistance via modem linked to the scientists in their labs. Programs disseminated through the National Diffusion Network, such as DASH and FAST, provide and require training of staff for schools adopting their programs. The AIMS Foundation also provides training for staff either at the school site or in regional training sessions.

The Best Schools — Staff Development Illustrations

SHEPARD, TX

Staff development is an ongoing focus at Shepard. The district provides six half-days and two full days for inservice. In addition, courses are offered on a voluntary basis or for credit toward the salary guide. Teachers also participate in summer inservice. Those faculty members attending the fifth grade camp program receive two days of specific inservice for the activities. In 1990–91, Shepard teachers logged over 1000 hours of teacher training beyond the minimum twenty hours required by the state of Texas. All teachers at each grade level have a common forty-five–minute per day common planning period, which allows for the development of thematic units, grade level planning, and collaboration.

MILILANI-UKA, I II

Staff development is a major focus of the school and the state of Hawaii. Teachers in the school are involved in professional development, curriculum development, and piloting of new programs and approaches. In the area of science, the staff benefits from inservice instruction from the science resource teacher. Co-teaching with the science center teacher provides classroom teachers with the opportunity to expand their knowledge of science and their ability to plan and implement lessons. The staff and students also benefit from a partnership with the high school science department. Teachers from Mililani-uka also participate in indepth training programs such as that required to implement Developmental Approach to Science and Health Technology (DASH) and participation in the Summer Physical Science Institute.

FUNDING DEVELOPMENT

The major cost for all instruction, including science, is for staff. In comparison, costs for equipment, field trips, materials, supplies, and staff training are small. However, the Best Schools invest in the tools of science and in staff and curriculum development. Many of the tools of science used at the elementary level, such as hand lenses and calculators, are inexpensive, while computers, software, and laser discs can be costly. The Best Schools frequently redirect funds that would normally be spent on textbooks to the acquisitions of hands-on materials and equipment for science. Partnerships, PTAs and local businesses are also frequently involved in providing equipment for the study of science. For example, at Eura Brown, Alabama, a group of doctors provided microscopes for the school. In addition, speakers used to enrich the program usually donate their time.

Effective staff and curriculum development requires time. The Best Schools invest heavily in development. Inservice training is provided through scheduled inservice days, summer and after-school workshops, college courses, and special training programs associated with adopted curriculum. Release time is provided to staff to observe instruction within the school and district and in other districts. A number of states have requirements for continuing education, thus facilitating professional development. Costs for inservice training usually involve the costs for substitutes for release time, travel to training sessions, summer workshop pay, inservice credits that may affect movement on salary guides, workshop fees, and in some cases consultants. Many schools use their funds from the Education for Economic Security Dwight D. Eisenhower Mathematics and Science Education Act funds for inservice. Schools that have hired a science specialist have added to the overall cost of the science program. While there are some costs associated with much of staff and curriculum development, the staffs of the Best Schools characteristically voluntarily involve themselves in a wide range of professional activities.

Field trips are another expense associated with the science program. In some cases, these may be trips to local areas for a few hours, to museums and science centers for the day, or to a camp setting for a week. Some schools pay for these trips as part of the school budget, and some are supported by PTAs or PTOs, other fund-raisers, or partnerships; in other cases, parents pay for the field experiences. Students whose parents cannot afford the expense are subsidized by district or donated funds. The Best Schools, because of their commitment to staff and program development, have managed to find the resources for development regardless of their economic status.

The Best Schools — Funding Illustrations

SHEPARD, TX

The per pupil cost of education in Plano is about $4000, which is typical for the area, but lower than in some districts. The district provides the funds for the multi-media science program, computers, and other technology. Funds for staff development come from the district and from school-generated activity funds (picture sales, ice cream sales). Teachers who have prime responsibility for the fifth grade camping experience are paid for two days of training in the summer and a stipend for the week at camp. Other teachers volunteer to participate. Students individually pay approximately $130 for the week of camping. The PTA and the district provide funds to support children who cannot afford the expense.

MILILANI-UKA, HI

The state of Hawaii provides for school-based discretion in the use of funds. Mililani-uka made the decision to allocate their discretionary funds to the development of the Science Discovery Room and the hiring of a certified science resource teacher.

OUR LADY OF FATIMA, WV

The school staff has worked to improve the instructional program by adding new programs, learning new teaching methods, attending workshops, reading educational periodicals, and meeting to update and integrate curriculum. Grants have been applied for and received for equipment and materials. In 1989, the school principal and a primary teacher participated in Project E.A.S.T. (Exemplary Approaches of Science Teaching), focused on K−3 students. Through this program, funds were received to purchase hand-held microscopes, a class bio-scope, magnets, simple machine kits, a primary science kit, and teacher resource materials. The fifth grade teacher received a grant to purchase materials to teach energy and alternative energy sources in the intermediate grades. The school has also worked with community groups to provide services to the school. The parent-teacher organization has provided funds for materials.

CRAYCROFT, AZ

The hands-on learning environments have been created by students, staff, and community. Over a period of years, businesses contributed in excess of $35,000 in material and labor. The environments that have been developed include Life Learning Center, Science Lab, Stellarium Planetarium, Kids Kitchen Center, First Interstate Banking/Math Lab, Sonoran Desert Cave Habitat (indoors with talapia pond, waterfall, mineral samples, etc.), a quarter mile Desert Learning Trail, the Outdoor Environmental Lab (utilizing reclaimed water to supply garden centers) and a mini-biosphere.

SUMMARY

Science programs in the Best Schools have many of the characteristics of instruction advocated for development of scientific literacy goals for the 21st century. Instruction is based on a constructionist's view of how children learn. Curriculum has been developed based on the recognition that ''less is more,'' that it is more important for students to gain indepth understanding of concepts, the methods of science, and scientific ''habits of mind'' than to cover large quantities of surface information about science. New forms of performance-based assessment are being utilized. The Best Schools, urban, suburban, and rural, have developed their programs over time and have a commitment to continuous development. Extensive staff development is characteristic of the Best Schools. Underlying all their efforts and programs is the commitment that science is for all students and that all students can achieve scientific literacy.

REFERENCES

AIMS Education Foundation. (1989). "Project AIMS Update," Fresno, CA.

American Association for the Advancement of Science. (1993). *Benchmarks for Science Literacy.* Project 2061, Oxford University Press, New York, NY.

Association for Supervision and Curriculum Development. (1992). *ASCD Curriculum Handbook: A Resource for Curriculum Administrators*. Alexandria, VA.

Association for Supervision and Curriculum Development. (1989). *Toward the Thinking Curriculum: Current Cognitive Research*. L. B. Resnick and L. E. Klopher, eds., Alexandria, VA.

Bennett, William J. (1986). *First Lessons: A Report on Elementary Education in America*. Washington, D.C.: U. S. Government Printing Office.

Bennett, William J. (1988). *James Madison Elementary School*. Washington, D. C.: U. S. Government Printing Office.

California State Department of Education. (1990). *Science Framework for California Public Schools: Kindergarten Through Grade Twelve*. Sacramento, CA.

Educational Testing Service, Center for the Assessment of Educational Progress. (1991). *The 1991 IAEP Assessment: Objectives for Mathematics, Science, and Geography*. Princeton, NJ.

Fort, Deborah. (1993). "Science Shy, Science Savvy, Science Smart," *Kappan*, 74(9).

Loucks-Horsley, Susan, et al. (1990). *Elementary School Science for the '90s*. Alexandria, VA: Association for Supervision and Curriculum Development.

National Assessment of Educational Progress (NAEP). (1990). *America's Challenge: Accelerating Academic Achievement*. Princeton, NJ: Educational Testing Service.

National Assessment of Educational Progress (NAEP). (1988). *The Science Report Card: Elements of Risk and Recovery.* Princeton, NJ: Educational Testing Services.

National Assessment of Educational Progress (NAEP). (1987). *Learning by Doing: A Manual for Teaching and Assessing Higher-order Thinking in Science and Mathematics*. Princeton NJ: Educational Testing Service.

National Committee on Science Education Standards and Assessment. (1993). *National Science Educational Standards: July '93 Progress Report.* Washington, D. C. National Research Council.

Oakes, J. et al. (1990). "Multiplying Inequalities: The Effects of Race, Social Class, and Tracking on Opportunities to Learn Mathematics and Science," Report No. R-3928-NSF, Rand Co., Santa Monica, CA.

Rutherford, F. James and Andrew Ahlgren. (1990). *Science for All Americans*. New York: Oxford University Press.

U. S. Department of Education. (1991). *America 2000: An Educational Strategy*. Washington, D. C.

CHAPTER 10

The Arts

IN 1988, the National Endowment for the arts reported that schools were giving increasing attention to the arts as an essential and valued part of the academic curriculum, with as many teachers of the arts employed by districts as science teachers. In 1993, a survey of principals of the nationally recognized Blue Ribbon Elementary Schools listed visual and performing arts initiatives as their top curriculum priority. This chapter looks at the following questions concerning the role of the arts in preparing children for the 21st Century:

- What does theory say about what children should learn and how they should be taught the arts?
- How have the Best Schools successfully translated theory into practice in the arts?
- How do the Best Schools assess what children know and what they can do?
- How have effective programs been developed and implemented; what were the resources needed for development and support?

WHAT CHILDREN SHOULD LEARN

To some who remember their school art experiences as little more than finger painting and the singing of cute songs, the arts seem like the last arena of the curriculum that would be able to define what children should know and be able to do in measurable terms. However, this is not the case. While the arts were not specifically mentioned among the academic subjects in the national goals, the arts were written into federal law with the passage of *Goals 2000: Educate America Act* and a separate task force completed work on National Standards for the Arts. The Consortium of National Arts Education Associations was charged with defining ''what every young American should know and be able to do in the arts.'' They saw no contradiction between the arts as a creative individual process and the desirability of defining what should be the outcomes of arts education in grades K−12.

Art in the National Standards Project means creative works and the processes of production, as well as the whole body of art works that make up intellectual and cultural heritage. The art disciplines include dance, music, theater, and the visual arts. Within each discipline, the standards are organized based on three learning tasks:

- creating and performing
- perceiving and analyzing
- understanding cultural and historical contexts

While the standards recognize the importance of maintaining the integrity of each discipline, the importance of making connections among the disciplines has also been recognized by the task force.

197

Essentially, the standards ask that students should know and be able to do the following by the time they have completed secondary school:

- They should be able to communicate in the four arts disciplines (dance, music, theater, and visual arts). This includes knowledge and skills in the use of the basic vocabulary, materials, tools, techniques, and the intellectual methods of each arts discipline.
- They should be able to communicate proficiently in at least one art form, including the ability to define and solve artistic problems with insight, reason, and technical proficiency.
- They should be able to develop and present basic analyses of works of art from structural, historical, and cultural perspectives and from multiples of those perspectives. This includes the ability to understand and evaluate work in the various arts disciplines.
- They should have an informal acquaintance with exemplary works of art from a variety of world cultures and historical periods and a basic understanding of historical development in the arts disciplines, across the arts as a whole, and within cultures.
- They should be able to relate various types of arts knowledge and skills within and across the arts disciplines. This includes mixing and matching competencies and understandings in art-making, history and culture, and analysis in any arts-related project. (National Standards for Arts Education, 1994)

Specific curriculum and achievement standards provide guidelines within each discipline for grades K−4, 5−8, and 9−12. Following are examples from the National Standards for Arts Education:

Music Grades K−4

Content Standard:

Composing and arranging music within specified guidelines

Achievement Standard:

a. create and arrange music to accompany readings or dramatizations
b. create and arrange short songs and instrumental pieces within specified guidelines
c. use a variety of sound sources when composing

Dance Grades K−4

Content Standard:

Making connections between dance and other disciplines

Achievement Standard:

a. create a dance that reveals understanding of a concept or idea from another discipline (such as pattern in dance and science)
b. respond to a dance using another art form; explain the connections between the dance and their response to it (such as stating how their paintings reflect the dance they saw)

Theatre Grade 5−8

Content Standard:

Researching by using cultural and historical information to support improvised and scripted scenes

Achievement Standard:

a. apply research from print and nonprint sources to script writing, acting, design, and directing choices

Visual Arts Grades 5—8

Content Standard:

Choosing and evaluating a range of subject matter, symbols, and ideas

Achievement Standard:

a. integrate visual, spatial, and temporal concepts with content to communicate intended meaning in their artwork
b. use subjects, themes, and symbols that demonstrate knowledge of contexts, values, and aesthetics that communicate intended meaning in artworks

The project recognizes that there are many paths to development of the envisioned competencies in each of the arts disciplines. The standards do not represent a national curriculum; rather, they provide the standards for curriculum development and establish the expected outcomes of arts instruction for all children.

HOW CHILDREN LEARN—HOW CHILDREN ARE TAUGHT

The shift in emphasis in the other academic disciplines, away from rote memorization and discreet sequential learning of basic skills toward a curriculum focused on the development of thinking skills, connections, reflection, and the construction of knowledge, has also impacted on instruction in the arts. First, the retreat in other areas from repetitive drill and practice of multitudes of ''basic skills'' has increased the time available to the arts in many schools. Second, the restructuring of other academic areas has facilitated integration of subject matter, especially of the arts. Third, the methodologies currently advocated based on research on learning in other subject areas are congruent with those of effective instruction in the arts.

In order to accomplish the objectives of arts education, it is essential that students be actively involved in a comprehensive, sequential, and articulated curriculum from year to year. Less comprehensive approaches may result in skill development in specific areas and even exceptional performances; however, without an encompassing articulated framework, these remain only pieces and parts, with little potential for all children to meet the objectives of arts education.

The National Endowment for the Arts (1988), in a report to the President and to Congress, described the characteristics of a desired school program for the arts:

- Is comprehensive across all grades for all students, and defines the curriculum content in the arts that all students, not just the gifted and talented or college bound, should have, particularly in terms of the knowledge and skills, concepts and principles, necessary to be knowledgeable and appreciative of the arts;
- Encompass, over the course of 13 years of schooling, all of the arts disciplines and assures students opportunities for the study of history and criticism of the arts in a sequential and structured curriculum, as well as the making, exhibiting, and performing of art;
- Interrelates components of various art forms where appropriate while providing for interdisciplinary learning across non-arts subject areas where relevant;
- Utilizes, as part of an integrated system of art education, specially trained arts teachers, supported by general elementary and teacher specialists in other areas who are

well-grounded in the arts, along with artists and scholars in residency programs and field trips to museums and performances;

- Provides for ongoing professional growth in the arts and humanities for all staff, including general teachers, arts specialists, administrators, superintendents and board members;
- Assesses and measures students' achievement and program effectiveness;
- Takes place in school facilities which are compatible with program goals;
- Is supported by instructional and reference materials and supplies which are both appropriate and adequate in numbers; and
- Finally, uses media and modern technology both as a curriculum content and a process to learn about the arts.

In the past, the art education program in most schools was focused almost entirely on art production designed to encourage creativity. While students still produce art in schools, the importance of skill development has been established, and there is recognition that participation is not the same as education. In addition to art production, students should develop the ability to analyze and critically view the arts. The history of the arts and the relationship of the arts to culture and history are important parts of the arts curriculum. The Discipline-Based Arts Education (DBAE) is the approach that has been broadly disseminated and supported by the Getty Center for Arts Education and has impacted on art education in many schools. DBAE advocates development of a program in the arts, which engages students every year in the study of four disciplines: art history, criticism, production, and aesthetics.

HOW LEARNING SHOULD BE ASSESSED

The arts have a long history of the use performance and product-based assessment techniques, such as portfolio assessment in the visual arts and auditions in dance, music, and theater. These techniques are representative of the types of authentic assessments that other academic disciplines are seeking to develop. While the arts are experienced with individual assessment techniques, there have been few attempts to assess the outcomes of art instruction for large groups of children exposed to specific types of instruction, to assess outcomes across programs, or to determine the national levels of achievement of children in the arts. In most cases, the assessment of student achievement in the arts and evaluation of arts programs have been left to local school initiative.

The National Assessment of Educational Progress, however, is developing a framework for the national assessment of the arts by 1996, which will coincide with the voluntary national standards. The project is jointly funded by the Getty Center for Education in the Arts and the National Endowment for the Arts.

THE BEST SCHOOLS—THE ARTS: THEORY INTO PRACTICE

In 1989–90, the U. S. Department of Education invited Doug Herbert of the National Endowment for the Arts, Kathy Walsh-Piper of the National Gallery of Art, and Pat Mitchell of the Fillmore Arts Center, D.C. Public Schools to reread applications of the elementary schools selected for Blue Ribbon School recognition to see what kinds of exemplary arts education programs were among the group. Seventeen model programs were found from a wide variety of communities. The reviewers found that all of the seventeen schools shared the following characteristics:

- a philosophy that holds that arts education is a basic and necessary component of a balanced educational program for pre-kindergarten through grade 8 students

- a broad understanding of arts curricula and pedagogy that is matched with the highest quality instructors available—arts specialists, artists/teachers, and highly trained classroom teachers
- a balance of art forms, including music, dance, drama, poetry, creative writing, and visual and media arts (Music, visual arts, and drama were offered most frequently; poetry, creative writing, dance and media arts, less frequently.)
- a realization that the arts need time, space, and financial and administrative support (Time spent in direct arts instructions ranged from two to seven hours per week. The ratio of arts teacher to students ranged from 1:80 to 1:250.)
- an understanding of the instructional power that comes from using the arts as part of an integrated approach to teaching (Every school infused the arts into other parts of the curriculum.)
- a commitment to *all* students that ensures access to instruction in the basic art areas and also provides for differentiated levels of instruction based on student motivation and talent
- a strong and vital connection to the local arts community and an awareness that successful arts programs lead to wider community support for education in general

The Best Schools have evolved their programs in the arts over many years and are continuing to give priority to these areas of the curriculum. Changes in other academic subjects have resulted in increased recognition of the arts as a valuable part of a more integrated school curriculum. Programs have been developed to fit within the context of each school.

The Best Schools—Four Case Studies in the Arts: The Context

WALLINGFORD ELEMENTARY SCHOOL, WALLINGFORD, PA

Wallingford Elementary School is located in a suburban community near Philadelphia. The principal and staff see the school as a place where students are developing the necessary information-gathering and analysis skills to function productively in the 21st Century, and where their search for knowledge should be an intrinsically exciting adventure in which they discover the joy of learning for its own sake. The median scores in reading and mathematics are above the 93rd percentile on standardized tests. In addition to being recognized as a Blue Ribbon School, Wallingford received special recognition for its arts program in 1989.

Robert Rice, *Principal, Grades 1 – 5, 381 Students*

GULLIVER ACADEMY, CORAL GABLES, FL

Gulliver Academy, a co-educational, nonsectarian day school, was established in 1926. It is the largest independent school in Dade County. The twenty-acre campus enjoys the quiet beauty of residential Coral Gables and yet offers ready access to the cultural amenities of the greater Miami area. The student body reflects the diverse ethnic composition of the area. Approximately 30% are of Hispanic origin, many of whom come with limited knowledge of English. In addition, representatives of over forty foreign countries are in attendance each year. These children richly enhance the school by helping to broaden the students' view of the world.

Joseph Krutulis, *Principal, Nursery – 8, 1040 Students*

IRWIN SCHOOL, EAST BRUNSWICK, NJ

Irwin School is one of eight elementary schools in the suburban multi-ethnic middle to upper middle socioeconomic community of East Brunswick. The school provides a creative, caring, and cooperative environment, which makes it possible for every student to achieve at a very high level and to develop positive self-esteem.

Lucille Fisher, Principal, Grades K – 5, 542 Students

SUSAN LINDGREN INTERMEDIATE CENTER, ST. LOUIS PARK, MN

Susan Lindgren serves children in the eastern half of St. Louis Park, a first ring suburb of Minneapolis. The community is an urban mix of residential, business, and industrial property. Citizens traditionally support tax referendums to finance school programs, and expenditures are among the highest in the state. A site management council of educators, parents, business representatives, and community members has governed the school with the encouragement of the district since 1983.

Harry Hoff, Principal, Grades 3 – 6, 460 Students

CLASS ORGANIZATION AND INSTRUCTIONAL TIME

The National Endowment for the Arts recommends that, at the elementary and middle school levels, 15% of instructional time be devoted to the arts. Many of the Best Schools meet this criteria, and some exceed it. The arts in these schools are considered an integral part of the total educational process. Heterogeneous grouping has always been the rule in elementary art programs, as it has been accepted that instruction in the classroom can and should allow for differences in ability or talent. However, the arts have also recognized the need for individual and group study for those students who have special talent and/or interest in an art form. Especially in music, schools have provided for and encouraged choral and instrumental groups. The Best Schools also provide opportunities, usually starting in fourth grade, for all interested students to learn to play an instrument. Special opportunities are provided in the Best Schools for children interested in other art forms through electives and/or special projects and teaching artists.

The Best Schools—Class Organization Illustrations

WALLINGFORD, PA

There is a full-time art and full-time music teacher at Wallingford. A music teacher from the high school is also involved in teaching instrumental music, particularly strings, to fourth and fifth grade students. Students are scheduled for music and art one hour a week each. In addition, the music and art teachers schedule all children for seminar groups and to work on projects. In music, children also schedule time with the teacher to work on the computers. Beginning in fourth grade, students can elect to study instrumental music. The performing arts are taught by the classroom teacher with assistance from the art, music, physical education, and library specialists. Teaching artists spend from two to four weeks working with teachers and students; usually, their work is related to the year-long theme adopted each year at Wallingford. One year's theme was "South of the Border." One of the teaching artists was a Mexican mask maker, while another artist was a dancer/choreographer who worked with fourth and fifth grade students for a month to enhance understanding of dance and movement and to develop a dance presentation with a Latin theme.

GULLIVER ACADEMY, FL

The fine arts department is staffed by artist-teachers with experience in both the teaching profession and the arts. Classes are held in specially designed studios. Diverse programs of the fine arts department are designed to provide opportunities for students to be exposed to the fine arts.

All students in grades 1 −4 receive art class instruction forty-five minutes per week. In grades 5 −8, children can elect art. Electives meet every day for forty-five minutes. There are three full-time art teachers, each with a fully equipped studio.

Grades 1 −3 attend music/chorus classes, sixty to ninety minutes per week. Fourth graders may choose weekly band and music/chorus classes, which last forty-five to ninety minutes. Music is elective in grades 5 −8. Students may choose chorus or intermediate or advanced band. These classes are held forty-five minutes daily. After-school instrument lessons are required of all band members in grades 4 −8.

In preprimary, every day begins with dramatics in areas such as the housekeeping, dress-up or block corners. A full-time and part-time instructor work together in drama with all children from grades 1 −8. Electives courses are offered in grades 5 −8.

IRWIN, NJ

Music and the visual arts are taught by certified specialists. In grades 1 −3, instruction in each area averages sixty minutes a week; in grades 4 −5, this increases to eighty minutes a week. The study of art is also integrated into the social studies program. Instrumental music is an elective for interested fourth and fifth grade students. The performing arts flourish at Irwin through the unique teaching artists from Lincoln Center in New York and an extensive Cultural Arts Program provided by matching funds from the board of education and PTA.

SUSAN LINDGREN, MN

One example of Susan Lindgren's commitment to holistic, quality education for all children is the fine arts program, a combination of visual arts and vocal/instrumental music departments. Fine arts instruction averages fifty-five minutes per day. This is accomplished by staggering visual arts instruction with other subjects throughout the week.

A second component of the fine arts curriculum is vocal/instrumental music. Students are scheduled for four 30-minute class sessions and may opt for more instruction by participating in the grade 4 −6 orchestra programs or the grades 5 −6 band program.

CURRICULUM

The Best Schools have structured sequential curricula in the arts. Skill development, as well as creativity, is fostered across the grades in art production. Art history, criticism, and aesthetics education is embedded in the programs at each grade level. In addition to scheduled group art instruction, the arts are integrated into other areas of the school curriculum. Provision in the Best Schools is made for the development of individual talents and interests.

The Best Schools−Curriculum Illustrations

WALLINGFORD, PA

The visual arts program at Wallingford Elementary schools is exemplary. The three main reasons for the success of this program are 1) an outstandingly talented and gifted art educator who is creative, imaginative, and of great energy; 2) a principal who is philosophically convinced of the importance of art in our culture and who supports the arts program financially through the school budget; and 3) the enthusiastic response and participation of the students and the entire community. The art program is based on a written and sequential curriculum and is discipline based. Current findings by the Getty Center for Education in the Arts were inspirational in developing this program. The visual arts program is designed to include all four disciplines—production, art history, art criticism, and aesthetics—with emphasis on production but with each lesson incorporating one or more of the other disciplines. For example, the interdisciplinary "Celebration of the Future" was introduced in 1984. The excitement and energy that visual arts generate can be felt upon entering the school. The explanation accompanying one exhibit, "Bateman Invades WES," captures the essence of the visual arts program. It says,

> The fifth grade art classes present their version of Bateman accessories. The objective of this art project was to stretch thinking beyond the ordinary. Students brainstormed and shared ideas. Some looked, planned, and sketched until their ideas had been formulated. At last, they were ready to convert their ideas into visual art. Creative thinking is very contagious, and the results are exciting.

The music program is also based on a written and sequential curriculum. The youngest children are introduced to music through body movement, while older students begin to learn rhythmic development, pitch discrimination, and form recognition. The development of positive attitudes toward music remains the primary goal. Two Apple GS computers are used by the music teacher to develop ear training and music reading skills (Music Studio, ActiVision); an additional software program (Brass Fingerings, Wenger Corp.) teaches brass instruments' fingering; and a programmed self-instruction course teaches students to read rhythms (Count Me Out, Temperal Acuity Products). Music composition is also taught at the fourth and fifth grade levels using Pyware Music Writer. The music program also includes a fourth and fifth grade music composition course for gifted children. Last year, more than ninety children were part of the school band.

In the performing arts, taught by the classroom teacher with assistance from the art, music, physical education, and library specialists, an attempt is made to provide each student with the opportunity to participate and to experience success. Some recent all-school performances have included *Charlotte's Web*, *Shoemaker and Elves*, *Kapok Tree*, and *The Wizard of Oz*. Supported by the student council at the end of the year, an all-school talent show is an eagerly awaited event.

GULLIVER ACADEMY, FL

In the Visual Arts program, in the preprimary, many of the art projects complement an ongoing classroom activity and range from making something specific for a holiday theme to open-ended activities. For example, the children make large dinosaur models for a "Dinosaur Museum" when they study prehistoric animals.

Teachers in the visual art department attempt to make students think of art as both an approach to critical thinking (perspective, color, balance, dimension, scale, and proportion) and as a means of communication. Small class size allows a daily critique with each student, ensuring meaningful and timely progress. The art teachers collaborate monthly with classroom teachers, not only in grades 1–4, but also with the social sciences and language arts classes in grades 5–8. Recent examples are African masks, Renaissance art, and Egyptian hieroglyphics. The structured arts are a major part of the curriculum; for example, facial structure is taught in both two- and three-dimensional form. Art history is integrated into the curriculum from the prehistoric to current Western Art. The evolution of art is stressed, while various artists are spotlighted and their lives, styles, and techniques are studied. Slide presentations and other visual aids help to develop the student's "critical eye." Field trips to local museums and visits from professionals add to the endeavor. Students are encouraged to apply their own standards of aesthetics to whatever they create or see.

Drafting/architectural drawing is an elective course for eighth grade students. Weekly projects allow students to improve upon their developing skills in drafting. United States history and western civilizations are covered in the course through the study of architectural history from ancient civilizations to the 20th Century.

In Gulliver Academy's musical arts curriculum, the children in preprimary are given the chance to enjoy music many times during the day. They may begin with circle time morning songs, sing while cleaning up or switching activities, and end the day with a goodbye song. In addition, preprimary classes meet twice weekly for twenty-five minutes with the music specialist. Songs are taught and coordinated with the curriculum. Also, students learn specific skills dealing with tempo, pitch, and rhythm through songs. Each spring, students participate in a musical. Over 100 kindergartners perform in the rhythm band under the direction of the music teacher.

The music department strives to promote music literacy by developing aesthetic sensitivity; mastery of musical skills; and an awareness of the nature, structure, and meaning of music. Music objectives are designed and taught in sequence. Advanced work is encouraged, and group and individual assessments are in the form of written quizzes and evaluation of performance. Classroom teachers are supplied with tapes and word sheets containing seasonal and event songs. Relationships of historical significance to social studies, song texts to language arts, foreign language texts to language arts, and rhythm and pitch to mathematics integrate musical and academic study. The unique features of the program include the instrumental program that begins in grade 4 and the private instrumental lessons available on campus. There is also an abundance of recordings, instruments, and other related resources for the department.

In preprimary, dramatic arts begin every day in areas such as the housekeeping, dress-up, or block corners. Here, children are able to express their individuality and be imaginative and creative with a minimum of adult direction. At other times, teachers lead children in drama through finger plays, puppet plays, and the dramatization of plays or stories.

The drama department includes instruction in both performance and technical skills. Students are exposed to a variety of dramatic experiences in all grade levels. The drama chairperson acts as coordinator/facilitator for all performances in grades 1−4. In grades 5−8, elective courses are offered in puppetry, stagecraft (costuming, lighting and sound, make-up, set design), and acting. Classes are held forty-five minutes daily. The department presents skits for assembly programs; fall and spring evening performances; and pantomime, monologue, and comedy skits. Critiques of shows in publication are studied, short plays are written, origins of the theater are studied, and the idea of "theater for art's sake" is analyzed. The addition of specialized rooms (a little theater and a workshop for stage craft) has aided in the continual growth of this department. A full-time and part-time instructor work together in drama.

IRWIN, NJ

The arts are an integral and important aspect of Irwin School.

As content, the arts represent man's best work. Our children ought to have access to such work, and they should know that we care that they do. When we define our school curricula, we not only provide children with access to the intellectual and artistic capital of our culture, we also tell the young what we value for them. Surely the arts are among the things we ought to care about. — Elliot W. Eisner

The visual arts curriculum is formulated to include content from the disciplines of art production, art history, art criticism, and aesthetics. This follows the philosophical concepts developed by the Getty Center for Education in the Arts — an approach known as discipline-based art education (DBAE). The quality of this philosophy is evident when viewing the extensive and varied student-produced displays in the halls, the classroom, public library, and other community buildings. Students study about the arts through the use of art reproductions related to their art projects; for example, they study African masks prior to producing their own masks. In social studies, the arts are used to reflect the culture of the times. Through art exhibits, children learn to appreciate the technique and style of many different artists. Professional teaching artists work with children to develop understanding and appreciation of various mediums and styles.

The written music curriculum is based on a sequential learning process, including objectives for each grade level. The essential elements include singing as a means of personal expression, performance ensembles, musical elements, listening skills, music notation, appreciation of music, and American musical heritage, as well as the music of other cultures. Among the most exciting aspects of music are student productions in which all of the children in the school participate.

The goals of the Irwin School's arts program are supported by the performing art repertories. Several Irwin teachers have been trained in aesthetic education at Lincoln Center programs. This year, teaching artists will work with fourth and fifth grade teaching artists to prepare the children for *A Midsummer Night's Dream* production by artists from Lincoln Center. Teaching artists will also work with classes in support of a guitar concert by Dennis Coster.

The strength of the arts makes Irwin School unique. The students are encouraged to participate in the highest aspirations of the human spirit every day through a variety of activities, including an environment filled with student and historically and culturally significant art.

SUSAN LINDGREN, MN

"SmART," a discipline-based art curriculum, engages students in a sequential study of four disciplines: art history, criticism, production, and aesthetics. Students learn how to evaluate and interpret art forms, methods, and materials. The use of aesthetic scanning is an excellent concrete example of higher level thinking skills put into practice. A growing library of arts-oriented laser disks facilitates the classroom teaching of the art curriculum.

The school's strong commitment to fine arts education is exemplified by membership in the A.R.T. Exchange, a cultural organization that facilitates student art exchanges between American and Soviet classrooms. Plans are underway for a visit to Russia by the visual art instructor and other staff members.

Vocal music in all grades emphasizes a combination of singing, instrumental study, movement, music theory, music history, ethnic music, drama, and composition. Music theory, history, and music of various cultures is incorporated into song, dance, and listening activities. Instrumental students learn the technical aspects of performance on their instruments, musical concepts and the responsibility of performing in a group. Integration with other curricular areas is provided throughout the music program by comparing music and art concepts and emphasizing music from many cultures.

All vocal classes have CD/dual tape deck/phonograph stereo systems. There are two Casio C-Z I synthesizers in the school that are used by the students for sound exploration and performance. Students use computers for drill and practice on music theory, signs, and symbols and for composition.

ASSESSING WHAT STUDENTS KNOW AND CAN DO

Assessment of individual achievement in the arts takes place in the classroom based on the objectives of the curriculum. Children learn to critique each other's work and to understand the standards they and the teacher use in assessing works of art. Classroom assessment also includes knowledge and understanding of art history, criticism, and aesthetics. Some of the Best Schools use out-of-school individuals or committees to formally evaluate their arts programs every four to six years in the same way that they evaluate other academic areas of the curriculum.

The Best Schools—Assessment Illustrations

WALLINGFORD, PA

Evaluation occurs daily in the art classroom, with everyone participating in critiquing each other's work. The five-year community evaluation committee, which studied the district art program, identified Wallingford as a model program. This group has become an advocate for the arts to ensure that the arts continue to flourish in the district. They publish an arts newsletter once a month.

IRWIN, NJ

The art and music programs were evaluated this year by out-of-district professional educational evaluators. Both programs were commended for the breadth, depth, and quality of program offering. Supervisors and teachers will use the extensive evaluation data to further enhance the program and its effectiveness in teaching discipline-based arts.

THE BEST SCHOOLS—PROGRAM DEVELOPMENT AND SUPPORT IN THE ARTS

The Implementation Process

The seventeen schools selected for their model arts programs participated in a symposium in Washington, D.C. Following is some of the advice these schools gave for developing effective arts programs:

- Treat the arts as academics.
- Plan a curriculum thought out to integrate the arts with the other curricula.
- Encourage teachers to attend summer educational programs at museums and then bring back ideas to their classrooms.
- The location of the school and the unique community it serves largely determines the parameters of the community arts support that can be built, such as bridges to local museums and business partnerships. Locale can provide unique advantages.
- Involve senior citizen and other community members with or without children in the program.
- Engage in arts competitions. Recognition reinforces learning, encourages good teaching, and builds community support.
- The superintendent and school board are of vital importance in support of the arts; they need to be intimately involved in funding the arts. No one person can take total responsibility for building support for the arts; it must be shared responsibility.

STAFF DEVELOPMENT

In the Best Schools, staff development in the arts involves more than opportunities for art specialists. The role of the classroom teacher is recognized, and much of the inservice activity involves these teachers. Resources of universities, art galleries, orchestras, opera companies, museums, and local working artists are frequently used for staff development. In some cases, the training is specific and indepth, such as working with a teaching artist in the classroom for several weeks or attending one- to three-week workshops at a center for the arts. Other training takes place in short-term inservice programs designed to enhance the links between the classes in the arts and other areas of the school curriculum. In addition, the Best Schools encourage their art specialists to continue their own work as artists and encourage all teachers to participate in the arts.

The Best Schools—Staff Development Illustrations

WALLINGFORD, PA

Inservice workshops for teachers include visits to Philadelphia Art Museums, the Wallingford Art Center, Brandywine River Museum, gallery visits, and county-wide small group sharing sessions.

IRWIN, NJ

The East Brunswick School District takes advantage of its proximity to New York City through its participation with sixty other school districts in a partnership with the Lincoln Center Institute

(LCI). The LCI program is based on the belief that aesthetic education has its place among the basic learning experiences for young people. Teachers and students focus on developing skills of perception through greater understanding of art forms, of how artists make aesthetic choices, and how these understandings relate to other aspects of life. Teachers are involved in extensive workshop experiences at Lincoln Center (one to three weeks) to prepare for teaching artists who will work in the school during the year and performances such as Ballanchine Ballets and Shakespeare, are given in the district by Lincoln Center. In 1992−93, fifty district teachers participated in these workshops, and 4000 children in the district worked with teaching artists.

FUNDING DEVELOPMENT

The Best Schools provide support for the arts in terms of teaching specialists, materials, facilities, and staff development. Funds are budgeted for live performances at the school and for field trips to museums and performances. Frequently, the PTO or PTA provides additional funding for the arts. Volunteers are also recruited to work with staff or children.

The Best Schools—Funding Illustrations

WALLINGFORD, PA

In the Wallingford School District, each elementary school receives $148.28 per student, exclusive of salary, maintenance, and new textbook (first year of adoption only) expenses. Each school decides how these funds will be allocated. Wallingford allocates approximately $5600 for the arts program. In addition, the PTO provides $3841 toward teaching artists and programs.

IRWIN, NJ

The district budgets over $60,000 for expenses related to the Lincoln Center Institute (LCI) program (approximately $8.50 per child). These funds provide stipends to teachers attending LCI in the summer, support teaching artists in the schools and LCI productions brought to the district. Irwin spends approximately $10 per pupil for art and music supplies and materials.

The Irwin PTA has demonstrated its strong support for the arts through the Cultural Arts Council and by raising funds to bring outstanding arts productions to the school. In support of the arts, the board of education matches funds raised by the PTA for these productions. Some of the programs for children have included "Encore: 3-D," "Soft Sculpture," "Theater Works: Footprints on the Moon," "The Mask Man," "Festival Percussion," "Pushcart Players: Betwixt-n-Between," and even a performance by the Children's Play Touring Theater of original poems and stories written by Irwin School children.

SUMMARY

The Best Schools consider the arts as important academic subjects. Structured sequential curricula include not only art production, but art history, criticism, and aesthetic education. Specialists in the arts provide instruction, and classroom teachers and, in many cases, teaching artists provide additional instructional support. Staff development provides opportunity for the classroom teacher and administration, as well as the art specialists. Individual or small group instrumental lessons are made available to interested students. Art productions enliven the total school program. A significant portion of the elementary school budget contributes to supporting the arts programs; in addition, PTO or PTA are active supporters of the arts in the schools. Finally, the Best Schools reach out to local artists, centers for the arts, universities, and museums.

REFERENCES

Consortium of National Arts Education Association. (1994). *National Standards for Arts Education: Dance, Music, Theatre, Visual Arts: What Every Young American Should Know and Be Able to Do in the Arts.* Reston, VA.

National Endowment for the Arts. (1988). ''The Arts in America: A Report to the President and to the Congress,'' Washington, D. C.

Report on Educational Research. (1993) ''Artists, Educators Craft Standards for Arts Education,'' *Report on Educational Research*

U. S. Department of Education, Office of Educational Research and Improvement. (1990). ''Model Arts Programs in Blue Ribbon Schools,'' Blue Ribbon School Program, Washington, D. C.

U. S. Department of Education, Office of Educational Research and Improvement. (1991). ''Notes of the Blue Ribbon Schools Arts Symposium, September 24, 1991,'' Blue Ribbon Schools Program, Washington, D. C.

U. S. Department of Education, Office of Educational Research and Improvement. (1993). ''A Profile of Principals: Facts, Opinions, Ideas and Stories from Principals of Recognized Elementary Schools of 1991 – 1992,'' Blue Ribbon Schools Program, Washington, D. C.

CHAPTER 11

Preparation for Life in the Information Age

WHAT CHILDREN SHOULD LEARN

ACCORDING to the National Goals of Education,

> . . . Every school in America will ensure that all students learn to use their minds well, so they may be prepared for responsible citizenship, further learning, and productive employment in our modern economy.

> Every adult American will be literate and will possess the knowledge and skills necessary to compete in a global economy and exercise the rights and responsibilities of citizenship.

What does it mean to learn to use your mind well? How do you prepare children for further learning? What are the knowledge and skills necessary to compete in a global economy? One thing is clear: the answers to these questions cannot be found in one course or even a series of courses. The national goals envision behaviors, skills, and knowledge that should be the outcomes of the total school experience. However, there are specific learning opportunities that schools need to provide within courses and that transcend individual courses that are essential for achievement of the goals and life in the information-based society of the 21st Century.

As we prepare to enter the next century, information is being generated at a dizzying rate in all fields. Information is coming at the individual with lightning speed and, often, the information is contradictory. Information has become the new capital of the global economy. Those who know what questions to ask and where and how to get and exchange information; who can interpret, analyze, and synthesize data; and who can apply "information-based products" to problems are the new capitalists. Children now cannot only study other cultures and places from textbooks, but now they can actively participate with children across the street, across the country, or around the globe to exchange and create information and cooperatively solve problems and develop projects. Telecommunication provides students with direct opportunities to practice the skills needed for global understanding and future participation in a global economy. It is clear that the old school curriculum, with its emphasis on rote memorization material and selection of *THE* right answer on paper-and-pencil tests, is inadequate to meet the needs of students in the 21st Century. The new skills needed are reflected in some of the new subject matter-related standards, in the research on how students learn complex skills, and in the work done by individual schools and universities.

The development of standards or statements concerning what students should be able to do to demonstrate information literacy has not received a separate focus of attention from the national efforts to articulate standards in subject areas. However, elementary information literacy standards might include the following sample:

STANDARDS: INFORMATION LITERACY

Students will be able to
- formulate questions and plan strategies for finding solutions

- find, collect, and analyze information from multiple sources to solve subject specific and trans-curricular questions
- exchange, interpret, and develop information-based products cooperatively with other students within the school and through telecommunications with other students
- critique information in terms of validity and reliability of sources
- use research to propose solutions to everyday problems
- produce information-based products using multiple technologies

Students will demonstrate the skills to use tools necessary for information literacy by

- finding information using print sources, video, CD-ROM, laser and computer data bases through telecommunication
- developing data bases and spread sheets using technology
- developing one-, two-, and three-dimensional and technology-generated visual representations of information
- using keyboarding, word processing, scanning and desktop publishing skills to produce documents
- producing products incorporating multi-media

HOW CHILDREN LEARN—HOW THEY ARE TAUGHT

Schools have traditionally viewed the teacher and the textbook as the dispensers of knowledge; however, this paradigm cannot be used to prepare children to function effectively in the Information Age. There is simply too much information, and the information itself is generated, revised, and discarded at too astonishing a rate. If children are going to learn processes and gain the flexibility of thinking required to meet ever-changing information and intellectual demands, then instructional methodology must also change.

A distinction needs to be made between how children are to be taught to operate the tools of information literacy and the methods used to assist students internalize the processes necessary to function effectively by using, interpreting, analyzing, creating, and communicating information. Learning to use the tools is fairly straightforward. Keyboarding skills can be taught by a teacher, by the use of computer software, or by a combination of both, usually beginning around grade three. Simple word-processing programs can be introduced as early as kindergarten, with more complex functions introduced over the years as student products gain sophistication. Skills for accessing information from books, CD-ROM, and laser disc sources can be taught as part of a library media curriculum or introduced at times when children need access to a source for a specific project. Skills for accessing and retrieving information through telecommunications can be taught in the library, using such sources as Dow Jones Retrieval, or in classrooms as students have the need to access such programs as KidsNet or the AT&T Learning Network.

Development of a student's ability to effectively use sources to find, analyze, interpret, draw conclusions from, and communicate information is much more complex from an instructional point of view than learning to operate the tools of information literacy. Just as learning to hold a pencil and to form letters is very different from learning to write effectively, there is also a big difference between learning to use the keyboard and being able to effectively gather, analyze, and communicate information. Learning research and theory indicates that, if children are going to make connections between what they learn in school and real-life situations, learn to apply basic skills to complex problems, and develop the very high level thinking skills required for true information literacy, the instruction must provide for the active learning and application of these skills.

Instruction across the curriculum has to be structured in such a way as to require students to pose questions, seek information, and evaluate alternative solutions. The standards emerging in the individual subject areas are problem solving?based. There is a growing congruency among individual content areas in their views of how children learn and how they should be taught. In addition to a focus on the development of problem-solving skills, there is also an ever-increasing trend toward integration of curriculum. Clearly, as children and adults encounter life in the Information Age, the perceived boundaries between fields continue to fade.

In order for students to have the opportunity to learn to use the tools of information literacy, schools must have available not only traditional print materials, but also computers, CD-ROM, modems for telecommunication, calculators, video disc players, satellite dishes, cable television, retrieval services, access to remote data bases, software, laser discs, CDs, video- and audiotapes. They must have these technologies available in sufficient quantity and quality to make their use by the student body feasible and realistic. The opportunity to use technology must be available to all students, and all students must be actively engaged in problem defining and solving. Some information resources, such as VCRs or a telecommunication equipped computer for KidsNet, can be shared by an entire class or, in some cases, among a group of classes. Some tools are used primarily by the teacher to prepare lessons to more actively engage students in learning, such as HyperCard for Mac's or LinkWays for IBM or bar coded laser discs such as Windows on Science from Optical Data. Some activities are best carried out in cooperative groups and require only a computer for each group. However, other information-processing applications, such as word processing, require individual student access to computers for sustained periods of time. The computer has become the ''pencil'' of the Information Age, and scheduling the use of one or two of these modern ''pencils'' among an entire class is neither efficient nor effective for most purposes.

Equal educational opportunity is a major consideration in the use of technology. The school can be reasonably certain that all students have access to pencils and paper at school and at home, and research data shows that almost all households have calculators. However, not all homes have computers, nor do all children in homes that do have computers have access to them. Educators must be careful not to widen the gap between the ''knows'' and the ''non-knows'' in using information processing. Providing ample opportunity within the school day is one way of ensuring equity; extending hours of access, i. e., keeping the library/computer centers open after regular hours and loaning hardware and software for home use, are some of the ways of ensuring equity.

A three-year study and development project by a team of researchers from Education Development Center (EDC) and Technical Education Research Centers (TERC) found that, if technology is to meet the diverse needs of children in the classroom, essential and interdependent elements must be in place at the curriculum, instructional, and organizational levels. The principal must assume the overall leadership by communicating a vision of the value of technology in meeting the needs of students and the goals of the curriculum, fostering a spirit of inquiry among staff, providing motivation and resources, and allowing for individual differences in interest and expertise among staff in the use of technology. There is a need for a strong facilitator, an advocate who can work with teachers, providing training and guiding curriculum development. Finally, on the organizational level, there is a need for a team consisting of administrators, facilitator, and teachers within each school building to guide curriculum development. Within this curriculum, interdisciplinary and thematically based programs assist students to inquire, link, and synthesize ideas. Decisions concerning hardware acquisition, allocation, and scheduling should focus on curriculum goals and teacher expertise. When a mechanism to narrow software choices is matched to the curriculum, teachers are more apt to integrate technology into instruction.

At the instructional level, EDC advocates the use of an "I-search or We-search" process based on the work of Ken Macrorie (1988). By using a theme as a basis, students are engaged in a process of making meaning through posing an interesting question, gathering information, integrating information to build concepts and generate ideas, and refining their thinking and writing about how they have carried on their investigation and what they have learned. Instruction should also include the use of cooperative learning to enhance shared creativity and strengths and to build social skills and respect for each other. Finally, students should use, on a regular basis, a variety of technological applications to pose questions and solve problems, construct knowledge, and communicate ideas.

Staff development is an essential component of any plan to use technology effectively. EDC/TERC found that "in-service workshops contribute to acquisition of knowledge, but are insufficient in helping teachers use this knowledge in their work with students. Teachers best learn to integrate technology successfully through ongoing school-based support and structures for collaboration and communication" (in Zorfass et al., 1992; ASCD, 1993, p. 11.54). In addition, if teachers are to use technology regularly, someone must be responsible for maintaining hardware and for solving technical problems.

HOW LEARNING SHOULD BE ASSESSED

Accessing the students' skills in operating information processing tools is, in many ways, an easier process than accessing basic skills in content-related areas. In some cases, the assessment is built into the learning process. For example, software that teaches students to type usually includes routines that also record the speed at which the student has learned to type. The proof of a student's ability to access a data base is that the connection is made and the data retrieved; in addition, the length of the connection and the specific data base accessed is frequently reported on a regular basis back to the school as part of the billing process. Word-processing skills can be assessed by having students produce documents or edit text. Data searches can be monitored to determine how quickly and effectively a student can use descriptors to narrow and complete a search for specific information.

Assessing the student's ability to effectively use the information tools to solve problems and communicate results is more challenging. A very limited amount of knowledge can be assessed through traditional paper-and-pencil tests. For example, this form of traditional assessment can be used to determine if students can identify the best sources for obtaining certain kinds of data in certain situations. However, complex problem solving takes not only access to data, but time. Students need to learn to define problems, explore data sources, deal with conflicting or incomplete information, draw and justify conclusions, and produce and communicate a product. The complex and most important forms of information processing need to be assessed based on the process and the product. Most often, projects developed over time and in various content areas are used to access outcomes by using criteria such as

- problem definition
- appropriateness and variety of sources used
- accuracy of data reporting
- justification of conclusions reached
- effectiveness of mode of communication, i.e., graphs, charts, and narratives

In summary, assessment of information literacy distinguishes between *surface knowledge*, i.e., learning to use tools, procedures, and rote applications, and *meaningful knowledge*, connected learning that requires active problem solving and communication. There are at least six assumptions that underlie emerging standards in information literacy:

- It is not possible to teach, or for students to learn, all the information needed for life in the 21st or, in fact, the 20th Century.
- Learning how to pose questions, accessing, processing, and analyzing information and applying the results to real-life problems are essential skills transcending individual content areas or courses.
- Children must be actively engaged in real problem solving; children should learn to select and choose from among multiple resources and become proficient in using each approach.
- Learning to efficiently operate information tools is only a necessary step toward effectively learning to use these tools to solve meaningful problems.
- Information processing is needed by all students, and equal access needs to be ensured.
- Assessment is best embedded in the educational process; in other words, it is part of the instructional process, rather than an add-on to instruction. Assessment should provide evidence of what a student can do, as well as what a student knows. As much as possible, it should be performance-based.

THE BEST SCHOOLS – THEORY INTO PRACTICE IN INFORMATION PROCESSING

The Best Schools are keenly aware of the need for students to become information literate at a very high level. Information literacy goes far beyond the common objective of development of computer literacy. The latter is usually limited to the knowledge of and ability to use a computer, including keyboarding, booting programs, history of the computer, and a little knowledge of programming. The Best Schools assume that children have to learn to use technology, just as they have to learn to hold a pencil, print, and learn to write script, and they teach students these basic technology operation skills. However, the Best Schools also have as their prime instructional goals the ability of students to process, evaluate, use, and communicate information and solve problems. Since learning to use technology is the means to the ends, not the ends, information resources include not only computers, but also calculators, televisions, CD-ROM, laser discs, telecommunication links, camcorders, fax machines, and a wide range of print material, including books, charts, magazines, and prints.

The Best Schools recognize that access to information resources is key to accomplishing instructional goals. All students have the opportunity for repeated and sustained access to technology. Their visions of what technology to use, the location of that technology, and the use of technology are very consistent. Few of the Best Schools have totally implemented their visions; however, they have made large strides in the use of technology and have specific plans to expand access. Components of their systems commonly include, or they have plans to include:

- the library/media center as the central hub for technology access and distribution
- one or more labs for word processing, publishing, and exploration
- four to six computers in every classroom
- all computers networked to server in library
- access from labs and classrooms to card catalogs (in school library, county, district, university libraries), CD-ROM encyclopedias, telecommunication (other schools,

national data bases, worldwide data bases and exchanges, bulletin boards), videos, and cable TV
- a computer loan system to ensure equal access
- multi-use software available to all students, such as Microsoft Works, as well as software for specific purposes
- ability to use different platforms in network mode (PC, Apple)
- ability to expand access to homes
- ability to take advantage of programs via satellite
- ability to access library resources from the community

The new paradigms for instruction in language arts, science, mathematics, and social studies, grounded as they are in the development of complex problem-solving skills, make the development of information literacy essential in each of the several disciplines. Similarity in the goals for language arts, science, mathematics, and social studies also reinforces the interdisciplinary nature of learning and the use of interdisciplinary problems and projects in the learning process. In the Best Schools, technology is used to enhance learning in individual disciplines and in integrated units and projects. In this chapter one school will be used as the primary example of the development of information literacy so that the full range of multidisciplinary use of technology in subject areas and the specific instruction related to information literacy used can be shown. However, the school used as an example is similar to many others in its plans for and current use of technology. The school is also typical of many schools nationwide in terms of its socioeconomic status, student population, and financial resources.

The Best Schools—A Case Study In Information Literacy: The Context

MIDWAY HEIGHTS ELEMENTARY SCHOOL, COLUMBIA, MO

The Information Age of the 21st Century is already in full swing at Midway Heights Elementary School. The school is one of eighteen elementary schools in the District of Columbia. The school serves a full spectrum of students, from 17% who are eligible for free/reduced lunch to those from affluent homes. Recognizing the blend of community support (6739 volunteer hours, PTA, Toastmaster Business Partnership, University of Missouri Partnership), technology expertise of the principal, and academic achievement, the district designated Midway as the Technology Pilot School for the district, with the mission to develop a model elementary program that would provide advanced technological opportunities for all students. Technology is only one aspect of this outstanding school's total program where 90% of the students meet the mastery level of the instructional objectives in grades 1–6.

Midway Heights Elementary School was also named by *Redbook* as an ''Overall School of Excellence'' in 1993. The Columbia School District was designated by the Governor's Conference as one of the sixteen model districts in the United States in 1989. There are five other Blue Ribbon Schools in the district.

Dr. Liz Schmitz, *Principal, K–6, 322 Students*

INFORMATION PROCESSING GOALS AND OBJECTIVES

Many of the Best Schools have developed specific goals and objectives for the development of technology skills and the use of technology as a research tool; other schools have developed objectives that are embedded in subject specific learning objectives. With the exception of keyboarding skills, skills related to learning how to use particular hardware or software are usually introduced in conjunction with the student's need to use the hardware or software. For example, if a project requires the use of a camcorder, then instruction in how to operate the camera is introduced in conjunction with the assignment. Word-processing skills are introduced, as needed, in the classroom as students write using "user friendly" software such as Word Processing for Kids, Bank Street Writer III, MacWrite, LogoWriter, Fredwrite, or The Writing Center. Keyboarding skills, however, are usually taught in a formal manner in a lab setting. The most frequent grade level for keyboarding instruction appears to be grade three, with follow-up instruction at higher grade levels. Instruction usually is scheduled once or twice a week for approximately thirty minutes per session. The classroom teacher is most often the person responsible for instruction at the elementary level. However, instructional software such as CommuniKeys, MicroType, TIES Keyboarding Program, or Touch Typing for Beginners is used to provide individualized pacing of and instruction in skills.

Goals for information processing or research are frequently developed by grade level and may be interdisciplinary in nature. For example, the Lawrence Brook School, New Jersey, and Irwin School, NJ, use a research/style manual developed by the district, which has objectives for and research project requirements starting in grade four. The style portion of the manual establishes formats and mechanics for papers and products at each grade level. In another example, Highland Elementary School, Minnesota, fifth grade students are using Hypercard to format research into multi-media systems for presentations that allow them to tie the computer, video camera, and video presentations into one report.

The Best Schools—Information Processing Goals and Objectives Illustration

MIDWAY HEIGHTS, MO

Goal: Through a program that effectively integrates technology into the total school curriculum, students will be able to successfully utilize computers as tools for written communication, problem solving, telecommunications, research, data collection, and management before they leave the elementary grades.

STUDENT OUTCOMES

(1) The students will demonstrate the word-processing competencies necessary to compose, edit, and finalize a written product.
(2) The students will utilize proper keyboarding techniques.
(3) The students will develop the systematic problem-solving skills necessary to utilize technology systems such as computers, telecommunications, CD-ROM, information retrieval, interactive video, and still video imaging.
(4) The students will produce documents with graphics integrating desktop publishing capabilities.
(5) The students will be able to collect, organize, and analyze data (for example, Science Probe Data).
(6) The students will understand how to author a program.

RESEARCH

There is a great deal of curriculum integration at Midway. This is particularly apparent in the area of research, analysis, and production. Research is produced on a regular basis, starting in grade 1. There are special projects for each grade level. Students use the library and technology lab to access information not only from laser and CD-ROM data bases and books, but also from around the globe through Internet and Bitnet (under an agreement with the University of Missouri). Students are able to direct questions and collect data, throughout the world, from other schools, as well as research facilities and individuals.

For example, in the fifth grade, students researched why early Americans (1600s) came to America. They used CD-ROM, laser disc, print materials, and Internet. When they had gained all available information, they met in their cooperative learning groups to determine what information was vital to their end product. From their research information, they produced tri-fold travel brochures to encourage early Americans to come to America. They scanned pictures to import into their document; used the video camcorder or Zap Shot Camera (Cannon) to digitize images into their documents; wrote text using ClarisWorks, Children's Writing Center, or Pagemaker; imported graphics; and prepared the format. The project integrated history, geography, and research skills with technology life skills.

A three-day-a-week media specialist, the technology lab specialist, classroom teachers, and a cadre of twenty-five to thirty trained volunteers provide assistance to students as they conduct their research (one to five is the adult to student ratio). Students are brought to the laboratory by grade or class on a fluid schedule to access data, work in cooperative groups, and produce documents.

Technology life skills are assessed through a portfolio approach using student end products that demonstrate the use of the technology.

INFORMATION PROCESSING BY GRADE

In order to insure that students are involved in developmentally appropriate information processing and technology use and, at the same time, to insure that students have the opportunity to master a full range of technology applications, some of the Best Schools have developed grade-level specific scope and sequences that cut across subject matter areas. For example, Salanter Akiba Riverdale Academy, New York, lists the following grade-level outcomes in its computer curriculum:

- GRADE 1: Use EZ LOGO using printers.
- GRADE 4: Develop an Indian data base.
- GRADE 5: Use a United States data base in conjunction with a social studies project.
- GRADE 6: Develop a writing project from first draft to final copy using word processing.
- GRADE 7: Do math research using Connectany disks. Use a modem to exchange findings with other classes throughout the United States.

The library/media center of the Best Schools plays a central role in the development of information processing. The use of technology in no way reduces the importance of books and print materials; the Best Schools are proud of their book collections and the high level of circulation to all children. In most of the Best Schools, the library/media center catalog and circulation systems are computerized, and in many, computer stations have replaced card catalogs. Technology is having a profound effect on the reference sections of the library in that CD-ROM interactive video encyclopedias such as *Grolier's* and *Compton's* are being used extensively. These encyclopedias allow even very young students to conduct sophisticated searches for information, identify multiple sources, allow students to select references for indepth study, and on most topics, provide video footage based on actual events. For example, if a child is interested in why President Truman gave the order to drop the atomic bomb, the student can find a listing of many sources, narrow the search using additional ''search words, actually read material (on screen or printout), and watch and listen to President Truman explain to the nation the reasons for his decision. Unlike regular encyclopedias, the interactive video encyclopedias are updated regularly. Another resource widely available in library/media centers is *NewsBank*. This resource brings to the elementary library magazine resources that are beyond the funds available for individual subscriptions, is easier for children to use, and reduces the need for storage and shelf space. However, even with these sources, libraries still maintain subscriptions to frequently used magazines and newspapers.

Library/media centers in the Best Schools are also equipped for telecommunications. Via modem, the library/media center is linked to electronic networks outside of the school. Such a service is Dialog, which allows the librarian or teacher to conduct on-line searches for material not available through more child friendly sources. Dow Jones provides a reduced rate to schools so that students can access their data bases through DowLine. This latter source provides much more than stock information; however, it is often used in conjunction with the Stock Market Game. Prodigy is another source that provides a low- cost connection to multiple data bases and, like DowLine, is easy to use. Library/media centers are also frequently linked to other libraries in the district and/or to town- or county-level libraries via modem and fax. These connections allow students to search further for resources and allow libraries to share resources. A number of the Best Schools have developed links with universities and businesses to access not only their data bases, but also their professional staff. For example, in Lawrence Brook School, New Jersey, students can access scientists in their labs at BellCore to gain input and information concerning math and science projects.

In order to access the various forms of information available in the library/media centers, the facilities are equipped with computers, CD-ROM, laser disc players, videocorders, camcorders, scanners, and printers. One goal of the Best Schools is to constantly expand the availability of resources, have students access their resources, make decisions concerning relevance of information for solving specific problems, evaluate information in terms of credibility, use information to solve problems, justify their conclusions, and communicate results. In order to accomplish this, the Best Schools have plans for or have already linked the library/media technology sources by networks to four to six computers in individual classes. In order to ensure equal access for all students, libraries are also loaning hardware (computers and calculators) and software to students (Mirabeau Lamar, TX).

Computer laboratories are usually adjacent to the library/media centers and allow for whole class, small group, and individual computer work. Classroom teachers bring students to the facility to work on projects. In some schools, a trained technology assistant is available in the lab, and in a number of schools, volunteers are used to assist classroom teachers and students. Teachers also use the lab computers to prepare materials for lessons; in some schools, there is also a computer in each classroom for the teacher's use.

The Best Schools—Technology Emphasis by Grade Illustration

MIDWAY HEIGHTS, MO

Kindergarten

- picture drawing and learning computers (KidsPix)
- story writing (The Writing Center/Clifford Big Book Maker)

First Grade

- story writing (The Writing Center/Clifford Big Book Maker/KidsPix)
- mathematics skills
- sound/symbol relationships

Second Grade

- story writing with graphics (The Writing Center/KidsPix/MacWrite
- mathematics skills
- introduction to research skills (Information Resource Network, *NewsBank*, *Grolier's* and *Compton's Interactive CD-ROM Encyclopedias)*

Third Grade

- keyboarding (two or three thirty-minute sessions per week utilizing MicroType)
- composition and editing (MacWrite/The Writing Center)
- mathematics skills
- research skills (ClarisWorks, Information Resource Network, *NewsBank*, *Grolier's* and *Compton's Interactive CD-ROM Encyclopedias*)

Fourth Grade

- language and writing objectives integrated with social studies and science (PAWS Language Arts/The Writing Center)
- telecommunications (KidsNet)
- review of keyboarding and word-processing techniques (MicroType/The Writing Center)
- research skills (Information Resource Network, *NewsBank*, *Grolier's* and *Compton's Interactive Video Encyclopedias*)

Fifth Grade

- literature enrichment (Electronic Bookshelf)
- composition and editing (The Writing Center/ClarisWorks)
- social studies [TimeLine, Oregon Trail, GTV (National Geographic Social Studies Program on laser disc), Jenny's Journey, Carmen Sandiego series]
- problem solving (ClarisWorks, other various programs)
- mathematics [KidsNet, How the West Was Won $1+3\times4$, King's Rule, ClarisWorks, Jasper (Optical Data laser disc)]
- telecommunications [KidsNet, Missouri University Partners Program, FredMail (inter-schools problem solving)]
- research skills (Information Resource Network, *NewsBank*, *Grolier's* and *Compton's Interactive Video Encyclopedias*)
- science [Interactive video with Windows on Science (Optical Data), KidsNet]
- art (interactive video with Louvre and National Gallery and design in art with KidsPix)

Sixth Grade

- literature enrichment (Electronic Bookshelf)
- composition and editing (The Writing Center, ClarisWorks)
- social studies (Carmen Sandiego, Oregon Trail)
- problem solving (various programs)
- mathematics (ClarisWorks, King's Rule, How the West Was Won $1\times2+3$)
- research skills (Information Resource Network, *NewsBank*, *Grolier's* and *Compton's Interactive Video Encyclopedias*

Special Education

- sight vocabulary
- spelling

- story writing (The Writing Center, MacWrite)
- picture construction with sound (KidsPix)
- keyboarding (MicroType)

INFORMATION PROCESSING IN THE CONTENT AREAS

The curriculum in the content areas in the Best Schools is experiential and problem solving based. Technology is widely used, as sources of information to organize and analyze data; chart and visually present information; and produce documents. Laser discs are used by teachers to incorporate visual material into the classroom. For example, art and social studies teachers can access artwork from the National Gallery or the Louvre laser discs in their classrooms. Computer-assisted design programs such as MacDraw enhance art programs. Software programs such as ClarisWorks allow students to create data bases, import information, analyze data, and create graphs. Computer technology is used to support problem solving, rather than for "skill and drill." In some states, educational television is used to enhance specific areas of the curriculum; for example, current events information is downloaded to videotape and used in the classroom to connect studies to real-world events.

One of the most powerful uses of technology is the opportunity now available to link students across the district, the nation, and the world. KidsNet (National Geographic) is such a program used in many of the Best Schools. With the program, children are linked with children in other schools. Data is collected concerning real problems such as weather. Local data and data from linked schools is analyzed, conclusions are drawn, and students then interact with scientists concerning their findings and a report is developed. Another program, AT&T Learning Network, connects seven to nine distant classrooms via telecommunications into learning circles that provide the opportunity for students to expand perspectives, generate new ideas and solutions, and cooperatively develop products through units such as "Society's Problems," "Global Issues," "Energy and the Environment," and "Mind Works." For example, during the Gulf War, children in East Brunswick communicated daily via modem with children in Saudi Arabia, sharing insights about the effect of the conflict on the lives of children. Each of the previous chapters also includes numerous examples of how technology has become tools of instruction.

The Best Schools—Integration of Technology by Subject Illustration

MIDWAY HEIGHTS, MO

LANGUAGE ARTS

Students in grades K–6 are involved in keyboarding, word processing, language skills, telecommunication, composition, researching, and publishing. ClarisWorks (Claris, Inc.), an integrated package that includes word processing, spread sheet, data base, graphing, and telecommunication capabilities, is used in the technology lab and in classes equipped with Mac's. The Children's Writing Center (The Learning Company) is used in kindergarten and in other grades where there are Apple IIe's. Students use the full range of software capability in researching, analyzing, and publishing their projects. At each grade level, there are thematic research projects, which have a spectrum of research and production requirements.

Electronic Bookshelf (Electronic Bookshelf, Frankfurt, Indiana) is another example of software used in language arts. It is used by students in the classroom to check literature comprehension in grades 4–5 and as part of the school-wide language arts program. The Electronic Bookshelf is not correlated with the sets of literature read as part of the in-class shared literature. However, students are required to read a certain number of additional books per month and are tested via computer on each of these books. The students enjoy the program, and it is credited with increasing the quantity of literature read by students.

MATHEMATICS

Mathematics is taught based on concepts and outcomes. Textbooks are only used as a supplement in the program. Manipulatives are used extensively. Using ClarisWorks integrated software package, children are directly involved in data collection, graphing, and publishing. For example, students in grade 4 collected information about pets in different families; they then entered the information into a spread sheet and formed charts and graphs depicting the data numerically. Another software program that is frequently used is How the West Was Won $1+3\times4$ (Wings/Sunburst) in grades $4-6$. The skill and drill type software has been virtually eliminated, since it is incompatible with the overall teaching approach of the school. It was also found that this type of software was no more effective than worksheets, which are also rarely used in the school. The interdisciplinary Kidsnet (National Geographic) is used at grades 4 and 5. Telecommunication access to Kidsnet at grade 4 is through Apple GS's and at grade 5 through Mac's. Jasper (Optical Data), a laser disc-based program, was introduced into the fifth grade math program in the fall of 1993.

SCIENCE

Technology is utilized in science through the wide range of interactive video materials in Windows on Science (Optical Data) and the telecommunications of KidsNet. In addition, students research science topics in language arts through Midway's integrated thematic program. Students are taught to access, assimilate, and produce science information using technology.

HISTORY/GEOGRAPHY

Technology plays a role in history through the use of videotapes, interactive videos, and computer software. Examples are Time Line, Oregon Trail, GTV (National Geographic Social Studies Program on Laser Disc), Louvre and National Gallery of Art laser discs, and CD-ROM research using *Grolier's* and *Compton's Encyclopedias* and *Newsbank* (twenty-one newspapers on CD-ROM).

The Carmen Sandiego series (grades $3-6$), with Jenny's Journey and Oregon Trail (grades $2-6$,) are used as part of the geography program.

ASSESSING WHAT STUDENTS KNOW AND CAN DO

Assessment of the ability of students to operate a particular technology is quite straightforward. For example, many of the programs used to teach keyboarding keep track of individual student achievement as part of the program. In other cases, the products produced attest to the student's ability to use the technology. Valid and reliable assessment of information processing, however, holds the same challenges as assessment of higher level skills in all subject areas. Some aspects, such as the student's ability to locate multiple sources of information or the student's ability to narrow a search to specific documents, can be assessed directly. Higher levels of information processing and problem solving are most frequently assessed in terms of products produced by individuals, groups, or even classes of students. South Brunswick Township (Greenbrook School) has developed, with Education Testing Service, a sixth grade assessment—a process that combines the assessment of many of the school's learning objectives. In this model, each sixth grade student submits three research questions to the teacher. One question is selected by the teacher to be researched by the child. Each student is given eight hours of time over two or more days to research the question and produce a paper (word processing required) and a visual and oral presentation. The library/media center, computers, and school resources are available to these students. No attempt is made by staff to structure the time or the project for the students, and no work may be brought home or brought to school. Assessors who are teachers from other grades and schools, parents, board members, staff from other districts, and business people are trained for two hours in scoring the written product and visual and oral presentation. Incorporating their prepared visual, students give the oral presentation for the assessors; at the end of the presentation, the student gives the assessors the written document. Two assessors score each product and the parents and children receive a report of their achievements. The data is used districtwide to benchmark achievement and for curriculum development.

THE BEST SCHOOLS – PROGRAM DEVELOPMENT AND SUPPORT IN INFORMATION PROCESSING

Technology and Research Implementation Process

The Best Schools began to introduce technology six to ten years ago. In some cases, they began with a computer lab, and in others, they began by placing a single computer in as many individual classrooms as possible. Much of the initially available software was either the "skill and drill" type or games. However, the schools saw the potential of the technology, and these initial efforts have developed along with the technology and applications. Commodore and Apple 64 K computers were replaced with slightly more powerful machines, and these, in turn, are being replaced by much more powerful computers. However, in most cases, these highly durable second generation machines purchased by districts are still being used for some purposes. Other technology such as laser disc, CD-ROM, satellite dish, and VCRs have been introduced as they have become available.

The Best Schools, like most schools, began instruction using computers by focusing on computer literacy. The aim was to teach children about computers how to boot a program, how a program was written. Children enjoyed playing computer games, and teachers complained about the lack of relevance and quality of software. The Best Schools have not only upgraded software but have developed plans and curriculum to utilize computers and other technologically powerful learning tools. They recognize that new technology will constantly appear in the marketplace. Some of the new technology will find immediate application in their schools; however, each new contender will be reviewed in terms of what it really adds to the instructional process. For example, more powerful and faster computers are appearing all the time; however, these machines are not necessary for elementary school-level word processing. The schools move the technology around, placing the available machines where they can be most appropriately used. New technology is then placed where it can be most effectively used. The Best Schools do not wait for the "ultimate" technology; they buy what is adequate for their curriculum and as much as possible what is compatible with what they already own. However, they recognize that, just as textbooks become outdated, even the most carefully purchased technology will become obsolete.

The Best Schools – Implementing a Technology Plan Illustration

MIDWAY HEIGHTS, MO

Although technology began to appear at Midway Heights seven years ago, it was not until 1990 that the school was officially designated the Technology Pilot School for the district. The principal's extensive background as an instructional materials director in the district was a significant factor in the district's decision to make Midway the lead school for development in technology.

A building-level committee of grade-level representative teachers, a technology specialist, and the principal are responsible for development of technology. They review software and are responsible for allocating the very limited resources available for the purchase of software each year. No piece of software is purchased unless it is clear how it fits into the curriculum. Each year, a different grade has been the focus of technology development.

STAFF DEVELOPMENT

Teachers and administrators in the schools today did not grow up with technology beyond television, nor did they learn to use technology as part of their degree training. The training of staff is an essential part of any effective technology program. Not only do staff members have to learn to operate technology, they also need to become comfortable in using it and must see the value of its use in the education process. A recent survey of schools show that 90% planned to spend money on technology training in 1992–93. Nineteen percent of the schools surveyed planned more than ten hours of training per person (Technology & Learning, 1993). The Best Schools provide extensive and continuous staff development. In the early years of computer use in the schools, staff development was usually provided by the "school computer hackers." Unfortunately, they frequently "turned off" their colleagues by attempting to teach programming to teachers. Today's technology is much more user friendly than earlier models, and hard drives and networks make access to programs much easier than in the past. Training has also changed; now, the focus is on teaching how technology and specific software can be used to implement the curriculum. Every effort is made to make the use of technology simple and understandable, and staff receive training in specific applications with computers being available for their use and practice. Many schools encourage teachers to take computers home for weekends and vacations. Because a goal of most of the Best Schools is for every teacher to have a computer, in some schools there already is a computer on every teacher's desk. In addition, some schools have also initiated plans to assist teachers in buying computers for home use.

The Best Schools—Staff Development Illustration

MIDWAY HEIGHTS, MO

Staff development at Midway has been continuous. The principal and/or the technology lab specialist provides after-school training once or twice a month, with virtually all teachers attending these voluntary workshops. In addition, teachers are released for half a day to attend workshops twice a year. Intensive technology work is done in the technology lab by grade-level teams. Training in the use of software is enhanced by materials developed by the principal and/or the technology specialist. Complicated, often unclear software manuals are rewritten into two- to four-page materials that teachers can use and understand easily.

The technology laboratory specialist is a paraprofessional who has a real interest in technology and who has developed expertise over time. She works with children and teachers in the lab, works on the teacher version of software documentation, and provides training for teachers in technology.

Volunteers play an essential part in the support of all programs at Midway; in 1992–93, 6739 volunteer hours were clocked. Twenty-five to thirty volunteers provide direct support for student research in the technology lab and library/media center.

The principal and technology specialist provide training for volunteers, with initial training of volunteers to support research being approximately ten hours. However, training is ongoing and skills are enhanced as they work as consultants to children working on actual research projects.

HARDWARE

Hardware in most schools has been purchased over time. The type of computers used depends largely on the availability and desirability of software at the time of purchase. For example, most in-class computers purchased four or more years ago are Apple IIe's. These machines were relatively inexpensive, and most of the classroom software was available for this platform. Many of these machines are being replaced by Mac LCs, a much more powerful and flexible computer, but one that can use the software purchased for the Apple IIe's. On the other hand, software for computerizing libraries was available first for IBM PCs or compatible machines (Columbia Library, Winnebago or Follette Library systems), and many of the schools adopted PCs for library use. In some cases, computer labs were purchased for specific software applications that required specific hardware, for example, IBM's Writing to Read program. Today, while much of the software is available for both Apple and PC formats, there is still specific, and often excellent, software being developed, which requires either the Mac or IBM platform. Technology now allows the networking of these various types of computers throughout the school. The aim of the Best Schools is to network all technology in the school.

The schools also have CD-ROM equipped computers for interactive video encyclopedias, laser disc players for such programs as Windows on Science, modem-equipped computers for telecommunication, VCRs and cable for accessing television, and in many cases, satellite dishes to access instructional television.

The Best Schools – Technology Illustration

MIDWAY HEIGHTS, MO

Technology laboratory: In the laboratory located adjacent to the library, there are twenty-seven Mac LCs and LCIIs plus eight Apple IIe's which are networked for printer use with Local Talk. The laboratory is primarily used for production. In addition to computers, there are a laser printer, two color dot matrix printers, and an Apple I 300 dot matrix scanner (with Omni Page Professional and Ofoto software). A still video camera and camcorder allow for images to be captured for viewing on monitors or placed in computer-generated documents through the video digitizing process. Two Mac stations are provided in the lab for teacher use.

The library/media center: The library circulation system is computerized (Follett), and there are six networked (Novell) IBM student stations, which provide card catalog search capability integrated with a CBIS network that allows for the stacking of CD-ROMs for *World Book* and *Newsbank* searches. All stations can access the *World Book Encyclopedia*. All of the libraries in the district are connected through Internet. In addition, there is a Macintosh LC dedicated to telecommunications for accessing Internet and Bitnet. Finally, the library/media center contains two Mac stations for use by staff members. The goal is to link the library resources to each classroom.

Classrooms: Each classroom has at least one computer; however, some have as many as three. The goal is for each classroom to have six Mac's. Currently, the classroom computers are a combination of Apple IIe's, Apple GS, and Mac LCs. At the fourth and fifth grade level, each class has a Mac equipped for telecommunications for accessing Kidsnet, GTV, and Internet. Every room has a printer.

Rolling interactive video stations: Three rolling carts are equipped with Mac Classics with CD-ROM and laser disc players and monitors. These are moved from classroom to classroom as needed.

Homework hotline: Parents and students can maintain contact with the fifth and sixth grade teachers through what is considered a "low tech" homework hotline. Two inexpensive message machines with five-minute message capability are used. Teachers of 5th grades share one machine, and the sixth grade teachers share a second machine. Students and parents call a number assigned to each grade to get homework assignments and messages from the teacher.

FUNDING DEVELOPMENT

Technology is expensive. While prices have been reduced consistently over the years, technology, in the quantities needed for effective instruction, still requires a significant and ongoing commitment of funds. Except for new construction where it is not uncommon to include the technology as part of the bonding cost, or in the few cases where districts have issued bonds solely for technology, most schools are faced with the acquisition of equipment over time. As new and more powerful equipment is purchased, older, less powerful, but still usable machines are moved to classrooms that can make use of older technology. Funding for technology has been provided in most schools by numerous sources, including the PTAs and PTOs, district funds, redemption of coupons, donations, grants, and partnerships with business and industry. Federal Chapter 2 grant monies have been widely used for purchase of technology hardware.

The Best Schools—Technology Costs Illustration

MIDWAY HEIGHTS, MO

Midway Heights is not a wealthy community and has had a very limited school budget. During the past seven years, the PTA, through fund-raisers, has provided nearly $50,000 for the purchase of technology. State grants received in 1992 ($19,000) and 1993 ($17,000) have supported Project Interact, which has provided funds to increase the time of the media specialist from two to three days per week and provided funding for the Mac's in the lab. In addition, the district has provided approximately $50,000 over the past seven years for technology support. This was a special allotment of capital improvement funds from the district.

The only extra staff provided at the school in relationship to the use of technology is the technology lab specialist who works three days a week and is paid on the clerical scale. Volunteers are used extensively. Staff training has taken place on limited release time. The principal/technology lab specialist training for teachers has taken place primarily once or twice a month on a voluntary basis after school hours.

A business partnership with Toastmaster has provided valuable expertise in setting up the system, as well as donations of wiring. Computer specialists at the University of Missouri have provided technical assistance and access to Internet and Bitnet; they have also helped to identify telecommunication mailboxes worldwide to assist students to access data.

SUMMARY

The Best Schools have goals, objectives, and curriculum for information literacy, which go far beyond computer literacy. Technology is used within individual subjects to support instruction of higher level thinking skills and is also used to support integration of instruction. All students in the Best Schools use a widerange of technology and software. The library/media center is the hub for technology; however, technology is also available in individual classrooms and in labs. In most cases, this technology has been purchased over time and through multiple funding sources. Staff development has been extensive and is a continuing part of an overall plan for achieving the goal of information literacy.

REFERENCES

AT & T Learning Network. P. O. Box 4012, Bridgewater, NJ 08807.

National Geographic Society. (1993). KidsNet, National Geographic Educational Technology, Washington, D. C.

Macrorie, K. (1988). *The I-Search Paper*. Portsmouth, NH: Boynton/Cook Publishers.

Zorfass, J. et al. (1992). ''A School-Based Approach to Technology Integration,'' *ASCD Curriculum Handbook*, Alexandria, VA: ASCD.

Zorfass, J. M., C. C. Morocco and N. Lacy. ''A School-Based Approach to Technology Integration.'' *ASCD Curriculum Handbook*. Association for Supervision and Curriculum Development, Alexandria, VA 1992.

CHAPTER 12

Other Areas of the Curriculum

IN addition to the dimensions of the elementary curriculum covered in the previous chapters, schools also provide physical and health education and other subjects that address goals and objectives that they consider important for children to learn. This chapter looks at the following questions concerning other areas of the curriculum:

- What are some of the additional subjects that round out the elementary curriculum?
- What are some examples of how these are implemented in the Best Schools?

FOREIGN LANGUAGE

Goal Three of the National Goals for Education, "By the year 2000 . . . every school in America will ensure that all students learn to use their minds well, so they may be prepared for responsible citizenship, further learning, and productive employment in our modern economy," and the specific objective "competence in more than one language." Two types of programs potentially address this objective—first, the teaching of a non-English language to English speaking children, and second the teaching of English to children whose native language is other than English.

Foreign language instruction, whether English or other than English, aims today to develop the ability of students to function in real-life situations in the target language. Instruction focuses on the development of student competencies in speaking, listening, reading, and writing; and the assessment of proficiency includes actual demonstration by students of their ability to speak, write, read, and comprehend the spoken language. Leadership in the area of assessment has been provided by the American Council on the Teaching of Foreign Languages (ACTFL), which has defined eleven performance levels ranging from "no ability to speak the language" to that of "native speaker." Performance levels have also been developed in reading, listening, and writing.

To achieve communicative competence requires a continuous and sustained sequence of instruction. Research indicates that it takes a highly motivated adult with an aptitude for foreign language 720 hours of intense instruction (equivalent to five and a half years of one-period-per-day instruction) to achieve high levels of proficiency (Liskin-Gasparro, 1982). Spanish and French oral proficiency studies in East Brunswick Public Schools show that the average student reaches the "Intermediate-Mid" level on the ACTFL scale after four years in a foreign language program. The studies also show that students achieve an "Intermediate" level of writing ability in four years, with students achieving "Intermediate-High and "Advanced" levels at the end of the fifth year in Advance Placement courses (Lester, 1992).

The focus of instruction needs to be on communicative tasks. Instruction in a second language attempts to mirror the natural ways children acquire their native tongue. Because a successful foreign language program teaches students to communicate in the language, rather than solely demonstrate knowledge about it, emphasis is on use of language in real-life, culturally appropriate contexts. This is accomplished through listening, speaking, reading, and writing at predetermined levels of accuracy. However, in learning a second language, the child is usually at a disadvantage in that he/she is not a part of a nonschool group that regularly uses the language to communicate. The same factors that characterize good teaching in general are also those that characterize good foreign language teaching. East Brunswick Public Schools has identified the following features that should characterize a foreign language classroom:

TEACHER BEHAVIORS

- Teachers "de-mystify" the language by focusing on and teaching to meaningful and achievable goals.
- Teachers state objectives in terms of communicative functions/tasks.
- Teachers use the target language with ease.
- Teachers use the target language in instruction whenever appropriate.
- Teachers employ a variety of communicative/interactive activities to meet instructional goals in listening, speaking, reading, and writing, focusing on the learning styles of the students.
- Teachers use a variety of instructional strategies that are functional, meaningful, and contextualized; integrate the language skills; and provide opportunities for personalization.
- Teachers utilize questions in a manner that invites/facilitates normal conversation.
- Teachers provide opportunities, including use of audio, video, and computer technology, for language practice leading to creative language use.
- Teachers provide an instructional language-rich environment with many authentic foreign language books, magazines, newspapers, games, visuals, cultural displays, and other realia.
- Teachers demonstrate a sensitivity to individual students and, in turn, foster student sensitivity to others.
- Teachers demonstrate authentic cultural behaviors.
- Teachers present grammar as a "tool" for communication.
- Teachers use the textbook as a "springboard."
- Teachers accept oral and written errors as a natural part of the language learning process.
- Teachers use a flexible classroom organization, incorporating pairing, grouping, and moving about of students and teacher.
- Teachers use assessment, which reflects instructional techniques and learning styles.

STUDENT BEHAVIORS

- Students engage in meaningful activities that have real-world functions and purposes.
- Students participate in activities that allow for the development of listening and speaking skills.
- Students talk and write about ideas they have read and heard.
- Students work in large and small groups as well as one-on-one with the teacher.
- Students are involved in activities that reflect the beliefs and customs of other cultures.

FOREIGN LANGUAGE IN THE BEST SCHOOLS

Cognizant of the length of time required to achieve communicative proficiency in a second language, many of the Best Schools begin formal instruction in one or more languages at the elementary level. Other schools focus on developing the motivation and interest in foreign language study, which will then be pursued indepth at the middle or junior high level.

The Best Schools—Foreign Language Illustrations

EURA BROWN ELEMENTARY, GADSDEN, AL

Eura Brown Elementary School draws its students from a high socioeconomic area of the town. High standards are set for pupil achievement, and there is a significant amount of parental involvement.

Foreign language plays an important role in the school's curriculum. Students in grades 1–4 receive instruction in French twenty minutes per week for twelve weeks, and the fifth grade students receive instruction twenty minutes per week for thirty weeks. This provides a foundation for conversational French and gives the students a broader scope of the world. French customs, current events, and geography are integrated into language teaching, with vocabulary, songs, games, and cultural awareness among topics of study. Decision making and other critical thinking skills are employed as in a lesson on the "Chunnel."

The chance for students to experience how a language is learned is exciting, since acquisition of their primary language occurs before their ability to recognize the process. Students' natural curiosities are aroused, and all students begin on equal footing in this arena. Their willingness to try new sounds, make mistakes, and accept cultural differences adds to the total student concept of being ready to try whatever comes next.

Charlotte Crosson, *Principal, K–5, 325 Students*

ASHLEY RIVER CREATIVE ARTS ELEMENTARY SCHOOL

Ashley River Creative Arts Elementary School is a suburban magnet school located in Charleston County, South Carolina. The school has a population that is sociologically mixed, ranging from upper middle- to very low-income families, with 15% eligible for free or reduced price lunch. Students are admitted to the school on a first come, first served basis. The child-centered school focuses on individual gains through an arts-enriched curriculum, using innovative instructional approaches aimed at meeting students' learning styles and providing hands-on participation.

Spanish is taught in kindergarten through fifth grade, with grades 1–5 receiving eighty minutes weekly in two forty-minute classes. The Spanish curriculum includes study of the culture, history, geography, and customs of Spanish-speaking people throughout the world and projects involving computer graphics, word processing, study of current events in Spanish-speaking countries, and research. Students learn the language through games, dances, music, and other activities. Spanish-speaking community members are invited to speak to the classes or to demonstrate aspects of their culture such as traditional dress, foods, and celebrations.

Rose Maree Myers, *Principal, Grades K–5, 479 Students.*

LAKE SENECA ELEMENTARY SCHOOL, GERMANTOWN, MD

Lake Seneca Elementary is located in the outer reaches of suburban Washington. The students come from high density housing within a "created" community that did not exist ten years ago. Twenty-five percent of the attendance area is single-family homes, with the rest being rental apartments, townhouses and condominiums. A large number of the students come from single-parent, blended-family, and/or step-parent homes. In a majority of the two-parent households, both parents work and commute long distances, creating a typical twelve-hour day away from their children. Indeed, because of the large number of after-school and day-care options available at the school site, Lake Seneca has established a tradition of a "dawn to dusk" school.

The Spanish program was designed to give students in grades 3–5 the opportunity to learn a foreign language as early as possible. A communicative-based approach is used in language instruction, and the class is taught almost entirely in Spanish. This approach enables the language teacher to draw foreign language practice activities from all content areas of the elementary school curriculum (math, social studies, etc.), to make the language more meaningful. Children participate in a variety of activities that include dramatizations and musical presentations. They also learn about the culture of Spanish-speaking countries. Classroom teachers are present during language instruction and are actively involved in learning Spanish with the children. An end-of-year evaluation involves assessment of student language achievement, cultural knowledge, and overall program effectiveness. The parents continuously praise the program and consider themselves fortunate to have such a program available to their children.

Elizabeth Morgan, *Principal, Grades K–6, 480 Students*

ENGLISH AS A SECOND LANGUAGE

It is estimated that by the year 2000, one in three people in the United States will be either African-American, Hispanic, or Asian-American (ASCD, 1993). The largest non–English-speaking minority group is Hispanic; however, many other native languages are spoken by students. Facilitating the language and cultural transition to English is the aim of English as a second language programs (ESL). The focus of the curriculum is to enable students to learn English to the degree necessary to function in an English-speaking classroom. English is spoken exclusively in the ESL classroom, and in any given class, there may be children who speak several different native languages. Bilingual education differs from ESL in that, while the student is gaining competence, he/she also receives academic instruction in his/her native language. In terms of classroom instruction in English, there is little observable difference between a classroom where children are learning English and a classroom where native English speakers are learning a second language.

The rate at which a child learns a second language varies; however, the motivation for learning and the amount of time spent using and hearing the second language affect the speed and quality of acquisition. Educators frequently remark on how quickly a non–English-speaking child learns English. Unable to communicate with peers or to participate in English-speaking classes, these children are usually highly motivated to learn English. In addition, the child is exposed to English outside of the ESL class for as much as five hours per day in school, and that time may be extended through play time and, in some cases, at home. In communities with high concentrations of a particular non–English-speaking population, children may take longer to become proficient in English, since there may be many people who communicate with the child in the native language and, therefore, less motivation to learn English and less exposure time to English.

The non–English-speaking population in the United States is not distributed evenly across school districts. Some districts have students who speak many different languages (i.e., East Brunswick, New Jersey, with fifty-five native languages), while other districts draw students from only one or two non–English language groups; still other districts have no non–English-speaking students. For many districts, non–English-speaking students represent only a small fraction of the population; however, in other districts, more than 80% of their student body may have a native language other than English. Children who maintain their native language and become fluent in English achieve the national objective of fluency in two languages.

The Best Schools provide ESL and/or bilingual education based on the needs of their population.

The Best Schools—English as a Second Language Illustrations

WASHINGTON ELEMENTARY SCHOOL, MEDFORD, OR

Washington Elementary School is located in an area of the city with a population mainly of retired citizens and lower income families. There is an annual student mobility rate of 42 %, and 54 % of the students qualify for free or reduced price lunch. Washington School defies the statistics for schools serving similar populations. Students score at or above district- and statewide comparison groups on the standardized tests in reading, mathematics, and writing.

The Hispanic population in Medford has grown since 1988 and far exceeds state averages. The English as a Second Language (ESL) program, which dealt with students in a single pull-out classroom, was replaced several years ago by a program funded by HB2020 funds. Now ESL children are mainstreamed into regular classrooms; however, the program offered unique types of support. Each morning, a teacher meets with eight to ten children from 7:30 to 8:15 to work on English skills. At 8:15, they eat breakfast, and they begin regular classes at 8:45. During the morning, they are pulled out for an additional half hour to practice English skills. This lasts for eight weeks, until a new group begins the ESL program.

The grant funds support a teacher/facilitator who works with ESL students and coordinates ESL activities. Among the other functions performed by the teacher/facilitator are

- providing inservice training for staff in methods and techniques to aculturate portions of the school population
- encouraging staff to implement multi-language techniques in the classrooms
- coordinating parent volunteer workers to assist students in learning

In addition, foster grandparents who have been trained in ESL techniques take small groups of ESL students to work with each day. The combination of community volunteers working in the school, a business partnership with KOGAP Lumber Company, peer coaching, collegial support, mentoring, and the teacher/facilitator and classroom teachers help ESL students reach their potential and experience success in school.

Stephanie Johnson, *Principal, Grade K—6, 414 Students*

HEALTH EDUCATION

In response to societal concerns such as AIDS, teen pregnancy, and drugs, the health curriculum in schools has expanded over the years in terms of topic coverage and the need for depth of understanding. Furthermore, many states have legislated or issued administrative mandates for specific forms of health-related education, which have impacted on the curriculum of the schools and training and retraining of teachers. The health curriculum is only one aspect of a more comprehensive health program in most schools, as health-related services may include counseling, parent education, student referral committees, and nursing. Some schools house health clinics within their buildings. The health program may involve classroom teachers, school nurses, police department staff, doctors, student assistance specialists, social workers, counselors, and/or community volunteers. Many of the functions of the school health program have already been addressed in Chapter 4.

While other areas of the curriculum seek the means to make connections between classroom learning and the "real world" of children, this has always been the focus of a good health curriculum. Staff development and staff assignment for health instruction are areas of continuing concern in many schools. Elementary classroom teachers generally have had little formal training in health education and may only feel confident to teach basic health and safety concepts. Effective age appropriate teaching of topics such as sex education, AIDS prevention, and drug abuse education often requires either extensive training of classroom teachers or the use of trained specialists to implement at least parts of the health curriculum.

The Best Schools have comprehensive health education programs and services. While some schools have developed their own curriculum, most of the schools use or supplement their curriculum with *Growing Healthy* (NDN) developed by the National Health Education Center, the *Here's Looking at You 2000* developed by the Educational Services District #121 in Seattle, and/or the D.A.R.E. (Drug Abuse Resistance Education) program developed by the Los Angeles Police Department and the Los Angeles Unified School District. All of these programs require staff inservice in order to implement them in the school. The Best Schools have made a commitment to staff, as well as curriculum development.

The Best Schools—Health Illustrations

HEIGHTS ELEMENTARY SCHOOL, FT. MYERS, FL

Heights Elementary is located in southwest Lee County, Florida, in the small community of Harlem Heights. The population reflects the disparate socioeconomic groups presently in the area. As a result of the reputation of the school's academic program, parents specifically purchase homes within the school boundaries.

The school's philosophy of teaching the whole child demands that each child's needs are identified and addressed. Each week, sixty minutes are allocated to the *Growing Healthy Program* (NDN), which features a specific emphasis on study and skills acquisition for each grade level and helps students learn to make appropriate choices and decisions for a healthier and safer life.

Growing Healthy uses a hands-on approach to guiding students through the decision-making process as they discover what they do today can make a difference tomorrow. Teachers utilize community speakers and health groups, media presentations, individual counseling by the guidance counselors, and student organizations such as "Just Say No to Drugs," to convey the curriculum. Student progress is monitored through district- and teacher-made tests and worksheets. Vision, hearing, height, weight, and skinfold checks are made on a regular schedule to monitor the personal health of the students. Classroom teachers meet semi-annually with the nurse to review the health forms of K−3 and new to the district intermediate students for correctable health problems. The state fluoride program is an integral part of the students' weekly health maintenance. The health contact teacher attends weekly health meetings and provides inservice instruction and subject area integrating ideas to the teachers. This comprehensive health program features manipulatives, models, audiovisual materials, and some printed materials, but no textbook. The program is constantly revised to meet the changing needs of students.

Paul Cochrane, *Principal, Grades K−5, 876 Students*

HAZELWOOD ELEMENTARY SCHOOL, RENTON, WA

Hazelwood Elementary School opened in 1963 in a period of rapidly increasing population. It is a large, traditional brick school with ample playgrounds. Classrooms are light, airy, and spacious. Most students live in single-family dwellings built from 1960 to the present; however, a large apartment complex provides ethnic and socioeconomic diversity.

The major goals of the health curriculum are to understand the importance of family; to display positive attitudes toward self and others; and to develop the skills and knowledge base to make responsible, healthful decisions. Health occupies 3 – 5 % of the day. The text focuses on current physical, social, and emotional health issues. Through extended activities, crucial elements of the program are emphasized, such as inappropriate touching (reinforced by the Open Door Theater), drug abuse awareness and refusal skills (*Here's Looking at you 2000* materials and D.A.R.E), and HIV/AIDS information and prevention. Opportunities are provided for parent review of curriculum and materials. Eight members of the staff have taken "Impact" training, which deals with families in crisis, and the KLUE (Kids Like Us Are Everywhere) program supports students living in chemically abusive situations. The nurse is actively involved in health education on an informal (one-on-one) and formal (guest appearances in the classroom) basis with students. As a direct result of the self-study needs assessment, Hazelwood is providing additional education in the areas of self-esteem and peer interaction, using a variety of resources including the building K – 3 counselor, the resource room teachers, and the after-school programs for at-risk students.

Marsha Kay Hallett, *Principal (Vera Risdon, Principal at time of recognition),*
Grades K – 6, 554 Students

HOWARD C. REICHE COMMUNITY SCHOOL, PORTLAND, ME

Reiche School is located in the center of Maine's largest city. The area encompasses some of the district's most affluent sections and also some of the very poorest sections of the city. More than 81 % of the students come from low-income families, while the rest of the student body comes from the highest socioeconomic strata. In order to be responsive to the varied educational, social, health, and recreational needs of the community, the school has incorporated within the building a neighborhood health station, adult education rooms, a community kitchen, greenhouses, swimming pool, gym, a branch of the Portland Public Library, and a Community Recreation Program.

The health and safety programs at Reiche are designed to meet the unique community of students. The most integral thread of the entire program is the support of both the teaching staff and the parental community in the programs. Collaboration between health educators, nurse, teachers, administrators, social workers, and guidance counselor reinforces information, provides follow-up for children and families, and provides a consistent message of caring. Additionally, the nature of all of the programs is positive, with the focus being on the ways children can care for themselves, both physically and mentally. A community health clinic is housed within the building and other social services are available on-site.

The *Growing Healthy* curriculum goal is to provide comprehensive, sequential health education in grades K – 4. It is designed to equip children with the knowledge and skills to make choices that are conducive to good health and to help children to establish good health habits. There is a minimum of one class period per week per grade level, ranging from twenty minutes to sixty minutes. The health curriculum uses an approach where students suggest applications for all information and concepts in their daily lives.

Miriam Remar, *Principal, Pre-K – 5, 585 Students*

PHYSICAL EDUCATION

For the elementary age child, what happens on the playground has profound effect on how he/she feels about school and how he/she relates to peers. The child who views himself or herself or is perceived by other children as unable to participate adequately in games is handicapped in the society of the child. Not surprisingly, what happens on the playground has impact in the classroom. Failure to develop sufficient physical skill to "hold one's own" with peers outside of school or in noninstructional play situations is a common cause for poor peer relations, failure to like school, and feelings of alienation. All of these are negative characteristics associated with school failure, dropouts, and risk of drug abuse (Ogden and Germinario, 1988).

In some elementary schools, all of the physical education instruction is provided by the classroom teacher; in some schools, a specialist provides the instruction. While some activities can be carried out in a regular classroom, space is a requirement of many physical education activities. It is estimated that thirty cents of every educational dollar spent on facilities goes for building physical education and athletic facilities.

Elementary physical education should be developmental in nature; it should be approached in the same manner as any other subject. The achievement and physical fitness levels of students should be assessed, specific objectives set, and instruction designed to meet the objectives. The curriculum should be inclusive, not exclusive. In other words, activities should not eliminate the least able, while giving the most able more practice. An example of such practice is having students jump over a rope, where after each jump the rope is raised. When a student misses, he is eliminated. Thus, the most skilled child in the class ends up with the most practice. If the rope is slanted all children can continue to jump and increase their level based on their ability (Mosston, 1966; Mosston and Ashworth, 1990). No one would reduce the time a poor reader spends on developing reading skills; however, it happens too frequently in physical education classes that focus on competition.

In addition to development of specific skills, the physical education program should be designed to develop agility, strength, balance, and flexibility. This developmental program can take place in the classroom and on the playground, as well as in the designated physical education class.

PHYSICAL EDUCATION IN THE BEST SCHOOLS

The Best Schools have developed physical education programs that de-emphasize competition and that are clearly focused on development of skills, physical fitness, understanding of movement; assessment of skills and fitness levels plays an important part in individual, as well as program, development. In most cases, the programs are taught at least in part by a physical education specialist.

The Best Schools—Physical Education Illustrations

PINSON ELEMENTARY SCHOOL, PINSON, AL

The school is in the multi-ethnic, primarily blue collar community of Pinson. Single-family homes, low-income apartments, and mobile home parks provide housing for the large student population. A model in both written and oral communication, the school has developed a process-centered and technology-enriched program.

An essential area of the curriculum is the physical education program, which is linked to the school goals. The strength of the program lies in the two full-time physical education professionals who teach a complete and structured program. Students receive two or three thirty- to forty-minute classes of physical education a week. Focus is on the development of body management and manipulative and locomotor skills. Beginning with gross motor movement and progressing to fine motor skills, the child develops specific sport skills as he/she grows. The program includes units of study adapted to the ability and developmental levels of students. Physical education is easily integrated with academic areas, for example, hands-on mathematics and science activities using measurement and observation techniques and historical and cultural enrichment through rhythm, music, dance, and games.

In addition to classroom activities, interested students can participate in Jump Rope for Heart, the Square Dance Team, and the school track team.

Gloria Solomon, *Principal, K – 5, 1334 Students*

FRANCISCO MATIAS LUGO, CAROLINA, PR

Francisco Matias Lugo is an urban elementary school. Sixty-five percent of the students qualify for free or reduced price lunch. The school was the first in Latin America to begin a Spanish project called V.A.L.E., in which students learn to read through writing on the computer.

The physical education class is built around multiple activities that are designed so that students work individually or in small groups. The teacher has the opportunity to observe and to guide the students to reach their maximum potential. The selected activities help each child in his/her physical, motor, and social development. The school's two physical education teachers believe that a child with good physical and motor development will have a better and increasing acceptance of his/her self-worth. The experiences in the physical education class are structured so that students gain skills that they can practice in their own free time.

Nancy Rivera, *Principal, K – 6, 835 Students*

WASHINGTON ELEMENTARY SCHOOL, MEDFORD, OR

Dissatisfaction with the physical education program led the teaching staff to utilize all of their annual inservice monies to send a cadre of teachers to a three-day workshop entitled "Awesome Physical Education Activities for Elementary School Children." At least one teacher from each grade level was selected to attend the workshop. Upon completion of the training, equipment was purchased for the program. First grade children do Chinese Ribbon Dancing to improve rhythm and coordination, while third grade students are learning ball handling skills and fourth graders are involved in jump rope activities to improve their timing and coordination skills.

All of the students undergo physical fitness testing in fall and spring to evaluate their overall physical fitness and to provide teachers with information so that appropriate activities may be provided. The staff uses strategies that allow for differences in student ability. Student progress in all activities is monitored. A team of teachers designs the mastery curriculum to teach essential concepts and skills. The activities in the program are taught through whole-class, cooperative learning groups, enrichment activities, and activities designed for students to do on their own.

Stephanie Johnson, *Principal, K – 6, 414 Students*

OTHER SUBJECTS IN THE BEST SCHOOLS

Private schools among the recognized schools frequently have specialized programs that are central to their mission. For example, the Hebrew Academies devote as much as 50% of the instructional day to religious instruction and Hebrew. Other schools affiliated with religious groups also incorporate religious curricula. Multicultural, global, and character education are also taught as a distinct part of the curriculum in some private, as well as public schools.

Many of the Best Schools are also working toward development of a totally integrated curriculum, examples of this are found in previous chapters.

The Best Schools—Other Curriculum Illustration

SALANTER AKIBA RIVERDALE ACADEMY, RIVERDALE, NY

The school is a modern co-educational orthodox Jewish day school located in the Riverdale section of the Bronx. While primarily serving the Bronx community, students are also drawn from Manhattan, Queens, Westchester, and Rockland counties. The community is blessed with diverse cultural and educational institutions such as the Wave Hill Ecological Center, the Riverdale Hebrew Home for the Aged, the Bronx Zoo, the Bronx Botanical Gardens, the Hudson River Museum, the College of Mt. Saint Vincent, Manhattan College, Yeshiva University, and the Riverdale YMHA.

As could be expected of a Jewish day school, religious training is a central component of the school's curriculum, and the students receive one and a half hours of instruction daily in such courses as Talmud, Jewish Philosophy, and Jewish Law. Heavy emphasis is also placed on the study of the Hebrew language. That the students have excelled in their religious studies is evident from their outstanding scores on standardized tests given by the Jewish Board of Education and their fine showing in the national Bible contest of the World Zionist Organization.

However, the school downplays rote memorization of material in favor of deeper understanding of the ethical implications of religious texts and, especially, the practical application of these religious and ethical ideals. Thus, students are constantly reminded to show respect for and appreciation of their elders through programs such as Intergenerational Day, in which students' grandparents are invited to join their grandchildren for a full day of study and special programs.

Through courses in Jewish history, trips to sites like the Lower East Side and Ellis Island, and special programs like Model Seders commemorating Jewish holidays, S/A/R students gain greater appreciation of their spiritual heritage and enhanced self-image as a part of a historic people. At the same time, assemblies featuring community leaders of all religious denominations have impressed upon students the need to foster harmony among all groups and to seek the common good.

Videos are used extensively to illustrate ideas and concepts. Students write and perform skits to depict Jewish customs and ceremonies and analyze current TV shows as indicative of ethical dilemmas. They have painted murals depicting religious scenes as part of their annual Maccabean contest on Chanukah, and they have learned to express their knowledge of the Bible through song and dance at public assemblies for the younger grades.

Rabbi Yonah Fuld, *Principal, Pre-K – 8, 554 Students*

SUMMARY

In addition to language arts, mathematics, social studies, science, the arts and information processing, the Best Schools make provision for health and physical education. Furthermore, many schools provide for the learning of a second language, whether that be English for non-English speakers or a second language for native English speakers. Religion is often a part of the curriculum in private sectarian schools. Other areas of the curriculum in some schools are global, multicultural, and/or character education. Most of the Best Schools are working toward a more integrated curriculum, making connections among subject areas, and thereby reducing an overall curriculum often burdened with content, but with little time left for development of indepth understanding.

REFERENCES

Fitzmahan, Roberts and Associates. (1986). *Here's Looking at You 2000*. Educational Services District #121, Seattle, WA.

Germinario, Vito, Janet Cervalli, and Evelyn Ogden. (1992). *All Children Successful: Real Answers for Helping At-Risk Elementary Students*. Lancaster PA: Technomic Publishing Co., Inc.

Lester, Kenneth. (1992). "Foreign Language Program Evaluation: East Brunswick Public Schools," East Brunswick, NJ.

Liskin-Gasparro, Judith. (1982). "ETS Oral Proficiency Testing Manual," Princeton, NJ: Educational Testing Service.

Los Angeles Police Department and the Los Angeles Unified School District. (1990). *D.A.R.E. Drug Abuse Resistance Education*. Los Angeles Unified School District, Los Angeles, CA.

Malarz, Lynn. (1992). "Bilingual Education: Effective Programming for Language—Minority Students." *ASCD Curriculum Handbook*. Association for Supervision and Curriculum Development, Alexandria, VA.

Mosston, Muska. (1966). *The Teaching of Physical Education*. Columbus, OH: Charles E. Merrill.

Mosston, Muska and Sara Ashworth. (1990). *The Spectrum of Teaching Styles: From Command to Discovery*. New York: Longman.

National Center for Health Education. (1986). *Growing Health*. Topeka, KA: Temco, Inc.

Ogden, Evelyn and Vito Germinario. (1988). *The At-Risk Student: Answers for Educators*. Lancaster, PA: Technomic Publishing Co., Inc.

Rosiello, Linda. (1989). "Envisioning East Brunswick's Foreign Language Program," East Brunswick Public Schools, East Brunswick, NJ.

PART THREE

THE ROLE OF THE DISTRICT IN EFFECTIVE SCHOOL DEVELOPMENT

CHAPTER 13

The Effective School District

THE emphasis in the literature and in the media on the individual school as the focal point of educational reform has frequently distorted or overlooked the role of the district in school improvement. It is true that effective instruction occurs classroom by classroom, school by school. However, if successful schools are to become the rule rather than the exception, the role of the district in providing a unified mission, instructional leadership, and support must be recognized. There are over 110,000 schools in the country, but only 16,000 school districts. Standards for the 21st Century will not be met merely by hoping that 110,000 effective principals will emerge spontaneously and, with only inconsequential central organizational support, "create" 110,000 successful schools. "The individual school may be the unit of change but frequently change is the result of system initiatives that live or die based on the strategies and supports offered by the larger organization" (Fullan, 1991, p. 73). "Researchers who have studied innovation in general [have] found that it is most likely to be successful when it combines elements of 'bottom up' planning and decision making with 'top-down' stimuli and support in setting directions and guiding the change process" (Levine and Lezotte, 1990, p. 44). This chapter looks at the following questions concerning the roles of school districts in providing effective education for students:

- What does theory and research say about effective school districts?
- What is the role of the district in effective school development?
- What do effective districts do to foster and support the Best Schools?

CHARACTERISTICS OF EFFECTIVE SCHOOL DISTRICTS

School districts operate in a manner consistent with their underlying belief systems. "Conventional" and "congenial" districts operate much like the less than fully effective conventional and congenial schools (see Chapter 1). The leadership of these districts focus on operational matters; they determine which schools are "good," based on efficiency of operations and the opinion of the community as expressed by significant individuals or groups concerned with each individual school. There may be a multitude of district-defined practices, procedures, textbooks, curricula guides, and testing procedures and curriculum, which may give the appearance of centralized control; however, in fact, principals are left to function pretty much as they see fit. Interaction among schools is minimal and usually limited to operational concerns. In these types of districts, effective principals are viewed as "born" and "seasoned by experience," not made. Whom the central leadership and the board of education hires at the central office and principal levels and which administrative behaviors central leadership reinforces reflect their underlying beliefs about education and determine the culture, climate, and, ultimately, the effectiveness of the district.

Unfortunately, since conventional and congenial-type schools predominate, it follows that there is also a predominance of conventional or congenial districts in the nation. Conventional and congenial districts are the sum of their parts at any specific time in any specific place; there are no mechanisms, no vital forces, no perceived incentives within the district to transform it or improve it. Any force for change comes from outside. With little experience in planning, little knowledge of the change process, little knowledge of effective practices, the response to outside forces that cannot be ignored is usually the "quick fix," the solution that will impact least on the staff and business as usual.

Fortunately, there are districts that demonstrate through their actions, beliefs, values, and goals congruence with those factors associated with effective schools research and student outcome-based schools. Lawrence Lezotte (1992) describes four kinds of schools that exist within districts:

(1) Effective and still improving
(2) Not yet effective, but improving
(3) Effective but not improving
(4) Neither effective nor improving

Effective schools are those that have met standards of accomplishment. An improving school is one that is able to show continuing progress toward achievement of the standards. Effective and/or improving school districts are those striving to have only the first type of schools, which provide consistent support for both the first and second kinds of schools and which will not tolerate the third and fourth types of schools.

Just as the characteristics of effective schools are not very different than the characteristics associated with the effective classroom, the characteristics of the effective district are not very different than those of the effective school (Lezotte, 1992):

• strong instructional leadership
• a clear and focused mission
• a climate of high expectations for success of all children
• a safe, orderly environment
• the opportunity to learn and adequate time spent on academic tasks
• frequent monitoring of student progress
• positive home-school relations

The board of education is at the top of the pyramid in provision of district and school leadership. What the board believes and values provides the basis for its definition of its own roles and the powers it bestows on and the roles it defines for the superintendent. The superintendent, in turn, empowers and defines the roles of central- and building-level administrators. It is the superintendent who "is the single most important individual for setting the expectations and tone of the pattern of change within the local district" (Fullan, 1991, p. 191).

The need for continuous improvement is necessary even in the most effective district. Improvement requires change. Recognition of the continuous need for change, refinement, and adjustment in the local educational system's practices, programs, and approaches to "doing business" may be the most fundamental of all differences between effective districts and those less effective districts that are organized to maintain the status quo and that initiate change only when external pressures demand.

The roles of the central office in the ongoing journey of school improvement have many dimensions. Clarifying the beliefs of the district and communicating what is valued is one of these. This may be done through the development of a district mission statement, belief statements, and/or explicit statements of expected student learning outcomes. However, much more is involved than the development and dissemination of written documents. The central office must "talk the talk and walk the walk." School staff have often learned "not to take change seriously unless central administration demonstrates through actions that they should" (Fullan, 1991, p. 74). This means that central administration's day-to-day interactions with individuals and with groups, both inside and outside of the schools, reflect the commitment to the mission and the values of the district. What the district leadership does is far more important than what it says is important. How resources are allocated, where and on which issues time is spent, which behaviors are supported and which criticized, which activities are monitored and evaluated, the type of individuals hired for positions, the way staff is evaluated all speak powerfully to what is "actually" valued in the district. Effective districts reflect in their mission and act on their beliefs that "all students in a district are capable of achieving mastery in all areas of the curriculum and that the teachers and administrators accept responsibility for making this a reality" (Lezotte and Jacobs, 1992, p. 85).

A study by Pajak and Glickman about school districts that have demonstrated sustained improvement over time identified variables that contributed to their success:

> . . . The superintendent and central office supervisors played critical roles in improving the quality of instruction. . . . Each of the superintendents communicated to the community and to the district's faculty that "children come first." These superintendents also sought financial support from the community for improving instruction in the district.

> A common language which centered on instruction and curriculum refinement was found in each district. . . . Talking about students, lessons, and curriculum was the norm, not an aberration.

> . . . Districts put into place an organizational structure in which supervisory support was established to encourage instructional dialogue. These districts established either supervisory positions at the central office level or an instructional lead teacher at each building whose primary responsibility was to engage teachers in talking about pedagogy, students' progress, and curriculum. These districts also committed time to allow teachers to meet for the purpose of analyzing information, planning strategies, and sharing ways of implementing new techniques.

> . . . Each superintendent established and articulated a clear purpose for the. . . [organization]. This message was clear to the administrators, teaching staff and community. . . . [Each district] also approached the task of improving student learning as a collective effort and recognized the talent and leadership that existed within the district—both in the administration and in the ranks. [From abstract of Pajak and Glickman in *Effective Schools Research Abstracts*, 4(2):62, reported in Lezotte and Jacoby, 1992, pp. 31–32].

Other studies speak to the important role of advocacy in successful districts.

> Initiation of school improvement efforts never occur without an advocate (or advocates). The efforts of the superintendent and other district administrators are usually the most critical in initiating and/or supporting school improvement. Even when the source of school improvement initiation is elsewhere in the system, perhaps at the building level, a powerful determining factor is how the superintendent and others in central office react. The superintendent and other district administrators are such powerful influences on change that they can advance or block progress in school improvement efforts. [Lezotte and Jacoby, 1992]

> . . . Except in the case of isolated maverick schools that have become effective largely on their own, success . . . requires considerable direction and support of central leadership. [Levine and Lezotte, 1990, p. 40]

Creating a climate of high expectations for staff, as well as students, is an essential role of instructional leadership. While all central administrators contribute to the establishment and reinforcement of expectations, it is the superintendent who is the single most important individual in this regard. One of the ways a climate of high expectations is actualized is through the personnel hiring and evaluation system. Effective districts seek professionals who have the knowledge, attitude, and skills that will contribute to ongoing school improvement, whether that be in the classroom, at the building level, or in the central office. Job descriptions should reflect what is important to the district. For administrators, particularly principals, leadership roles and expectations should be clearly stated and outcome-based. Teacher job descriptions should be performance-based, reflect research on effective teaching, and establish the expectation for continuing professional growth. The evaluation system at all levels in the organization should be centered on instructional outcomes. The evaluation system should serve as a basis for ongoing improvement and development and make provision for terminating those who cannot or will not contribute to the overall mission of the district.

Another important role of the central office, in particular the superintendent, is ''in ensuring continuity of [effective] leadership at the building level'' (Lezotte and Jacobs, 1992, p. 33). However, continuity is important at all levels of the administration. Change in leadership can lead to positive examples of turn-around schools and districts or can quite quickly turn a successful or improving school or district into a less and less effective school or district. Successful practices and programs carefully implemented can quickly be derailed with a change in expectations and priorities of new leadership.

''One of the key beliefs of [administrators of] effective schools is that the people in the schools are already doing the best they know how to do, given the conditions under which they find themselves'' (Lezotte and Jacobs, 1992, p. 209). In some cases, change can be brought about by changing conditions, i.e., adding materials, changing equipment, building facilities. However, change most often must occur in what people know. This requires investment in staff development at all levels of the organization. The typical school district in the United States spends less than 2% of its resources on staff development. Effective school districts recognize the ongoing need for growth in the knowledge of their staff, and they allocate substantial resources to this area. Staff development means more than ''what happens on staff inservice day''; it includes the district's observation and assessment process, curriculum and program development, individual guided staff development, training programs related to specific program changes, observations of practices outside of the district, peer observations, opportunities for staff to share ideas and expertise, opportunities to receive feedback on implementation of practices, involvement in networks, professional association, and leadership projects.

Planning is another critical role of central administration. It begins with a belief that there is a need for ongoing improvement and a belief that planning is essential in bringing about positive change. Lawrence Lezotte and Barbara Jacoby (1992) point out in *Sustainable School Reform*, ''. . . that school improvement planning is a meaningful process – a journey – not an event.'' Every district administrator gives lip service to the importance of planning; however, most districts show few signs of systematic planning as a basis for either major or minor change. Most of what passes for planning is the quickly adopted solution implemented in response to ''crisis'' or the periodic establishment of committees to review new textbooks. Resource allocation is an essential aspect of planning. First, planning takes time – time to assess information concerning needs; time to disaggregate and analyze data; time to study research and effective practices; time to collaborate; time to define clearly the expected outcomes of change; time to train staff for plan implementation; and time to implement, monitor, refine, and revise practice. Effective districts value planning as the base for large-scale changes and for changes in the myriad practices and programs in the district. A major factor in the successful implementation of planned change is the commitment that central office staff makes to monitoring and nurturing the activities incorporated in the plan. Effective superintendents and supervisors are "cheerleaders" for planned change.

Another essential role of the district is to ensure that all students will achieve mastery in all curriculum areas. The district needs to have a process for defining "mastery," developing and implementing curriculum, and assessing what is learned. School administrators may do many things in a day, which are only indirectly involved in instruction; however, children and teachers spend 8500 hours from kindergarten through grade 8 directly involved in the learning process. When the district says "all" students, it implies that the expected outcomes of instruction will apply equally to the outcomes of all the schools in the district. The role of the district in curriculum development is essential. The first step in the process is the identification of what is worth learning – the statements of proficiency expected of all students as outcomes of their instruction. Curriculum development then follows from the expected outcomes and should be based on the research on learning and effective programs and practice in each area. Finally, means must be identified and/or developed to determine if mastery has occurred. In effective districts, schools, and classrooms, the written, taught, and tested curriculum is aligned (English, 1990); the instruction reflects the relationship between intended outcomes, instructional processes, and instructional assessment (Cohen, 1987). It seems as if this would be standard practice in all school and districts; however, this is not the case: "Lack of excellence in American schools is not caused by ineffective teaching, but mostly by misaligning what teachers teach, what they intend to teach, and what they assess as having been taught" (Alan Cohen, 1989, in Lezotte and Jacoby, 1992). The district's role is to ensure that expectations for learning are set, curriculum based on research is written, and valid assessment procedures are established; further, it is the central administration's responsibility, along with that of building administrators, to ensure that curriculum and instructional alignment occurs at the classroom level.

An additional role of the central office is to communicate to the community, parents, and the board of education the mission, goals, programs, and practices of the district and the need for and direction of change. How well the district staff, primarily the superintendent, does this is often critical in maintaining school improvement efforts. It is essential that the stakeholder understand and support what is happening in the schools. Effective district superintendents are decisive in carrying out this role.

Finally, it is the role of the district administration to operate the district, ensure a safe environment, hire staff, manage buildings, build budgets, pay bills, respond to "crises," and meet the mandates of state and federal agencies. Both effective and less effective districts, however, usually do these things well.

ROLE OF THE DISTRICT IN SCHOOL DEVELOPMENT

The relationship between the district and the individual school is crucial. The district must provide support for the school as an entity with a mission and, at the same time, insure that the school is also a functioning part of the larger entity – the school district. Levine and Lezotte (1990) describe this as "a kind of directed autonomy" (p. 44).

The central office needs to take the initiative in the development of the district mission in the establishment of the district and school planning process, in the determination of desired outcomes, and in the setting of guidelines for evaluation of outcomes. However, the central office must also encourage initiative at the school level, within the overall context of the district mission. One of the ways districts accomplish this balance is through the establishment of planning guidelines, which require each school to develop improvement plans using district-established criteria. The central office staff plays a significant role in supporting the efforts of the school staff in implementing the plan and in ongoing monitoring of milestones, and ultimately, it must hold the school accountable for outcomes.

Another important function of the central office is the coordination of plans and activities among the schools. This requires the development of a sense in each school that they are part of a greater district mission. The involvement of principals and teachers in districtwide planning is one means of accomplishing this. Principal/central office meetings used to discuss school improvement and to provide the opportunity to share instructional initiatives and concerns is another important strategy for supporting coordinated development among schools and the central office. Central office also needs to take an active role in monitoring programs districtwide; collecting, disaggregating, and analyzing data; and communicating findings as a basis for further program development.

Selection of building leadership is a critical central office role. What criteria district leadership and boards of education use in selecting principals reflects what they believe and value in their schools. Their ability to select the leaders who reflect and who can operationalize those values and beliefs and define which behaviors are encouraged, reinforced, or discouraged, once the principal is in place, determine to a great degree the type of schools in the district. Regardless of the process used, a central office committee or a committee involving parents, teachers, and other administrators, a process needs to be established that will insure the selection of building administrators with the characteristics of effective principals. In the case of a school with a long history of "status quo leadership," building staff may have no experience and no basis for identifying other forms of leadership. Fear of the unknown may steer teachers away from selection of a principal with a different, yet effective, leadership style. In such cases, involvement of building staff needs to be balanced with others' involvement to maximize the potential for selection of the most effective candidate.

In some districts, Best School principals were hired with full knowledge of the district leadership that they possessed the characteristics to develop Best Schools; in others they have been hired because of their personality and/or management skills; however, they brought more than "expected" and, in some cases, more than desired to the job in terms of educational knowledge, commitment to change, and willingness to take risks. There are also cases where district leadership has changed and conventional and congenial principals have been swept up, revitalized, and transformed into instructionally successful principals. Unfortunately, there are also cases at the building and district level where changes in central leadership and/or boards of education have resulted in regression of successful schools into conventional molds.

THE ROLE OF THE DISTRICT IN THE BEST SCHOOLS

Successful schools can be found in districts that have few characteristics of effective districts. In these cases, the relationship between the school staff and the district leadership can, at best, be described as indifferent and, at worst, antagonistic. The problem stems from their differing views, values, and beliefs concerning the form of the "elephants" we call districts and schools. A district in which the board of education and central administration hold values and beliefs congruent with the less effective "conventional or congenial school" will not understand the priorities and goals of a school staff that is acting on beliefs congruent with those of "student outcome-based/professional/collegial" schools. It takes particularly strong, self-initiating, and clever leadership within such schools to persist, survive, and succeed despite the mismatch of school and district culture. Frequently, in such districts, outside recognition of a school for excellence is valued only for its publicity value. In other districts, an individual successful school may never even be allowed to seek any kind of special recognition, because such recognition might rock the boat for the other schools, or the risk of criticism, should the school fail in its attempt to gain recognition, is considered too great.

There is no formal Blue Ribbon School District recognition program and therefore no specific process in place for examining the districts of which the Best Schools are but a part. However, a review of the Blue Ribbon Schools list for 1991 – 92 reveals that more than 50% of them were from districts in which at least one other school has been recognized and some where many have been recognized. It can be inferred from the number of multiple school recognitions emanating from these districts that, at a minimum, the district and the schools share the beliefs and values characteristic of effective schools and that there is active support for excellence.

The Best Schools – The Role of the District Illustrations

Flowing Wells School District in Arizona is clearly such an effective district, with six of the district's seven schools recognized as Blue Ribbon Schools.

FLOWING WELLS SCHOOLS, TUCSON, AZ

The Flowing Wells School District, located in a northwest suburban section of Tucson, Arizona, is a district of 6000 students. The district has experienced significant population growth in the past ten years, and its neighborhoods are a mixture of modest homes, trailer parks, and light industry.

The community is characterized as low- to low middle-income, with many of the district's families surviving with the assistance of social services. Over half of the district's seven schools have at least 50% student enrollment in the federal free or reduced meal program. Many of the adults in the community are on fixed incomes, and, in fact, only 17% of the adult population has school-age children. Student mobility averages 39% annually.

With the challenge of a large disenfranchised senior adult population and a low-income level of subsistence, the district has been unusually successful in involving the total community in the schooling of its children. Through comprehensive public information programs, extensive community utilization of facilities, an aggressive adult volunteer campaign, and business partnerships, the district has developed a relationship with the community that has produced strong alliances. During the past decade, three financial initiatives have successfully passed with comfortable margins in contrast to failed attempts in neighboring districts. Additionally, the district has continued to experience a widely respected reputation that has resulted in many wait-listed requests from those living outside its boundaries seeking to attend its schools.

Six of the district's seven schools have been recognized. The blueprint of the effectiveness of these schools can be attributed to many factors unique to the focus of each site. However, of equal significance is the district vision of excellence, which has established an "institutional culture" that permeates the schools' overall direction.

Borrowing heavily from the basic principals of Peters and Waterman's book *In Search of Excellence*, the district has embraced the concept of "simultaneous loose-tight properties." This is to say that there is a centrality of purpose in fostering a climate where there is a dedication to the basic values of the organization.

These values are inherent in the practicing framework of all Flowing Wells Schools. The development of culture commences with a staff induction program that departs from the usual explanation of procedural mechanics to a well-designed approach of organizational "storytelling" and modeling of successful practices. All teachers new to the district spend their first five days in the workplace attending the Flowing Wells Institute of Growth and Renewal. A series of successive training modules continues over the course of the employees' work experience, consistently stressing expectations. This training is coupled with a "coaching" component requiring teachers to demonstrate their acquired skills to their trainer colleagues. Professional vitality is further enhanced by the district's offer to pay the total cost of a Master's degree program. In a shared agreement with a state university, approximately a third of the courses are taught by district employees in an adjunct capacity.

School climate is a significant yardstick of organizational effectiveness, and all schools participate yearly in ascertainment reviews that analyze the customer service components of each site's operation. The assessment instrument, sent to a randomly selected survey group for each school, elicits a high return rate. Data is analyzed, results are shared with all site employees, and action plans are developed.

Moreover, the district's goals, established through an extensive collaborative effort of all community stakeholders, become a roadmap by which schools chart their strategies, measure short- and long-term successes, and define their future direction.

While school site-based management is clearly encouraged and actively functioning, the inherent center of their efficacy is a shared school/district relationship.

J. Robert Hendricks, *Superintendent, K – 12, 6000 Students*

Moorestown is another public school district that illustrates the district role in the development of effective schools.

MOORESTOWN TOWNSHIP PUBLIC SCHOOLS, NJ

The Moorestown Township Public Schools is a comprehensive K – 12 district located in a suburban community in the southern portion of New Jersey, located approximately twenty miles from Philadelphia. The school district has maintained a long history of excellence in education. During the past five years, all three of the district's elementary schools have received national Blue Ribbon School awards.

A foundation of the district's success is its commitment to a systematic planning process. The district has been guided by a strategic plan since its development in 1987. This plan is an organic document that serves as the basis for budgeting, curriculum development, staff development, and strategic school improvement initiatives. Specifically, through the collective governance of K – 12 Subject Advisory Committees, five-year operational objectives are developed from the more general strategic plan goals. These objectives are prioritized by the superintendent and his central administrative team. The annual school/district's objectives are presented to the school board for funding as "Program Initiatives." Each year, the district supports 1/2 – 1% of the annual operating budget for initiatives directly associated with the implementation of school improvement (strategic) projects. Using a variety of financing strategies, the district typically commits from $250,000 to $300,000 annually toward this effort.

The curriculum development process is guided by a systematic assessment of student performance and program needs. This is accomplished by curriculum audits. These audits, which have been conducted by district staff (internal) or by noted educators with specialized knowledge and skills in a content area (external), form the basis of establishing the direction for curricular change. Using current research to provide a benchmark for the "ideal curriculum" (e.g., NCTM Standards, Project 2061 – Science, etc.), these audits carefully assess the status and utility of current content and curricular standards and provide short- and long-term direction for program improvement.

The district places considerable emphasis on staff development, instructional support systems, and supervision to ensure quality and consistency in daily instruction. A District Instructional Model provides the foundation for essential teaching skills in the district. Originally developed in 1988, this instructional framework has been modified to reflect the latest research on how students learn best. Each staff member in the district has participated in at least ten hours of intensive inservice training by the superintendent on the nature of the model and how it can be integrated into the planning and delivery of daily lessons. Although not a categorical model for effective teaching, the model ensures a core set of teaching skills for all teachers, provides a common language by which school staff can focus professional dialog and is the basis for the evaluation of novice and advanced beginning teachers.

As teachers demonstrate proficiency in the delivery of daily instruction, they begin to integrate more complex instructional strategies into daily lessons. The district provides a wide variety of staff development opportunities for its proficient and expert teachers. Topics such as cooperative learning, teaching through student learning styles, whole language, TESA, etc., are available to promote ongoing professional dialog and skill development for experienced staff. Often, these teachers will utilize their skills and knowledge to conduct inservice training in their schools or by mentoring a novice or advanced beginning teacher.

Student academic achievement has been consistently well above state and national benchmarks. Student progress is monitored on an ongoing basis with special attention given to students who fail to take advantage of the educational opportunities offered in his/her school. To this end, the district has implemented a Student Assistance Program. This program, which has gained state and national recognition, utilizes a team [principal, teacher(s), school nurse, member of the Child Study Team] approach to identify and program for the success of at-risk students. Through collaborative efforts with parents, a wide variety of intervention strategies are put in place to help the students achieve and find success both in and out of school. Strategies that have proven to be particularly successful include the district's Grandparent Unlimited Program, which provides a support system for identified elementary at-risk students by matching them with trained senior citizens; mentorships that provide social and academic support for middle school students by matching identified at-risk students with staff members; and the "Teens Need Teens" program, which provides peer support and referral for high-risk high school students.

Recently, planning for school improvement has become increasingly decentralized. Through the formation of school-based planning committees, the school principal, staff, community members, and students (at middle school and high school) meet to discuss school needs and plan for school improvement. Specifically, each school has the responsibility of developing at least two multi-year challenge goals to maintain or improve a student-centered phenomenon in the school. To maintain a sense of parity among the schools, these goals may be unique to the school but must be developed and implemented within the framework of district curriculum and school board policy. Through these initiatives, a sense of collective autonomy has developed in the schools. It is hoped that participation by the major stakeholders within the schools will help focus the objectives of school improvement efforts and foster an increased sense of ownership within the school community.

Finally, the district school board has consistently placed its policy development and financial resources toward instructional and student learning outcomes. Moreover, through the leadership of the school board, administration, and staff, the citizens of Moorestown have acknowledged the success of the school district and have demonstrated their support by consistently passing school budgets and building referendums.

It is through this sense of commitment toward students, systematic planning, school climate, and instructional improvement that the Moorestown Schools continue to promote educational excellence. Yet, although successful, the staff of the district continues to recognize the need for ongoing school improvement. "We're good, but we can be better" is an attitude that is instilled within each member of the school community. This predisposition of high expectations for staff and students has been a cornerstone of this fine school district.

Vito Germinario, Superintendent, K – 12, 2643 Students

SUMMARY

While there is no Blue Ribbon Award for school districts, it is clear there are districts of excellence. Among the characteristics exhibited by these districts are many of the characteristics associated with the individual effective school. These districts are committed to and believe that each of their schools can meet the highest standards of excellence, and they provide the leadership, practices, processes, programs, and resources necessary to accomplish their mission. They provide effective balance between control and autonomy and between encouragement and accountability. In the Best Districts, the individual schools are active participants in the accomplishment of a shared district vision. The number of districts with multiple Blue Ribbon Schools is evidence of the powerful and specific roles the central district leadership and school boards can play in the development of schools of excellence.

REFERENCES

Black, John A. and Fenwick W. English. (1986). *What They Don't Tell You In Schools of Education About School Administration.* Lancaster, PA: Technomic Publishing Co.

Caulfield, James M. (1989). *The Role of Leadership in the Administration of Public Schools.* Union, NJ: Nevfield Press.

English, Fenwick W. (1988). *Curriculum Auditing.* Lancaster, PA: Technomic Publishing Co.

Fullan, Michael G. (1991). *The New Meaning of Educational Change.* New York: Teachers College Press.

Joyce, Bruce, et al. (1993). *The Self-Renewing School.* Alwxandria, VA: Association for Supervision and Curriculum Development.

Levine, Daniel U. and Lawrence W. Lezotte. (1990). *Unusually Effective Schools: A Review and Analysis of Research and Practice.* Madison, WI: The National Center for Effective Schools Research and Development.

Lezotte, Lawrence W. (1991). *Correlates of Effective Schools: The First and Second Generation.* Okemos, MI: Effective Schools Products, LDT.

Lezotte, Lawrence W. and Barbara C. Jacoby. (1992). *Sustainable School Reform: The District Context for School Improvement.* Okemos, MI: Effective Schools.

Pajak, Edward F. and Carl D. Glickman. (1989). "Dimensions of School District Improvement," *Educational Leadership,* 46(8):61–64.

Waterman, Robert H., Jr. (1987). *The Renewal Factor.* New York: Bantam Books.

PART FOUR

THE NATIONAL RECOGNITION PROCESS

CHAPTER 14

On Becoming a Blue Ribbon School of Excellence

OF the nation's 110,000 public and private elementary, middle, and secondary schools, a total of 2809 have been awarded national recognition as Blue Ribbon Schools of Excellence since the program's inception in 1982. Schools from every state, from very small to very large schools, from rural to inner-city schools, from schools serving very low to very high socioeconomic areas, have been among the approximately 2.5% of the schools nationwide that have met the standards of excellence necessary for national recognition. This chapter looks at the following questions concerning the development and recognition of schools of excellence:

- What are the purposes of the Blue Ribbon School Program?
- What is the process for application to become a Blue Ribbon School?
- What is the process for selection?
- What are the standards of excellence for schools?
- How can a school use the standards as part of the process for self-assessment and -improvement?
- What is the value to the school, community, state, and nation of meeting the standards for recognition?

The purpose of the Blue Ribbon School Program, begun in 1983, is to identify and give recognition to public and private schools across the United States, which are truly effective in meeting the goals of education for all students. These model schools collectively serve as evidence that schools can successfully provide education for children now and for the 21st Century, in many different community contexts, and within the full range of socioeconomic and multicultural backgrounds that comprise American society. Foundations, magazines, professional organizations, researchers, states, and individual federal programs have long recognized the importance of identifying models in education. The Blue Ribbon Schools Program differs from other recognition programs in that 1) the achievements of the total educational program are used for identification, rather than a specific program or set of programs, i.e., Chapter 1, Drug Free, mathematics programs; 2) a broad range of criteria based on research on effective schools and school practices are used as the basis of the selection process: criteria cover all aspects of the educational process, rather than criteria being limited to such items as test scores; 3) all schools, both public and private, are eligible for recognition; and 4) credibility of the recognition process is established through the multistage selection process starting at the local and state levels, followed by a three-stage national review, which included two reviews of written documents and an independent on-site validation process.

THE BLUE RIBBON APPLICATION PROCESS

Public and private elementary schools with some combination of grades K–8 may apply for recognition every other year. In alternating years, secondary schools may apply. Applications are distributed through each state's department of education.

The application has seven sections:

(1) Leadership

(2) Teaching environment

(3) Curriculum and instruction

(4) Student environment

(5) Parental and community support

(6) Indicators of success

(7) Organizational vitality

Each section is further divided into subsections that require specific information concerning each of the areas. In addition, there are two areas of special interest designated each year. These are areas in which the U.S. Department of Education is seeking outstanding model programs. These are optional areas, and a school is not penalized for not applying for special recognition.

Applications are usually developed by committees; however, the actual writing is usually done by one or two people. Response space is limited in the narrative section to twenty-eight pages. Clarity of response is the most important writing criteria, since many topics must be covered in limited space. From their reading of the application, panels of reviewers must be able to visualize and understand the programs, practices, and outcomes of the school. The preceding chapters contain many examples of application responses from winning schools. Several people at the local level, including a good editor and one or two people not terribly familiar with the programs in the school, should read the application to be sure that it is clear and understandable.

In addition to describing each program and practice required in the application, schools that are applying for a second or third time (they must skip at least one round after each recognition) must highlight changes and improvements since they were previously honored.

The completed application must be certified as to its accuracy by the principal, the superintendent, and in the case of public schools, the president of the board of education.

HOW SCHOOLS ARE SELECTED FOR RECOGNITION

Each state administers its own program for selecting public schools to be nominated to the national level. Panels of reviewers are used in most states; in a few cases, on-site visits are also part of the state selection process. Frequently, states provide their own form of recognition for schools selected at the state level. Schools selected within the state are nominated by the chief state school officer to the U.S. Department of Education. The number of schools a state can nominate in a given year is indexed to the state's population. The Council for American Private Education nominates private schools, and officials of the Bureau of Indian Affairs and the Department of Defense Dependent Schools also nominate schools.

At the national level, the applications are reviewed by a panel of some 100 outstanding public and private school educators, college and university staffs, school board members, medical professionals, business representatives, and the general public. Subpanels of three to four members review fifteen to twenty applications. Not only is training provided for all panel members, but each panel has as a facilitator a person who is knowledgeable of the broad range of educational research, programs, and practices associated with effective schools.

Special attention is paid to assigning schools, particularly private and special type schools, to reviewers with relevant experience. Panel members do not review schools from their own states or those with which they have had previous personal or professional involvement.

The standards for school identification are based on research concerning practices and processes associated with high academic achievement and demonstrated learning outcomes. Standards within curricular areas are reflective of the national goals, recognized curriculum, and program standards in each area and research on learning. Standards for leadership, student services, and parent and community involvement are consistent with research in those areas. Over the history of the program, the standards have been revised to reflect new research findings and evolving program standards; however, the basic framework for Blue Ribbon School standards has remained unchanged.

National Review Panels begin the selection process in Stage I, by rating each section of the application as individuals and then developing consensus ratings as a group, using the following scale and criteria.

U. S. Department of Education Blue Ribbon School Rating Scale

- exemplary—This segment of the program is truly excellent, that is, within the top 5% of the nation. It describes something that "knocks your socks off" and could be used as a model for presentation to any school.
- strong—Although a very good program and above the norm, this component does not have the quality of an exemplary program. This part of the school program would exceed that of 60% of the schools in the nation.
- adequate—This segment meets the general standards of quality expected of schools and represents the norm for schools of this type.
- inadequate—This segment has serious deficiencies and is clearly below the norm for this type of school.
- no evidence—There is insufficient evidence in the application to make any kind of judgment about this aspect of the program, or the section is not addressed.

Blue Ribbon Schools Program for Elementary Schools Review Panel Instrument

Following is the Review Panel Instrument that is used to evaluate each school.

_____ School Code

U. S. DEPARTMENT OF EDUCATION
1992–1993 BLUE RIBBON SCHOOLS PROGRAM FOR ELEMENTARY SCHOOLS
Review Panel Instrument

Recommended for recognition?

School Name_____ _____Yes _____ No

Honors Candidate?

_____ Science

_____ Math

Justification for Decision: (Include any extenuating circumstances.)

_____
_____
_____
_____
_____
_____
_____
_____
_____
_____
_____
_____

For research and referral purposes:

1. Based on your review of the entire nomination form, do you think that the context and abstract statements accurately reflect the school's nomination? (Circle one)
   a. Yes, to a great extent. b. Somewhat. c. Not as closely as it should.
2. Did you find any particularly exceptional or unique program(s), strategy(ies), approach(es) at this school that might be of value to other schools? _____Yes _____No. If yes, please complete the following:

Program title or focus   Nomination page number
_____
_____
_____

LEADERSHIP

E S A I NE
○ ○ ○ ○ ○   **A1.** Goals and priorities appear appropriate for the school and are clearly articulated. Goals and priorities are developed with input from the school's major constituents, formally reviewed and revised regularly, and effectively communicated to staff, students, parents, and the wider community.

○ ○ ○ ○ ○   **A2.** The principal and staff have a clear vision for the school and its students. This vision is operationalized in terms of specific objectives and the policies, programs, and resources needed to accomplish the school's goals and priorities. School leadership has created a sense of shared purpose among faculty, students, parents, and community to accomplish the school's mission.

○ ○ ○ ○ ○   **A3.** The principal and staff have a common understanding concerning the importance and structure of instructional leadership within the school. There are written guidelines concerning who performs the various functions.

TEACHING ENVIRONMENT

○ ○ ○ ○ ○   **B1.** Teachers are substantively involved in decisions about curriculum, instruction, discipline policy, teacher and program evaluation, and

E S A I NE   other activities. Teacher input is instrumental in the operation of the school.

○ ○ ○ ○ ○ **B2.** Staff collaborate in instructional planning and delivery. They routinely have opportunities for meaningful interaction and are encouraged to work collaboratively.

○ ○ ○ ○ ○ **B3.** Teachers are formally and informally supervised and evaluated on a regular basis by designated individuals, provided with useful feedback, and monitored to ensure that evaluations effect improvement.

○ ○ ○ ○ ○ **B4.** Special provisions are made for the support and training of beginning teachers and those new to the school. Recruitment and selection procedures appear appropriate to the school.

○ ○ ○ ○ ○ **B5.** The recognition of excellent teachers is supported and encouraged both formally and informally at the school level and beyond.

○ ○ ○ ○ ○ **B6.** A variety of opportunities are provided to expand or alter teachers' roles to enhance effectiveness with students, improve job satisfaction, and reduce teacher turnover.

○ ○ ○ ○ ○ **B7.** A significant number of staff members participate in staff development activities directly related to school priorities and in programs aimed at strengthening subject-matter expertise in the five core subjects.

CURRICULUM AND INSTRUCTION

○ ○ ○ ○ ○ **C1.** Differing student needs and the school's mission are reflected in school and classroom organization. Instructional placement procedures are reasonable and fair. Students have flexibility of movement among instructional/academic groups as their skills and interests change.

○ ○ ○ ○ ○ **C2.** Ongoing curriculum development has resulted in a rigorous and rich curriculum offered for all students in:

   a. English
   b. Mathematics
   c. Science
   d. History
   e. Geography
   f. Foreign Languages

○ ○ ○ ○ ○ **C3.** The school has highlighted a well-conceived course that clearly contributes to schoolwide curriculum goals.

○ ○ ○ ○ ○ **C4.** The school has implemented specific strategies for ensuring that students learn to write effectively and has an assessment process to measure progress.

○ ○ ○ ○ ○ **C5.** Special programs are provided by the school to adapt the academic program to meet the needs of specific groups of students. The identification and placement of students is equitable. Individual progress is closely monitored, and there is clear evidence that strat-

E S A I NE   egies/programs are effective. Suitable programs are provided for the following:

a. Special education students.

b. Students requiring Chapter 1 services, limited-English-proficient students, returning students, and students in need of remediation.

○ ○ ○ ○ ○   **C6.** A variety of advanced study or enrichment opportunities are provided for unusually talented or motivated students. If participating students do not represent student body diversity, a defensible explanation has been provided.

○ ○ ○ ○ ○   **C7.** The library/media center is an integral component of the school's overall instructional program and plays a key role in developing students' information literacy.

○ ○ ○ ○ ○   **C8.** Regular, systematic, building-level program evaluation efforts result in identifiable instructional improvement.

STUDENT ENVIRONMENT

○ ○ ○ ○ ○   **D1.** For elementary schools, school policies, practices, and outreach services ensure that children entering the school can participate successfully in formal schooling.

For middle schools, school policies and practices ensure that beginning students and transfer students can participate successfully in all aspects of school life.

○ ○ ○ ○ ○   **D2.** The school uses incentives, motivational programs, and/or special instructional strategies to help develop and sustain students' interest in learning.

○ ○ ○ ○ ○   **D3.** Opportunities to build sustained relationships with counselors, teachers, or other adults are varied and readily available. Programs are in place to provide counseling and advisement, and these approaches are systematically reviewed for effectiveness. A significant number of students representative of the student body take advantage of these opportunities.

○ ○ ○ ○ ○   **D4.** Effective procedures are employed for identifying, counseling, and assisting potential dropouts and other at-risk and underachieving students. A significant number of these identified students are served.

○ ○ ○ ○ ○   **D5.** A variety of extracurricular activities are available for students. Participation is encouraged, and a substantial number of students representative of the student body regularly take part.

○ ○ ○ ○ ○   **D6.** A sound, well-articulated discipline policy prevents violence and encourages students to behave in an orderly fashion without excessive constraints.

○ ○ ○ ○ ○   **D7.** Student use of weapons and drugs, including alcohol and tobacco, is prohibited at school and is discouraged away from school through

E S A I NE   a comprehensive "no use" drug prevention program and broad-based community efforts.

○ ○ ○ ○ ○   **D8.** Students play an active role in influencing classroom and school policy. Student input is valued, and student participation in problem solving is representative of the student body.

○ ○ ○ ○ ○   **D9.** School programs, practices, policies, and staff foster the development of sound character, democratic values, ethical judgment, good behavior, and the ability to work in a self-disciplined and purposeful manner.

○ ○ ○ ○ ○   **D10.** The school effectively employs curricular and other strategies to prepare students to live productively and harmoniously in a society that is culturally and economically diverse.

○ ○ ○ ○ ○   **D11.** The school effectively employs curricular and other strategies to prepare students to live productively and harmoniously in a society that is globally competitive.

PARENT AND COMMUNITY SUPPORT

○ ○ ○ ○ ○   **E1.** The school provides evidence of various types of parent involvement. A substantial number of parents are involved, and they are representative of the student body.

○ ○ ○ ○ ○   **E2.** Student progress and overall school performance are regularly communicated to parents through formal and informal means, and a mechanism is in place to receive feedback from parents and the community.

○ ○ ○ ○ ○   **E3.** The school encourages and helps parents to provide a supportive learning environment in the home and informs them about other learning opportunities.

○ ○ ○ ○ ○   **E4.** The school makes a concerted effort to support the diverse needs of families.

○ ○ ○ ○ ○   **E5.** The school provides specific evidence of valuable collaboration with other educational institutions and community groups to support school activities and programs, promote learning outside the school, and provide integrated services to children and their families.

INDICATORS OF SUCCESS

○ ○ ○ ○ ○   **F1.** Through the use of tests developed and normed at the national or state level:

         a. The school reports student achievement results in a manner readily interpretable.

         b. Student outcomes are more positive than those reported in schools with similar demographic characteristics.

E S A I NE   c. Improvements in student outcomes have been realized over the past three years, or results are consistently outstanding.

○ ○ ○ ○ ○   **F2.** Through the use of performance-based measures or other non-traditional assessments, the school provides convincing evidence of student achievement.

○ ○ ○ ○ ○   **F3.** Student and teacher attendance and the number of students involved in serious disciplinary incidents compare favorably with those of similar schools.

○ ○ ○ ○ ○   **F4.** The school, staff, and students have received a variety of noteworthy awards and recognition over the last five years indicative of school success.

ORGANIZATIONAL VITALITY

○ ○ ○ ○ ○   **G1.** The school's climate reflects its mission and provides an atmosphere that is orderly, purposeful, conducive to learning, respectful of diversity, and open to change.

○ ○ ○ ○ ○   **G2.** A school improvement planning process is in place, with evidence of leadership, support, and progress.

○ ○ ○ ○ ○   **G3.** School staff are cognizant of the findings and recommendations of major educational reform studies, national assessments, and the National Goals and have implemented or are considering related changes.

○ ○ ○ ○ ○   **G4.** The school has effectively introduced changes and/or overcome problems and impediments to educational excellence over the last five years while sustaining those conditions that have contributed most to its success.

○ ○ ○ ○ ○   **G5.** Major educational challenges the school must face in the next five years are realistically understood and reflect a careful assessment of changing student needs.

SPECIAL EMPHASES: SCIENCE AND MATHEMATICS

○ ○ ○ ○ ○   **H1.** The school provides a content-rich program in science that encompasses the kind of science program described on page ii of the nomination package and stimulates interest and achievement among all students.

○ ○ ○ ○ ○   **H2.** The school provides a content-rich program in mathematics that encompasses the standards developed by the National Council of Teachers of Mathematics [NCTM] and stimulates interest and achievement among all students.

          NA Total

__ __ __ __ __   __   __   Conditions A1 through H2 (Total number of items is 58)

There is no calculation of a total score, nor is there a set number of ''exemplary'' or ''strong'' ratings required for recognition. Based on the total application, the panel either recommends that the school should continue to Stage II of the review process, the site visit, or be eliminated from further consideration. Panels are not limited in terms of the number of schools that can be recommended for visits. Experience over the years has shown that from 40% to 60% of the schools that reach the national level are recommended for site visits by the review panels. The panel's recommendation to site visit means that 1) based on the review of the application, the school is judged worthy of recognition; the purpose of the site visit is to validate the practices, programs, and outcomes reported in the application; or 2) the school has many exemplary and strong programs and practices; however, there are some concerns or needs for clarification that the site visit may be able to clarify or answer during the visit, which would allow the panel to recommend recognition; in addition, each section of the application must be validated by the on-site reviewer.

Two-day site visits are conducted at each school recommended at Stage I of the process. Site visitors are educators with extensive public and/or private school experience. The role of the site visitor is to verify the accuracy of the information in the nomination form and provide answers to specific questions posed by the review panel. Site visitors receive special training and follow carefully prepared guidelines in conducting their school reviews. During the visit, they observe in many, if not all, classrooms; meet with parents, students, staff, and administrators; and review achievement data. They arrange part of their time schedule in advance to insure that they see all aspects of the program and talk with all constituencies; however, much of the time on-site is not structured. During this unstructured time, the visitor may have lunch with students, drop into classes, talk to parents who happen to be in the school, review student work in classrooms, and talk informally with staff. For two days, the site visitor is totally immersed in the school. Then, the site visitor reports his/her findings back to the review panel. For each section of the application, the reviewer states whether he/she found the school's description as ''overstated,'' ''understated,'' or ''accurately stated''; narrative comments are made for each section. In addition, the site visitor reports his/her findings concerning specific concerns or questions. The on-site reviewer does not decide if a school will be recognized.

The review panel meets for a second time, Stage III, to review the site reports. Based on the report, the review panel decides whether their original ratings of each area were ''too low,'' ''too high,'' or ''accurate'' and then, based on all the information available to them, whether or not the school will be recommended to the Secretary of Education for recognition.

In addition to the individual panels, there is a group of five panel members who review the actions on all nominated schools within state or private school communities where no schools have been recommended for site visits to insure that at least one school from each state and private school community is visited. However, there is no requirement that a school from each state or private school community will be recognized. In addition, this special panel reviews applications referred by other panels because of unusual circumstances. This panel has the authority to reverse the original panel. However, once a decision is made, no appeals are permitted. All schools reviewed at the national level receive a copy of the panel rating and a narrative statement concerning the reasons for the decision.

Schools selected for recognition are notified by phone and by letter of their selection. The schools are invited to send their principal and two other representatives to Washington for an award ceremony at the White House and reception at which the schools receive the ''Blue Ribbon Flags of Excellence,'' which will fly over their school and plaques for the schools. The principals also receive recognition from the National Association of Elementary Principals. Communities, districts, and schools celebrate the award in many different ways.

SELF-ASSESSMENT AND -IMPROVEMENT: DECIDING WHEN AND IF A SCHOOL SHOULD APPLY FOR RECOGNITION

The Review Panel Instrument can be used as the basis for an assessment of all aspects of the school's programs, services, practices, and achievements. Frequently, an initial "quick and dirty" informal assessment is made by the principal and a few staff members. This usually identifies areas for further study and/or development. Initial assessment is then followed by a more comprehensive review by one or more committees of principal and teachers and, not infrequently, parents, who take each Blue Ribbon Standard; seek specific standards, reports, and research concerning effective practice in each area; and then rate their school's own practices against these criteria. For example,

C2. On-going curriculum development has resulted in rigorous and rich curriculum offered for all students in (b) mathematics

requires schools to review their mathematics program in the light of research on the learning of mathematics, the NCTM Curriculum Standards for Mathematics, and the outcomes envisioned in national goals and in developing standards, asking the questions concerning their curriculum, instructional strategies, and outcomes for *all* students in the school.

The five ratings used by the National Review Panel can be used as a shorthand rating in each area. However, justification for the self-assessment rating should be documented so that it can be shared with the staff as a whole, serve as a basis for improvement, and/or be used in the application process.

Early in the self-assessment process, the committees may find that they have to rate parts of their programs or practices as "No Evidence." As staff focus in on specific programs and practices, it often becomes necessary to better define what the actual practice is in the school and/or collect data concerning effectiveness. For example, the committee may be able easily to find a list of staff development activities in which teachers were involved or which were offered by the district; however, it may be necessary to collect additional information in order to determine the extent of involvement of all staff in development programs, the relationship of the involvement to school priorities, and the need for subject matter expertise and to determine how actual practice was affected in the classroom.

The self-assessment process itself has been characterized by many Blue Ribbon principals as one of the best forms of "staff development" undertaken by themselves and their faculties. In order to determine the status of practices and programs, much work must be done in terms of reviewing research concerning learning and program. Whether or not the match is close between the ideal and current practice, the staff learns much about what the ideal should be, reflects on current practice, and either validates their practices or is provided with the basis for planning improvement strategies. They also learn a great deal about the school as a whole and the full range of problems, strengths, and services within the school. In the words of five of the successful principals, the impact of applying for national recognition was:

The Blue Ribbon Schools nomination process brought teachers, parents, and students together for a common cause. It provided a focus and single-mindedness to the entire school community.

The process permitted faculty to focus on positive aspects of the school. In a school where everyone wants to do her or his best, the focus easily shifts to our flaws and results in disenchantment. But this process generated pride in the enterprise.

A phenomenal team-building activity that magnified our knowledge of school programs, curriculum, and activities.

There emerged a kind of pride that words are too anemic to describe. There now is an aura of academic supremacy that prevails among students, staff, and community. And we'll work hard to preserve that sense of achievement.

We examined our school with a collective microscope. The process afforded us the opportunity to reflect critically on what we really are all about and to increase our understanding of where we are headed. (U. S. Department of Education, 1993)

Based on the self-assessment, the school is in position to decide if they will seek formal recognition as a Blue Ribbon School. While the Blue Ribbon School standards encompass all aspects of the school program and practices, it is not necessary for a school to be rated "exemplary" on each standard. Successful applicants usually have a mix of "exemplary" and "strong" ratings. Occasionally, a school with a rating of "adequate" in an area may be recognized if there are very high ratings in all other areas. It is not uncommon for schools to apply for recognition and, if rejected, then use the experience as a springboard for school improvement. Some schools have been rejected twice before recognition finally came. Discussions with principals in these schools indicate that, while they were disappointed in not being selected the first or even the second time, the process was a powerful agent for self-improvement and definitely worth the effort.

Time is also a factor in the development of Blue Ribbon Schools. In the preceding chapter, the time lines involved in evolving and implementing successful programs frequently extend over many years. A school that rates itself as "adequate" or "inadequate" in many areas will have to set priorities, establish program improvement objectives, plan staff development programs, and make a commitment to change and persist in development over a period of years. Those who have worked extensively with schools of excellence frequently conclude that it takes three to five years with the *right* leadership for an "adequate/inadequate" school to become a school of overall excellence. In addition, it takes leadership and commitment to excellence on the part of the district or at least a willingness on the part of the district to let a school strive for excellence. This would seem to be a simple criterion; however, the leadership in far too many districts is afraid to take risks, to rock the boat, to assess and expose weaknesses, or to implement program changes that may be initially uncomfortable for teachers or PTA parents. Another concern of business-as-usual or "play-it-safe" districts is the fear that, if one school is recognized, the school will "stand out from the rest," creating unwelcome pressure for change at the district level and on other schools in the district. There are, unfortunately, many stories of struggles on the part of principals and staffs to succeed with little encouragement outside the walls of the school. However, there are also many cases where district leadership has supported excellence at all levels over time; these are the districts with multiple Blue Ribbon Schools. If there were a district-level award, these would be the Blue Ribbon Districts of Excellence.

THE VALUE TO THE SCHOOL, COMMUNITY, STATE, AND NATION OF THE BLUE RIBBON SCHOOL PROGRAM

School and District

For the school, the Blue Ribbon School pre-application review process can be a powerful tool for self-improvement. Many schools have used the process to determine needs, to establish improvement objectives, and to make changes in practices and programs.

In addition to improving programs, the review and application process itself is often credited by Blue Ribbon Schools with increasing the unity of staff, parents, community, and students. The sharing of the ''microscope'' as the practices and programs are reviewed leads to many immediate, sometimes major, sometimes minor, improvements and enhances the understanding of the roles of all those involved in the success of the school. Some schools that have completed this stage of the process postpone formal application for recognition until the next round, while others go forward with application development. School districts also can find application of the criteria for recognition as a valuable form of assessment and use this as a basis for long- and short-term planning of school improvement.

Recognition as a Blue Ribbon School of Excellence is the public confirmation to all concerned that ''this is a successful school.'' The announcing phone call sets off a professional ''high'' in the school, among parents, and the community, which is unparalleled. Even schools that have been previously rejected one or even two times believe that it was worth all the effort and prior disappointments. There is no other award offered in education that matches the Blue Ribbon School of Excellence designation. Receiving the flag and plaque in Washington, the White House ceremony with the President of the United States, and the raising of the flag of excellence above the school are frequently described as the highlights in the professional careers of recipients. Educators, so often painted with the broad brush of criticism based on reports about ''average'' or poor practices and results, need the public confirmation that excellence can also be a characteristic of education.

Designation as a Blue Ribbon School does not mean that the self-improvement work of the school is complete. Just the opposite is true. Constant review, revision, and assessment is characteristic of the Best Schools, and the award just stimulates the schools to continue to reach for perfection. In fact, seventy-nine schools have applied for and received recognition twice during the ten years of the program. In discussions with Best School principals, one of the messages that comes through most clearly is their commitment to future improvement. Discussions concerning what their schools are doing now, or what they have done, quickly turn to what the school is going to do this year and the following year or over the next five years to make the program even better for students. Also impressive is the knowledge of principals and the staff concerning newly developed materials, technology, research, assessments, large-scale state and national improvement projects, reports, and practices in other schools. For example, the day after Apple Computer introduced the new Newton Computer, a principal in Texas brought the conversation around to speculating on all the ways this new technology could further enhance instruction in his school. He couldn't wait to talk to staff about the potential.

Designation of a school as a Blue Ribbon School of Excellence has considerable impact on the district as a whole. Schools do not function in isolation within the district. Best Schools are willing to take risks to improve instruction; these schools are most often found in districts that also focus on continuous improvement of program for children and that encourage innovation and risk taking. In many cases, programs in Best Schools have been initiated with the encouragement and support of the district. Priorities concerning planning, funding, staffing, curriculum, materials, and equipment at the school level reflect decisions and priorities at the central district level. Therefore, the district as a whole rightfully shares in the glory of even a single school's recognition. Where central district practices and programs parallel and support Blue Ribbon School standards, it is not unusual for multiple schools to be designated Blue Ribbon schools over a period of years. Unfortunately, however, in other districts, the Blue Ribbon School reached its high level of excellence in spite of laissez-faire or indifferent district support.

Another positive effect of having Blue Ribbon Schools in the district is in the recruitment of new teachers, subject supervisors, and principals. Districts report frequently that outstanding professional candidates state that the fact that the district had one or more Blue Ribbon

Schools was a major factor in their decision to apply. They see the award as an important indicator of a professional school and/or district committed to and willing to support excellence.

The success of one school in the district many times encourages other schools to work toward Blue Ribbon School recognition by stimulating interest in self-assessment and program development. However, the fact that another school has won the flag can also cause anxiety in some schools, based on fear that to apply and fail could be viewed negatively. Where district leadership supports risk taking, focuses on continuous improvement and growth as a district goal, and allows the school staff to decide when they are ready to apply for recognition, the effect of school fears can be minimized. Many districts in the country have multiple Blue Ribbon Schools and a few, such as Flowing Wells, Arizona, are close to having 100% of their schools recognized. In many districts with multiple winners, some of the winning schools were recognized the first time they applied, and others were not recognized until the second or third attempt.

Parents and Community

Parents have a gut-level feeling about the quality of the school their child attends; however, their perceptions are usually limited to such indicators as their child "likes" or does "not like" the school, the principal and teachers seem "caring" or seem "indifferent," and/or the school's and their child's standardized test scores are "high" or "low." Assessment of the school's practices and programs in the light of Blue Ribbon School standards provides the confirmation that the opportunities enjoyed by their child are congruent with what is known about the most effective approaches and programs. This is important to parents. The enthusiasm of parents when a school receives Blue Ribbon status usually matches that of the staff and children. The community as a whole also gains confidence and pride, not only in the designated school, but frequently in the entire school district. Realtors report that, where parents have the financial flexibility to select the community they want to live in, the quality of the schools is a major factor in their determination of where to settle. Having one or more Blue Ribbon Schools in a district affects home-purchasing decisions, property values, and ultimately, support for the schools.

State and Nation

Many of the reports on education released over the past ten years could easily lead the public and even educators to believe that education in the country is a complete disaster. On national surveys, even parents who rate their own child's school at a fairly high level believe that education in other places is in bad shape. Educators are frequently little more positive than the public at large. At the local level, school and program failures are frequently blamed on parents and even the children themselves. At the state and national level, policymakers, researchers, and educational reporters seem to be determined to find flaws in and discard every program or practice that begins to receive positive reports. Groups that are advocating for a particular program or organizational pattern seem to feel compelled to minimize achievements of any other practice, program or standard.

Blue Ribbon Schools represent only 2.5% of the nation's schools; however, they serve as ongoing testimony that education can successfully meet world-class standards. Undoubtedly, there are many, many more schools across the country that meet standards of excellence, and hopefully, they will be recognized in the future.

Educators do use models to improve programs and practices. This is particularly true of the Best Schools. Visits to other schools to observe particular programs are almost always mentioned as a starting point for evolving new programs or revising old ones. Release time for observing in other schools is part of the Best Schools' plans for staff development. Frequently, the principal and key teachers are the ones to go first to observe a promising practice in operation. Once a decision is made to adapt or adopt a practice or program, staff are frequently trained by staff from the school where the model is in place. The National Diffusion Network, which disseminates programs validated as effective, has long recognized the importance of model programs and the need for multiple sites where observations and training can take place. Blue Ribbon Schools are frequently the developers of new programs and practices and, in many cases, have served as demonstration sites for other schools.

The existence of over 2000 Blue Ribbon Schools of every socioeconomic type means that other schools can observe the programs and practices of schools with similar demographics to their own. The existence of Blue Ribbon Schools make it impossible for educators and the public to sit back and say, "It can't be done with our population of students." Inner-city and schools serving low socioeconomic students are definitely not the only ones who can benefit from Blue Ribbon Schools, for many times it is even more difficult to initiate program improvement in middle- and upper-class communities. The limited nature of most assessments, i.e., standardized math and reading scores, which show high "achievement," make the need for more comprehensive assessment and program development a risk that many educators are not inclined to take. In other words, "If the basic skills test scores are high and parents are relatively happy, why "rock the boat"? The dissemination of results, practices, and programs from federal and state levels can provide the education for parents, community members, administrators, and teachers, which can stimulate motivation to move beyond the "safe" to the "effective."

Blue Ribbon Schools are located in every state in the nation. States with aggressive school improvement efforts make maximum use of their knowledge about how schools change and of the existence of their Blue Ribbon Schools. Texas, with many of the Best Schools, is an example of a state that broadly disseminates the standards for Blue Ribbon School status, encourages schools to use the standards for self-assessment, reports on the practices and programs in Blue Ribbon Schools, and actively involves principals of Blue Ribbon Schools and higher education in training of school administrators and teachers statewide. South Carolina is another state which uses the Blue Ribbon School Process to effectively promote school improvement.

SUMMARY

Approximately 2.5% of the nations' 110,000 public and private schools have met the standards as a Blue Ribbon School of Excellence since 1982. These recognized schools are in every state and serve the full range of student populations and community types, from inner-city to rural to suburban. Recognition is a powerful energizer for further improvement in recognized schools, as well as a stimulus for continued efforts by schools striving for excellence. The recognized schools serve as models for other schools seeking excellent programs and practices; they serve as testimony about what is right about education. The standards for the recognition as a Blue Ribbon School can serve as a basis for self-assessment and school improvement. Based on their own assessments, schools can decide whether to apply for and participate in the Blue Ribbon process and seek to fly the flags of excellence over their own schools.

REFERENCES

Lezotte, Lawrence W. and Barbara C. Jacoby. *Sustainable School Reform: The District Context for School Improvement.* Effective Schools, Okemos, Michigan, 1992.

U. S. Department of Education. Blue Ribbon Schools 1993–94 Elementary Program: Nomination Requirements and Application. Blue Ribbon Schools Program, Programs for Improvement of Practice, Office of Educational Research and Improvement, 555 New Jersey Avenue, Washington, D.C. 20208-5645, (202) 219-2149.

U. S. Department of Education. "Review Panel Manual," Blue Ribbon Schools Program, Washington, D.C.

U. S. Department of Education, Office of Educational Research and Improvement. (1993). "A Profile of Principals: Facts, Opinions, Ideas and Stories from Principals of Recognized Elementary Schools of 1991–1992," Blue Ribbon Schools Program, Washington, D. C.

U. S. Department of Education. "A Profile of Principals." Blue Ribbon Schools Program, Program for the Improvement of Practice, Office of Educational Research and Improvement, 555 New Jersey Avenue, Washington, D. C. 1992.

The Complete List of Elementary, Middle, and Secondary Schools Recognized 1982–1983 through 1993–1994

For further information, contact:
Blue Ribbon Schools Program
Programs for the Improvement of Practice
Office of Educational Research and Improvement
U. S. Department of Education
555 New Jersey Avenue, NW
Washington, D. C. 20208–5645
(202) 219–2149

SCHOOL	CITY	YEAR(S) RECOGNIZED
ALABAMA		
Academy for Academics and Arts	Huntsville	87–88
Bob Jones High School	Madison	92–93
Bush Middle School	Birmingham	83–84
C. F. Vigor High School	Prichard	83–84
Cahaba Heights Community School	Birmingham	85–86
Corpus Christi School	Mobile	89–90
East Highland Middle School	Sylacauga	84–85
Edgewood Elementary School	Homewood	91–92
Elvin Hill Elementary School	Columbiana	87–88
Enterprise High School	Enterprise	83–84
EPIC Elementary School	Birmingham	93–94
Eura Brown Elementary School	Gadsden	91–92
Grantswood Community School	Irondale	91–92
Hewitt-Trussville High School	Trussville	92–93
Homewood High School	Homewood	83–84
Homewood Middle School	Homewood	83–84
Indian Valley Elementary School	Sylacauga	89–90
Ira F. Simmons Junior High School	Birmingham	84–85
Julian Newman Elementary School	Athens	87–88
Leeds Elementary School	Leeds	93–94
Mars Hill Bible School	Florence	86–87, 92–93
Mars Hill Bible School (Elementary)	Florence	87–88
Maryvale Elementary School	Mobile	93–94
Mountain Brook High School	Mountain Brook	83–84, 92–93
Muscle Shoals High School	Muscle Shoals	90–91
Oak Mountain Elementary School	Birmingham	93–94

SCHOOL	CITY	YEAR(S) RECOGNIZED

ALABAMA (*continued*)

SCHOOL	CITY	YEAR(S) RECOGNIZED
Pinson Elementary School	Pinson	91–92
Riverchase Middle School	Birmingham	84–85
S. S. Murphy High School	Mobile	86–87
Saint Ignatius School	Mobile	87–88
Shades Cahaba Elementary School	Homewood	93–94
St. Paul's Episcopal School	Mobile	88–89
South Side Elementary School	Gadsen	89–90
Sylacauga High School	Sylacauga	84–85
Tarrant Elementary School	Tarrant	93–94
Valley Elementary School	Pelham	85–86
Vestavia Hills Elementary School	Vestavia Hills	85–86
Vestavia Hills High School	Vestavia Hills	90–91
W. P. Davidson High School	Mobile	90–91
Westlawn Elementary School	Decatur	89–90

ALASKA

SCHOOL	CITY	YEAR(S) RECOGNIZED
East Anchorage High School	Anchorage	90–91
Gruening Junior High School	Eagle River	84–85
Homer High School	Homer	88–89
Kenai Junior High School	Kenai	83–84
Mendenhall River Community School	Juneau	93–94
North Star Elementary School	Nikiski	93–94
Petersburg High School	Petersburg	86–87
Romig Junior High School	Anchorage	84–85
Rosamond Weller Elementary School	Fairbanks	87–88
Soldotna High School	Soldotna	82–83
Soldotna Junior High School	Soldotna	82–83
Tok School	Tok	85–86
Valdez High School	Valdez	82–83
West Anchorage High School	Anchorage	92–93
Yakutat Elementary School	Yakutat	87–88

ARIZONA

SCHOOL	CITY	YEAR(S) RECOGNIZED
Agua Fria Union High School	Avondale	82–83
Amphitheater High School	Tucson	83–84
Baboquivari Junior High School	Sells	86–87
Booker T. Washington School	Mesa	85–86
Centennial Elementary School	Tucson	93–94
Chandler High School	Chandler	82–83, 86–87
Cherokee Elementary School	Paradise Valley	87–88
Craycroft Elementary School	Tucson	91–92
Del Rio Elementary School	Chino Valley	93–94
Desert Cove Elementary School	Phoenix	87–88

SCHOOL	CITY	YEAR(S) RECOGNIZED

ARIZONA (*continued*)

SCHOOL	CITY	YEAR(S) RECOGNIZED
Desert Shadows Middle School	Scottsdale	86−87
Desert Sky Middle School	Glendale	90−91
Dobson High School	Mesa	86−87
Echo Mountain Elementary School	Phoenix	89−90
Flowing Wells High School	Tucson	86−87, 90−91
Flowing Wells Junior High School	Tucson	84−85
Frye Elementary School	Chandler	87−88
Green Fields Country Day School	Tucson	84−85
Greenway Middle School	Phoenix	86−87
Harvey L. Taylor Junior High School	Mesa	84−85
Indian Bend Elementary School	Phoenix	87−88
John J. Rhodes Junior High School	Mesa	82−83, 92−93
Kino Junior High School	Mesa	84−85
Laguna Elementary School	Tucson	85−86
Manzanita School	Tucson	93−94
Mesa High School	Mesa	83−84
Mohave Middle School	Scottsdale	92−93
Mountain View High School	Mesa	84−85
Page Elementary School	Page	85−86
Palomino Elementary School	Phoenix	89−90
Poston Junior High School	Mesa	83−84
Rancho Viejo School	Yuma	87−88
Richardson Elementary School	Tucson	87−88
Safford Engineering/Technology Magnet Middle School	Tucson	92−93
Saint Mary-Basha Catholic Elementary School	Chandler	93−94
Sandpiper Elementary School	Scottsdale	91−92
Santa Rita High School	Tucson	84−85
Sequoya Elementary School	Scottsdale	91−92
Shea Middle School	Phoenix	83−84
Show Low Primary School	Show Low	91−92
Shumway Elementary School	Chandler	93−94
Sirrine Elementary School	Chandler	89−90
Utterback Junior High School	Tucson	83−84
Veora E. Johnson Elementary School	Mesa	87−88
Walter Douglas Elementary School	Tucson	89−90
Weinberg Elementary School	Chandler	85−86
Westwood High School	Mesa	83−84
Willis Junior High School	Chandler	82−83
Xavier College Preparatory School	Phoenix	90−91
Yavapai Elementary School	Scottsdale	89−90

ARKANSAS

SCHOOL	CITY	YEAR(S) RECOGNIZED
Annie Camp Middle School	Jonesboro	82−83

SCHOOL	CITY	YEAR(S) RECOGNIZED

ARKANSAS (*continued*)

Arkadelphia High School	Arkadelphia	90−91
Conway High School	Conway	84−85
Douglas MacArthur Middle School	Jonesboro	82−83
Jonesboro High School	Jonesboro	82−83
Louisa E. Perritt Primary School	Arkadelphia	87−88
Northside High School	Fort Smith	92−93
Parson Hills Elementary School	Springdale	93−94
Root Elementary School	Fayetteville	91−92
Southside High School	Fort Smith	82−83, 86−87
Thurman G. Smith Elementary School	Springdale	87−88
Westwood Elementary School	Springdale	89−90
White Hall High School	Pine Bluff	83−84

BUREAU OF INDIAN AFFAIRS

Cherokee Central Schools	Cherokee, North Carolina	88−89
Cherokee Elementary School	Cherokee, North Carolina	87−88
Dzilth-na-o-dith-hle Community School	Bloomfield, New Mexico	86−87
St. Stephens Indian School	St. Stephens	93−94
Santa Clara Day School	Espanola, New Mexico	89−90
Santa Fe Indian School	Santa Fe, New Mexico	86−87
Sky City Community School	Acoma, New Mexico	90−91

CALIFORNIA

Academy of Our Lady of Peace	San Diego	88−89, 92−93
Admiral Akers School	NAS Lemoore	86−87
Alameda High School	Alameda	92−93
Alamo Elementary School	Alamo	85−86, 91−92
Alvarado Middle School	Union City	83−84
Amy Blanc Elementary School	Fairfield	85−86
Anacapa Middle School	Ventura	90−91
Andersen Elementary School	Newport Beach	87−88
Anza Elementary School	Torrance	89−90
Argonaut Elementary School	Saratoga	93−94
Armijo High School	Fairfield	88−89
Arroyo Elementary School	Santa Ana	89−90
Artesia High School	Lakewood	83−84
Audubon Junior High School	Los Angeles	86−87
Balboa Boulevard Gifted/High Achievement Magnet School	Northridge	87−88
Bishop Amat Memorial High School	West Covina	83−84
Bishop O'Dowd High School	Oakland	90−91
Bishop's Peak Elementary School	San Luis Obispo	87−88
Black Mountain Middle School	San Diego	90−91

SCHOOL	CITY	YEAR(S) RECOGNIZED

CALIFORNIA (*continued*)

SCHOOL	CITY	YEAR(S) RECOGNIZED
Borel Middle School	San Mateo	83–84
Borrego Springs High School	Borrego Springs	84–85
Brea Olinda High School	Brea	92–93
Brightwood Elementary School (grades 5–8)	Monterey Park	92–93
Bryant Ranch School	Yorba Linda	93–94
Brywood Elementary School	Irvine	91–92
Bullis Purissima School	Los Altos Hills	91–92
Cajon Park School	Santee	92–93
Carmenita Junior High School	Cerritos	90–91
Caroline Davis Intermediate School	San Jose	92–93
Castro Valley High School	Castro Valley	84–85, 88–89
Cate School	Carpinteria	86–87
Cayucos School	Cayucos	86–87
Chadbourne Elementary School	Fremont	89–90
Chaparral Elementary School	Poway	91–92
Charles E. Teach Elementary School	San Luis Obispo	91–92
Charlotte Wood Middle School	Danville	92–93
Chico Senior High School	Chico	88–89
Chula Vista High School	Chula Vista	83–84
Claremont High School	Claremont	86–87
Clovis High School	Clovis	86–87, 92–93
Clovis West High School	Fresno	88–89
Collins School	Cupertino	87–88
Country Club Elementary School	San Ramon	93–94
Convent of the Sacred Heart High School	San Francisco	92–93
Corona del Mar High School	Newport Beach	84–85
Cuddeback Union Elementary School	Carlotta	93–94
Culver City High School	Culver City	92–93
D. Russell Parks Junior High School	Fullerton	86–87
Davidson Middle School	San Rafael	82–83
Del Cerro Elementary School	Mission Viejo	87–88
Del Dayo Elementary School	Carmichael	87–88
Del Mar Hills Elementary School	Del Mar	87–88
Diegueno Junior High School	Encinitas	92–93
Discovery Bay Elementary School	Byron	85–86
Dr. Jonas Salk School	Anaheim	89–90
Dry Creek Elementary School	Clovis	93–94
E. O. Green Junior High School	Oxnard	92–93
Earl Warren Junior High School	Solana Beach	90–91
Edison-Computech 7/8 School	Fresno	90–91
Eisenhower High School	Rialto	92–93
El Morro Elementary School	Laguna Beach	87–88
Eugene Padan Elementary School	Vacaville	87–88
Fairmont Private Junior High School	Anaheim	90–91
Fallbrook Street School	Fallbrook	87–88

SCHOOL	CITY	YEAR(S) RECOGNIZED

CALIFORNIA (*continued*)

Fallbrook Union High School	Fallbrook	83 – 84
Ferndale Elementary School	Ferndale	86 – 87
Foothill Elementary School	Saratoga	91 – 92
Fort Washington Elementary School	Fresno	85 – 86, 91 – 92
Fred L. Newhart School	Mission Viejo	93 – 94
Fruitvale Junior High School	Bakersfield	90 – 91
Fullerton Union High School	Fullerton	88 – 89
Garden Gate Elementary School	Cupertino	85 – 86
Gardenhill Elementary School	La Mirada	93 – 94
George Leyva Junior High School	San Jose	82 – 83
George W. Kastner Intermediate School	Fresno	84 – 85
Glenn E. Murdock Elementary School	La Mesa	91 – 92
Gomes Elementary School	Fremont	87 – 88
Graystone Elementary School	San Jose	91 – 92
Greenville Fundamental Elementary School	Santa Ana	85 – 86
Greenville Junior/Senior High School	Greenville	92 – 93
Gretchen Whitney High School	Cerritos	86 – 87, 90 – 91
Grover Heights Elementary School	Grover Beach	93 – 94
Harbor View Elementary School	Corona del Mar	85 – 86
Harkham Hill Hebrew Academy	Beverly Hills	93 – 94
Harvard School	North Hollywood	88 – 89
Helen Estock Elementary School	Tustin	89 – 90
Hewes Middle School	Santa Ana	92 – 93
Highland High School	Bakersfield	88 – 89
Highlands Elementary School	Saugus	89 – 89
Hillsdale High School	San Mateo	92 – 93
Holy Names High School	Oakland	84 – 85, 90 – 91
Homestead High School	Cupertino	86 – 87
Horace Mann Academic Middle School	San Francisco	86 – 87
Hyde Junior High School	Cupertino	88 – 89
Irvine High School	Irvine	88 – 89
J. Haley Durham Elementary School	Fremont	93 – 94
Jacoby Creek Elementary School	Bayside	89 – 90
James Logan High School	Union City	82 – 83, 86 – 87
Jerabek Elementary School	San Diego	87 – 88
Joaquin Miller Intermediate School	San Jose	86 – 87
John F. Kennedy Junior High School	Cupertino	92 – 93
John Marshall Elementary School	Glendale	87 – 88
Julian Elementary School	Julian	89 – 90
K. R. Smith Elementary School	San Jose	87 – 88
Kastner Intermediate School	Fresno	92 – 93
La Cañada High School	La Cañada	92 – 93
La Mesa Middle School	La Mesa	90 – 91
La Paz Intermediate School	Mission Viejo	92 – 93
Laguna Hills High School	Laguna Hills	92 – 93

SCHOOL	CITY	YEAR(S) RECOGNIZED

CALIFORNIA (*continued*)

SCHOOL	CITY	YEAR(S) RECOGNIZED
Lakeside Middle School	Irvine	90—91
Lakewood Elementary School	Modesto	93—94
Leroy Anderson Elementary School	San Jose	87—88
Levi Bemis Elementary School	Rialto	87—88
Lincoln Elementary School	Fresno	89—90
Lindero Canyon Middle School	Agoura Hills	84—85
Los Alamitos High School	Los Alamitos	88—89, 92—93
Los Altos Intermediate School	Camarillo	86—87
Los Angeles Center for Enriched Studies	Los Angeles	92—93
Los Gatos High School	Los Gatos	86—87, 90—91
Los Primeros Structured School	Camarillo	87—88
Los Ranchos Elementary School	San Luis Obispo	89—90
Lowell High School	San Francisco	82—83
Lupin Hill Elementary School	Calabasas	85—86
Manhattan Beach Intermediate School	Manhattan Beach	90—91
Marina High School	Huntington Beach	84—85
Mayfield Junior School of the Holy Child	Pasadena	91—92
McFadden Intermediate School	Santa Ana	88—89
Meadowbrook Middle School	Poway	84—85
Meadows Elementary School	Valencia	93—94
Melvin Avenue School	Reseda	85—86
Mendocino High School	Mendocino	88—89
Mendocino Middle School	Mendocino	85—86
Menlo-Atherton High School	Atherton	86—87
Mesa Union School	Somis	86—87
Miramonte High School	Orinda	86—87, 90—91
Mission Avenue Open School	Carmichael	87—88
Mission Junior High School	Riverside	83—84
Mission San Jose High School	Fremont	86—87
Mission Viejo High School	Mission Viejo	88—89
Monte Gardens Elementary School	Concord	91—92
Montebello Intermediate School	Montebello	83—84
Montgomery High School	Santa Rosa	90—91
Moreau High School	Hayward	83—84, 88—89
Morning Creek Elementary School	San Diego	93—94
Mount Carmel High School	San Diego	88—89
Mountain View Elementary School	Fresno	93—94
Mountain View High School	Mountain View	88—89
Nathaniel Bowditch Middle School	Foster City	92—93
Neil Armstrong Elementary School	Diamond Bar	89—90
Nelson Elementary School	Pinedale	91—92
Newhall Elementary School	Newhall	93—94
Nick G. Parras Middle School	Redondo Beach	92—93
North Monterey County High School	Castroville	84—85
Norwood Creek Elementary School	San Jose	93—94

SCHOOL	CITY	YEAR(S) RECOGNIZED

CALIFORNIA (*continued*)

Notre Dame Academy	Los Angeles	90−91
Nueva Learning Center	Hillsborough	87−88
O'Neill Elementary School	Mission Viejo	85−86
O. B. Whaley School	San Jose	89−90
Oak Grove Middle School	Jamul	88−89
Oak Hills Elementary School	Agoura	91−92
Oak Park High School	Agoura	92−93
Oakbrook Elementary School	Fairfield	91−92
Olive Peirce Middle School	Ramona	92−93
Orange Glen High School	Escondido	86−87
Pacific Union Elementary School	Arcata	93−94
Pacific Union College Elementary School	Angwin	85−86
Palms Junior High School	Los Angeles	86−87
Palo Alto High School	Palo Alto	86−87
Park Dale Lane Elementary School	Encinitas	87−88
Pepper Drive School	El Cajon	87−88
Piedmont High School	Piedmont	84−85
Pioneer Elementary School	Union City	85−86
Pioneer High School	Whittier	82−83
Pliocene Ridge Elementary School	North San Juan	93−94
Polytechnic School	Pasadena	84−85
Pomerado Elementary School	Poway	89−90
Poway High School	Poway	90−91
Presentation High School	Berkeley	84−85
Quailwood Elementary School	Bakersfield	91−92
R. J. Neutra Elementary School	NAS Lemoore	87−88, 91−92
Ralph Waldo Emerson Junior High School	Davis	88−89
Ramona Convent Secondary School	Alhambra	92−93
Rancho Buena Vista High School	Vista	90−91
Raymond J. Fisher School	Los Gatos	88−89
Red Bank Elementary School	Clovis	93−94
Redondo Union High School	Redondo Beach	88−89
Regnart Elementary School	Cupertino	87−88
Rio Vista Elementary School	Canyon Country	91−92
Rolling Hills Middle School	Los Gatos	88−89, 92−93
Rosedale North Elementary School	Bakersfield	93−94
Rosemont Middle School	La Crescenta	84−85, 92−93
Ruth Paulding Middle School	Arroyo Grande	92−93
Saint Anthony's School	Fresno	85−86
Saint Francis High School	Mountain View	90−91
Saint John the Baptist School	El Cerrito	87−88
Saint Joseph High School	Santa Maria	92−93
Saint Simon Catholic School	Los Altos	91−92
St. David's Elementary School	Richmond	85−86
St. Elizabeth High School	Oakland	83−84

SCHOOL	CITY	YEAR(S) RECOGNIZED

CALIFORNIA (*continued*)

SCHOOL	CITY	YEAR(S) RECOGNIZED
St. Ignatius College Preparatory School	San Francisco	83–84
St. Isadore School	Danville	93–94
St. James Episcopal School	Los Angeles	93–94
St. Joseph Elementary School	Alameda	93–94
St. Mary's College High School	Berkeley	84–85
St. Thomas the Apostle School	Los Angeles	91–92
Samuel Curtis Rogers Middle School	San Jose	92–93
San Diego Hebrew Day School	San Diego	91–92
San Lorenzo High School	San Lorenzo	90–91
San Mateo High School	San Mateo	90–91
Santa Rita Elementary School	Los Altos	91–92
Santana High School	Santee	83–84
Santee Elementary School (grades 6–8)	Santee	92–93
Saratoga High School	Saratoga	88–89
Sequoia Elementary School	Santa Rosa	89–90, 93–94
Sierra Canyon School	Chatsworth	89–90
Silver Spur School	Rancho Palos Verdes	87–88
Skyline School	Solana Beach	87–88
Solana Vista School	Solana Beach	89–90
Sonoma Elementary School	Modesto	89–90
Southwest High School	San Diego	86–87
Stevens Creek School	Cupertino	87–88
Strawberry Elementary School	Santa Rosa	87–88
Sundance Elementary School	San Diego	87–88
Taper Avenue Elementary School	San Pedro	87–88
Terrace Hills Junior High School	Grand Terrace	82–83
The Bishop's School	La Jolla	90–91
The Crossroads School	Santa Monica	83–84
The Thacher School	Ojai	90–91
The York School	Monterey	90–91
Torrey Pines High School	San Diego	86–87, 92–93
Twin Peaks Middle School	Poway	83–84, 90–91
University High School	Irvine	86–87
Vacaville High School	Vacaville	86–87
Valley Center Middle School	Valley Center	88–89
Valley Christian High School	Cerritos	83–84
Valley High School	Sacramento	86–87
Valley Oak Elementary School	Fresno	93–94
Van Buren Elementary School	Riverside	93–94
Venado Middle School	Irvine	82–83
Village Elementary School	Santa Rosa	91–92
Vista High School	Vista	88–89
Walnut High School	Walnut	92–93
Walter White School	Ceres	85–86
Walters Junior High School	Fremont	88–89

SCHOOL	CITY	YEAR(S) RECOGNIZED

CALIFORNIA (*continued*)

West High School	Torrance	83 – 84
West Hillsborough School	Hillsborough	93 – 94
West Orange Elementary School	Orange	87 – 88
West Valley Elementary School	Sunnyvale	85 – 86
Westlake School for Girls	Los Angeles	84 – 85
Westminster High School	Westminster	92 – 93
Westwood Elementary School	Santa Clara	93 – 94
White Oak Elementary School	Westlake Village	85 – 86, 93 – 94
Whitmore Union Elementary School	Whitmore	86 – 87
William H. Crocker School	Hillsborough	82 – 83, 88 – 89
Willow Elementary School	Agoura Hills	91 – 92
Woodbridge High School	Irvine	86 – 87
Woodside School	Woodside	93 – 94

COLORADO

Alameda Junior High School	Lakewood	84 – 85
Arapahoe High School	Littleton	92 – 93
Beth Jacob High School of Denver	Denver	83 – 84
Carmody Junior High School	Lakewood	82 – 83
Cherry Creek High School	Englewood	92 – 93
Cheyenne Mountain High School	Colorado Springs	82 – 83
Douglass Valley School	Colorado Springs	85 – 86
Eagle Valley Middle School	Eagle	92 – 93
Evergreen Junior High School	Evergreen	86 – 87
Heritage High School	Littleton	90 – 91
Holmes Junior High School	Colorado Springs	83 – 84
Indian Ridge Elementary School	Aurora	89 – 90
Lutheran High School	Denver	90 – 91
Mrachek Middle School	Aurora	82 – 83
Pioneer Elementary School	Colorado Springs	91 – 92
Rampart High School	Colorado Springs	90 – 91
Regis Jesuit High School	Denver	84 – 85
St. Mary's Academy	Englewood	91 – 92
Smoky Hill High School	Aurora	90 – 91
South Elementary School	Castle Rock	93 – 94
Thomson Elementary School	Arvada	87 – 88
Westridge Elementary School	Littleton	93 – 94
Wheat Ridge High School	Wheatridge	83 – 84
Woodland Park Middle School	Woodland Park	88 – 89

CONNECTICUT

Alcott Middle School	Wolcott	90 – 91
Amity Regional High School	Woodbridge	82 – 83

SCHOOL	CITY	YEAR(S) RECOGNIZED

CONNECTICUT (*continued*)

SCHOOL	CITY	YEAR(S) RECOGNIZED
Amity Regional Junior High School	Bethany	83—84
Amity Regional Junior High School	Orange	82—83
Anna M. Reynolds School	Newington	93—94
Avon Middle School	Avon	84—85
Benjamin Franklin School	Meriden	87—88
Bess and Paul Sigel Hebrew Academy	Bloomfield	89—90
Bi-Cultural Day School	Stamford	87—88
Cider Mill School	Wilton	85—86
Columbus Magnet School	South Norwalk	89—90
Conard High School	West Hartford	84—85
Conte Arts Magnet School	New Haven	83—84
Darien High School	Darien	86—87
East Catholic High School	Manchester	88—89
East Ridge Junior High School	Ridgefield	83—84
Eastern Middle School	Riverside	91—92
Edward Morley School	West Hartford	87—88
Edwin O. Smith High School	Storrs	92—93
Eric G. Norfeldt Elementary School	West Hartford	91—92
Fairfield College Preparatory School	Fairfield	86—87
Flanders Elementary School	East Lyme	93—94
Flood Intermediate School	Stratford	83—84
Gideon Welles Junior High School	Glastonbury	84—85
Granby Memorial Middle School	Granby	86—87, 90—91
Greenwich High School	Greenwich	88—89
Haddam-Killingworth Middle School	Higganum	88—89
Illing Junior High School	Manchester	82—83
Irving A. Robbins Junior High School	Farmington	86—87
Joel Barlow High School	West Redding	88—89, 92—93
John Wallace Middle School	Newington	92—93
King Philip Middle School	West Hartford	86—87
Mansfield Middle School	Storrs	91—92
Martin Kellogg Middle School	Newington	86—87
Memorial Middle School	Middlebury	88—89
Middlebrook School	Wilton	82—83
Middlesex Middle School	Darien	84—85
Mitchell Elementary School	Woodbury	93—94
Naubuc School	Glastonbury	89—90
New Canaan Country School	New Canaan	93—94
New Fairfield High School	New Fairfield	84—85
Newington High School	Newington	88—89
Noah Wallace School	Farmington	93—94
Northeast Elementary School	Vernon	91—92
Northwest Catholic High School	West Hartford	88—89
Notre Dame Catholic High School	Fairfield	84—85
Plainfield Central School	Plainfield	92—93

SCHOOL	CITY	YEAR(S) RECOGNIZED
CONNECTICUT (*continued*)		
Roger Sherman School	Meriden	93−94
Saint Brendan School	New Haven	89−90
Saint Francis School	New Haven	85−86
Sacred Heart Academy	Hamden	92−93
Shelton Intermediate School	Shelton	88−89
Silas Deane Middle School	Wethersfield	90−91
Southington High School	Southington	92−93
Stratfield School	Fairfield	87−88, 93−94
Tashua School	Trumbull	89−90
The Peck Place School	Orange	87−88
The Rectory School	Pomfret	93−94
Tilford W. Miller School	Wilton	87−88
Torringford School	Torrington	87−88
Union School	Unionville	91−92
Watkinson School	Hartford	83−84
West Hill School	Rock Hill	89−90
Weston Middle School	Weston	87−88
William H. Hall High School	West Hartford	84−85
Wilton High School	Wilton	82−83
Wooster Intermediate School	Stratford	82−83

DELAWARE

SCHOOL	CITY	YEAR(S) RECOGNIZED
Brandywine High School	Wilmington	82−83
Caesar Rodney Senior High School	Camden	83−84
Christiana High School	Newark	83−84
Corpus Christi School	Wilmington	89−90
Dover High School	Dover	86−87
St. Matthew School	Wilmington	91−92
Shue Middle School	Newark	82−83
Skyline Middle School	Wilmington	84−85

DEPARTMENT OF DEFENSE DEPENDENTS SCHOOLS

SCHOOL	CITY	YEAR(S) RECOGNIZED
Aschaffenburg American School	Aschaffenburg, Germany	87−88
Bahrain Elementary School-High School	Manama, Bahrain	84−85
Bonn American High School	Bonn, Germany	86−87
Coevorden American School	Coevorden, Netherlands	91−92
Curundu Junior High School	Curundu, Panama	88−89
Ft. Kobbe Elementary School	DODDS−Panama Region	89−90
Frankfurt American High School	Frankfurt, Germany	83−84
Hahn American High School	Hahn Air Base, Germany	90−91
Heidelberg High School	Heidelberg, Germany	83−84, 92−93
Heidelberg Middle School	Heidelberg, Germany	84−85
Nile C. Kinnick High School	Yokosuka, Japan	88−89

SCHOOL	CITY	YEAR(S) RECOGNIZED

DEPARTMENT OF DEFENSE DEPENDENTS SCHOOLS (*continued*)

School	City	Year(s) Recognized
Rhein Main Junior High School	Rhein Main, Germany	83–84
Seoul American High School	Seoul, Korea	84–85
Sollars Elementary School	APO AP Honshu, Japan	93–94
Wuerzburg American Middle School	Wuerzburg, Germany	92–93

DISTRICT OF COLUMBIA

School	City	Year(s) Recognized
Alice Deal Junior High School	Washington	83–84
Benjamin Banneker Academic High School	Washington	90–91
Brookland Junior High School	Washington	82–83
Browne Junior High School	Washington	84–85, 88–89
Bunker Hill Elementary School	Washington	85–86, 91–92
Duke Ellington School of the Arts	Washington	92–93
Georgetown Visitation Preparatory School	Washington	86–87
Horace Mann Elementary School	Washington	89–90, 93–94
Jefferson Junior High School	Washington	82–83, 86–87
Julius W. Hobson Senior Middle School	Washington	83–84
Lemon G. Hine Junior High School	Washington	90–91
Paul Laurence Dunbar Senior High School	Washington	92–93
Robert Brent Elementary School	Washington	87–88
Sidwell Friends Lower School	Washington	85–86
Smothers Elementary School	Washington	85–86

FLORIDA

School	City	Year(s) Recognized
Academy of the Holy Names	Tampa	93–94
Alimacani Elementary School	Jacksonville	93–94
American Senior High School	Hialeah	83–84
Apopka High School	Apopka	92–93
Ascension Catholic School	Melbourne	85–86
Azalea Middle School	St. Petersburg	88–89
Bay Haven School of Basics Plus	Sarasota	89–90
Bayview Elementary School	Fort Lauderdale	85–86
Boca Raton Christian School	Boca Raton	89–90
Bonita Springs Middle School	Bonita Springs	90–91
Brandon High School	Brandon	82–83
C. H. Price Middle School	Interlachen	90–91
Caloosa Elementary School	Cape Coral	85–86
Caloosa Middle School	Cape Coral	90–91
Cape Coral High School	Cape Coral	88–89
Cardinal Gibbons High School	Fort Lauderdale	86–87
Chaminade-Madonna College Preparatory	Hollywood	92–93
Clearwater Central Catholic High School	Clearwater	88–89
Conway Middle School	Orlando	88–89
Coral Gables Elementary School	Coral Gables	93–94

SCHOOL	CITY	YEAR(S) RECOGNIZED
FLORIDA (*continued*)		
Coral Springs Middle School	Coral Springs	90–91
Dade Christian Schools	Hialeah	84–85
Dixie Hollins High School	St. Petersburg	83–84
Dr. W. J. Creel Elementary School	Melbourne	85–86
Eccleston Elementary School	Orlando	87–88
Eisenhower Elementary School	Clearwater	89–90
Fairway Elementary School	Miramar	89–90
Finegan Elementary School	Atlantic Beach	85–86
Floranada Elementary School	Fort Lauderdale	87–88
Forest Glen Middle School	Coral Springs	92–93
Fort Myers High School	Fort Myers	84–85
Fort Myers Middle School	Fort Myers	90–91
Gemini Elementary School	Melbourne Beach	87–88
Greenwood Lakes Middle School	Lake Mary	88–89
Griffin Elementary School	Cooper City	91–92
Gulf Elementary School	Cape Coral	87–88
Gulliver Academy	Coral Gables	91–92
Gulliver Preparatory School	Miami	90–91
H. B. Plant High School	Tampa	90–91
Hawkes Bluff Elementary School	Davie	93–94
Heights Elementary School	Fort Myers	91–92
Hendricks Avenue Elementary School	Jacksonville	85–86
Highland Oaks Junior High School	North Miami Beach	83–84
Horace O'Bryant Middle School	Key West	84–85
Hyde Grove Elementary School	Jacksonville	93–94
Interlachen Elementary School	Interlachen	93–94
J. P. Taravella High School	Coral Springs	88–89
Jackson Heights Middle School	Oviedo	85–86
Jefferson Davis Junior High School	Jacksonville	82–83
Jesuit High School	Tampa	86–87
John Gorrie Junior High School	Jacksonville	83–84
John N. C. Stockton School	Jacksonville	85–86
Kate Sullivan Elementary School	Tallahassee	85–86
Kirby-Smith Junior High School	Jacksonville	86–87
Largo Middle School	Largo	83–84
Loggers' Run Community Middle School	Boca Raton	90–91
Lyman High School	Longwood	84–85
Mainland High School	Daytona Beach	83–84, 90–91
Melbourne Central Catholic High School	Melbourne	90–91
Miami Country Day School (Elementary)	Miami	87–88
Miami Country Day School, Inc.	Miami	88–89
Miami Palmetto Senior High School	Miami	88–89
Miami Shores Elementary School	Miami Shores	87–88
Murdock Middle School	Port Charlotte	92–93
N. B. Broward Elementary School	Tampa	91–92
Neptune Middle School	Kissimmee	92–93

SCHOOL	CITY	YEAR(S) RECOGNIZED

FLORIDA (*continued*)

SCHOOL	CITY	YEAR(S) RECOGNIZED
New World School of the Arts	Miami	92–93
Nob Hill Elementary School	Sunrise	91–92
Norland Middle School	Miami	86–87
North Dade Center for Modern Languages	Miami	91–92
North Miami Beach Senior High School	North Miami Beach	84–85
Nova Blanche Forman Elementary School	Fort Lauderdale	93–94
Nova High School	Davie	88–89
Oak Hill Elementary School	Jacksonville	91–92
Ormond Beach Elementary School	Ormond Beach	93–94
Our Lady of Lourdes Academy	Miami	86–87
Pensacola Catholic High School	Pensacola	92–93
Pine Crest Preparatory School	Fort Lauderdale	84–85
Pine Crest Preparatory School (Elementary)	Fort Lauderdale	87–88
Pine Trail Elementary School	Ormond Beach	85–86
Pinecrest Elementary School	Miami	85–86
Rabbi Alexander S. Gross Greater Miami Hebrew Academy	Miami Beach	85–86
Ramblewood Middle School	Coral Springs	92–93
Ribault High School	Jacksonville	82–83
Rodney B. Cox Elementary School	Dade City	93–94
Rogers Middle School	Fort Lauderdale	92–93
Saint Patrick School	Miami Beach	87–88
St. David Catholic School	Davie	93–94
St. Gregory School	Plantation	87–88
St. Joseph Catholic School	Palm Bay	93–94
St. Petersburg High School	St. Petersburg	83–84
St. Rose of Lima School	Miami Shores	85–86, 93–94
St. Thomas Aquinas High School	Fort Lauderdale	84–85
Sandalwood Junior-Senior High School	Jacksonville	84–85
Sanibel Elementary School	Sanibel	91–92
Seabreeze High School	Daytona Beach	88–89
Sealey Elementary School	Tallahassee	89–90
South Plantation High School	Plantation	82–83
Southside Junior High School #211	Jacksonville	86–87
Southwood Junior High School	Miami	84–85
Spessard Holland Elementary School	Satellite Beach	89–90
Spruce Creek High School	Port Orange	92–93
Stanton College Preparatory School	Jacksonville	86–87
Terry Parker High School	Jacksonville	83–84
The Cushman School	Miami	91–92
The King's Academy	West Palm Beach	85–86
Thomas Jefferson Junior High School	Merritt Island	83–84
Thomas Jefferson Middle School	Miami	91–92
Westchester Elementary School	Coral Springs	91–92
Windy Ridge Elementary School	Orlando	93–94

SCHOOL	CITY	YEAR(S) RECOGNIZED

GEORGIA

School	City	Year(s) Recognized
A. L. Burruss Elementary School	Marietta	91—92
Benjamin E. Banneker High School	College Park	92—93
Benjamin Elijah Mays High School	Atlanta	86—87
Benteen Elementary School	Atlanta	89—90
Boynton Elementary School	Ringgold	89—90
Brandon Hall School	Dunwoody	84—85
Brookwood High School	Snellville	86—87
Burroughs-Molette Elementary School	Brunswick	85—86
Christ the King School	Atlanta	85—86
Cook Middle School	Adel	91—92
Conyers Middle School	Conyers	84—85
County Line Elementary School	Winder	93—94
Crabapple Middle School	Roswell	87—88
Dalton High School	Dalton	83—84
Dalton Junior High School	Dalton	86—87
Dolvin Elementary School	Alpharetta	89—90
Duluth High School	Duluth	90—91
Duluth Middle School	Duluth	85—86
East Cobb Middle School	Marietta	89—90
Eastvalley Elementary School	Marietta	93—94
Edwards Middle School	Conyers	87—88
Elm Street School	Newnan	93—94
Five Forks Middle School	Lawrenceville	87—88
Frederick Douglass High School	Atlanta	83—84
Garden Hills School	Atlanta	85—86
George L. Edwards Middle School	Conyers	93—94
Glynn Middle School	Brunswick	83—84
Graysville Elementary School	Graysville	91—92
Greater Atlanta Christian Schools, Inc.	Norcross	88—89
Hardaway High School	Columbus	84—85
Harlem Comprehensive High School	Harlem	88—89
Hebrew Academy of Atlanta, Inc.	Atlanta	85—86
Heritage High School	Conyers	88—89
Jonesboro Junior High School	Jonesboro	88—89
Knight Elementary School	Lilburn	87—88
Lakeside High School	Atlanta	84—85
Lee County Primary School	Leesburg	89—90
Lincoln County High School	Lincolnton	86—87
Luke Garrett Middle School	Austell	83—84
Marist School	Atlanta	86—87
McCleskey Middle School	Marietta	91—92
Mount de Sales Academy	Macon	90—91
Mt. Bethel Elementary School	Marietta	85—86
Mundy's Mill Middle School	Jonesboro	92—93
Murdock Elementary School	Marietta	87—88

SCHOOL	CITY	YEAR(S) RECOGNIZED

GEORGIA (*continued*)

SCHOOL	CITY	YEAR(S) RECOGNIZED
Myers Middle School	Savannah	92–93
Newton County High School	Covington	86–87
North Fulton High School	Atlanta	84–85
North Whitfield Middle School	Dalton	84–85
Otwell Middle School	Cumming	90–91
Parkview High School	Lilburn	84–85
Pinckneyville Middle School	Norcross	91–92
R. D. Head Elementary School	Lilburn	91–92
St. John Neumann Regional Catholic School	Lilburn	93–94
St. John the Evangelist Catholic School	Hapeville	93–94
St. Marys Elementary School	St. Marys	91–92
St. Simons Elementary School	St. Simons Island	89–90
St. Thomas More Catholic School	Decatur	87–88
Shiloh Middle School	Lithonia	86–87
Sope Creek Elementary School	Marietta	87–88
South Cobb High School	Austell	92–93
Southeast Bulloch High School	Brooklet	92–93
Southside Elementary School	Milledgeville	85–86
Staley Middle School	Americus	89–90
Stephens County High School	Toccoa	86–87
Swainsboro High School	Swainsboro	92–93
Tapp Middle School	Powder Springs	84–85
The Howard School	Atlanta	85–86
The Savannah Country Day School	Savannah	91–92
Thomson High School	Thomson	90–91
Trickum Middle School	Lilburn	90–91
Walton Comprehensive High School	Marietta	83–84
Warner Robins High School	Warner Robins	90–91
William Milton Davis Elementary School	Marietta	93–94
Yeshiva High School	Atlanta	84–85

HAWAII

SCHOOL	CITY	YEAR(S) RECOGNIZED
Aikahi Elementary School	Kailua	89–90
ASSETS School	Honolulu	91–92
Hanahauoli School	Honolulu	85–86
Iolani School	Honolulu	84–85
James B. Castle High School	Kaneohe	92–93
Kaala Elementary School	Wahiawa	87–88
Kahuku High and Intermediate Schools	Kahuku	88–89
Kailua High School	Kailua	88–89
Kalaheo High School	Kailua	90–91
Kapunahala Elementary School	Kaneohe	91–92
Leilehua High School	Wahiawa	92–93

SCHOOL	CITY	YEAR(S) RECOGNIZED
HAWAII *(continued)*		
Linapuni School	Honolulu	93 – 94
Manoa Elementary School	Honolulu	85 – 86
Mililani-uka Elementary School	Mililani	91 – 92
Moanalua High School	Honolulu	86 – 87
Nuuanu Elementary School	Honolulu	85 – 86
Pearl Ridge Elementary School	Aiea	93 – 94
Princess Miriam K. Likelike Elementary School	Honolulu	91 – 92
Punahou School	Honolulu	84 – 85
Seabury Hall School	Makawao	92 – 93
Waiahole Elementary School	Kaneohe	89 – 90
Waiakea High School	Hilo	88 – 89
Walhe' s School	Wailuku	93 – 94

IDAHO

SCHOOL	CITY	YEAR(S) RECOGNIZED
Frontier School	Boise	89 – 90
Jefferson Junior High School	Caldwell	84 – 85
Lincoln Elementary School	Caldwell	85 – 86
Lowell Elementary School	Boise	93 – 94
Morningside Elementary School	Twin Falls	93 – 94
Mullan Junior-Senior High School	Mullan	83 – 84
Pierce School	Pierce	85 – 86
Pocatello High School	Pocatello	88 – 89
Silver Hills Junior High School	Osburn	84 – 85
Weiser High School	Weiser	86 – 87
Westside Elementary School	Idaho Falls	87 – 88

ILLINOIS

SCHOOL	CITY	YEAR(S) RECOGNIZED
Academy of Our Lady	Chicago	84 – 85
Adlai E. Stevenson High School	Prairie View	86 – 87, 90 – 91
Adler Park School	Libertyville	91 – 92
Alan B. Shepard Junior High School	Deerfield	84 – 85
Amos Alonzo Stagg High School	Palos Hills	90 – 91
Arnett C. Lines School	Barrington	93 – 94
Arnold J. Tyler School	New Lenox	91 – 92
Avoco West Elementary School	Glenview	89 – 90
Barrington High School	Barrington	92 – 93
Bernard Zell Anshe Emet Day School	Chicago	87 – 88
Booth Tarkington School	Wheeling	93 – 94
Boylan Central Catholic High School	Rockford	86 – 87, 90 – 91
Brehm Preparatory School	Carbondale	92 – 93
Brother Rice High School	Chicago	84 – 85
Butterfield School	Libertyville	93 – 94
Carl Sandburg High School	Orland Park	84 – 85

SCHOOL	CITY	YEAR(S) RECOGNIZED

ILLINOIS *(continued)*

Carmel High School for Girls	Mundelein	84—85
Caroline Bentley School	New Lenox	91—92
Carrie Busey School	Champaign	89—90
Champaign Central High School	Champaign	88—89
Champaign Middle School at Columbia	Champaign	86—87
Cherokee School	Lake Forest	87—88
Community High School	West Chicago	92—93
Community High School North	Downers Grove	83—84
Crete-Monee Junior High School	Crete	88—89
Crete-Monee Middle School	Crete	93—94
Daniel Wright Middle School	Lake Forest	86—87
De La Salle Institute	Chicago	84—85
Deer Path Junior High School	Lake Forest	86—87, 90—91
Deer Path Middle School	Lake Forest	87—88
Deerfield High School	Deerfield	92—93
Dr. Howard Elementary School	Champaign	89—90
Edgewood Middle School	Highland Park	88—89
Elm Place Middle School	Highland Park	82—83
Everett School	Lake Forest	85—86
Fairview South School	Skokie	85—86
Fenwick High School	Oak Park	83—84
Frankfort Junior High School	Frankfort	93—94
Franklin Middle School	Wheaton	87—88
Garden Hills Elementary School	Champaign	85—86
Glenbrook North High School	Northbrook	83—84
Glenbrook South High School	Glenview	83—84
Grove Avenue School	Barrington	91—92
Hadley Junior High School	Glen Ellyn	85—86
Haines School	New Lenox	93—94
Hales Franciscan High School	Chicago	84—85
Hawthorn Intermediate School	Vernon Hills	87—88
Hawthorn Junior High School	Vernon Hills	87—88
Highland Upper Grade Center	Libertyville	90—91
Hoffman Estates High School	Hoffman Estates	84—85
Holy Angels School	Aurora	87—88
Holy Cross School	Deerfield	85—86
Homewood-Flossmoor High School	Flossmoor	82—83
Immanuel Lutheran School	Palatine	87—88
Indian Trail School	Highland Park	87—88
John Hersey High School	Arlington Heights	88—89
John W. Gates Elementary School	Aurora	85—86
Kenneth E. Neubert Elementary School	Algonquin	85—86
La Grange Highlands Elementary School	La Grange	85—86
Lake Bluff Junior High School	Lake Bluff	91—92
Lake Forest Country Day School	Lake Forest	93—94

SCHOOL	CITY	YEAR(S) RECOGNIZED

ILLINOIS (*continued*)

School	City	Year(s) Recognized
Laura B. Sprague School	Lincolnshire	85 – 86, 91 – 92
Leyden East Campus	Franklin	84 – 85
Leyden West Campus	North Lake	84 – 85
Libertyville Community High School	Libertyville	90 – 91
Lincoln Elementary School	Highland Park	87 – 88
Luther High School South	Chicago	83 – 84
Madonna High School	Chicago	90 – 91
Mahomet-Seymour High School	Mahomet	86 – 87
Maine Township High School East	Park Ridge	84 – 85
Maine Township High School South	Park Ridge	88 – 89
Maine Township High School West	Des Plaines	90 – 91
Marian Catholic High School	Chicago Heights	84 – 85
Marist High School	Chicago	86 – 87
Medinah Elementary School	Roselle	83 – 84
Mother McAuley Liberal Arts High School	Chicago	86 – 87, 90 – 91
Mt. Carmel High School	Chicago	83 – 84
Mundelein High School	Mundelein	92 – 93
New Trier Township High School	Winnetka	90 – 91
Niles North High School	Skokie	90 – 91
Niles West High School	Skokie	90 – 91
Nob Hill School	Country Club Hills	85 – 86
Northbrook Junior High School	Northbrook	91 – 92
Notre Dame High School	Chicago	84 – 85
O'Fallon Township High School	O'Fallon	86 – 87
Oak Terrace School	Highwood	87 – 88
Old Orchard Junior High School	Skokie	83 – 84
Oliver Wendell Holmes Junior High School	Wheeling	86 – 87
Palatine High School	Palatine	92 – 93
Prospect High School	Mount Prospect	92 – 93
Ravinia School	Highland Park	85 – 86
Regina Dominican High School	Wilmette	92 – 93
Rich South High School	Richton Park	83 – 84
Riverton Middle School	Riverton	87 – 88
Rockland School	Libertyville	89 – 90
Roosevelt School	River Forest	88 – 89
Saint Louise de Marillac High School	Northfield	86 – 87
Saint Matthias School	Chicago	85 – 86
Saint Stanislaus Bishop and Martyr School	Chicago	87 – 88
St. Damian School	Oak Forest	91 – 92
St. Isaac Jogues School	Hinsdale	89 – 90
St. Joan of Arc School	Lisle	85 – 86
St. Luke School	River Forest	91 – 92
St. Rita High School	Chicago	86 – 87
Schaumburg High School	Schaumburg	92 – 93

SCHOOL	CITY	YEAR(S) RECOGNIZED

ILLINOIS (*continued*)

Sheridan School	Lake Forest	85—86, 91—92
Sparta Primary Attendance Center	Sparta	89—90
Springman Junior High School	Glenview	84—85
The Avery Coonley School	Downers Grove	87—88
The School of Saint Mary	Lake Forest	89—90
Thomas Junior High School	Arlington Heights	83—84
Trinity Lutheran School	Roselle	91—92
University of Chicago Laboratory High School	Chicago	86—87
Washington School	Mundelein	91—92
Weber High School	Chicago	88—89
Westbrook School	Glenview	87—88
Wheeling High School	Wheeling	86—87
William Fremd High School	Palatine	86—87
Wilmette Junior High School	Wilmette	90—91
Wilmot Elementary School	Deerfield	87—88
Wilmot Junior High School	Deerfield	83—84
Winston Churchill School	Homewood	85—86
Wood View Elementary School	Bolingbrook	87—88
York Community High School	Elmhurst	82—83

INDIANA

Amy Beverland Elementary School	Indianapolis	93—94
Ben Davis High School	Indianapolis	83—84
Ben Davis Junior High School	Indianapolis	86—87
Boston Middle School	LaPorte	90—91
Brumfield Elementary School	Princeton	87—88, 91—92
Carmel High School	Carmel	82—83
Carmel Junior High School	Carmel	84—85
Cathedral High School	Indianapolis	88—89
Chesterton High School	Chesterton	84—85
Clay Junior High School	Clay	82—83
College Wood Elementary School	Carmel	85—86
Concordia Lutheran High School	Fort Wayne	84—85, 88—89
Culver Academy	Culver	83—84
East Elementary School	Pendleton	89—90
Eastbrook Elementary School	Indianapolis	89—90
Eastern Elementary School	Greentown	89—90
Eastwood Middle School	Indianapolis	84—85
Edward Eggleston Elementary School	South Bend	91—92
Fegely Middle School	Portage	84—85
Harold Handley Elementary School	LaPorte	91—92
Hebrew Academy of Indianapolis	Indianapolis	89—90, 93—94
Henry W. Eggers Middle School	Hammond	88—89

SCHOOL	CITY	YEAR(S) RECOGNIZED

INDIANA (*continued*)

SCHOOL	CITY	YEAR(S) RECOGNIZED
Holy Cross Lutheran School	Fort Wayne	85 – 86
Indian Creek Elementary School	Indianapolis	89 – 90
Indian Meadows Elementary School	Fort Wayne	87 – 88
Jefferson High School	Lafayette	84 – 85, 92 – 93
John F. Kennedy School	South Bend	85 – 86
John J. Young Middle School	Mishawaka	90 – 91
John Marshall High School	Indianapolis	84 – 85
Kesling Middle School	LaPorte	86 – 87, 92 – 93
Klondike Elementary School	W. Lafayette	91 – 92
LaSalle High School	South Bend	88 – 89
Lawrence Central High School	Indianapolis	84 – 85
Lawrence North High School	Indianapolis	83 – 84
Longfellow Elementary School	Muncie	85 – 86
Marian Heights Academy	Ferdinand	86 – 87
Mary Evelyn Castle Elementary School	Indianapolis	87 – 88
Muessel School	South Bend	87 – 88
North Central High School	Indianapolis	82 – 83
Perley Elementary School	South Bend	93 – 94
Roncalli High School	Indianapolis	92 – 93
St. Joseph's High School	South Bend	84 – 85
St. Lawrence School	Indianapolis	93 – 94
St. Mark Catholic School	Indianapolis	85 – 86
St. Paul Lutheran School	Fort Wayne	85 – 86
Skiles Test Elementary School	Indianapolis	85 – 86
Southport Elementary School	Southport	85 – 86
Southport Middle School	Indianapolis	88 – 89
Tecumseh-Harrison Elementary School	Vincennes	87 – 88
The Stanley Clark School	South Bend	85 – 86
The Summit Elementary Program	Fort Wayne	89 – 90
Thompkins Middle School	Evansville	86 – 87
Trinity School at Greenlawn	South Bend	88 – 89, 92 – 93
Valparaiso High School	Valparaiso	82 – 83
Warren Central High School	Indianapolis	82 – 83
Westchester Middle School	Chesterton	82 – 83
Westlane Middle School	Indianapolis	83 – 84
Winchester Village Elementary School	Indianapolis	87 – 88

IOWA

SCHOOL	CITY	YEAR(S) RECOGNIZED
Alden Community Elementary School	Alden	93 – 94
Ames Junior High School Central-Welch Campuses	Ames	82 – 83
Ames Senior High School	Ames	82 – 83
CAL Elementary School	Latimer	91 – 92
CAL High School	Latimer	86 – 87

SCHOOL	CITY	YEAR(S) RECOGNIZED

IOWA (*continued*)

SCHOOL	CITY	YEAR(S) RECOGNIZED
Central Catholic Elementary School	Mason City	87 – 88
Clive Elementary School	Des Moines	87 – 88
Cody Elementary School	Pleasant Valley	85 – 86
Erskine Elementary School	Cedar Rapids	89 – 90
Franklin Junior High School	Cedar Rapids	83 – 84
Franklin Pierce Elementary School	Cedar Rapids	87 – 88
Fredericksburg Community School	Fredericksburg	88 – 89
Garfield Elementary School	Davenport	93 – 94
George Washington High School	Cedar Rapids	83 – 84, 90 – 91
Grant Wood Elementary School	Cedar Rapids	91 – 92
Greenwood Elementary School	Des Moines	85 – 86
Grinnell Community Middle School	Grinnell	90 – 91
Harding Middle School	Cedar Rapids	90 – 91
Indian Hills Junior High School	Des Moines	82 – 83
Keokuk Middle School	Keokuk	82 – 83
Kirn Junior High School	Council Bluffs	83 – 84
Linn-Mar High School	Marion	84 – 85
Linn-Mar Junior High School	Marion	83 – 84
Metro High School	Cedar Rapids	84 – 85, 92 – 93
Northwest Junior High School	Coralville	84 – 85
Pella Christian Grade School	Pella	93 – 94
Pella Christian High School	Pella	84 – 85
Pleasant Valley Community High School	Pleasant Valley	83 – 84
Pleasant View Elementary School	Pleasant Valley	87 – 88
Regina Elementary School	Iowa City	91 – 92
St. Katherine's-St. Mark's School	Bettendorf	85 – 86
South East Junior High School	Iowa City	82 – 83
South Winnishiek Senior High School	Calmar	86 – 87
Thomas Jefferson Senior High School	Cedar Rapids	84 – 85
Trinity Lutheran School	Davenport	89 – 90
Valley High School	West Des Moines	83 – 84
Woodrow Wilson Junior High School	Council Bluffs	88 – 89

KANSAS

SCHOOL	CITY	YEAR(S) RECOGNIZED
Belinder Elementary School	Shawnee Mission	93 – 94
Blue Valley High School	Stilwell	88 – 89
Blue Valley Middle School	Overland Park	86 – 87
Blue Valley North High School	Overland Park	90 – 91
Brookridge Elementary School	Shawnee Mission	89 – 90
Cherokee Elementary School	Shawnee Mission	93 – 94
Christa McAuliffe Elementary School	Lenexa	93 – 94
Countryside Elementary School	Olathe	91 – 92
Earhart Environmental Magnet Elementary School	Wichita	89 – 90

SCHOOL	CITY	YEAR(S) RECOGNIZED
KANSAS (*continued*)		
Hocker Grove Middle School	Shawnee Mission	89 – 90
Horace Mann Alternative Middle School	Wichita	83 – 84
Indian Creek Elementary School	Olathe	91 – 92
Leawood Elementary School	Leawood	91 – 92
Leawood Middle School	Leawood	88 – 89
Meadowbrook Junior High School	Shawnee Mission	84 – 85
Morse Elementary School	Olathe	87 – 88
Northview Elementary School	Manhattan	87 – 88
Oak Hill Elementary School	Overland Park	91 – 92
Olathe South High School	Olathe	90 – 91
Oregon Trail Junior High School	Olathe	83 – 84, 92 – 93
Overland Trail Elementary School	Overland Park	93 – 94
Oxford Middle School	Overland Park	91 – 92
Ridgeview Elementary School	Olathe	93 – 94
Robinson Middle School	Topeka	84 – 85
Roosevelt-Lincoln Junior High School	Salina	83 – 84
Roseland Elementary School	Shawnee Mission	93 – 94
St. Mary Queen of the Universe School	Salina	85 – 86
Salina High School	Salina	84 – 85
Santa Fe Trail Junior High School	Olathe	84 – 85
Seaman High School	Topeka	84 – 85
Shawnee Mission South High School	Shawnee Mission	83 – 84
Shawnee Mission West High School	Shawnee Mission	83 – 84
Sumner Academy of Arts and Science	Kansas City	84 – 85
Tomahawk Elementary School	Olathe	85 – 86, 93 – 94
Topeka High School	Topeka	88 – 89
Topeka West High School	Topeka	83 – 84
Valley Park Elementary School	Overland Park	89 – 90
Village Elementary School	Emporia	85 – 86

KENTUCKY

Arnett Elementary School	Erlanger	85 – 86
Assumption High School	Louisville	88 – 89, 92 – 93
Ballard High School	Louisville	86 – 87
Belfry High School	Belfry	92 – 93
Blessed Sacrament School	Fort Mitchell	93 – 94
Centerfield Elementary School	Crestwood	89 – 90
Clark Elementary School	Paducah	85 – 86
Crestwood Elementary School	Crestwood	93 – 94
Crittenden County Elementary School	Marion	85 – 86
Danville High School	Danville	90 – 91
duPont Manual-Magnet High School	Louisville	90 – 91
Elizabethtown High School	Elizabethtown	92 – 93
Fort Campbell High School	Fort Campbell	92 – 93
Goshen Elementary School	Goshen	85 – 86

SCHOOL	CITY	YEAR(S) RECOGNIZED

KENTUCKY (*continued*)

SCHOOL	CITY	YEAR(S) RECOGNIZED
Helmwood Heights Elementary School	Elizabethtown	85–86
Highlands High School	Fort Thomas	84–85
Holmes High School	Covington	84–85
Jackson Elementary School	Fort Campbell	87–88
Liberty Elementary School	Goshen	87–88
Louisville Male High School	Louisville	88–89
Mahaffey Middle School	Fort Campbell	90–91
Marshall Elementary School	Fort Campbell	91–92
Maryhurst School	Louisville	86–87
Murray High School	Murray	83–84
Oldham County High School	Buckner	86–87
Oldham County Middle School	Buckner	84–85
Robert D. Johnson Elementary School	Fort Thomas	91–92
Saint Xavier High School	Louisville	83–84, 88–89, 92–93
Southern Elementary School	Lexington	89–90
Stanton Elementary School	Stanton	93–94
Thomas Jefferson Middle School	Louisville	84–85
Trinity High School	Louisville	90–91
Virginia Wheeler Elementary School	Louisville	91–92
Wassom Middle School	Fort Campbell	88–89
Williamsburg High School	Williamsburg	92–93
Woodlawn Elementary School	Danville	89–90

LOUISIANA

SCHOOL	CITY	YEAR(S) RECOGNIZED
Alfred Bonnabel High School	Metairie	86–87
Alice M. Harte Elementary School	New Orleans	87–88
Archbishop Chapelle High School	Metairie	86–87, 90–91
Archbishop Rummel High School	Metairie	88–89
Baton Rouge High School	Baton Rouge	82–83
Benjamin Franklin Senior High School	New Orleans	88–89
Bissonet Plaza Elementary School	Metairie	85–86
Broadmoor Elementary School	Lafayette	89–90
Broadmoor Middle Laboratory School	Shreveport	86–87
Brother Martin High School	New Orleans	86–87
Caddo Middle Magnet School	Shreveport	84–85
Captain Shreve High School	Shreveport	82–83
Catholic High School	Baton Rouge	88–89, 92–93
Christ the King School	Bossier	93–94
Cope Middle School	Bossier	93–94
Edgar Martin Middle School	Lafayette	86–87
Edward Haynes School	New Orleans	87–88
Episcopal High School	Baton Rouge	86–87, 90–91
Episcopal School of Acadiana	Cade	86–87
Gentilly Terrace Creative Arts Magnet School	New Orleans	91–92
Grace King High School	Metairie	82–83

SCHOOL	CITY	YEAR(S) RECOGNIZED

LOUISIANA (*continued*)

Isidore Newman Lower School	New Orleans	87 – 88
Isidore Newman School	New Orleans	84 – 85
Jean Gordon Elementary School	New Orleans	89 – 90
Jesuit High School-New Orleans	New Orleans	86 – 87
Lafayette Elementary School	Lafayette	83 – 84
Lakewood Junior High School	Luling	82 – 83
Leesville High School	Leesville	82 – 83
Little Oak Elementary School	Slidell	89 – 90
Lockport Junior High School	Lockport	84 – 85
Lusher Alternative Elementary School	New Orleans	87 – 88
M. R. Weaver Elementary School	Natchitoches	85 – 86
Mandeville Middle School	Mandeville	89 – 90
Marie B. Riviere Elementary School	Metairie	87 – 88
McDonogh 35 Senior High School	New Orleans	92 – 93
McKinley Middle Magnet School	Baton Rouge	83 – 84
McMain Magnet Secondary School	New Orleans	90 – 91
Metairie Park Country Day School	Metairie	86 – 87
Mount Carmel Academy	New Orleans	92 – 93
New Iberia Senior High School	New Iberia	88 – 89
Norbert Rillieux Elementary School	Waggaman	85 – 86
Northeast Elementary School	Pride	93 – 94
Our Lady of Divine Providence School	Metairie	93 – 94
Our Lady of Fatima School	Lafayette	85 – 86, 89 – 90
Parkway High School	Bossier City	84 – 85
Raceland Junior High School	Raceland	82 – 83
Romeville Elementary School	Convent	86 – 87
Ruston High School	Ruston	83 – 84
Saint Joseph's Academy	Baton Rouge	90 – 91
Saint Michael Catholic School	Crowley	85 – 86
Saint Rosalie School	Harvey	91 – 92
St. Anthony of Padua School	New Orleans	87 – 88
St. Bernard Elementary School	Breaux Bridge	87 – 88
St. Christopher School	Metairie	93 – 94
St. Francis Xavier Cabrini School	New Orleans	93 – 94
St. Leo the Great Elementary School	New Orleans	89 – 90
St. Martin's Episcopal School	Metairie	85 – 86
St. Mary's Dominican High School	New Orleans	88 – 89
St. Thomas More Catholic High School	Lafayette	86 – 87, 92 – 93
Scott Middle School	Scott	84 – 85
Trinity Episcopal School	New Orleans	87 – 88
Upper Little Caillou School	Chauvin	85 – 86
Ursuline Academy	New Orleans	90 – 91
Woodlake Elementary School	Mandeville	93 – 94
Woodvale Elementary School	Lafayette	87 – 88
Xavier University Preparatory School	New Orleans	86 – 87, 90 – 91
Youree Drive Middle School	Shreveport	83 – 84

SCHOOL	CITY	YEAR(S) RECOGNIZED

MAINE

SCHOOL	CITY	YEAR(S) RECOGNIZED
Action Elementary School	East Lebanon	93−94
Auburn Middle School	Auburn	83−84
Biddeford Middle School	Biddeford	91−92
Bowdoin Central School	Bowdoin	91−92
Camden-Rockport High School	Camden	84−85
Deering High School	Portland	82−83
Gray-New Gloucester Junior High School	Gray	84−85
Greely High School	Cumberland	86−87
Greely Junior High School	Cumberland Center	84−85
Howard C. Reiche Community School	Portland	91−92
Jordan Small School	Raymond	87−88
Junior High School of the Kennebunks	Kennebunk	83−84
Katahdin High School	Sherman Station	82−83
Kennebunk High School	Kennebunk	82−83, 90−91
King Middle School	Portland	82−83
Lake Region Junior High School	Bridgton	89−90
Miller School	Waldoboro	93−94
Mount Desert Island High School	Northeast Harbor	83−84
Mt. Ararat School	Topsham	82−83
Old Orchard Beach High School	Old Orchard Beach	90−91
Park Street School	Kennebunk	85−86
Portland High School	Portland	83−84
Presque Isle High School	Presque Isle	90−91
Skowhegan Area High School	Skowhegan	86−87
Yarmouth Junior-Senior High School	Yarmouth	86−87

MARYLAND

SCHOOL	CITY	YEAR(S) RECOGNIZED
Archbishop Keough High School	Baltimore	86−87
Archbishop Spalding High School	Severn	92−93
Arlington Baptist High School	Baltimore	84−85
Atholton High School	Columbia	92−93
Baltimore School for the Arts	Baltimore	90−91
Bells Mill Elementary School	Potomac	87−88
Burtonville Elementary School	Burtonville	93−94
Calvert Hall College High School	Towson	84−85, 88−89
Candlewood Elementary School	Rockville	91−92
Centennial High School	Ellicott City	84−85
Chevy Chase Elementary School	Chevy Chase	93−94
Clarksville Elementary School	Clarksville	87−88
College Gardens Elementary School	Rockville	85−86
Columbia Park Elementary School	Landover	87−88
Connelly School of the Holy Child	Potomac	88−89
DeMatha Catholic High School	Hyattsville	83−84, 90−91
Diamond Elementary School	Gaithersburg	89−90

SCHOOL	CITY	YEAR(S) RECOGNIZED

MARYLAND (*continued*)

SCHOOL	CITY	YEAR(S) RECOGNIZED
Eleanor Roosevelt High School	Greenbelt	90−91
Elizabeth Seton High School	Bladensburg	84−85
Frances R. Fuchs Special Center	Beltsville	91−92
Frederick High School	Frederick	92−93
Gaithersburg Elementary School	Gaithersburg	89−90
Glenelg High School	Glenelg	84−85
Good Counsel High School	Wheaton	92−93
Governor Thomas Johnson High School	Frederick	90−91
Greenbelt Center Elementary School	Greenbelt	91−92
Havre de Grace High School	Havre de Grace	90−91
Heather Hills Elementary School	Bowie	89−90
Hebrew Academy of Greater Washington	Silver Spring	87−88, 92−93
Ivymount School	Rockville	89−90, 93−94
Kenmoor Middle School TAG Magnet Center	Landover	88−89
Kettering Middle School	Upper Marlboro	92−93
La Reine High School	Suitland	84−85
Lake Seneca Elementary School	Germantown	91−92
Linganore High School	Frederick	92−93
Loyola High School of Baltimore, Inc.	Towson	86−87
Martin Luther King, Jr. Middle School	Beltsville	92−93
Mercy High School	Baltimore	84−85
Middletown Elementary School	Middletown	89−90
Middletown High School	Middletown	86−87
Milton M. Somers Middle School	La Plata	84−85
Mount Saint Joseph High School	Baltimore	88−89
Mt. Harmony Elementary School	Owings	85−86
North Chevy Chase Elementary School	Chevy Chase	89−90
Northfield Elementary School	Ellicott City	85−86
Notre Dame Preparatory School	Towson	84−85
Parkland Junior High School	Rockville	84−85
Perryville Middle School	Perryville	90−91
Poolesville Junior-Senior High School	Poolesville	86−87
Redland Middle School	Rockville	84−85, 88−89, 92−93
Richard Montgomery High School	Rockville	90−91
Riderwood Elementary School	Towson	93−94
Saint Jane de Chantal School	Bethesda	87−88
Saint Rita School	Baltimore	85−86
St. Andrew Apostle School	Silver Spring	89−90
St. Catherine Laboure	Wheaton	93−94
St. Elizabeth School	Rockville	85−86
Stone Ridge-School of the Sacred Heart	Bethesda	86−87, 92−93
Suitland High School	Forestville	88−89
TRI-Services Center School	Chevy Chase	87−88
The Bryn Mawr School	Baltimore	83−84
The Gilman School	Baltimore	83−84
The Park School of Baltimore	Brooklandville	83−84

SCHOOL	CITY	YEAR(S) RECOGNIZED

MARYLAND (*continued*)

School	City	Year(s)
Thomas S. Wootton High School	Rockville	84–85
Trinity School	Ellicott City	89–90
Washington Episcopal School	Bethesda	93–94
Westland Intermediate School	Bethesda	90–91
Whetstone Elementary School	Gaithersburg	87–88
White Oak Intermediate School	Silver Spring	88–89
Wilde Lake Middle School	Columbia	84–85
William H. Farquhar Middle School	Olney	86–87
Winston Churchill High School	Potomac	90–91
Yellow Springs Elementary School	Frederick	93–94

MASSACHUSETTS

School	City	Year(s)
Abraham Edwards Elementary School	Beverly	89–90
Acton-Boxborough Regional High School	Acton	83–84
Alice M. Barrows School	Reading	87–88
Broad Meadows Middle School	Quincy	90–91
Cathedral High School	Springfield	83–84
Charles Sumner Pierce Middle School	Milton	84–85
Claypit Hill School	Wayland	85–86
Coyle and Cassidy High School	Taunton	90–91
Dartmouth High School	North Dartmouth	84–85
Deerfield Academy	Deerfield	83–84
Fay School	Southborough	91–92
Glenbrook Middle School	Longmeadow	84–85
Groton School	Groton	83–84
Hawlemont Regional School	Charlemont	85–86
Henry C. Sanborn Elementary School	Andover	91–92
Holliston High School	Holliston	88–89
Holyoke Street School	Holyoke	83–84
James P. Timilty Middle School	Roxbury	88–89
John Glenn Middle School	Bedford	89–90
Jonas Clarke Middle School	Lexington	92–93
Josiah Quincy School	Boston	85–86
Lighthouse School	Chelmsford	84–85, 91–92
Mansfield High School	Mansfield	90–91
Marshall Simonds Middle School	Burlington	90–91
Martha's Vineyard Regional High School	Oak Bluffs	88–89
Milton High School	Milton	86–87
Monument Mountain Regional High School	Great Barrington	92–93
Nessacus Middle School	Dalton	84–85
New Bedford High School	New Bedford	83–84
Northfield Mount Hermon School	Northfield	86–87
Oliver Ames High School	North Easton	84–85
Pine Grove School	Rowley	87–88
Raymond J. Grey Junior High School	Acton	88–89

SCHOOL	CITY	YEAR(S) RECOGNIZED

MASSACHUSETTS (*continued*)

Rockland Junior High School	Rockland	83 – 84
Snug Harbor Community School	Quincy	93 – 94
South Elementary School	Plymouth	87 – 88
Steward School	Topsfield	87 – 88
Summer Street School	Lynnfield	85 – 86
Sutton Elementary School	Sutton	87 – 88
Thayer Academy	Braintree	84 – 85
The Advent School	Boston	91 – 92
The May Institute, Inc.	Chatham	87 – 88
The Meadowbrook School	Weston	87 – 88
The Williston Northampton School	Easthampton	90 – 91
Tower School	Marblehead	89 – 90
Tucker School	Milton	85 – 86
W. S. Parker Middle School	Reading	84 – 85
Wayland High School	Wayland	86 – 87
Wilson Junior High School	Natick	84 – 85

MICHIGAN

Abbott Middle School	Orchard Lake	84 – 85
Andrews Academy	Berrien Springs	84 – 85
Ann Arbor Huron High School	Ann Arbor	83 – 84
Ann J. Kellogg School	Battle Creek	85 – 86
Berkshire Middle School	Birmingham	84 – 85
Bingham Farms School	Birmingham	87 – 88
Bishop Foley High School	Madison Heights	83 – 84
Bloomfield Hills Andover High School	Bloomfield Hills	83 – 84
Bloomfield Hills Lahser High School	Bloomfield Hills	82 – 83
Bloomfield Hills Middle School	Bloomfield Hills	88 – 89
Bridgman High School	Bridgman	83 – 84
Brighton High School	Brighton	86 – 87
Brooks Middle School	Detroit	84 – 85
Caledonia Elementary School	Caledonia	87 – 88
Carl H. Lindbom Elementary School	Brighton	91 – 92
Cass Technical High School	Detroit	83 – 84, 90 – 91
Chesterfield Elementary School	Mt. Clemens	89 – 90
Covington Middle School	Birmingham	92 – 93
Cranbrook Kingswood School	Bloomfield Hills	86 – 87
Creative Arts Academy	Benton Harbor	87 – 88
De La Salle Collegiate High School	Warren	92 – 93
Dickinson Area Catholic School	Iron Mountain	85 – 86
Doherty Elementary School	West Bloomfield	85 – 86
East Grand Rapids High School	Grand Rapids	84 – 85
East Grand Rapids Middle School	East Grand Rapids	92 – 93
East Hills Middle School	Bloomfield Hills	90 – 91

SCHOOL	CITY	YEAR(S) RECOGNIZED

MICHIGAN (*continued*)

SCHOOL	CITY	YEAR(S) RECOGNIZED
Eastover Elementary School	Bloomfield Hills	91−92
Edwardsburg High School	Edwardsburg	92−93
Four Towns Elementary School	Waterford	93−94
Fox Elementary School	Macomb	93−94
Garber High School	Essexville	86−87
Gaylord High School	Gaylord	83−84
Gaylord Middle School	Gaylord	84−85
George P. Way Elementary School	Bloomfield Hills	89−90
Golightly Educational Center of Liberal Arts and Sciences	Detroit	93−94
Grand Rapids Christian School	Grand Rapids	83−84
Green Elementary School	West Bloomfield	87−88
Grosse Pointe North High School	Grosse Pointe Woods	84−85
Grosse Pointe South High School	Grosse Pointe	82−83
Harlan Elementary School	Bloomfield Hills	91−92
Hartland High School	Hartland	92−93
Hawkins Elementary School	Brighton	89−90
Hickory Grove Elementary School	Bloomfield Hills	87−88
Highmeadow Common Campus	Farmington Hills	93−94
Holland Christian Middle School	Holland	85−86
Holt High School	Holt	92−93
Hornung Elementary School	Brighton	87−88
Interlochen Arts Academy	Interlochen	83−84
John Page Middle School	Madison Heights	83−84
Kalamazoo Christian High School	Kalamazoo	84−85
Lakewood Elementary School	Milford	87−88
Lamphere High School	Madison Heights	86−87
L'Anse Creuse Middle School Central	Harrison Township	93−94
Lansing Catholic Central High School	Lansing	86−87
Larson Middle School	Troy	86−87
Lawton Community High School	Lawton	86−87
Longstreet Elementary School	Saginaw	85−86
Lutheran High School North	Mount Clemens	86−87
Lutheran High School West	Detroit	86−87
Maltby Middle School	Brighton	88−89
McCord Renaissance Center	Benton Harbor	92−93
Meadow Lake Elementary School	Birmingham	89−90
Mercy High School	Farmington Hills	83−84
Monteith Elementary School	Grosse Pointe Woods	89−90
Newaygo High School	Newaygo	90−91
North Christian School	Kalamazoo	87−88
North Farmington High School	Farmington Hills	92−93
Northview High School	Grand Rapids	83−84
Novi High School	Novi	86−87
Oak Ridge Elementary School	Royal Oak	89−90

SCHOOL	CITY	YEAR(S) RECOGNIZED

MICHIGAN (*continued*)

Oakley Park Elementary School	Walled Lake	87 – 88
Okemos High School	Okemos	83 – 84
Orchard Hills Elementary School	Novi	85 – 86
Orchard Lake Middle School	West Bloomfield	90 – 91
Parcells Middle School	Grosse Pointe Woods	86 – 87
Parkwood-Upjohn School	Kalamazoo	85 – 86
Petoskey Middle School	Petoskey	86 – 87
Pinckney Middle School	Pinckney	90 – 91
Quarton Elementary School	Birmingham	85 – 86
Rochester Adams High School	Rochester Hills	88 – 89, 92 – 93
Rockford Middle School	Rockford	92 – 93
Roscommon High School	Roscommon	82 – 83
St. Clare of Montefalco Catholic School	Grosse Pointe Park	93 – 94
St. Francis Elementary School	Traverse City	87 – 88
St. Joan of Arc School	St. Clair Shores	93 – 94
St. John Lutheran School	Rochester	85 – 86
St. Lorenz Lutheran School	Frankenmuth	85 – 86
St. Mary Cathedral School	Gaylord	85 – 86
Sashabaw Junior High School	Clarkston	88 – 89
Scotch Elementary School	West Bloomfield	89 – 90
Seaholm High School	Birmingham	84 – 85
Shay Elementary School	Harbor Springs	85 – 86
Slauson Intermediate School	Ann Arbor	83 – 84
Southfield Christian School	Southfield	90 – 91
Southfield Senior High School	Southfield	83 – 84, 88 – 89
Southfield-Lathrup Senior High School	Lathrup Village	90 – 91
Southwest Elementary School	Howell	91 – 92
Sturgis Public High School	Sturgis	82 – 83
Sunset Lake Elementary School	Vicksburg	87 – 88
Sylvester Elementary School	Berrien Springs	85 – 86
The Grosse Pointe Academy	Grosse Pointe Farms	87 – 88, 91 – 92
Traverse City Area Junior High School	Traverse City	83 – 84, 90 – 91
Troy Athens High School	Troy	92 – 93
Walter R. Bemis Elementary School	Troy	87 – 88
Waukazoo Elementary School	Holland	93 – 94
West Bloomfield High School	West Bloomfield	86 – 87, 92 – 93
West Hills Middle School	West Bloomfield	86 – 87
West Ottawa Middle School	Holland	82 – 83

MINNESOTA

Apple Valley High School	Apple Valley	90 – 91
Aquila Primary Center	St. Louis Park	89 – 90
Blake Lower School	Wayzata	93 – 94
Breck School	Minneapolis	87 – 88, 92 – 93

SCHOOL	CITY	YEAR(S) RECOGNIZED

MINNESOTA (*continued*)

SCHOOL	CITY	YEAR(S) RECOGNIZED
Cambridge Middle School	Cambridge	84−85
Cedar Island Elementary School	Maple Grove	89−90
Cedar Manor Intermediate Center	St. Louis	93−94
Centennial Senior High School	Circle Pines	86−87
Clara Barton Open School	Minneapolis	87−88
Clear Springs Elementary School	Minnetonka	91−92
Creek Valley Elementary School	Edina	93−94
Dassel Elementary School	Dassel	89−90
Dassel-Cokato Senior High School	Cokato	90−91
Deephaven Elementary School	Wayzata	91−92
Edina High School	Edina	83−84
Fridley Middle School	Fridley	88−89
Greenvale Park Elementary School	Northfield	93−94
Groves Learning Center	St. Louis Park	83−84, 91−92
H. O. Sonnesyn Elementary School	New Hope	89−90, 93−94
Hastings Middle School	Hastings	84−85, 88−89, 92−93
Hayes Elementary School	Fridley	89−90
Highland Elementary School	Apple Valley	91−92
Holy Family School	St. Louis Park	85−86
Hopkins High School	Minnetonka	82−83
Hopkins North Junior High School	Minnetonka	83−84
Hopkins West Junior High School	Minnetonka	83−84
Hosterman Middle School	New Hope	91−92
Hutchinson High School	Hutchinson	92−93
Irondale High School	New Brighton	92−93
John Adams Junior High School	Rochester	82−83
John F. Kennedy Senior High School	Bloomington	84−85
Mankato West High School	Mankato	92−93
Minnetonka High School	Minnetonka	88−89
Mounds Park Academy-Lower School	St. Paul	91−92
New Hope Elementary School	New Hope	87−88
Oak Grove Intermediate School	Bloomington	93−94
Oak Grove Junior High School	Bloomington	86−87
Oak Park Elementary School	Stillwater	89−90
Oak-Land Junior High School	Lake Elmo	83−84
Peter Hobart Primary Center	St. Louis Park	87−88
Pike Lake Elementary School	New Brighton	85−86
Poplar Bridge Elementary School	Bloomington	85−86
Regina High School	Minneapolis	84−85
Richfield Senior High School	Richfield	83−84
Rosemount High School	Rosemount	84−85
Saint Louis Park High School	St. Louis Park	86−87
St. Louis Park Junior High School	St. Louis Park	88−89
South St. Paul High School	South St. Paul	84−85
South View Junior High School	Edina	86−87

SCHOOL	CITY	YEAR(S) RECOGNIZED
MINNESOTA (*continued*)		
Stillwater Junior High School	Stillwater	83−84
Stillwater Senior High School	Stillwater	84−85
Stonebridge Elementary School	Stillwater	87−88
Susan Lindgren Intermediate Center	St. Louis Park	91−92
Technology Learning Campus	Robbinsdale	87−88
The Blake Lower School	Hopkins	89−90
The Blake School	Minneapolis	92−93
Valley Middle School	Apple Valley	84−85, 90−91
Valley View Junior High School	Edina	86−87
Wadena Elementary School	Wadena	87−88
Wayzata East Junior High School	Plymouth	88−89
Wayzata Senior High School	Plymouth	90−91
Wayzata West Junior High School	Wayzata	88−89

MISSISSIPPI

SCHOOL	CITY	YEAR(S) RECOGNIZED
Brookhaven High School	Brookhaven	83−84
Carver Middle School	Meridian	88−89
Clinton High School	Clinton	82−83
D. T. Cox Elementary School	Pontotoc	89−90
Hall's Ferry Road Elementary School	Vicksburg	85−86
Kate Griffin Junior High School	Meridian	86−87
Marion Park Elementary School	Meridian	85−86
McComb High School	McComb	82−83
Meridian Senior High School	Meridian	84−85
Northside Elementary School	Pearl	85−86
Oak Grove School	Hattiesburg	86−87, 92−93
Pearl High School	Pearl	90−91
Pontotoc Junior High School	Pontotoc	92−93
Sudduth Elementary School	Starkville	93−94
Thomas Street Elementary School	Tupelo	89−90
Tupelo High School	Tupelo	83−84
Van Winkle Elementary School	Jackson	87−88
Vicksburg High School	Vicksburg	88−89

MISSOURI

SCHOOL	CITY	YEAR(S) RECOGNIZED
Ballwin Elementary School	Ballwin	93−94
Barretts School	Manchester	89−90
Bellerive Elementary School	Creve Coeur	91−92
Blue Springs High School	Blue Springs	82−83
Blue Springs Junior High School	Blue Springs	86−87
Brentwood Middle School	Brentwood	83−84, 88−89
Bryan Elementary School	Nevada	93−04
Camdenton Junior High School	Camdenton	88−89

SCHOOL	CITY	YEAR(S) RECOGNIZED

MISSOURI (*continued*)

Cardinal Ritter College Prep High School	St. Louis	83−84
Central Institute for the Deaf	St. Louis	85−86
Clayton High School	Clayton	84−85
Cler-Mont Community School	Independence	93−94
Cor Jesu Academy	St. Louis	90−91
Cross Keys Middle School	Florissant	88−89
David H. Hickman High School	Columbia	84−85
De Smet Jesuit High School	St. Louis	84−85
E. E. Swinney Elementary School	Kansas City	89−90
Fairview Elementary School	Columbia	85−86
Farmington High School	Farmington	92−93
Flynn Park School	University City	87−88
Genesis School	Kansas City	90−91
Green Trails Elementary School	Chesterfield	87−88
H. F. Epstein Hebrew Academy	St. Louis	85−86
Hanna Woods Elementary School	Ballwin	87−88
Highcroft Ridge School	Chesterfield	85−86
Holman Middle School	St. Ann	84−85
Horton Watkins High School	St. Louis	82−83
Immanuel Lutheran School	St. Charles	89−90
J. A. Rogers Academy of Liberal Arts and Sciences	Kansas City	92−93
Jackson Park Elementary School	University City	85−86
James Lewis Elementary School	Blue Springs	91−92
Jefferson Junior High School	Columbia	92−93
Jennings Junior High School	Jennings	84−85
John Ridgeway Elementary School	Columbia	85−86
Kikapoo High School	Springfield	82−83
Knob Noster Elementary School	Knob Noster	91−92
Ladue Junior High School	St. Louis	83−84
Lewis Middle School	Excelsior Springs	83−84
Lutheran High School North	St. Louis	83−84
Lutheran High School South	St. Louis	92−93
Mason Ridge School	Creve Coeur	85−86
McCluer North High School	Florissant	83−84
Meramec Elementary School	Clayton	85−86
Midway Heights Elementary School	Columbia	91−92
Missouri Military Academy	Mexico	84−85
Monett Elementary School	Monett	85−86
Nerinx Hall High School	Webster Groves	90−91
New Franklin Elementary School	New Franklin	89−90
Notre Dame de Sion	Kansas City	84−85
Oakland Junior High School	Columbia	88−89
Old Bonhomme Elementary School	Olivette	91−92
Palmer Junior High School	Independence	86−87

SCHOOL	CITY	YEAR(S) RECOGNIZED

MISSOURI *(continued)*

SCHOOL	CITY	YEAR(S) RECOGNIZED
Parkway Central High School	Chesterfield	86−87
Parkway Central Junior High School	Chesterfield	88−89
Parkway East Junior High School	Creve Coeur	86−87
Parkway North High School	Creve Coeur	84−85
Parkway South High School	Manchester	86−87
Parkway West Senior High School	Ballwin	82−83
Pattonville Heights Middle School	Maryland Heights	83−84
Pattonville High School	Maryland Heights	92−93
Pershing School	University City	93−94
Pond Elementary School	Grover	93−94
Ralph M. Captain Elementary School	Clayton	89−90
River Bend Elementary School	Chesterfield	91−92
Robinwood Elementary School	Florissant	89−90
Rock Bridge Senior High School	Columbia	86−87
Rockwood Eureka Senior High School	Eureka	92−93
Rolla Middle School	Rolla	92−93
Rolla Senior High School	Rolla	92−93
Russell Elementary School	Hazelwood	93−94
St. Joseph's Academy	St. Louis	92−93
St. Monica School	Creve Coeur	85−86
St. Theresa's Academy	Kansas City	83−84
Spoede School	St. Louis	87−88
The Churchill School	St. Louis	89−90
Thomas B. Chinn School	Kansas City	85−86
Thorpe J. Gordon Elementary School	Jefferson City	93−94
Ursuline Academy	St. Louis	88−89
Villa Duchesne School	St. Louis	90−91
Washington Middle School	Maryville	90−91
Westminster Christian Academy	St. Louis	90−91
Wilkinson Early Childhood Center	St. Louis	93−94
Williams Southern Elementary School	Independence	93−94
William Volker Applied Learning	Kansas	93−94
Wydown Junior High School	Warson Woods	84−85
Wydown Middle School	Clayton	90−91

MONTANA

SCHOOL	CITY	YEAR(S) RECOGNIZED
Bozeman High School	Bozeman	88−89, 92−93
Chief Joseph Middle School	Bozeman	93−94
C. M. Russell Elementary School	Missoula	85−86
Garfield Elementary School	Billings	87−88
Geyser Public School	Geyser	86−87
Havre Middle School	Havre	91−92
Ponderosa Elementary School	Billings	89−90

SCHOOL	CITY	YEAR(S) RECOGNIZED

MONTANA (*continued*)

Sussex School	Missoula	87–88
Washington Middle School	Glendive	86–87
Will James Junior High School	Billings	84–85

NEBRASKA

Arbor Heights Junior High School	Omaha	83–84
Beatrice Senior High School	Beatrice	82–83
Bellevue East High School	Bellevue	84–85
Blair Junior-Senior High School	Blair	88–89
Boys Town High School	Boys Town	88–89
Christ the King Catholic School	Omaha	89–90
Creighton Preparatory School	Omaha	86–87
Father Flanagan High School	Omaha	83–84
Fremont Senior High School	Fremont	86–87
Grace Abbott Elementary School	Omaha	89–90
Gretna Junior-Senior High School	Gretna	90–91
Harry A. Burke High School	Omaha	83–84
Hastings Junior High School	Hastings	84–85
Holling Heights Elementary School	Omaha	89–90
Kearney Junior High School	Kearney	82–83
Kearney Senior High School	Kearney	83–84
Lincoln East Junior-Senior High School	Lincoln	83–84
Lincoln High School	Lincoln	83–84
Lincoln Southeast High School	Lincoln	88–89
Longfellow Elementary School	Scottsbluff	91–92
Marian High School	Omaha	92–93
McMillan Junior High School	Omaha	84–85
Millard Central Middle School	Omaha	90–91
Millard North High School	Omaha	83–84
Millard North Junior High School	Omaha	86–87
Millard South High School	Omaha	82–83
Montclair Elementary School	Omaha	87–88
Norfolk Public Senior High School	Norfolk	84–85
Norris Middle School	Firth	84–85
Ralston High School	Ralston	92–93
Raymond Central Elementary School	Valparaiso	89–90
Saint Cecilia's Cathedral Elementary School	Omaha	85–86
St. John Lutheran School	Seward	85–86
St. Mary's High School	O'Neill	88–89
St. Pius X-St. Leo School	Omaha	85–86
Tri County Senior High School	DeWitt	84–85
Valley Middle/High School	Valley	92–93
Valley View Junior High School	Omaha	84–85

SCHOOL	CITY	YEAR(S) RECOGNIZED
NEBRASKA *(continued)*		
Westbrook Junior High School	Omaha	84–85
Westside High School	Omaha	83–84

NEVADA

Brown Elementary School	Reno	91–92
Cannon Junior High School	Las Vegas	83–84, 88–89
Darrel C. Swope Middle School	Reno	82–83
Edward C. Reed High School	Sparks	84–85
Elko High School	Elko	82–83
Gardnerville Elementary School	Gardnerville	85–86
Grass Valley Elementary School	Winnemucca	87–88
Kenny C. Guinn Junior High School	Las Vegas	82–83
Las Vegas High School	Las Vegas	84–85
McGill Elementary School	McGill	93–94
Procter Hug High School	Reno	86–87
Reno High School	Reno	83–84
St. Viator School	Las Vegas	85–86
Stead Elementary School	Reno	85–86
Vegas Verdes Elementary School	Las Vegas	91–92
Walter Bracken Elementary School	Las Vegas	89–90

NEW HAMPSHIRE

Amherst Middle School	Amherst	86–87, 90–91
Exeter Area Junior High School	Exeter	83–84
Fairgrounds Junior High School	Nashua	88–89
Frances C. Richmond School	Hanover	87–88
Hanover High School	Hanover	82–83
Hollis Elementary School	Hollis	87–88
Kearsarge Regional High School	North Sutton	83–84
Lebanon Junior High School	Lebanon	82–83
Londonderry High School	Londonderry	86–87
Londonderry Junior High School	Londonderry	84–85
Moultonborough Central School	Moultonborough	85–86
Phillips Exeter Academy	Exeter	83–84
St. Paul's School	Concord	83–84
Stratham Memorial School	Stratham	85–86
Timberlane Regional Junior High School	Plaistow	88–89
Woodbury School	Salem	89–90
Woodman Park School	Dover	85–86

NEW JERSEY

Canfield Avenue School	Mine Hill	91–92

SCHOOL	CITY	YEAR(S) RECOGNIZED

NEW JERSEY (*continued*)

School	City	Year(s) Recognized
Christian Brothers Academy	Lincroft	83–84
Columbia High School	Maplewood	92–93
CPC Behavorial Healthcare, High Point Elementary School	Morganville	93–94
Crossroads School	Monmouth Junction	92–93
Delbarton School	Morristown	83–84
Dwight-Englewood School	Englewood	86–87
East Brunswick High School	East Brunswick	90–91
Eden Institute	Princeton	91–92
Fair Lawn High School	Fair Lawn	90–91
George C. Baker Elementary School	Moorestown	91–92
Greenbrook School	Kendall Park	91–92
Hebrew Academy of Atlantic County	Margate	89–90
Hillside School	Montclair	87–88
Ho-Ho-Kus Public School	Ho-Ho-Kus	89–90
Irwin School	East Brunswick	89–90
Jefferson School	Summit	89–90
Lawrence Brook School	East Brunswick	91–92
Leesburg School	Port Elizabeth	91–92
Mary E. Roberts School	Moorestown	89–90
Maurice Hawk	Princeton Junction	93–94
Mill Lake School	Monroe Township	91–92
Montgomery High School	Skillman	92–93
Moorestown Friends Lower School	Moorestown	91–92
Morris Catholic High School	Denville	84–85
Mount St. Mary Academy	Plainfield-Watchung	84–85
Mustard Seed School	Hoboken	87–88
Nishuane School	Montclair	89–90
Northern Highlands Regional High School	Allendale	86–87
Our Lady Star of the Sea School	Cape May	93–94
Paramus High School	Paramus	88–89
Parkway School	Paramus	87–88
Pompton Lakes High School	Pompton Lakes	86–87
Princeton Child Development Institute	Princeton	83–84
Queen of Peace High School	North Arlington	92–93
Richard M. Teitelman School	Cape May	90–91
Ridge High School	Basking Ridge	86–87
Ridgewood High School	Ridgewood	86–87
Rutgers Preparatory School	Somerset	92–93
Sacred Heart School	Trenton	87–88
St. Paul's School	Jersey City	87–88
St. Peter Elementary School	New Brunswick	85–86
South Brunswick High School	Monmouth Junction	90–91
South Valley School	Moorestown	87–88
Spotswood High School	Spotswood	92–93

SCHOOL	CITY	YEAR(S) RECOGNIZED

NEW JERSEY (*continued*)

The Midland School	North Branch	89–90
Upper Freehold Regional Elementary School	Allentown	93–94
Watchung School	Montclair	89–90, 93–94
West Windsor-Plainsboro High School	Princeton Junction	92–93

NEW MEXICO

Albuquerque Academy	Albuquerque	83–84
Albuquerque High School	Albuquerque	82–83
Barcelona Elementary School	Albuquerque	93–94
Carrizozo High School	Carrizozo	83–84
Cibola High School	Albuquerque	86–87
Corrales Elementary School	Albuquerque	85–86
Eisenhower Middle School	Albuquerque	84–85
Governor Bent Elementary School	Albuquerque	93–94
Highland High School	Albuquerque	84–85
Hillrise Elementary School	Las Cruces	89–90
Hoover Middle School	Albuquerque	82–83
Jefferson Middle School	Albuquerque	83–84
John Adams Middle School	Albuquerque	86–87
John Baker Elementary School	Albuquerque	87–88
Las Cruces High School	Las Cruces	84–85
Loma Heights Elementary School	Las Cruces	91–92
Longfellow Elementary School	Albuquerque	85–86
Manzano High School	Albuquerque	82–83
McCormick Elementary School	Farmington	87–88
McKinley Middle School	Albuquerque	88–89, 92–93
Polk Middle School	Albuquerque	86–87
Rehoboth Christian High School	Rehoboth	83–84
Roosevelt Middle School	Tijeras	92–93
Taft Middle School	Albuquerque	82–83
Van Buren Middle School	Albuquerque	84–85, 92–93
Washington Middle School	Albuquerque	86–87
West Mesa High School	Albuquerque	83–84

NEW YORK

A. Phillip Randolph Campus High School	New York	86–87
Academy of Mount Saint Ursula	Bronx	86–87
Academy of Our Lady of Good Counsel	White Plains	86–87
Alexander Hamilton High School	Elmsford	92–93
Anne M. Dorner Middle School	Ossining	88–89
Aquinas High School	New York	84–85
Archbishop Molloy High School	Briarwood	86–87
Astor Home for Children	Rhinebeck	93–94

SCHOOL	CITY	YEAR(S) RECOGNIZED

NEW YORK *(continued)*

SCHOOL	CITY	YEAR(S) RECOGNIZED
Baldwin Senior High School	Baldwin	90–91
Bedford Road School	Pleasantville	89–90
Benjamin Franklin Elementary School	Binghamton	93–94
Benjamin Franklin Middle School	Kenmore	93–94
Benjamin N. Cardozo High School	Bayside	83–84
Berkshire Junior/Senior High School	Canaan	92–93
Bishop Loughlin Memorial High School	Brooklyn	83–84
Blind Brook High School	Rye Brook	86–87
Blue Mountain Middle School	Peekskill	82–83
Bronxville High School	Bronxville	90–91
Brooklyn Technical High School	Brooklyn	82–83
Burnt Hills-Ballston Lake Senior High School	Burnt Hills	88–89
Byram Hills High School	Armonk	88–89
Campus East School	Buffalo	87–88
Canandaigua Primary School	Canandaigua	85–86
Carrie E. Tomkins Elementary School	Croton-on-Hudson	85–86
Catherine McAuley High School	Brooklyn	90–91
Cazenovia Junior-Senior High School	Cazenovia	88–89
Central School	Larchmont	85–86
Clayton A. Bouton Junior/Senior High School	Voorheesville	90–91
Clinton Middle School	Clinton	89–90
Clinton Senior High School	Clinton	88–89
Como Park Elementary School	Lancaster	91–92
Concord Road Elementary School	Ardsley	91–92
Convent of the Sacred Heart School	New York City	90–91
Daniel Webster Magnet School	New Rochelle	93–94
Davison Avenue School	Lynbrook	91–92
Dr. Roland N. Patterson Intermediate School #229	Bronx	86–87
Eastchester High School	Eastchester	92–93
Edgemont Junior-Senior High School	Scarsdale	83–84
Edward R. Murrow High School	Brooklyn	88–89
Elmer Avenue School	Schnectady	87–88
Elmont Memorial High School	Elmont	90–91
F. E. Bellows School	Mamaroneck	87–88
Fordham Preparatory School	Bronx	83–84
Friends Academy	Locust Valley	87–88
Fulmar Road Elementary School	Mahopac	89–90
Futures Academy #37	Buffalo	85–86
Garden City Junior High School	Garden City	84–85
Garden City Senior High School	Garden City	86–87
Gardnertown Fundamental Magnet School	Newburgh	87–88
George W. Miller Elementary School	Nanuet	89–90
Glenmont Elementary School	Glenmont	89–90
Gowana Junior High School	Clifton Park	88–89

SCHOOL	CITY	YEAR(S) RECOGNIZED

NEW YORK (*continued*)

SCHOOL	CITY	YEAR(S) RECOGNIZED
Greece Athena Senior High School	Rochester	83−84
H. J. Kalfas Early Childhood Magnet School	Niagara	93−94
Haldane Elementary School	Cold Spring	87−88
Harbor Hill School	Greenvale	85−86
Harrison Avenue School	Harrison	85−86
Harry Hoag School	Fort Plain	87−88
Hebrew Academy of the Five Towns and Rockaway	Lawrence	87−88
Herbert Hoover Elementary School	Kenmore	91−92
Hillel Academy of Broome County	Binghamton	87−88
Holmes Elementary School	Tonawanda	89−90
Holy Family School	Hicksville	89−90
Holy Trinity Diocesan High School	Hicksville	86−87
Horace Mann School	New York	84−85
Horizons-on-the-Hudson Magnet School	Newburgh	89−90, 93−94
Houghton Academy - P. S. #69	Buffalo	85−86
Hutchinson Central Technical High School	Buffalo	88−89
Irvington High School	Irvington	92−93
Irvington Middle School	Irvington	86−87
Jamaica High School	Jamaica	84−85
James P.B. Duffy School No. 12	Rochester	89−90
Jericho High School	Jericho	90−91
John Bowne High School	Flushing	92−93
John F. Kennedy High School	Somers	83−84
Kenmore East High School	Tonawanda	92−93
Koda Junior High School	Clifton Park	86−87
L. P. Quinn Elementary School	Tupper Lake	87−88
La Salle Institute	Troy	86−87, 90−91
Lake George Elementary School	Lake George	85−86, 91−92
Lincoln Elementary School	Scotia	85−86
Liverpool High School	Liverpool	84−85
Livonia Primary School	Livonia	89−90
Long Island Lutheran High School	Brookville	88−89
Longwood Middle School	Middle Island	90−91
Louis Armstrong Middle School	East Elmhurst	82−83
Louis M. Klein Middle School	Harrison	93−94
Loyola School	New York	88−89
Lynbrook High School	Lynbrook	90−91
Maine-Endwell Middle School	Endwell	88−89
Malverne High School	Malverne	88−89
Mandalay School	Wantagh	93−94
Manhasset Junior-Senior High School	Manhasset	88−89
Marion Street Elementary School	Lynbrook	85−86
McQuaid Jesuit High School	Rochester	86−87
Mercy High School	Riverhead	88−89

SCHOOL	CITY	YEAR(S) RECOGNIZED

NEW YORK (*continued*)

SCHOOL	CITY	YEAR(S) RECOGNIZED
Midwood High School at Brooklyn College	Brooklyn	86−87
Miller Place High School	Miller Place	83−84
Milton School	Rye	93−94
Moriches Elementary School	Moriches	89−90, 93−94
Mother Cabrini High School	New York	86−87
Mount Markham Middle School	West Winfield	90−91
Mount Saint Michael Academy	Bronx	90−91
Mount Vernon High School	Mount Vernon	86−87
Nazareth Academy	Rochester	83−84
New Hyde Park Memorial Junior/Senior High School	New Hyde Park	92−93
New Rochelle High School	New Rochelle	83−84
Newburgh Free Academy	Newburgh	86−87
Niskayuna High School	Schenectady	82−83
North Salem High School	North Salem	88−89
North Salem Middle School	North Salem	86−87
North Shore High School	Glen Head	90−91
Northport High School	Northport	83−84
Oneida Middle School	Schenectady	86−87
Orchard School	Yonkers	89−90, 93−94
Orenda Elementary School	Clifton Park	89−90
Osborn School/ Julia Dyckman Andrews Memorial	Rye	91−92
Our Lady of Lourdes School	West Islip	85−86
Our Lady of Mercy School	Hicksville	87−88
Our Lady of Peace School	Lynbrook	89−90
Our Lady of the Hamptons Regional Catholic School	Southhampton	93−94
Our Saviour Lutheran School	Bronx	87−88
Oyster Bay High School	Oyster Bay	88−89
P. S. 183, General Daniel ''Chappie'' James, Jr.	Brooklyn	87−88
P. S. 189, Bilingual School	Brooklyn	85−86
P. S. 206, M.-Jose C. Barbosa School	New York	87−88
Park Early Elementary School	Westbury	85−86
Paul D. Schreiber High School	Port Washington	84−85
Paul J. Gelinas Junior High School	Setauket	86−87
PEARLS Elementary School #32	Yonkers	91−92
Pelham Memorial High School	Pelham	92−93
Pequenakonck Elementary School	North Salem	87−88
Pierre Van Cortlandt Middle School	Croton-on-Hudson	84−85
Pittsford Middle School	Pittsford	86−87
Pleasantville High School	Pleasantville	90−91
Poestenkill Elementary School	Poestenkill	93−94
Port Jefferson Junior High School	Port Jefferson	86−87
Purchase School	Purchase	87−88

SCHOOL	CITY	YEAR(S) RECOGNIZED

SCHOOL	CITY	YEAR(S) RECOGNIZED
Regis High School	New York	84 – 85
Ridge Street School	Rye Brook	85 – 86
Robert Cushman Murphy Junior High School	Stony Brook	83 – 84
Sacandaga Elementary School	Scotia	85 – 86, 93 – 94
Sacred Heart/Mt. Carmel School of the Arts	Mount Vernon	93 – 94
Saddle Rock Elementary School	Great Neck	93 – 94
Saint Catharine Academy	Bronx	92 – 93
St. Agnes Cathedral School	Rockville Centre	89 – 90
St. Francis Prep School	Fresh Meadows	83 – 84
St. Ignatius Loyola School	New York	85 – 86
St. Isidore School	Riverhead	87 – 88
St. Joseph's School	Long Island City	89 – 90, 93 – 94
St. Thomas of Canterbury School	Cornwall-on-Hudson	87 – 88
Sts. Peter and Paul School	Bronx	85 – 86
Salanter Akiba Riverdale Academy	Riverdale	91 – 92
Scarsdale High School	Scarsdale	82 – 83
School #54-ECC	Buffalo	85 – 86
School #59-Science Magnet	Buffalo	84 – 85
Scotia-Glenville High School	Scotia	86 – 87
Scotia-Glenville Junior High School	Scotia	88 – 89
Seth Low Intermediate School #96	Brooklyn	86 – 87
Sewanhaka High School	Floral Park	92 – 93
Shaker High School	Latham	84 – 85
Shaker Junior High School	Latham	92 – 93
Shelter Rock Elementary School	Manhasset	91 – 92
Shenendehowa High School	Clifton Park	90 – 91
Shoreham-Wading River High School	Shoreham	86 – 87
Shoreham-Wading River Middle School	Shoreham	82 – 83
Shulamith High School for Girls	Brooklyn	86 – 87, 92 – 93
Skaneateles High School	Skaneateles	90 – 91
South Park High School	Buffalo	88 – 89
Springhurst Elementary School	Dobbs Ferry	87 – 88
Stewart School	Garden City	87 – 88
Stratford Avenue School	Garden City	87 – 88
Stuyvesant High School	New York	82 – 83
Susan E. Wagner High School	Staten Island	88 – 89
Syosset High School	Syosset	92 – 93
The Academy of the Holy Names	Albany	92 – 93
The Astor Learning Center	Rhinebeck	87 – 88
The Brearley School	New York	83 – 84
The Bronx High School of Science	Bronx	82 – 83, 88 – 89
The Calhoun School	New York	85 – 86
The Douglaston School	Douglaston	85 – 86
The Fieldston School	Riverdale	83 – 84
The Fox Lane Middle School	Bedford	83 – 84

SCHOOL	CITY	YEAR(S) RECOGNIZED

NEW YORK *(continued)*

SCHOOL	CITY	YEAR(S) RECOGNIZED
The Herman Schreiber School	Brooklyn	87–88
The Nichols School	Buffalo	84–85
The Ursuline School	New Rochelle	84–85
Theodore Roosevelt Elementary School	Kenmore	93–94
Thomas Edison Elementary School	Tonawanda	93–94
Thomas Jefferson Elementary School	Buffalo	89–90
Thomas K. Beecher School	Elmira	85–86
Tottenville High School	Staten Island	86–87
Townsend Harris High School at Queens College	Flushing	88–89
Triangle Academy	Buffalo	89–90
Vestal Senior High School	Vestal	84–85
Voorheesville Elementary School	Voorheesville	91–92
Wantagh Elementary School	Wantagh	91–92
Wantagh Middle School	Wantagh	90–91
Ward Melville High School	Setauket	88–89
Waterford-Halfmoon Elementary School	Waterford	87–88
Weedsport Elementary School	Weedsport	85–86
West Corners Campus School	Endicott	87–88
West End School	Lynbrook	85–86
West Hertel Academy	Buffalo	85–86
Westbury Senior High School	Westbury	86–87
Westhill High School	Syracuse	92–93
White Plains High School	White Plains	86–87
White Plains Middle School	White Plains	86–87
William B. Ward Elementary School	New Rochelle	87–88
Woodmere Middle School	Hewlett	86–87
Xavier High School	New York	90–91
Yeshiva of Central Queens	Flushing	93–94

NORTH CAROLINA

SCHOOL	CITY	YEAR(S) RECOGNIZED
Blessed Sacrament School	Burlington	89–90
Brevard Elementary School	Brevard	85–86
Brewster Middle School	Camp Lejeune	88–89
C. G. Credle Elementary School	Oxford	89–90
Carmel Junior High School	Charlotte	83–84
Carolina Friends School	Durham	83–84
Charlotte Latin School	Charlotte	86–87
China Grove Elementary School	China Grove	89–90
Crest Senior High School	Shelby	86–87
Elon College Elementary School	Elon College	87–88
First Ward Elementary School	Charlotte	87–88
Gatesville Elementary School	Gatesville	86–87
Ira B. Jones Elementary School	Asheville	85–86
John A. Holmes High School	Edenton	84–85

SCHOOL	CITY	YEAR(S) RECOGNIZED
NORTH CAROLINA (*continued*)		
John T. Hoggard High School	Wilmington	90−91
Kinston High School	Kinston	86−87
Lee County Senior High School	Sanford	82−83
Lewis H. Powell Gifted and Talented Magnet Elementary School	Raleigh	91−92
Manteo High School	Manteo	83−84
McDowell High School	Marion	84−85
Mooresville Junior High School	Mooresville	86−87
Myers Park High School	Charlotte	86−87
Needham Broughton High School	Raleigh	83−84
North Davie Junior High School	Mocksville	84−85
Park View Elementary School	Morresville	85−86
Piedmont Middle School	Monroe	90−91
Piedmont Open Middle School	Charlotte	90−91
Providence Day School	Charlotte	86−87
Richmond Senior High School	Rockingham	90−91
Rowland Hill Latham Elementary School	Winston-Salem	93−94
Stone Street Elementary School	Camp Lejeune	87−88
W. G. Pearson Elementary School	Durham	85−86
Walter M. Williams High School	Burlington	92−93
West Rowan High School	Mount Ulla	90−91
William G. Enloe High School	Raleigh	82−83

NORTH DAKOTA

Belmont Elementary School	Grand Forks	91−92
Benjamin Franklin Junior High School	Fargo	82−83
Beulah High School	Beulah	90−91
Clara Barton Elementary School	Fargo	91−92
Century High School	Bismarck	92−93
Crosby Elementary School	Crosby	85−86
Divide County High School	Crosby	83−84
Hazen Public High School	Hazen	82−83
Hughes Junior High School	Bismarck	84−85
Northridge Elementary School	Bismarck	89−90
Shanley High School	Fargo	83−84
Washington School	Fargo	87−88

OHIO

Arbor Hills Junior High School	Sylvania	83−84
Aurora High School	Aurora	92−93
Barrington Elementary School	Upper Arlington	85−86
Bath Elementary School	Akron	85−86
Beachwood Middle School	Beachwood	92−93

SCHOOL	CITY	YEAR(S) RECOGNIZED

OHIO *(continued)*

Beaumont School	Cleveland Heights	90–91
Bellflower Elementary School	Mentor	91–92
Berea High School	Berea	84–85
Berwick Science/Math/Environmental Studies Alternative Elementary School	Columbus	87–88
Bishop Watterson High School	Columbus	88–89
Brunswick Middle School	Brunswick	84–85
Canton Country Day School	Canton	91–92
Center Street Village Elementary School	Mentor	89–90
Centerville High School	Centerville	83–84, 92–93
Central Catholic High School	Toledo	90–91
Chagrin Falls High School	Chagrin Falls	88–89
Chambers Elementary School	East Cleveland	85–86, 89–90
Chaminade-Julienne High School	Dayton	88–89
Columbus Alternative High School	Columbus	84–85
Columbus School for Girls	Columbus	92–93
Columbus School for Girls, Lower School	Bexley	93–94
Cottonwood Elementary School	Cincinnati	87–88
David Smith Elementary School	Delaware	87–88
Dublin Middle School	Dublin	86–87
East Muskingum Middle School	New Concord	83–84
Eastview Middle School	Bath	82–83
Edison Primary School	Dayton	85–86
Elda Elementary School	Hamilton	87–88
Elyria Catholic High School	Elyria	92–93
Evamere Elementary School	Hudson	85–86
Evendale Elementary School	Cincinnati	87–88
Fairfax Elementary School	Mentor	87–88
Fairfield North Elementary School	Hamilton	89–90
Forest Elementary School	North Olmsted	85–86
Francis Dunlavy Elementary School	Lebanon	85–86
Freedom Elementary School	West Chester	91–92
Gesu Catholic School	University Heights	87–88
Gibbs Elementary School	Canton	85–86
Glendale Elementary School	Cincinnati	87–88
Greensview Elementary School	Upper Arlington	87–88
Harrison Elementary School	Harrison	89–90
Hastings Middle School	Upper Arlington	84–85
Heritage Elementary School	Medina	87–88
Herman K. Ankeney Junior High School	Beavercreek	83–84
Hillcrest Primary School	Richfield	87–88
Hoffman School	Cincinnati	87–88, 91–92
Hopewell Elementary School	West Chester	91–92
Hopkins Elementary School	Mentor	87–88
Hudson High School	Hudson	83–84

SCHOOL	CITY	YEAR(S) RECOGNIZED

OHIO (*continued*)

School	City	Years
Hudson Junior High School	Hudson	83–84
Immaculate Conception School	Columbus	93–94
Incarnation Catholic School	Centerville	89–90
Independence Primary School	Independence	93–94
Indian Hill Elementary School	Cincinnati	87–88
Indian Hill High School	Cincinnati	83–84
J. F. Burns Elementary School	Kings Mills	93–94
Jennings Middle School	Akron	84–85
John F. Dumont Elementary School	Cincinnati	87–88
Jones Middle School	Columbus	83–84
Kilgour Elementary School	Cincinnati	91–92
Kirtland Middle School	Kirtland	93–94
Lakota High School	West Chester	92–93
Lewis Sands Elementary School	Chagrin Falls	87–88
Lial Elementary School	Whitehouse	91–92
Lomond Elementary School	Shaker Heights	85–86
Louisa Wright Elementary School	Lebanon	87–88
Madeira High School	Cincinnati	84–85
Magnificat High School	Rocky River	84–85
Mariemont High School	Cincinnati	84–85, 88–89
Mentor Shore Junior High School	Mentor	86–87, 92–93
Metro Catholic Parish School	Cleveland	93–94
Morgan Elementary School	Hamilton	87–88
Mount Notre Dame High School	Cincinnati	86–87
Nativity School	Cincinnati	87–88
Normandy Elementary School	Centerville	91–92
North Olmsted High School	North Olmsted	86–87
Oakwood High School	Dayton	90–91
Olde Sawmill Elementary School	Dublin	85–86
Orange High School	Pepper Pike	90–91
Orchard Elementary School	Cleveland	93–94
Ottawa Middle School	Cincinnati	84–85
Our Lady of Perpetual Help School	Grove City	87–88, 91–92
Pepper Pike Elementary School	Pepper Pike	93–94
Perkins Junior High School	Akron	82–83
Perry Middle School	Worthington	84–85
Pine Elementary School	North Olmsted	91–92
Princeton High School	Cincinnati	83–84, 92–93
Princeton Junior High School	Cincinnati	82–83, 92–93
Regina High School	South Euclid	90–91
Revere High School	Richfield	90–91
Robert E. Lucas Intermediate School	Cincinnati	85–86
Roselawn Condon School	Cincinnati	85–86
Saint Barbara School	Massillon	85–86
Saint Bernard-Elmwood Place High School	Saint Bernard	86–87

SCHOOL	CITY	YEAR(S) RECOGNIZED

OHIO (*continued*)

SCHOOL	CITY	YEAR(S) RECOGNIZED
Saint Xavier High School	Cincinnati	83–84
St. Agatha School	Columbus	85–86
St. Andrew School	Columbus	91–92
St. Columban Elementary School	Loveland	89–90
St. Francis DeSales High School	Columbus	92–93
St. Gertrude School	Cincinnati	87–88
St. Ignatius Jesuit High School	Cleveland	84–85
St. James White Oak School	Cincinnati	87–88, 91–92
St. John Bosco School	Parma Heights	91–92
St. John's High School	Toledo	88–89
St. Joseph Academy	Cleveland	90–91
St. Joseph Montessori School	Columbus	93–94
St. Jude Elementary School	Elyria	93–94
St. Mary School	Cincinnati	85–86, 93–94
St. Michael School	Worthington	87–88
St. Patrick of Heatherdowns School	Toledo	93–94
St. Paul Lutheran School	Napoleon	87–88
St. Peter Catholic School	Huber Heights	89–90
St. Therese of the Little Flower School	Cincinnati	93–94
St. Thomas More School	Brooklyn	93–94
St. Timothy School	Columbus	89–90
School for Creative and Performing Arts	Cincinnati	84–85
Shaker Heights High School	Shaker Heights	82–83
Shaker Heights Middle School	Shaker Heights	86–87
Sharonville Elementary School	Cincinnati	91–92
Solon High School	Solon	90–91
Springdale Elementary School	Cincinnati	93–94
Stewart Elementary School	Cincinnati	93–94
Sycamore Junior High School	Cincinnati	86–87
Symmes Elementary School	Loveland	93–94
Theodore Roosevelt High School	Kent	84–85
Three Rivers Middle School	Cleves	87–88
Tremont Elementary School	Upper Arlington	85–86
Upper Arlington High School	Upper Arlington	84–85
Urban Community School	Cleveland	87–88
Ursuline Academy of Cincinnati	Cincinnati	88–89
Villa Angela Academy	Cleveland	86–87
W. M. Sellman Middle School	Madeira	85–86
Walnut Hills High School	Cincinnati	84–85
Walsh Jesuit High School	Stow	84–85
Western Row Elementary School	Mason	93–94
Whitewater Valley Elementary School	Harrison	93–94
William Henry Harrison High School	Harrison	90–91
William Henry Harrison Junior High School	Harrison	83–84
Willoughby South High School	Willoughby	92–93

SCHOOL	CITY	YEAR(S) RECOGNIZED

OHIO (*continued*)

SCHOOL	CITY	YEAR(S) RECOGNIZED
Windermere Elementary School	Upper Arlington	85 – 86
Woodbury Junior High School	Shaker Heights	83 – 84
Woodlawn Elementary School	Cincinnati	87 – 88
Worthington Hills School	Worthington	85 – 86
Worthingway Middle School	Worthington	86 – 87
Wyoming High School	Wyoming	82 – 83

OKLAHOMA

SCHOOL	CITY	YEAR(S) RECOGNIZED
Ardmore High School	Ardmore	82 – 83
Ardmore Middle School	Ardmore	90 – 91
Booker T. Washington High School	Tulsa	82 – 83
Byng High School	Ada	83 – 84
Carnegie School	Tulsa	85 – 86
Cimarron Middle School	Edmond	93 – 94
Crosby Park Elementary School	Lawton	85 – 86
Deer Creek Elementary School	Edmond	89 – 90
Douglas Learning Center	Lawton	89 – 90
Gans Junior-Senior High School	Muldrow	83 – 84
Holland Hall Middle School	Tulsa	85 – 86, 89 – 90
Hugh Bish Elementary School	Lawton	93 – 94
James L. Dennis Elementary School	Oklahoma City	85 – 86
John Marshall High School	Oklahoma City	82 – 83
Maryetta School	Stilwell	87 – 88
McKinley Elementary School	Norman	87 – 88
Millwood High School	Oklahoma City	83 – 84
Monte Cassino School	Tulsa	93 – 94
Norman High School	Norman	88 – 89
Northeast High School	Oklahoma City	83 – 84
Piedmont Elementary School	Piedmont	89 – 90
Putnam City North High School	Oklahoma City	88 – 89
Quail Creek Elementary School	Oklahoma City	91 – 92
School of Saint Mary	Tulsa	87 – 88
Seiling Public Schools	Seiling	84 – 85
Summit Middle School	Edmond	92 – 93
West Mid High School	Norman	88 – 89
Western Hills Elementary School	Lawton	89 – 90
Whittier Elementary School	Lawton	87 – 88
Wiley Post Elementary School	Oklahoma City	89 – 90

OREGON

SCHOOL	CITY	YEAR(S) RECOGNIZED
Alameda Elementary School	Portland	87 – 88
Beaumont Middle School	Portland	84 – 85
Beaverton High School	Beaverton	84 – 85

SCHOOL	CITY	YEAR(S) RECOGNIZED

OREGON (*continued*)

SCHOOL	CITY	YEAR(S) RECOGNIZED
Bolton Middle School	West Linn	85–86
Burns High School	Burns	86–87, 90–91
Byrom Elementary School	Tualatin	87–88
Calapooia Middle School	Albany	82–83
Cedar Park Intermediate School	Beaverton	82–83
Centennial High School	Gresham	88–89
Chapman Elementary School	Portland	89–90
Clackamas High School	Milwaukie	83–84
Corridor School	Creswell	85–86
Crater High School	Central Point	82–83
Duniway Elementary School	Portland	87–88
Floyd Light Middle School	Portland	83–84
Gilbert Park School	Portland	89–90
Gladstone High School	Gladstone	86–87
Jesuit High School	Portland	88–89
Lake Oswego High School	Lake Oswego	82–83
Lake Oswego Junior High School	Lake Oswego	84–85
Lakeridge High School	Lake Oswego	86–87
Marist High School	Eugene	84–85
McLoughlin Junior High School	Milwaukie	83–84
Monroe Middle School	Eugene	83–84
North Bend High School	North Bend	86–87
Nyssa Elementary School	Nyssa	85–86
Nyssa High School	Nyssa	84–85
Oaklea Middle School	Junction City	82–83
Obsidian Junior High School	Redmond	84–85
Ogden Junior High School	Oregon City	86–87
Oregon City High School	Oregon City	84–85
Our Lady of the Lake School	Lake Oswego	89–90
Pleasant Hill High School	Pleasant Hill	83–84
Pringle Elementary School	Salem	87–88
Renne Intermediate School	Newburg	82–83
Rex Putnam High School	Milwaukie	84–85
Riverdale School	Portland	85–86
Saint Mary's Academy	Portland	83–84, 88–89
Seven Oak Middle School	Lebanon	85–86
Slater-Filmore Grade School	Burns	91–92
South Eugene High School	Eugene	82–83
South Salem High School	Salem	86–87
Sunset High School	Beaverton	82–83
Tualatin Elementary School	Tualatin	89–90
Walker Middle School	Salem	89–90
Washington Elementary School	Medford	91–92
West Linn High School	West Linn	83–84
Westridge Elementary School	Lake Oswego	87–88
Wilbur Rowe Junior High School	Milwaukie	86–87

SCHOOL	CITY	YEAR(S) RECOGNIZED

PENNSYLVANIA

School	City	Year(s)
Academy of Notre Dame de Namur	Villanova	86–87
Allentown Central Catholic High School	Allentown	83–84, 92–93
Ancillae-Assumpta Academy	Wyncote	85–86, 91–92
Arcola Intermediate School	Norristown	90–91
Bala Cynwyd Middle School	Bala Cynwyd	83–84
Baldwin School	Bryn Mawr	83–84
Benchmark School	Media	85–86
Boyce Middle School	Upper St. Clair	91–92
Buckingham Elementary School	Buckingham	85–86
Bywood Elementary School	Upper Darby	93–94
Carl Benner School	Coatesville	93–94
Carl R. Streams Elementary School	Upper St. Clair	89–90
Carson Middle School	Pittsburgh	93–94
Central Catholic High School	Pittsburgh	86–87
Central High School	Philadelphia	86–87
Chatham Park School	Havertown	85–86
Conestoga Senior High School	Berwyn	83–84
Crooked Billet Elementary School	Hatsboro	93–94
Cynwyd Elementary School	Bala Cynwyd	91–92
Delaware Valley Middle School	Milford	84–85
Dorothea H. Simmons School	Horsham	91–92
Downingtown Senior High School	Downingtown	84–85, 88–89
E. T. Richardson Middle School	Springfield	84–85
East Coventry Elementary School	Pottstown	93–94
East High School	West Chester	86–87, 92–93
East Junior High School	Waynesboro	84–85
Fort Couch Middle School	Upper St. Clair	86–87, 92–93
Fox Chapel Area High School	Pittsburgh	92–93
Franklin Elementary School	Sewickley	85–86
Franklin Learning Center	Philadelphia	92–93
Garrettford Elementary School	Drexel Hill	89–90
General Wayne Middle School	Malvern	84–85, 90–91
Glenwood Elementary School	Media	89–90
Great Valley High School	Malvern	86–87
Gwynedd Mercy Academy	Gwynedd Valley	90–91
Harriton High School	Rosemont	83–84, 92–93
Harvey C. Sabold Elementary School	Springfield	93–94
Haverford Senior High School	Havertown	86–87
Henderson High School	West Chester	86–87
Hereford Township Elementary School	Hereford	89–90
Highland Park School	Upper Darby	87–88
Hillcrest Elementary School	Drexel Hill	87–88
Holy Ghost Preparatory School	Bensalem	92–93
Independence Middle School	Bethel Park	92–93
J. R. Fugett Middle School	West Chester	90–91
John M. Grasse Elementary School	Sellersville	91–92

SCHOOL	CITY	YEAR(S) RECOGNIZED

PENNSYLVANIA (*continued*)

SCHOOL	CITY	YEAR(S) RECOGNIZED
Kathryn D. Markley School	Malvern	87−88
Keith Valley Middle School	Horsham	90−91
Kerr Elementary School	Pittsburgh	93−94
King's Highway Elementary School	Coatesville	93−94
La Salle College High School	Wyndmoor	84−85
Louis E. Dieruff High School	Allentown	84−85
Marlborough Elementary School	Green Lane	93−94
Mary C. Howse Elementary School	West Chester	85−86, 89−90
Mercy Vocational High School	Philadelphia	83−84
Mercyhurst Preparatory School	Erie	92−93
Merion Elementary School	Merion	85−86
Methacton High School	Fairview Village	88−89
Mount Saint Joseph Academy	Flourtown	92−93
Mt. Lebanon Junior High School	Pittsburgh	90−91
Mt. Lebanon Senior High School	Pittsburgh	83−84, 90−91
Nether Providence Middle School	Wallingford	86−87
New Eagle Elementary School	Wayne	85−86
North Allegheny Intermediate High School	Pittsburgh	88−89
North Allegheny Senior High School	Wexford	92−93
North Penn High School	Lansdale	90−91
O'Hara Elementary School	Pittsburgh	91−92
Orborne Elementary School	Sewickley	93−94
Overbrook Educational Center	Philadelphia	87−88
Penn Wynne School	Philadelphia	85−86
Pennsbury High School	Fairless Hills	84−85
Perkiomen Valley South Elementary	Collegeville	93−94
Philadelphia High School for Girls	Philadelphia	86−87
Quaker Valley High School	Leetsdale	92−93
Radnor High School	Radnor	83−84
Saint Bernadette School	Drexel Hill	85−86
Saints Philip and James School	Exton	89−90
St. Agnes School	West Chester	89 90
St. Gabriel's Hall School	Audubon	88−89
St. Joseph's Preparatory School	Philadelphia	84−85
Salford Hills Elementary School	Harleysville	93−94
Sandy Run Middle School	Dresher	83−84
Scenic Hills Elementary School	Springfield	85−86
Schenley High School Teacher Center	Pittsburgh	86−87
Scranton Preparatory School	Scranton	86−87
Sewickley Academy	Sewickley	92−93
Springfield High School	Springfield	88−89
Springside School	Philadelphia	84−85
State College Area High School	State College	92−93
Stonehurst Hills Elementary School	Upper Darby	89−90
Strath Haven High School	Wallingford	84−85
Sugartown Elementary School	Malvern	85−86

SCHOOL	CITY	YEAR(S) RECOGNIZED

PENNSYLVANIA (*continued*)

Swarthmore Rutledge School	Swarthmore	91–92
The Harrisburg Academy	Wormleysburg	92–93
The Mercersburg Academy	Mercersburg	90–91
The Miquon School	Miquon	85–86
Tredyffrin/Easttown Junior High School	Berwyn	86–87
Trinity High School	Camp Hill	92–93
Upper Darby High School	Upper Darby	88–89
Upper Perkiomen Middle School	East Greenville	92–93
Upper St. Clair High School	Upper St. Clair	83–84, 88–89
Villa Maria Academy	Malvern	88–89
Villa Maria Academy-Lower School	Immaculata	87–88
Wallingford Elementary School	Wallingford	89–90
Welsh Valley Middle School	Narberth	83–84
West Catholic High School for Boys	Philadelphia	83–84
William T. Gordon Middle School	Coatesville	92–93
Wissahickon Middle School	Ambler	84–85
Wyomissing Area Junior-Senior High School	Wyomissing	90–91

PUERTO RICO

Academia Maria Reina	Rio Piedras	88–89
Andres Grillasca Salas School	Ponce	89–90
Angela Cordero Bernard School	Ponce	87–88
Benito Cerezo Vazquez High School	Aguadilla	88–89
C. R. O. E. M. High School	Mayaguez	92–93
Colegio Ponceño	Coto Laurel	90–91
Colegio Ponceño	Ponce	91–92
Colegio Radians	Cayey	92–93
Colegio San Ignacio de Loyola	Rio Piedras	84–85
Francisco Matias Lugo School	Carolina	91–92
José Emilio Lugo Ponce De León High School	Adjuntas	90–91
Patria Latorre Ramirez High School	San Sebastián	92–93
Saint John's School	Santurce	86–87

RHODE ISLAND

Archie R. Cole Junior High School	East Greenwich	88–89
Bishop Hendricken High School	Warwick	92–93
Davisville Middle School	North Kingstown	90–91
Dr. James H. Eldredge Elementary School	East Greenwich	91–92
East Greenwich High School	East Greenwich	83–84
Hugh Bain Junior High School	Cranston	82–83
La Salle Academy	Providence	90–91
Lincoln Junior-Senior High School	Lincoln	82–83, 88–89
Mount Saint Charles Academy	Woonsocket	92–93

SCHOOL	CITY	YEAR(S) RECOGNIZED

RHODE ISLAND (*continued*)

SCHOOL	CITY	YEAR(S) RECOGNIZED
Narragansett Elementary School	Narragansett	85–86
Narragansett High School	Narragansett	86–87
Norwood Avenue School	Cranston	87–88
St. Luke School	Barrington	93–94
St. Mary Academy-Bay View	Riverside	90–91
St. Rocco School	Johnston	93–94
South Kingstown High School	Wakefield	86–87
South Kingstown Junior High School	Peace Dale	84–85
Western Hills Junior High School	Cranston	83–84

SOUTH CAROLINA

SCHOOL	CITY	YEAR(S) RECOGNIZED
Aiken Elementary School	Aiken	89–90
Ashley River Creative Arts Elementary School	Charleston	91–92
Augusta Circle Elementary School	Greenville	93–94
Baker's Chapel Elementary School	Greenville	91–92
Buena Vista Elementary School	Greer	89–90
C. E. Williams Middle School	Charleston	92–93
Camden High School	Camden	82–83
Clifdale Elementary School	Spartanburg	89–90
Conder Elementary School	Columbia	85–86
Conway High School	Conway	84–85
Conway Middle School	Conway	92–93
Cowpens Elementary School	Cowpens	85–86
Dent Middle School	Columbia	84–85
Dreher High School	Columbia	88–89
Dutch Fork Elementary School	Irmo	93–94
E. L. Wright Middle School	Columbia	83–84
Edwards Junior High School	Central	88–89
Greeleyville Elementary School	Greeleyville	93–94
Harbor View Elementary School	Charleston	93–94
Heathwood Hall Episcopal School	Columbia	83–84
Hillcrest Middle School	Simpsonville	84–85
Irmo High School	Columbia	82–83
Joseph Keels Elementary School	Columbia	85–86, 93–94
L. W. Conder Elementary School	Columbia	93–94
Lake City Primary School	Lake City	93–94
League Middle School	Greenville	82–83
Lemira Elementary School	Sumter	89–90
Lexington Middle School	Lexington	90–91
Lonnie B. Nelson Elementary School	Columbia	87–88
Mauldin High School	Mauldin	84–85
Mitchell Elementary School	Charleston	93–94
North Springs Elementary School	Elgin	87–88
Oakbrook Elementary School	Ladson	93–94

SCHOOL	CITY	YEAR(S) RECOGNIZED

SOUTH CAROLINA (*continued*)

Orange Grove Elementary School	Charleston	93 – 94
Richland Northeast High School	Columbia	84 – 85, 92 – 93
Rock Hill High School	Rock Hill	83 – 84
Satchel Ford Elementary School	Columbia	87 – 88
Shaw Heights Elementary School	Shaw Air Force Base	87 – 88
Socastee High School	Myrtle Beach	90 – 91
Spartanburg High School	Spartanburg	82 – 83, 88 – 89, 92 – 93
Spring Valley High School	Columbia	82 – 83
Summerville Elementary School	Summerville	93 – 94

SOUTH DAKOTA

Central High School	Aberdeen	86 – 87
Dell Rapids Elementary School	Dell Rapids	93 – 94
O'Gorman High School	Sioux Falls	84 – 85
Yankton Senior High School	Yankton	86 – 87

TENNESSEE

Alvin C. York Institute	Jamestown	88 – 89
Andrew Jackson Elementary School	Old Hickory	89 – 90
Big Ridge Elementary School	Chattanooga	93 – 94
Bradley Central High School	Cleveland	86 – 87
Brookmeade Elementary School	Nashville	91 – 92
Brown Middle School	Harrison	86 – 87
Central High School	Harrison	86 – 87
Cleveland High School	Cleveland	82 – 83
Collierville Middle School	Collierville	82 – 83
Craigmont Junior/Senior High School	Memphis	92 – 93
Dodson Elementary School	Hermitage	85 – 86
Dyersburg High School	Dyersburg	90 – 91
Eagleville School	Eagleville	92 – 93
Eakin Elementary School	Nashville	85 – 86
Farmington School	Germantown	87 – 88
Farragut Intermediate School	Knoxville	87 – 88
Farragut Middle School	Knoxville	86 – 87
Girls Preparatory School	Chattanooga	90 – 91
Glencliff High School	Nashville	88 – 89
Glendale Middle School	Nashville	91 – 92
Grahamwood School	Memphis	85 – 86
Haywood High School	Brownsville	86 – 87
Head Middle School	Nashville	89 – 90
Hillsboro High School	Nashville	84 – 85
Hixson High School	Hixson	84 – 85
Ingleside School	Athens	85 – 86, 89 – 90
Lakeview Elementary School	Nashville	87 – 88

SCHOOL	CITY	YEAR(S) RECOGNIZED

TENNESSEE (*continued*)

McCallie School	Chattanooga	88−89
Meigs Magnet School	Nashville	89−90
Memphis Catholic High School	Memphis	84−85
Miller Perry Elementary School	Kingsport	87−88
Millington South Elementary School	Millington	87−88
Oak Elementary School	Bartlett	93−94
Red Bank High School	Chattanooga	92−93
Richland Elementary School	Memphis	93−94
Sacred Heart Cathedral School	Knoxville	91−92
Saint Cecilia Academy	Nashville	90−91
St. Jude School	Chattanooga	87−88
St. Mary's Episcopal School	Memphis	90−91
Science Hill High School	Johnson City	90−91
Snow Hill Elementary School	Ooltewah	85−86
Snowden School	Memphis	82−83
Thrasher Elementary School	Signal Mountain	85−86
Vanleer Elementary School	Vanleer	89−90
Westminster School	Nashville	89−90
Whiteville Elementary School	Whiteville	91−92

TEXAS

Akiba Academy of Dallas	Dallas	85−86
All Saints Episcopal School	Lubbock	91−92
Anderson Elementary School	Spring	89−90
Anna Middle School	Anna	92−93
Arch H. McCulloch Middle School	Dallas	90−91
Armstrong Middle School	Plano	92−93
Arnold Junior High School	Houston	90−91
Austin Academy for Excellence	Garland	92−93
Bear Creek Elementary School	Houston	87−88
Bellaire Senior High School	Bellaire	83−84
Ben Milam Elementary School	McAllen	89−90
Big Springs Elementary School	Garland	87−88
Bishop Lynch High School	Dallas	90−91
Bleyl Junior High School	Houston	83−84, 90−91
Booker T. Washington Elementary School	Port Arthur	87−88
Booker T. Washington Junior High School	Conroe	92−93
Bradley Middle School	San Antonio	86−87
Brentfield Elementary School	Dallas	93−94
Bunker Hill Elementary School	Houston	91−92
Canyon Vista Middle School	Austin	90−91
Carroll Elementary School	Southlake	93−94
Castle Hills Elementary School	San Antonio	87−88
Charles M. Blalack Junior High School	Carrollton	92−93
Charlie Richard Lyles Middle School	Garland	92−93

SCHOOL	CITY	YEAR(S) RECOGNIZED
TEXAS (*continued*)		
Chisholm Trail Middle School	Round Rock	92 – 93
Christ the King Catholic School	Dallas	93 – 94
Christa McAuliffe Elementary School	Lewisville	91 – 92
Clark High School	Plano	92 – 93
Clear Lake High School	Houston	86 – 87
Clear Lake Intermediate School	Houston	86 – 87
Coke R. Stevenson Middle School	San Antonio	90 – 91
Corpus Christi Catholic School	Houston	89 – 90
Crockett Elementary-Intermediate School	El Paso	85 – 86
Daniel F. Ortega Elementary School	Austin	93 – 94
Dartmouth Elementary School	Richardson	89 – 90
Davis Elementary School	Plano	93 – 94
Desert View Middle School	El Paso	83 – 84
Dooley Elementary School	Plano	89 – 90
Douglas MacArthur High School	San Antonio	88 – 89
Duchesne Academy of the Sacred Heart	Houston	92 – 93
Dwight D. Eisenhower Middle School	San Antonio	88 – 89
E. B. Reyna Elementary School	La Joya	93 – 94
E. L. Kent Elementary School	Carrollton	93 – 94
East Side Elementary School	Palacios	89 – 90
Eisenhower High School	Houston	88 – 89
Fiest Elementary School	Houston	93 – 94
Florence Elementary School	Southlake	93 – 94
Flower Mound Elementary School	Flower Mound	93 – 94
Forest Trail Elementary School	Austin	89 – 90
Forman Elementary School	Plano	93 – 94
Fort Sam Houston Elementary School	San Antonio	93 – 94
Francone Elementary School	Houston	91 – 92
Frostwood Elementary School	Houston	89 – 90
Good Shepherd Episcopal School	Dallas	91 – 92
Greenhill School	Dallas	84 – 85
H. B. Carlisle Elementary School	Plano	87 – 88
Hamilton Park Pacesetter School	Dallas	85 – 86
Harwood Junior High School	Bedford	86 – 87
Hazel S. Pattison Elementary School	Katy	93 – 94
Hedgecoxe Elementary School	Plano	93 – 94
Highland Park Elementary School	Austin	91 – 92
Highland Park High School	Dallas	84 – 85
Highland Village Elementary School	Lewisville	93 – 94
Hill Country Middle School	Austin	90 – 91
Hill Elementary School	Austin	93 – 94
Holy Cross High School	San Antonio	83 – 84
Holy Family of Nazareth School	Irving	89 – 90
Huffman Elementary School	Plano	91 – 92
Hunters Creek Elementary School	Houston	93 – 94

SCHOOL	CITY	YEAR(S) RECOGNIZED

TEXAS (*continued*)

Immaculate Conception School	Grand Prairie	85–86
Incarnate Word Academy	Corpus Christi	84–85
J. J. Pearce High School	Richardson	88–89
Jack D. Johnson Elementary School	Southlake	93–94
James Bowie High School	Austin	92–93
Jesuit College Preparatory School	Dallas	90–91
John Foster Dulles High School	Sugar Land	84–85
John Marshall High School	San Antonio	92–93
John S. Armstrong Elementary School	Dallas	85–86
John S. Bradfield Elementary School	Dallas	89–90
Juan N. Seguin Elementary School	McAllen	85–86
Kimberlin Academy for Excellence	Garland	91–92
Kingwood High School	Kingwood	84–85
L. P. Montgomery Elementary School	Farmers Branch	91–92
L. V. Berkner High School	Richardson	88–89
Labay Junior High School	Houston	88–89, 92–93
Langham Creek High School	Houston	90–91
Las Colinas Elementary School	Irving	93–94
Laurel Mountain Elementary School	Austin	91–92
Lina Milliken Middle School	Lewisville	92–93
Live Oak Elementary School	Austin	91–92
Los Encinos Special Emphasis School	Corpus Christi	87–88
Lowery Elementary School	Houston	91–92
Lozano Special Emphasis School	Corpus Christi	85–86
Mayde Creek Elementary School	Houston	89–90
Memorial High School	Houston	88–89
Memorial Junior High School	Houston	88–89
Meridith Magnet School	Temple	87–88
Merriman Park Elementary School	Dallas	89–90
Mirabeau B. Lamar Elementary School	Corpus Christi	91–92
Monsignor Kelly High School	Beaumont	84–85, 90–91
Moss Haven Elementary School	Dallas	93–94
North Loop Elementary School	El Paso	87–88
North Oaks Elementary School	Austin	93–94
Northbrook Senior High School	Houston	88–89
Northside Health Careers High School	San Antonio	90–91
Nottingham Elementary School	Houston	91–92
Olle Middle School	Houston	90–91
Parkhill Junior High School	Dallas	92–93
Pine Tree High School	Longview	88–89, 92–93
Pine Tree Junior High School	Longview	90–91
Pine Tree Middle 6/7 School	Longview	92–93
Pines Montessori School	Kingwood	85–86
Plano East Senior High School	Plano	92–93
Plano Senior High School	Plano	84–85

SCHOOL	CITY	YEAR(S) RECOGNIZED

TEXAS (*continued*)

Pope Elementary School	Arlington	85–86
R. L. Turner High School	Carrollton	90–91
R. W. Carpenter Middle School	Plano	92–93
Raul Longoria Elementary School	Pharr	87–88
Richardson High School	Richardson	83–84
Richardson Junior High School	Richardson	90–91
River Oaks Baptist School	Houston	91–92
Robert E. Lee Elementary School	Austin	91–92
Robert G. Cole Junior/Senior High School	San Antonio	86–87, 90–91
Robert S. Hyer Elementary School	Dallas	91–92
Rockdale High School	Rockdale	84–85
Rose Shaw Special Emphasis School	Corpus Christi	85–86
Rummel Creek Elementary School	Houston	85–86
Sacred Heart School	Muenster	93–94
Saigling Elementary School	Plano	91–92
Saint Agnes Academy	Houston	83–84, 88–89
St. Elizabeth Catholic School	Dallas	87–88
St. James Episcopal School	Corpus Christi	91–92
St. Mark the Evangelist Catholic School	Plano	91–92
St. Mark's School of Texas	Dallas	86–87
St. Patrick School	Corpus Christi	85–86
St. Peter Prince of Apostles School	San Antonio	85–86
St. Thomas More Parish School	Houston	93–94
Scarborough Senior High School	Houston	86–87
Schimelpfenig Middle School	Plano	88–89
Schuster Elementary School	El Paso	87–88
Shepard Elementary School	Plano	91–92
Sidney Lanier Vanguard Expressive Arts School	Dallas	87–88
Spring High School	Spring	92–93
Stephen F. Austin High School	Austin	82–83
Strack Intermediate School	Klein	90–91
Stratford High School	Houston	83–84
T. F. Birmingham Elementary School	Wylie	91–92
T. H. Johnson Elementary School	Taylor	85–86
T. H. Rogers School	Houston	91–92
Tanglewood Elementary School	Fort Worth	91–92
The Lamplighter School	Dallas	93–94
The Parish Day School	Dallas	93–94
Thomas J. Stovall Junior High School	Houston	90–91
Travis Elementary School	Greenville	87–88
Travis Middle School	Port Lavaca	83–84
University Park Elementary School	Dallas	87–88
Ursuline Academy of Dallas	Dallas	92–93
V. W. Miller Intermediate School	Houston	88–89

SCHOOL	CITY	YEAR(S) RECOGNIZED

TEXAS (*continued*)

Vivian Field Junior High School	Farmers Branch	92–93
W. H. L. Wells Elementary School	Plano	91–92
Wake Village School	Wake Village	85–86
West Ridge Middle School	Austin	92–93
Westlake High School	Austin	88–89
Wilchester Elementary School	Houston	89–90
William H. Atwell Fundamental Academy	Dallas	86–87
Wilson Middle School	Plano	88–89
Winston Churchill High School	San Antonio	82–83
Woodway Elementary School	Waco	85–86

UTAH

Altara Elementary School	Sandy	85–86
Bonneville Elementary School	Salt Lake City	87–88
Bountiful High School	Bountiful	82–83
Brighton High School	Salt Lake City	82–83
Butler Middle School	Salt Lake City	82–83
Eastmont Middle School	Sandy	83–84
George Q. Knowlton Elementary School	Farmington	91–92
Granger High School	West Valley	92–93
Highland High School	Salt Lake City	82–83
Hillcrest Elementary School	Logan	85–86
J. A. Taylor Elementary School	Centerville	87–88
Judge Memorial Catholic High School	Salt Lake City	83–84, 88–89
Logan Junior High School	Logan	83–84
Logan Senior High School	Logan	82–83
Mound Fort Middle School	Ogden	84–85
Northwest Intermediate School	Salt Lake City	88–89
Northwest Middle School	Salt Lake City	93–94
Olympus High School	Salt Lake City	84–85
Olympus Junior High School	Salt Lake City	86–87
Rowland Hall-St. Mark's School	Salt Lake City	85–86
South High School	Salt Lake City	83–84
Timpview High School	Provo	83–84
Wasatch Elementary School	Salt Lake City	89–90
Wasatch Middle School	Heber City	82–83
West High School	Salt Lake City	88–89

VERMONT

Camels Hump Middle School	Richmond	88–89
Chamberlin School	South Burlington	91–92
Craftsbury Academy	Craftsbury Common	90–91

SCHOOL	CITY	YEAR(S) RECOGNIZED
VERMONT (*continued*)		
Essex Elementary School	Essex Junction	89−90
Hardwick Elementary School	Hardwick	87−88
Hazen Union School	Hardwick	83−84
Mater Christi School	Burlington	89−90
Proctor Junior/Senior High School	Proctor	92−93
Richmond Elementary School	Richmond	91−92
St. Johnsbury Academy	St. Johnsbury	90−91
Shelburne Middle School	Shelburne	88−89
South Burlington High School	South Burlington	84−85
South Burlington Middle School	South Burlington	86−87
Waitsfield Elementary School	Waitsfield	93−94
Waterbury Elementary School	Waterbury	85−86
Woodstock Union High School	Woodstock	86−87

VIRGIN ISLANDS

Antilles School	St. Thomas	91−92

VIRGINIA

Ashlawn Elementary School	Arlington	89−90
Bishop Denis J. O'Connell High School	Arlington	92−93
Breckinridge Junior High School	Roanoke	83−84
Brookland Middle School	Richmond	84−85
Cape Henry Collegiate School	Virginia Beach	92−93
Cave Spring High School	Roanoke	82−83
David A. Dutrow Elementary School	Newport News	85−86
Denbigh High School	Newport News	86−87
Dooley School	Richmond	86−87
Douglas Southall Freeman High School	Henrico County	92−93
Dunbar-Erwin Middle School	Newport News	83−84
E. C. Glass High School	Lynchburg	82−83, 92−93
Falls Church Elementary School	Falls Church	85−86
George Mason Junior-Senior High School	Falls Church	82−83
Glenvar High School	Salem	88−89
Hampton High School	Hampton	84−85
Heritage Elementary School	Lynchburg	85−86
Heritage High School	Lynchburg	92−93
Hermitage High School	Richmond	83−84
Hidden Valley Junior High School	Roanoke	83−84
Highland Park Learning Center Magnet School	Roanoke	91−92
Homer L. Hines Middle School	Newport News	86−87, 92−93
Huntington Middle School	Newport News	84−85
James Madison Junior High School	Roanoke	86−87
Kingston Elementary School	Virginia Beach	89−90

SCHOOL	CITY	YEAR(S) RECOGNIZED

VIRGINIA (*continued*)

SCHOOL	CITY	YEAR(S) RECOGNIZED
Linkhorne Elementary School	Lynchburg	93—94
Lynnhaven Junior High School	Virginia Beach	86—87
Menchville High School	Newport News	83—84
Mills E. Godwin High School	Richmond	88—89
Mountain View Elementary School	Roanoke	87—88
Norfolk Academy	Norfolk	84—85, 93—94
Northside Middle School	Norfolk	92—93
Norview High School	Norfolk	88—89
Oak Grove Elementary School	Roanoke	85—86
Oakridge Elementary School	Arlington	85—86
Poquoson Elementary School	Poquoson	87—88
Poquoson Primary School	Poquoson	93—94
Prospect Heights Middle School	Orange	82—83
R. C. Longan Elementary School	Richmond	85—86
Rawls Byrd Elementary School	Williamsburg	91—92
School for Contemporary Education	Annandale	92—93
Syms Middle School	Hampton	90—91
T. C. Williams High School	Alexandria	82—83
The Madeira School	Greenway	86—87
Washington-Lee High School	Arlington	84—85
William Fleming High School	Roanoke	88—89

WASHINGTON

SCHOOL	CITY	YEAR(S) RECOGNIZED
Anacortes High School	Anacortes	88—89
Battle Ground High School	Battle Ground	83—84
Bellarmine Preparatory School	Tacoma	83—84, 88—89
Blaine High School	Blaine	84—85
Blaine Middle School	Blaine	85—86
Capital High School	Olympia	86—87
Cashmere Middle School	Cashmere	82—83
Charles A. Lindbergh High School	Renton	83—84
Charles Wright Academy	Tacoma	88—89
Cherry Crest Elementary School	Bellevue	87—88
Colville High School	Colville	83—84, 88—89
Curtis High School	Tacoma	82—83
Curtis Junior High School	Tacoma	83—84
Custer Elementary School	Custer	93—94
Dick Scobee Elementary School	Auburn	89—90
Eastmont High School	East Wenatchee	88—89
Emily Dickinson School	Redmond	85—86
Enumclaw Junior High School	Enumclaw	88—89
Eton School	Bellevue	91—92
Ferndale High School	Ferndale	86—87
Garrison Junior High School	Walla Walla	86—87

SCHOOL	CITY	YEAR(S) RECOGNIZED

WASHINGTON (*continued*)

SCHOOL	CITY	YEAR(S) RECOGNIZED
Gonzaga Preparatory School	Spokane	92–93
Hanford Secondary School	Richland	82–83
Hazelwood Elementary School	Renton	91–92
Holy Names Academy	Seattle	84–85, 90–91
Holy Rosary School	Seattle	89–90
Jefferson Middle School	Olympia	83–84
Jemtegaard Middle School	Washougal	90–91
John Campbell Elementary School	Selah	85–86
John H. McKnight Middle School	Renton	84–85
John Muir Elementary School	Kirkland	89–90
Kent Junior High School	Kent	88–89
Kent-Meridian High School	Kent	92–93
Kentridge High School	Kent	84–85
Lacamas Heights Elementary School	Camas	85–86
Lake Washington High School	Kirkland	84–85
Lake Youngs Elementary School	Kent	85–86
McAlder Elementary School	Puyallup	93–94
Mead Junior High School	Mead	82–83
Meany Middle School	Seattle	86–87
Meridian Junior High School	Kent	84–85
Mount Rainier High School	Des Moines	84–85
New Century High School	Lacey	92–93
Omak Middle School	Omak	83–84
Pasco Senior High School	Pasco	82–83
Pine Tree Elementary School	Kent	89–90
Pleasant Valley Intermediate School	Vancouver	84–85
Redmond Elementary School	Redmond	87–88
Redmond High School	Redmond	83–84
Renton Park Elementary School	Renton	89–90
Ringdall Middle School	Bellevue	84–85
Sacajawea Junior High School	Spokane	82–83
Saint Edward School	Seattle	87–88
St. Paul School	Seattle	87–88
St. Philomena Catholic School	Des Moines	91–92
Shorewood High School	Seattle	82–83
Skyline Elementary School	Ferndale	91–92
Spring Glen Elementary School	Renton	91–92
Stevens Middle School	Port Angeles	84–85
Vista Middle School	Ferndale	88–89
Washington Elementary School	Auburn	93–94
Washington Elementary School	Mount Vernon	93–94
Wenatchee High School	Wenatchee	86–87
West Valley Junior High School	Yakima	84–85
Whitworth Elementary School	Seattle	85–86
Wilbur High School	Wilbur	83–84

SCHOOL	CITY	YEAR(S) RECOGNIZED

WEST VIRGINIA

Bridge Street Junior High School	Wheeling	82−83
Buckhannon-Upshur Middle School	Buckhannon	93−94
Capital High School	Charleston	92−93
Clay County High School	Clay	88−89
Clay County Junior High School	Clay	90−91
Clay Elementary School	Clay	93−94
DuPont Junior High School	Belle	92−93
East Dale Elementary School	Fairmont	87−88
Elm Grove Elementary School	Wheeling	91−92
George Washington High School	Charleston	83−84
High Lawn Elementary School	St. Albans	91−92
Jennings Randolph Elementary School	Elkins	85−86
Johnson Elementary School	Bridgeport	85−86
Lewisburg Elementary School	Lewisburg	93−94
Lory-Julian Elementary School	Julian	93−94
Our Lady of Fatima School	Huntington	91−92
Pleasants County Middle School	Belmont	92−93
St. Francis Central Catholic School	Morgantown	93−94
St. Marys High School	St. Marys	84−85
Tiskelwah Elementary School	Charleston	91−92
Triadelphia Junior High School	Wheeling	82−83
Troy Elementary School	Troy	93−94
Weberwood Elementary School	Charleston	87−88
West Milford Elementary School	West Milford	93−94
Wheeling Junior High School	Wheeling	82−83
Wheeling Park High School	Wheeling	83−84
Wyatt Elementary School	Wyatt	87−88

WISCONSIN

Alexander Hamilton High School	Milwaukee	86−87
Bay View Middle School	Green Bay	93−94
Brown Deer High School	Brown Deer	83−84
Butte des Morts Junior High School	Menasha	86−87
Columbus High School	Columbus	84−85
Crestwood Elementary School	Madison	91−92
Custer High School	Milwaukee	92−93
Divine Savior Holy Angels High School	Milwaukee	84−85
East High School	Madison	88−89
Edgewood High School of the Sacred Heart	Madison	86−87
Elm Grove Lutheran School	Elm Grove	85−86
Franklin High School	Franklin	86−87
Garfield Math/Science Elementary School	Milwaukee	87−88
Hales Corners Elementary School	Hales Corners	87−88

SCHOOL	CITY	YEAR(S) RECOGNIZED

WISCONSIN (*continued*)

SCHOOL	CITY	YEAR(S) RECOGNIZED
Harold S. Vincent High School	Milwaukee	86 – 87
Horace Mann Middle School	Sheboygan	90 – 91
Immanuel Lutheran School	Wisconsin Rapids	87 – 88
James Madison Memorial High School	Madison	90 – 91
Jefferson Elementary School	Menasha	91 – 92
John Burroughs Middle School	Milwaukee	83 – 84
John Muir Elementary School	Madison	91 – 92
Kohler High School	Kohler	88 – 89
LaFollette High School	Madison	83 – 84
Lincoln High School	Manitowoc	88 – 89
Lincoln High School	Wisconsin Rapids	86 – 87
M. J. Gegan Elementary School	Menasha	87 – 88
Magee Elementary School	Genesee Depot	93 – 94
Marquette University High School	Milwaukee	83 – 84
Martin Luther High School	Greendale	83 – 84
McFarland Elementary School	McFarland	85 – 86
Memorial High School	Eau Clair	82 – 83
Merrill Senior High School	Merrill	84 – 85
Milwaukee German Immersion School	Milwaukee	93 – 94
Milwaukee Lutheran High School	Milwaukee	84 – 85, 92 – 93
Milwaukee Trade and Technical High School	Milwaukee	92 – 93
Morse Middle School	Milwaukee	84 – 85
Neenah High School	Neenah	84 – 85
Nicolet High School	Glendale	90 – 91
Northwest Lutheran School	Milwaukee	85 – 86
Oconomowoc High School	Oconomowoc	90 – 91
Owen-Withee High School	Owen	83 – 84
Parkview Middle School	Green Bay	87 – 88
Phoenix Middle School	Delavan	84 – 85
Pius XI High School	Milwaukee	83 – 84
Rufus King High School	Milwaukee	82 – 83
St. Alphonsus School	Greendale	93 – 94
St. Joseph Academy	Green Bay	88 – 89
St. Margaret Mary School	Neenah	87 – 88
St. Paul's Lutheran School	Janesville	91 – 92
Seymour Middle School	Seymour	93 – 94
Sheboygan South High School	Sheboygan	86 – 87
South Milwaukee Senior High School	South Milwaukee	88 – 89
Spring Road School	Neenah	85 – 86
Stevens Point Area Senior High School	Stevens Point	84 – 85
Stoughton Middle School	Stoughton	84 – 85
Valley View Elementary School	Green Bay	89 – 90
Van Hise Middle School	Madison	86 – 87
Webster Transitional School	Cedarburg	82 – 83
West Senior High School	Madison	84 – 85

SCHOOL	CITY	YEAR(S) RECOGNIZED
WISCONSIN (*continued*)		
Whitman Middle School	Wauwatosa	84–85
Williams Bay High School	Williams Bay	86–87
Wilson Elementary School	Sheboygan	89–90

WYOMING

SCHOOL	CITY	YEAR(S) RECOGNIZED
Big Piney Middle School	Big Piney	92–93
Crest Hill Elementary School	Casper	87–88, 91–92
Douglas Middle School	Douglas	82–83
Jackson Hole High School	Jackson	86–87, 92–93
Kelly Walsh High School	Casper	83–84
Pine Bluffs High School	Pine Bluffs	82–83
Pinedale Elementary School	Pinedale	89–90
Pinedale Middle School	Pinedale	90–91
Sage Valley Junior High School	Gillette	86–87
Wilson Elementary School	Wilson	93–94

Blue Ribbon Schools Program
Office of Educational Research and Improvement
U. S. Department of Education

STATE LIAISONS 1993 – 94
Dr. Frank Heatherly
Mathematics Specialist
Alabama Department of Education
50 North Ripley Street
Montgomery, AL 36130-3901
(205) 242-8082

Ms. Rosemary Hagevig
Education Specialist
Alaska Department of Education
Goldbelt Place
801 West 10th Street, P. O. Box F
Juneau, AK 99811
(907) 465-8715

Mr. Thomas L. Cox
Coordinator, Recognition Programs
Arizona Department of Education
1535 West Jefferson
Phoenix, AZ 85007
(602) 542-3740

Mr. James A. Hester
Program Support Manager for Evaluation
Arkansas Department of Education
4 Capitol Mall
Little Rock, AR 72201
(501) 682-4371

Ms. Norma Carolan
Research Analyst
California Department of Education
Program Evaluation and Research
Division
721 Capitol Mall, P. O. Box 944272
Sacramento, CA 95814
(916) 657-3799

Ms. Erlinda Archuleta
Director
Regional Educational Services Unit
Colorado Department of Education
201 East Colfax Avenue
Denver, CO 80203
(303) 866-6638

Dr. Marie Della Bella
School Approval Consultant
State Department of Education
Box 2219
Hartford, CT 06145
(203) 566-3593

Dr. Horacio D. Lewis
State Supervisor, Human Relations
Delaware Department of Education
The Towsend Building
P. O. Box 1402
Dover, DE 19901
(302) 739-2770

Ms. Beth Boltz
Research Assistant
Information and Accountability Reports
Florida Department of Education
Suite 714 FEC
Tallahassee, FL 32399
(904) 488-1659

Ms. Gale E. Samuels
Special Projects Coordinator
Georgia Department of Education
2052 Twin Towers East
Atlanta, GA 30334-5010
(404) 656-2476

Dr. Elaine M. Takenaka
Special Programs Management Section
Hawaii Department of Education
3430 Leahi Avenue
Honolulu, HI 96815
(808) 735-9024

Ms. Judy Adamson
Elementary Supervisor
Idaho Department of Education
LBJ Office Building
Boise, ID 83720
(208) 334-2281

Dr. Anne Marie Fuhrig
Educational Consultant
Illinois State Board of Education
Textbooks and Scholarships Section,
 W-265
100 North First Street
Springfield, IL 62777
(217) 782-9374

Ms. Betty Johnson
Chief, Office of School Assistance
Indiana Department of Education
229 State House
Indianapolis, IN 46204
(317) 232-9141

Ms. Sharon Slezak
Administrative Coordinator
Communication Services
Iowa Department of Education
Des Moines, IA 50319-3294
(515) 281-3750

Mr. Robert L. Gast
Team Leader, Information and Marketing
Kansas State Board of Education
120 S. E. 10th Street
Topeka, KS 66612-1182
(913) 296-4961

Ms. Kay Anne Wilborn
Office of Communication Services
Kentucky Department of Education
Capitol Plaza Tower, 19th Floor
Frankfort, KY 40601
(502) 564-3421

Mrs. Kay Nelson
Program Manager
Bureau of Elementary Education
Louisiana Department of Education
P. O. Box 94064
Baton Rouge, LA 70804-9064
(504) 342-3366

Dr. Horace P. Maxcy, Jr.
Senior Planner
Division of Applied Technology
Maine Department of Education
State House Station 23
Augusta, ME 04333
(207) 287-1135

Mrs. Darla Strouse
Specialist
School Volunteer and Partnership Program
Maryland Department of Education
200 West Baltimore Street
Baltimore, MD 21201
(410) 333-2211

Ms. Jacqueline Peterson
Program Coordinator
Blue Ribbon Schools Programs
Massachusetts Department of Education
350 Main Street
Malden, MA 02148-5023
(617) 388-3300, Ext. 235

Ms. Ellen Carter Cooper
Education Consultant
School Improvement/Special
Development
Michigan Department of Education
P. O. Box 30008
608 West Allegan
Lansing, MI 48909
(517) 373-3608

Dr. Bounlieng Phommasouvanh
Minnesota Department of Education
550 Cedar Street
St. Paul MN 55101
(612) 296-1064

Dr. Samuel McGee
Director of Student Development
Office of Student Development
P. O. Box 771
Walter Sillers Building
Jackson, MS 39205-0771
(601) 359-5532

Ms. Joan Solomon
Director of Urban Education
Missouri Department of Elementary and
  Secondary Education
P. O. Box 480
205 Jefferson
Jefferson City, MO 65102
(314) 751-2931

Mr. Duane Jackson
Foreign Language Specialist
Office of Public Instruction
Capitol Station
Helena, MT 59620
(406) 444-3129

Dr. Dean Bergman
Administrative Assistant
Nebraska Department of Education
Centennial Mall South
Lincoln, NE 68509-4987
(402) 471-2437

Ms. Vicki M. Bulter
Education Consultant
Nevada Department of Education
Capitol Complex
Carson City, NV 89710
(702) 687-3136

Dr. Gerald Bourgeois
Program Administrator,
  School Approval
New Hampshire Department of Education
101 Pleasant Street
Concord, NH 03301
(603) 271-3859

Dr. John Dougherty
Program Evaluation Specialist
New Jersey Department of Education

Division of General Academic Education
225 West State Street
Trenton, NJ 08625
(609) 984-6304

Mrs. Mary Gervase
Assistant Director
School Programs and Professional
  Development
New Mexico Department of Education
Education Building
Santa Fe, NM 87501-2786
(505) 827-6673

Ms. Susan Shipe
Associate, Office for Statewide School
  Registration Programs
New York Department of Education
Room 675 EBA
Washington Avenue
Albany, NY 12234
(518) 474-5894

Mr. Dennis Stacey and
Mrs. Rebecca Banks
North Carolina Department of Education
116 West Edenton Street
Raleigh, NC 27603-2825
(919) 715-1632

Ms. Joan Estes
Assistant Director, Elementary Education
and Mr. Roger Rieger
  Assistant Director of Secondary Education
North Dakota Department of Education
600 Boulevard Avenue, East
Bismarck, ND 58505
(701) 224-2488

Ms. Hazel Flowers
Director, Division of Equal
  Educational Opportunities
Ohio Department of Education
106 North High Street, Second Floor
Columbus, Ohio 43266-0106
(614) 466-3318

Ms. Martha Michael
Director of Effective Schools

Oklahoma Department of Education
2500 North Lincoln Boulevard
Oklahoma City, OK 73105-4599
(405) 521-4513

Ms. Patricia L. Stewart
Regional Director, Division of
  School Based Improvement
Pennsylvania Department of Education
333 Market Street
Harrisburg, PA 17126-0333
(717) 783-2862

Ms. Nancy Lebron Iriarte
Special Assistant, Academic Programs
Department of Education
Office 800, Floor 8, Box 759
Hato Rey, Puerto Rico 00919
(809) 754-1315

Mr. Steve Nardelli
School Improvement Center
Rhode Island Department of Education
22 Hayes Street
Providence, RI 02908
(401) 277-2638

Dr. Bart Teal
Accreditation Supervisor
South Carolina Department of Education
707 Rutledge Building
Columbia, SC 29201
(803)734-8333

Ms. Shirlie Moysis
Gifted Education Director
South Dakota Department of Education
700 Governors Drive
Pierre, SD 57501
(605) 773-4662

Mrs. Mary Ann Lewis
Director of Elementary Education
Tennessee Department of Education
8th Floor Gateway Plaza
710 James Robertson Parkway
Nashville, TN 37243-0379
(615) 532-6267

Mr. Michael A. Gula
Director, Exemplary Instruction

Texas Education Agency
1701 North Congress Avenue
Austin, TX 78701-1494
(512) 463-9661

Ms. Eileen Rencher
Director of Public Information
Utah State Board of Education
250 East 500 South
Salt Lake City, UT 84111
(801) 538-7519

Mr. Edward Haggett
School Improvement Coordinator
Vermont Department of Education
120 State Street
Montpelier, VT 65602
(802) 828-2756

Mr. Vernon Wildy
Principal/Specialist Student
  Needs Assessment
Virginia Department of Education
P. O. Box 6Q
Richmond, VA 23216
(804) 371-6881

Ms. Henrita Barber
Office of Testing, Planning,
  Research, and Evaluation
44-46 Kongens Gade, Charlotte Amalie
St. Thomas, U.S. Virgin Islands 00802
(809) 774-0100, ext 3082

Ms. Chris McElroy
Supervisor, School Improvement and
  Accreditation Program
Washington Department of Education
Old Capitol Building
Olympia, WA 98504
(206) 753-1895

Mr. David Perrine
Coordinator of Early Childhood
  Education
Office of Professional Development
West Virginia Department of Education
Capitol Complex, Room B-330
1900 Kanawha Boulevard, East

Charleston, WV 25305
(304) 558-7805

Ms. Ann Conzemius
Executive Assistant to the State
 Superintendent of Instruction
Wisconsin Department of Public
 Instruction
P. O. Box 7841
Madison, WI 53707
(608) 266-1771

Mr. D. Leeds Pickering
Consultant, School Improvment Unit
Wyoming Department of Education
Hathaway Building
Cheyenne, WY 82002-0050
(307) 777-6265

Ms. Lana Shaughnessy
Education Specialist
Elementary and Secondary Branch
Bureau of Indian Affairs
U.S. Department of the Interior
Code 521, MS3525, MIB
1849 C Street, NW
Washington, D. C. 20245
(202) 219-1129

Ms. Joyce G. McCray
Executive Director
Council for American Private Education
1726 M Street, NW, Suite 1102
Washington, D. C. 20036
(202) 659-0016

Dr. Phyllis D. Hines
Executive Assistant

Office of Educational Programs and
 Operations
District of Columbia Public Schools
415 12th Street, NW, Suite 903
Washington, D. C. 20004
(202) 724-4980

Dr. Mary Johnson
Project Officer, Recognition Program
Department of Defense
Dependents Schools
4040 North Fairfax Drive
Room 916, Education Division
Alexandria, VA 22203
(703) 696-4490, Ext. 152

U. S. DEPARTMENT OF EDUCA-
TION STAFF-BLUE RIBBON
SCHOOLS
PROGRAM
Lois Weinberg
Director
School Recognition Programs

Kathryn E. Crossely
202-219-2154

Patricia A. Hobbs
202-219-2063

J. Stephen O'Brien
202-219-2141

Blue Ribbon Schools Program
555 New Jersey Avenue NW
Washington, D. C. 20208-5645
Telephone: 202-219-2149
FAX: 202-219-2106

Educational Program References

SOME of the programs available through the National Diffusion Network used in many of the Best Schools include: the following programs which have been nationally validated as effective by the U. S. Department of Education. Inservice training and materials are made available to schools throughout the country through the National Diffusion Network (NDN) and there are state facilitators available in every state to assist schools with adoption (see Appendix D for a list of state facilitators).

- *CSMP—Comprehensive School Mathematics Program*—has as an underlying assumption that students can learn and enjoy mathematics more than is usually the case. The content is presented as an extension of experiences children have encountered in their development, both in real life and at the fantasy level. Children are led through problem-solving situations. It is CSMP's conviction that mathematics is a unified whole and should be learned as such. CSMP is a complete K−6 curriculum. CSMP Project Director, 12500 E. Iliff Ave., Suite 201, Aurora, CO 80014.
- *DASH—Developmental Approaches in Science and Health*—is an elementary science, health, and technology program designed to narrow the gap between the way science is taught and the way science is used in a technological, health-oriented society. The program, which was created by the University of Hawaii Curriculum Research and Development Group, takes an interdisciplinary approach to science, health, and technology; is built on twenty years of research, and was ten years in the making. DASH lets science studies evolve naturally from a need to cope with experiences. DASH Project Manager, University of Hawaii−CRDG, 1776 University Ave., Honolulu, HI 96822.
- *FAST—Foundation Approaches in Science Teaching*—is a multidisciplinary, inquiry science program designed to meet the special needs of middle school students in three one-year courses: FAST 1, The Local Environments; FAST 2, The Flow of Matter and Energy Through the Biosphere; and FAST, Change over Time. The program uses carefully sequenced tasks and inquiries involving both students and teachers in defining concepts, generating and testing hypotheses, correcting misconceptions, and ultimately coming to consensus on the adequacy of explanations. Between 60% and 80% of class time is spent in laboratory or field studies. The remaining time is devoted to analysis of data, small group and class discussion, literature research, and report writing. There are separate teacher institutes for each course. Director FAST Dissemination Project, University of Hawaii−CRDG, 1776 University Ave., Honolulu, HI 96822.
- *Growing Healthy* is a comprehensive health education program designed to foster student competencies to make decisions enhancing their health and lives, for grades K−7. Growing Healthy includes a planned sequential curriculum, a variety of

343

teaching methods, a teacher training program, and strategies for eliciting community support for health education. Contact: Michelle Reich, School-Based Programs, National Council for Health Education, 72 Spring Street, Suite 208, New York, NY 10012, (212)334-9470.

- *H.O.T.S. — Higher Order Thinking* is an alternative approach to reading remediation, which consists solely of higher order thinking activities. The program has also been used for gifted children. The goal is to provide students with conceptual skills to learn content of the upper elementary school grades the first time it is taught in the classroom. The program was developed by Dr. Stanley Pogrow, University of Arizona. Chapter I H.O.T.S.: Higher Order Thinking Skills Project, University of Arizona, College of Education, Tucson, AZ 85721.

- *Junior Great Books* is a student-centered program of interpreting reading, writing, and discussion based on the shared inquiry method of learning developed by the Great Books Foundation. The curriculum provides intensive work in constructing meaning from literature. The Great Books Foundation, 35 East Wacher Drive, Suite 2300, Chicago, IL 60601-2298.

- *Reading Recovery* is a one-to-one intervention program for the lowest achieving children in first grade reading. The approach is based on the research of Marie M. Clay in New Zealand, where *Reading Recovery* is a nationally adopted program. The goal is to bring children to the average of the class through involvement in highly specialized individual thirty-minute daily lessons. The average length of instruction needed is 16.4 weeks. The aim is that once children successfully complete the program, they will never again need remediation. Many of the best schools use this approach. Reading Recovery Program, The Ohio State University, 200 Ramseyer Hall, 29 West Woodruff Avenue, Columbus, OH 43210.

- *STAMM — Systematic Teaching and Measuring Mathematics* is an elementary mathematics program that provides the curriculum and the means to assist in delivering the NCTM Standards. Teachers select from a variety of learning activities using concrete manipulatives, problem solving, and enrichment strategies. The program was developed to compliment existing textbooks, manipulatives, and teacher-made resources. STAMM Project Director, Jefferson County Schools, 1005 Wadsworth Blvd., Lakewood, CO 80215.

- *Talents Unlimited* is a teaching/learning model that integrates creative and critical thinking skills into any area in the regular curriculum. The program applies, at the classroom level, Dr. Calvin Taylor's research-based multiple talent approach to teaching. Talents Unlimited, 1107 Arlington Street, Mobile, AL 36605.

Some of the other programs frequently used in the Best Schools are

- *AIMS — Activities That Integrate Math and Science* is a program that establishes an intrinsic relationship between math and science. A whole series of math skills and science processes are interwoven in a single activity, creating a continuum of experiences, practice, and application. Students actively investigate questions that relate to the world of the student. Investigations are available in a series of books for grades K−9. Teacher training and other support materials are available. AIMS Education Foundation, P.O. Box 7766, Fresno, CA 93747.

- *D.A.R.E. — Drug Abuse Resistance Education* was developed by the Los Angeles Police Department and the Los Angeles Unified School District to prevent drug abuse in children. The K−12 curriculum is designed to help students recognize and resist the many subtle pressures that influence them to experiment with alcohol and marijuana. In addition, program strategies are planned to focus on feelings related to self-esteem, interpersonal and communication skills, and decision making. Lessons are conducted by police officers trained in program implementation. Contact: D.A.R.E., Los Angeles Unified School District, Los Angeles, CA.

- *Here's Looking at You 2000* is a sequenced K−12 program that includes all the activities and materials needed for implementing the program. The program teaches life skills, as well as providing drug prevention education. Contact: Robert, Fitsmahan and Associates. Educational Services District #121, Seattle, WA.

- *KidsNet—National Geographic Kids Network* is a program that uses easy-to-use computer software, hands-on materials, and telecommunications to allow children to work together around the world to conduct original scientific research on real-world issues. Students share findings (via modem) with ''research teammates'' in the United States and other countries. Help and advice is provided by participating professional scientists. Materials and software are purchased and owned by the school. Tuition and telecommunications is paid by subscription for each eight-week session. Units include Weather in Action, What's in Our Water?, Hello!, Too Much Trash, Solar Energy, Acid Rain, and What Are We Eating? National Geographic Society, Educational Services, Washington, D. C. 20036.

- *Project Jason* uses The Jason Classroom Network, offered through cable companies by Turner Educational Services, to carry live broadcasts from research sites. Scientists at multiple sites lead experiments and live discussions via satellite with students at interactive stations. The National Science Teachers Association has developed curriculum support materials. Lessons feature hands-on activities dealing with one or more topics the Jason expedition explores: technology, geology, physics, biology, geography, history, and social studies. The Jason Foundation for Education, 391 Totten Pond Rd., Waltham, MA 02154.

- *SCIS 3—Science Curriculum Improvement Study* is the third generation of a program originally developed in the post-Sputnik era of the 1960s, with funding from the National Science Foundation. SCIS 3 uses a thematic conceptual hands-on approach to actively engage students in physical, life, earth, and environmental science. Emphasis is placed on the concept of evidence as a foundation of modern science and on relationships between classroom science and everyday lives of students. Delta Education, Hudson, NH.

- *Voyage of the Mimi* is an interdisciplinary program that combines videos or video discs, computer software, and print material to present an integrated set of concepts in math, science, social studies, and language arts. The Voyage of the Mimi is based on the story of the ketch Mimi and her crew, who set out on the sea to locate and study whales. The Second Voyage of Mimi leads students on an adventure in Mexico to study the ancient Maya civilization. The programs were created by Bank Street College of Education, with funds from the U. S. Department of Education and the National Science Foundation, for students in grades 4−6. WINGS for Learning/Sunburst Communications, 1600 Green Hills Road, Scotts Valley, CA 95067-0002.

National Diffusion Network State Facilitators

FOR information concerning nationally validated programs disseminated by the National Diffusion Network Contact:

ALABAMA
Ms. Maureen C. Cassidy
Alabama Facilitator Project
Div. of Professional Services
Gordon Persons Building Rm 5069
50 North Ripley
Montgomery, AL 36130-3901
(205) 242-9834
Fax (205)242-9708

ALASKA
Ms. Sandra Berry
Alaska State Facilitator
AK State Department of Education
Mail to: 801 West 10th Street
Suite 200
Ship To: P.O. Box F
Juneau, AK 99801-1894
(907) 464-2824
Fax (907) 464-3396

ARIZONA
Dr. L. Leon Webb
Arizona State Facilitator
Ed. Diffusion Systems, Inc.
161 East First Street
Mesa, AZ 85201
(602) 969-4880
Fax (602) 898-8527

ARKANSAS
Ms. Jo Cheek
State Facilitator
Arkansas Department of Ed.
Office of the Director
#4 Capitol Mall/Room 204B
Little Rock, AR

(501) 682-4568
Fax (501) 682-1146

CALIFORNIA
Ms. Susan Boiko, SF
Association of California
  School Administrators
1575 Old Bayshore Highway
Burlingame, CA 94010
(415) 692-4300
Fax (415) 692-1508

COLORADO
Mr. Charles D. Beck, Jr.
The Education Diffusion Group
3607 Martin Luther King Blvd.
Denver, CO 80295
(303) 322-9323
Fax (303) 322-9475

CONNECTICUT
Mr. Jonathan P. Costa
Connecticut Facilitator
RESCUE Education Service Center
P. O. Box 909
355 Goshen Road
Litchfield, CT 06759-0909
(203) 567-0863
Fax (203) 567-3381

DELAWARE
Mrs. Linda Y. Welsh
State Facilitator Project
Dept. of Public Instruction
John G. Townsend Building
Management Information Division
P. O. Box 1402

Dover, DE 19903
(302) 739-4583
Fax (302) 739-3092

DISTRICT OF COLUMBIA
Ms. Susan C. Williams
District Facilitator Project
Eaton School
34th and Lowell Streets, NW
Washington, D. C. 2008
(202) 282-0056
Fax (202) 282-1127

FLORIDA
Ms. Judy Bishop
Florida State Facilitator
Florida Department of Education
424 FEC
325 West Gaines Street
Tallahassee, FL 32399-0400
(904) 487-1078
Fax (904) 487-0716

GEORGIA
Dr. Frances Hensley
Georgia Facilitator Center
607 Aderhold Hall, UGA
Carlton Street
Athens, GA 30602-7145
(706) 542-332 or 542-3810
Fax (706) 542-4032

HAWAII
Dr. Mona Vierra
State Facilitator
Department of Education
Office of Information and
  Telecommunication Services
P. O. Box 2360
Honolulu, HI 96808
(808) 735-3107
Fax (808) 735-5217

IDAHO
Ms. Lianne Yamamoto
State Facilitator
Idaho State Department of Ed.
Len B. Jordan Office Building
Boise, ID 83720-3650

(208) 334-3561
Fax (208) 334-2228 or 2636

ILLINOIS
Dr. Shirley Menendex
Project Director
Statewide Facilitator Project
1105 East Fifth Street
Metropolis, IL 62960
(618) 524-2664
Fax (618) 524-3535

INDIANA
Dr. C. Lynwood Erb
Project Director
Indiana Facilitator Center
Education Resource Brokers, Inc.
2635 Yeager Road
Suite D
West Lafayette, IN 47906
(317) 497-3269
Fax (317) 497-3461

IOWA
Ms. June Harris
State Facilitator
Iowa Department of Education
Bureau of Planning, Research,
  and Evaluation
Grimes Building
East 14th Street & Grand Ave.
Des Moines, IA 50310-0146
(515) 281-5288
Fax (515) 242-5988

KANSAS
Mr. James H. Connett
Kansas State Facilitator Project
Director, KEDDS/Link
Administrative Center-S. Bldg.
217 North Water
Wichita, KS 67202
(316) 833-4711
Fax (316) 833-4712

KENTUCKY
Ms. Jannet Stevens
Kentucky State Facilitator
Kentucky Department of Education

Capitol Plaza Tower Office Bldg.
500 Mero Street
Frankfort, KY 40601
(502) 564-2672
Fax (502) 564-6711

LOUISIANA
Ms. Brenda Argo
Facilitator Project Director
State Department of Education
ESEA Title II Bureau Office
Mail To: P. O. Box 94064
Baton Rouge, LA 70804-9064
Ship To: 654 Main St.-3rd Floor
Baton Rouge, LA 70802-9064
(504) 342-3375
Fax (504) 342-7367

MAINE
Ms. Sue Doughty
Ms. Elaine Roberts
Center for Educational Services
Mail To: P. O. Box 620
Auburn, Maine 04212-0620
Ship To: 223 Main Street
Auburn, ME 04210
(207) 783-0833
Fax (207) 783-9701

MARYLAND
Dr. Raymond H. Hartjen
Educational Alternatives, Inc.
P. O. Box 265
Harwood Lane
Port Tobacco, MD 20677
(301) 934-2992
(DC Line) (301) 870-3399
Fax (301) 034-2999 (Please call first)

MASSACHUSETTS
Ms. Nancy Love
THE NETWORK
300 Brickstone Square
Suite 900
Andover, MA 01810
(508) 470-1080 or 1-800-877-5400
Fax (508) 475-9220

MICHIGAN
Ms. Elaine Gordon

Michigan State Facilitator
MI Department of Education
Mail To: Box 30008
Lansing, MI 38909
Ship To: 608 W. Allegan St.
Lansing, MI 48933
(517) 373-1807
Fax (517) 373-2537

MINNESOTA
Ms. Diane Lassman and
Ms. Barbara Knapp
State Facilitator Office
The EXCHANGE AT CAREI
116 U Press Building
2037 University Avenue, S. E.
University of Minnesota
Minneapolis, MN 55414-3097
(612) 624-0584
Fax (612) 625-4880

MISSISSIPPI
Dr. Bobby Stacy
MS Facilitator Project
State Department of Education
P. O. Box 771, Suite 704
550 High
Jackson, MS 39205-0771
(601) 359-3498
Fax (601) 359-2198

MISSOURI
Ms. Jolene Schulz
Project Director
Missouri Facilitator Project
Suite A
555 Vandiver
Columbia, MO 65202
(314) 886-2165
Fax (314) 886-2160

MONTANA
Ms. Patricia B. Johnson
State Facilitator Project
MT Office of Public Instruction
State Capitol, Room 106
1300 11th Avenue
Helena, MT 59620
(406) 444-2736
Fax 9406) 444-3924

NEBRASKA
Dr. Elizabeth Alfred
Facilitator Project Director
Nebraska Department of Education
301 Centennial Mall
P. O. Box 94987
Lincoln, NE 68509
(402) 471-3440 or 471-2452
Fax (402) 471-2113

NEVADA
Ms. Doris B. Betts
State Facilitator
Nevada Department of Education
Capitol Complex
400 W. King Street
Carson City, NV 89710
(702) 687-3187
Fax (702) 786-4499

NEW HAMPSHIRE
Mr. Jared Shady
NH Facilitator Center
36 Coe Drive
Durham, NH 03824
(603) 224-9461
Fax (603) 224-8925

NEW JERSEY
Ms. Katherine Wallin or
Ms. Elizabeth Ann Pagen
Education Information and
  Resource Center
NJ State Facilitator Project
606 Delsea Drive
Sewell, NJ 08080-9199
(609) 582-7000
Fax (609) 582-4206

NEW MEXICO
Dr. Amy L. Atkins
New Mexico State Facilitator
Department of Educational
  Foundations
University of NM
College of Education
Onate Hall, Room 223
Albuquerque, NM 87131
(505) 277-5204
Fax (505) 277-7991

NEW YORK
Ms. Laurie Rowe
State Facilitator
New York Education Department
Room 469 EBA
Washington Avenue
Albany, NY 12234
(518) 473-1388
Fax (518) 473-2860

NORTH CAROLINA
Ms. Linda Love
Project Director
Division of Development Services
North Carolina Department of
  Public Instruction
301 North Wilmington Street
Raleigh, NC 27601-2825
(919) 715-1363
Fax (919) 733-3791

NORTH DAKOTA
Ms. Jolene Richardson
Division of Independent Study
North Dakota State University
State University Station
P. O. Box 5036
Fargo, ND 58105-5036
(701) 239-7287

OHIO
Ms. Mary Ellen Murray
Ohio Facilitation Center
Ohio Department of Education
Div. of Curriculum/Instruction
  and Professional Development
65 South Front Street
Columbus, OH 43266-0308
(614) 466-2761
Fax (614) 752-8148

OKLAHOMA
Ms. Deborah Murphy
Oklahoma Facilitator Center
123 East Broadway
Cushing, OK 74023
(918) 225-1882
Fax (918) 225-4711

OREGON
Dr. Ralph Nelsen

Columbia Education Center
11325 S. E. Lexington
Portland, OR 97266
(503) 760-2346
Fax (503) 760-5592

PENNSYLVANIA
Mr. Richard Brickley
Project Director
Facilitator Project, R. I. S. E.
200 Anderson Road
King of Prussia, PA 19406
(215) 265-6056
Fax (215) 265-6562

RHODE ISLAND
RI State Facilitator Center
RI Department of Education
Roger Williams Building
22 Hays Street
Providence, RI 02908
(401) 277-2638
Fax (401) 277-2734

SOUTH CAROLINA
Mrs. Catherine Thomas
NDN Facilitator Project
Department of Education
1429 Senate Street, Room 1114
Columbia, SC 29201
(803) 734-8446
Fax (803) 734-8624

SOUTH DAKOTA
Dr. Wendy Bonaiuto
State Facilitator
South Dakota Curriculum
  Center
435 South Chapelle
Pierre, SD 57501
(605) 224-6287
Fax (605) 224-8320

TENNESSEE
Dr. Peggy F. Harris
Tennessee State Facilitator
Tennessee Association for School
  Supervision and Administration
330-10th Avenue, North
Nashville, TN 37203-3436

(615) 251-1173
Fax (615) 259-8492

TEXAS
Dr. Judy Bramlett
Texas Facilitator Project-NDN
Education Service Center
  Region 6
3332 Montgomery Road
Huntsville, TX 77340-6499
(409) 295-9161
Fax (409) 295-1447

UTAH
Ms. Kathy Mannos
State Facilitator Project
Utah State Office of Education
250 East 500 South
Salt Lake City, UT 84111
(801) 538-7823
Fax (801) 538-7882

VERMONT
Mr. Howard Verman
Trinity College
McAuley Hall
208 Colchester Avenue
Burlington, VT 05401
(802) 658-7429
Fax (802) 658-7435

VIRGINIA
Ms. Judy McKnight
The Education Network of Virginia
3421 Surrey Lane
Falls Church, VA 22042
(703) 698-0487
Fax (703) 698-5106

WASHINGTON
Ms. Nancy McKay
Project Manager
Washington State Facilitator
Educational Service District 101
1025 West Indiana Avenue
Spokane, WA 99205-4400
(509) 456-7086
Fax (509) 456-2999

WEST VIRGINIA
Ms. Cornelia Toon
WV State Facilitator
Mail To: State Department
  of Education
Building #6, Room B-252
Ship To: 1900 Kanawha Boulevard, East
Charleston, WV 25305
(304) 558-2193
Fax (304) 558-0048

WISCONSIN
Mr. William Ashmore
State Facilitator
Department of Public Instruction
125 South Webster
P. O. Box 7841
Madison, WI 53703
(608) 267-9179
Fax (608) 267-1052

WYOMING
Ms. Nancy Leinius
State Facilitator
WY Innovation Network System
State Department of Education
Hathaway Building-Room 269
2300 Capitol Avenue
Cheyenne, WY 82002-0050
(307) 777-6226
Fax (307) 777-6234

PUERTO RICO
Ms. Maria del Pilar Charneco
Puretro Rico State Facilitator
General Council on Education
P. O. Box 5429
Hato Rey, PR 00919
(809) 764-0101
Fax (809) 704-0820

VIRGIN ISLANDS
Dr. Fiolina B. Mills
State Facilitator
Department of Education
Office of the Commissioner
44-46 Kongens Gade
Charlotte Amalie
St. Thomas, VI 00802
(809) 774-0100 X 225
Fax (809) 776-5687

AMERICAN SAMOA
Ms. Sharon Stevenson
NDN Facilitator
P. O. Box 1132
Pago Pago, AS 96799
(011) (684) 633-5654/2401
DC Office (202) 225-8577
Fax (011) (684) 633-5184

GUAM
Ms. Margaret Camacho
NDN Facilitator
Federal Program Office
Guam Department of Education
P. O. Box DE
Agana, Guam 96910
(011) (671) 472-8524 or 5004
or 8901 Extension 321
D. C. office (202) 225-1188
Fax (011) (671) 477-4587

NORTHERN MARIANA ISLANDS
Ms. Paz Younis
NDN Facilitator
CNMI Public School System
P. O. Box 1370
Saipan, MP 96950
(011) (670) 322-9311
D. C. office (202) 673-5869
Fax (011) (670) 322-4056

PALAU
Mr. Masa-Aki Emesiochl
State Facilitator
Department of Education
P. O. Box 189
Koror, Republic of Palau 96940
(011) (680) 488-2570 or 1003
Fax (011) (680) 488-2830

PRIVATE SCHOOL FACILITATOR
Dr. Charles Nunley
Private School Facilitator
Council for American Private Ed.
1726 M Street, NW
Suite 1102
Washington, D. C. 20036
(202) 659-0177
Fax (202) 659-0018

Parent Involvement Resources

Consumer Information Center
P.O. Box 100
Pueblo, CO 81002

National Committee for Citizens in
Education
10840 Little Patuxent Parkway
Suite 301
Columbia, MD 21044
(301) 997-9300

The National PTA
700 North Rush Street
Chicago, IL 60611
(312) 787-0977

National Association of Partners in
Education, Inc.
1501 Lee Highway, Suite 201
Arlington, VA 22209
800-48-NSPRA
FAX 703-528-7017

The Parent Institute
P.O. Box 7474
Fairfax Station, VA 22039-7474
FAX 703-569-9244

EVELYN HUNT OGDEN—Dr. Ogden received her Ed.D. from Rutgers University in Educational Evaluation, Psychological Measurement, and Statistics. She is the author of books, major studies, and reports on effective and ineffective schools, programs that work, strategies to increase student achievement, programs for at-risk students, reduction of school violence, and dissemination of successful practices. Dr. Ogden has served for many years on the U.S. Department of Education, Blue Ribbon Schools Selection Panel. She also serves on the U.S. Department of Education Program Evaluation Panel, which reviews and accepts or rejects research related to claims of program effectiveness. Her twenty-five years of administrative experience have included roles as Deputy Assistant Commissioner for Research, Planning, and Evaluation, New Jersey Department of Education; Director of the National Diffusion Network (NDN) Project; Director of Curriculum, Moorestown Public Schools, Moorestown, New Jersey; and her current position as Deputy Superintendent, East Brunswick, New Jersey. As a central office administrator, Dr. Ogden has worked directly with six schools that have been recognized as Blue Ribbon Schools of Excellence.

VITO GERMINARIO—Dr. Germinario received his Ed.D. from Rutgers University in Educational Administration and Supervision. He has teaching experience at the junior high, high school, and college level. He also taught at the Bordentown Youth Correctional Center for Men. Dr. Germinario has been an elementary and middle school principal and currently serves as Superintendent for the Moorestown Township Public Schools in New Jersey. Dr. Germinario has lectured and conducted workshops for numerous school districts and private organizations nationwide on such topics as the supervision of instruction, essentials of instruction, and at-risk students.